Development Dynamics in North East India

Development Dynamics in North East India

Edited by
Jayanta Kumar Ray
Rakhee Bhattacharya

Maulana Abul Kalam Azad Institute of Asian Studies, Kolkata

ANSHAH Anshah Publishing House

ISBN: 978-81-8364-046-6

First Published in India in 2008

Development Dynamics in North East India

Published by:
ANSHAH PUBLISHING HOUSE
Delhi
Sales Office : 115-A, Vikas Marg, Shakarpur, Delhi-110 092
Phone: 9810522367, 22500954

Preface

Northeast India has manifested itself as a problem-arena in the political and economic milieu of contemporary India. There has emerged a plethora of perspectives to deal with the manifold and multifaceted issues among the political, social, ethnic, economic, infrastructural and strategic aspects of Northeast India. Most of these perspectives have identified 'development' as the key issue that needs to be addressed with implications for economic growth and social equity. These issues are intimately connected with the removal of inter-regional disparities in the country and bringing the economically underdeveloped regions like Northeast India into the so called great Indian mainstream, admitting and implying thereby that there did exist a certain degree of alienation between the Northeast and the rest of India. A part of the academic and political intelligentia, of course, would have us believe that the ills of Northeast India are solely due to the central neglect and apathy for decades together, and all the insurgency in the region is a natural reaction to that apathy and colossal neglect. It was a mindset shared by a lot of people from all walks of life in the Northeast, and the feeling is reinforced and vindicated by the daily experiences and struggles of the people, in the near total absence of infrastructure even after 60 years of independence, in the absence of adequate employment and economic opportunities and, in the absence of the least bit of accountability among the ruling administrators and politicians in the region. This mindset also tends to ignore the rampant corruption prevalent, the dismal failure of governance in the region, the absence of any work culture as also the unwillingness to have one, and in the mentality that tends to overlook one's own shortcomings.

The States in this region, with a long history, along with failure of governance and rising corruption, could never focus on capacity building and self-sustenance of their economies. Due to shortage of revenue and meaningful productive activity generating resources, they are heavily dependent on central assistance to avoid a possible economic collapse. The result was that when India actually transformed from Licence-Permit Raj to the era of reforms and globalization, the rest of the country could enjoy the high economic growth trajectories brought by it, but the Northeastern States were deprived of the reforms and their fruits. This failure to develop a skill-based competitive attitude is partly due to the obsession of the perceived 'ethno-cultural identity', which has eventually failed to develop a mindset to accept the 'modern identity', which evolves through economic development, diversity and professionalism. The conflicting dynamics of 'insurgents'—encompassing secessionist movements, violent struggles against alleged 'colonisation' by the Indian state, scramble for homelands and resources, demands for autonomy and recognition – have brought the simmering political cauldron to the boil. Most of these movements have their respective agendas, and are not concerned with the development of the Northeast in general at all. The aim was never to resolve the conflicting internal dynamics and divergent agendas of the movements and discerning how despite internal variations, these movements have had an overall destructive impact on regional governance and development. Thus there was no attempt to address the real, living issues at a much deeper level. The aim was only a few short term gains or advantages of a few groups, with an eye on political power, also in the short term. Indeed, short-sightedness is the only name one can possibly give to the various movements and outfits in the region that miserably failed to foresee the future course, at any given point of time in history.

The region, which was once perceived as 'paradise' has become a 'problem' in perpetuity now with its badly managed economy and an absolute lack of political vision. Side by side, words like 'alienation', 'exploitation' and 'insecurity' started getting 'used' by a group of people across the region to instigate the dangerous problem of insurgency across the hills and valleys of this beautiful and idyllic part of the country. Insecurity, threats and a dismal failure of governance have crippled the emergence of a congenial social and economic atmosphere, holding at bay any prospect of further growth and prosperity. Lack of political stability, absence of pragmatic policy initiatives and mindless violence and extortion in various forms as a substitute for meaningful and productive employment gradually built up an atmosphere of insecurity and suspicion. As a result, disparity widened, more and more people became even more impoverished, and prospect for the region attracting investments and resources to make it self-sufficient receded into oblivion. This indeed is pathetic and besides the problem never disappeared but in fact accelerated in a multifaceted manner ranging widely from inaccessibility to insurgency. Over the years demands for various homelands, rights and independence actually had drifted the region far away from any possible economic turnaround.

All the while, Central assistance was pumped in generously for various developmental programmes, but their misutilisation, siphoning off money, absence of appropriate controls as well as of timely evaluation and adoption of corrective actions, had hindered and prevented achievement of the scheme deliverables. It is time to revisit and question the earlier policies in the light of present requirements, in order to explain through a multi-stage analysis – the problem and the paradox, the gap between economic potential and performance in Northeast India. One cannot ignore the fact that, in its entire journey through six decades of independence, this region has not experienced none else than neglect and damage inflicted both by outsiders as well as by its own people. It has neither fulfilled its economic nor its human potential. It has lost a huge number of young human capital (both tribal and non-tribal), who got their professional training from various prestigious institutes of India but never came back to the region either due to lack of opportunity or due to lack of security. This massive exodus and brain drain that has taken place over the last so many decades has created a severe void in human capital, with its consequently severe adverse impact on the economy to a very significant extent. It has also deprived the region of a pragmatic, honest and dedicated leadership that these migrating youths could have provided.

To be able to address these heterogeneous aspects, I believe that there can be two alternative ways. One is the macro perspective, which can make an overall assessment taking into account and recounting the contributions of all the relevant components together and the other is the micro perspective, which looks at the specific issues and its various components individually. Both these approaches are the needs of the hour to bring this region back from the wilderness of oblivion and alienation to the fold of the multi-cultural, multi-lingual and multi-ethnic cauldron that is India, where despite all the chaos, there is an unmistakable element of identity, an unmistakable unity and an almost undefinable but nevertheless unmistakable pride, with a perceptible sense of belongingness.

So in the macro perspective, one can have an integrated interdisciplinary model to look at this region. This also involves looking at the Northeast in a new way: not simply as a single problem-unit or entity, but as a sensitive, internally differentiated terrain where intra-regional specificities need to be given long-needed attention. The methodological thrust would be to achieve integration through a new assessment of the unique political, economic and social settings of the Northeast as a region, and also to understand the intricacies of intra-regional variations of the problems and their manifestations, their causes and consequences. Thus this perspective moves beyond a simplistic and stereotyped set of problems in different parts of the region, reviewing and re-addressing intricacies of distinct, sub-national and conflicting identities, their individual stresses and dimensions, and assessing whether or not they interrelate at a pan-regional level with the developmental dynamics.

On the other hand, if one takes up the micro perspective, then it boils down to some specific issues along with their multiple facets. This creates an ambience of an in-depth analysis of a specific problem and finding out a solution to it through both quantitative and qualitative assessments as well as comparative judgments with other parts of the country to see the existing gap and disparity. For example, one can make a comparative economic study on tourism between say, Mizoram and Goa (both being small and naturally beautiful states), and can find the wide gaps between them. The next step could be to see all the probable dimensions of tourism in Mizoram and the reasons behind these gaps, and then trying to look for a solution in developmental dynamics. Or, one can see the growth differences in Meghalaya and Himachal Pradesh. Both being hill states, with their difficult terrains and though both enjoy the status and benefits of special category states but are in altogether different growth paths, what are the reasons behind such a disparity? Unless the reasons are hammered and pointed out repeatedly, the solution will never come from within. Development theorists are strongly emphasizing now that the prosperity should come from 'within' through various endogenous growth models with the participation of endogenous people, so it is essential that the people take the initiative to fight against the odds and to generate revenues to look for a self sustaining development. Assistance from outside can provide a shield but not a sword for self defence. Northeast India, being one of the richest resource hubs in the world with so many ethnic and cultural diversities, can offer many unique things to the rest of India and to the world. This dream can be achieved only through a clean political vision and initiative from the people here. To me, regional cooperation at various levels among the eight Northeastern States can also turn this dream into a reality. The challenges are tough but certainly not unachievable.

In this research forum, I feel both these approaches are equally important and supplementary to each other. This can provide an integrated and all-encompassing framework towards addressing the situation, keeping 'development' as the pivotal and overarching factor. Even though the canvas becomes too wide for the purpose, it would give us an opportunity to elicit diverse views from a galaxy of scholars belonging to various disciplines of social science attempting to trace the roots of and connections between various aspects and ultimately forging a common strategy to address the issue of the lack of development in the region. The attempt is to bring together all concerned in a single forum to search for ways and means for translating the dream of development in Northeast India into a concrete reality. The region truly needs a break from its painful past as the future beckons it at the crossroad of an emerging Asia.

Rakhee Bhattacharya

Acknowledgement

The present volume is the product of a National Seminar that was held in Aizawl on 19th and 20th April 2007 as part of the Long Term Northeast India Research Programme of Maulana Abul Kalam Azad Institute of Asian Studies, Kolkata. The Institute has dedicated a part of its resources for developing and fostering an understanding of this region by continuous academic pursuits in the form of seminars, symposia, dialogues, and collaborations with scholars, academicians and people from all the Northeastern States, with a view to searching for a solution in the development paradigm.

We would like to take the privilege of expressing our deep appreciation to all those, whose inspiration, help and suggestions have provided us with immense strength to bring out this volume. Our foremost thanks go to Prof. B.B. Bhattacharya, Vice-Chancellor, Jawaharlal Nehru University, New Delhi, who is the adviser of our Northeast India Research Programme. We thank Prof. H.S. Vasudevan, Ambassador Krishnan Srinivasan, Dr. Amiya Choudhuri, Dr. P.K. Sengupta, Mr. Kausik Bandyapadhyaya, Dr. Binoda Mishra, Mr. Mainak Sen and Mr. S.K. Mitra for their co-operation and academic inputs in this ambitious programme. We are indebted to all the distinguished authors of this volume who in spite of their own pressing commitments have contributed well researched and analytical papers. Our sincerest thanks to everybody whose names we could not take but without whose earnest efforts this volume would not have seen the light of the day.

Jayanta Kumar Ray
Rakhee Bhattacharya

Contents

List of Tables

Introduction

The North East Region of India (NER) consists of eight States of the Indian Union: Arunachal, Assam, Manipur, Meghalaya, Mizoram, Nagaland, Sikkim and Tripura. The region, except Sikkim, suffers from terrorist activities of varying degrees. A study of all the papers in this volume indicates that these activities are partly propelled by the greed and shortsightedness of ruling politicians and administrators, but are inordinately strengthened by the flow of funds, arms and training from abroad, notably from the Inter-Services Intelligence (ISI) of Pakistan, and the Directorate General of Forces Intelligence (DGFI) of Bangladesh.

It is easy for some observers to suggest that terrorism in the NER has its roots in relative economic deprivation. This prompts an inquiry into the comparative figures of per capita income (as of 2003-04) for a number of Indian States. Sikkim has a per capita income of Rs. 22,062, and is free from terrorism, but Assam has Rs. 6,466, Arunachal Rs. 9,678, Manipur Rs. 8,751, Meghalaya Rs. 10,795, Nagaland Rs. 12,292, and Tripura Rs. 9,969. It is not advisable to oversimplify the complex phenomenon of terrorism and attribute it to economic grievances, especially to low per capita income. This will be clear if we refer to the per capita income (a convenient though rough measurement of economic success or failure) of some other Indian States whose per capita income is less than, or near to, that of Nagaland, but do not suffer from terrorism in the same way as, e.g. Nagaland does. For example, Madhya Pradesh has Rs. 8,284 as per capita income, Rajasthan Rs. 9,685, Uttar Pradesh Rs. 6,138, and Kerala Rs. 12,328.

It is pertinent to argue that instability in the NER (including terrorism) has its major roots in (1) the British policy of Divide And Rule, (2) the harmful consequences of Partition in 1947; and (3) chronically and acutely bad governance in the post-1947 era. The British probably have an unrivalled record of practicing Divide And Rule in many parts of the world. But, in the NER, they seemed to have surpassed all their previous records.

The British first tried to subjugate the hill people militarily. But the British found it too difficult and expensive, for, many of these people, with diverse ethnicities, had a warlike tradition, and did not hesitate to raid British installations. In order to preempt these raids, and set the indigenous people against one another, the British imported the Kuki-Chin people from the Chin Hills in Burma (Myanmar), and arranged their settlement in locations between the habitats of Mizos and Nagas on one side, and the Cachar/Manipur areas (occupied by the British) on the other. The Kuki-Chin people were hardly aware that the British were not only using them as a cushion against sudden attacks by Mizos or Nagas, but also exacerbating rivalries/hostilities between these various ethnic groups. The revolt of 1857 in India taught the British how to refine their age-old policy of Divide And Rule. They stopped the movement of people between the hills and plains of the NER. Moreover, they imposed arbitrary boundaries, and administered the boundaries in such a way as to aggravate animosities between different ethnic groups.

In order to reinforce the military and administrative aspects of Divide and Rule, the British attempted a cultural conquest. Christian missionaries followed the military, and helped in the consolidation as well as expansion of territories under British domination. The British coined such deceptive phrases as 'tribal people' or 'tribal societies' in order to convey the false message that the ethnic/racial groups in the NER did not have varying shares of the civilized thought and belief systems of such old religions, as Buddhism. Actually, they did, and retained some features of the old religion even after they got converted to a new religion, viz. Christianity. So tricky were the British that, initially, many of the converts were not even aware that they were being converted. Moreover, it is significant that inroads by Christian missionaries in the NER started approximately at a time when the British were planning to conquer Myanmar (Burma).

This Divide And Rule policy left a legacy of instability for free India, which was aggravated by partition. For many people in the NER, partition was a geographical-economic monstrosity. It cut them off from the larger land mass of India (an excessively narrow link being provided by the Siliguri Corridor), and destroyed their mutually profitable economic connection with East Bengal (East Pakistan/ Bangladesh). Before partition, the NER people had satisfactory exchanges of commodities with the territory forming East Bengal. Subsequently, they noted that their exports did not fetch the minimum expected price across the Siliguri Corridor, whereas imports from the rest of India cost much more than imports from East Bengal.

Partition produced further unrest in the NER, as a large number of Hindus were compelled to leave East Bengal. The response of New Delhi was typical: it could not fathom (or simply did not recognize) the spread and depth of the anti-Hindu policies in East Bengal, as also their disruptive fallout in the NER. It formulated a policy that could be characterized by a phrase that gained currency in the 1990s viz: the doctrine of non-reciprocity vis-à-vis neighbouring countries. The Indo-Pak agreement of 1950 (known as the Nehru-Liaquat Pact) provided for the return of refugees to East Bengal and India, as also the restoration of their property and honour. Although a relatively insignificant number of Muslims in Assam (and, e.g. West Bengal) left for East Bengal around 1947, nearly all of them returned to India after the conclusion of the Nehru-Liaquat Pact. In contrast, very few Hindus – perhaps none – could return to East Bengal and enjoy the benefits of rehabilitation. Whereas Hindu refugees became a source of tension in the NER (especially Assam), in the long run, the return of Muslims from East Bengal to Assam (as also West Bengal) created a menace from which the NER has so far failed to extricate itself.

This requires some explanation. When the Muslims took advantage of the Nehru-Liaquat Pact, and returned to Assam, they also brought many of their brethren and encouraged many more to move to Assam (and the NER) on account of comparably greater economic opportunities in the NER. Muslims entered the NER (especially Assam) in such unmanageably large numbers as to pose a threat to the political-social-cultural identity of the Assamese. From the 1970s, on account of Pakistani sponsorship of International Islamic Terrorism (IIT), this threat assumed much more dangerous dimensions.

It must be added, however, that, in order to counteract the threat from Muslim Bangladeshi migrants, an organization such as the United Liberation Front of Assam (ULFA) came into being. Subsequently, the ULFA itself due to a queer gyration of circumstances in which the failures of policymakers in New Delhi and State capitals were probably the most prominent – turned into an appendage of the ISI and DGFI. It is now one of the 24 outfits in the NER receiving arms, money and training from Pakistan/Bangladesh. The Government of India appears to be a helpless practitioner of the doctrine of non-reciprocity vis-à-vis Bangladesh and Pakistan.

Currently, there are around fifty militant organizations in the NER, some of them representing tiny ethnic groups, and their origin mostly could be traced to ceaselessly bad governance at Union and State levels. Some examples of sheer inefficiency on the part of Union and State Governments may be sampled.

The Naga insurgency is the oldest and most powerful insurgency in the NER. Yet, a minimum of competence and ruthlessness on the part of Union/State Governments could have nipped the Naga insurgency in the bud. For, there are around twenty Naga groups in Nagaland, and their dominant characteristics are ethnic-cultural distinctions causing incurable mutual hostilities. In addition, in Assam, Arunachal Pradesh, Manipur (and Myanmar) there are around fifteen Naga groups. All these thirty-five Naga groups have not even one common language. Not to speak of capitalizing divisions among Nagas, and thereby liquidating Naga insurgency at its infancy, Union/State Governments have abetted the same. Such abetment is rooted in complete abhorrence of the dictum that a stitch in time saves nine. The chronic governmental tendency has been to remain apathetic to transparent dangers till the time when even nine stitches are of no avail. Thus Naga insurgency has not only grown, it has incited insurgencies among numerous groups (many of them numerically negligible), e.g. Mizos, Meitheis, Khasis, Bodos, Brus, Hmars, Tripuris, Karbis, Dimasas, Kukis, Garos, etc.

An important reason why these rebel groups (with a deceptive ethnic colour) have emerged is the successful demonstration by Nagas that even in the absence of any moral or ideological strength they can carry out continuous and large scale extortions. Whereas the ordinary people languish largely because of extortion undermining economic development, the rebel leaders enjoy an enviably luxurious lifestyle in India or abroad (notably in Bangladesh, where they are allowed to run lucrative businesses). Authorities at Union/State levels have been fully aware of all this. As early as 1981, the Seventh Report of the National Police Commission (headed by Dharma Vira) deplored the unsystematic attempts of authorities to deal with the continuing turbulence, which was causing instability and insecurity. Authorities were supplying enormous amounts of development funds to the region. But, as the 1981 Report stressed, benefits of development, instead of reaching the ordinary people, flowed to a small group of corrupt and incompetent political leaders, businessmen, and officials. In these circumstances, policing remained ineffective in coping with the insurgency.

Evidently, corruption legitimized extortion, which spread in the following decades so much so that the fundings of the aforesaid 1981 Report were not only repeated but reinforced by the 2000-01 Annual Report of the Government of India's Ministry of Home Affairs (MHA). This MHA Report underlined the absence of any ideological content in the militant movements as also the abundance of a craze for money-making by extortion, accompanied by kidnapping and murder, whenever necessary. The MHA report also points to (what has already been stressed in this note) the unfriendly conduct of neighbouring countries which not only provide shelter, arms, finance and training to these militants, but also organize the infiltration of illegal migrants with experience/skills in terrorist activities.

But an important question arises. If extortion and not ideology remains the principal motivation of rebels in the NER, do they survive because of large scale collusion with the authorities? The answer is, regrettably, in the affirmative. As many reports of Comptroller and Auditor General of India (CAG) have disclosed, contractors receive project contracts without competitive bidding, and materials for construction of roads, etc. fetch inordinately high prices. The obvious aim is to share the booty with officials and militants (robbing the common people of benefits of development funds). Actually, CAG reports do not reveal anything that is new. They only confirm the vicious and all-polluting operation of what (for lack of a better phrase) can be called the quadrangular alliance of politicians, officials, businessmen and militants. All are extortionists, and one may wonder who are the most dangerous extortionists. Probably, ruling politicians and officials can be placed in this category. For, they have the capacity to extinguish militancy but they do not. In Assam, for instance, several Chief Ministers have called off operations by security forces at moments when they were about to liquidate the militants. Evidently, the survival of militancy can ensure the sustainability and profitability of the activities of the quadrangular alliance. Politicians use rebels as vote banks as also informal banks from which extortion proceeds can be partially accessed. As to government officials/employees, they cause enormous harm even when they do not accept bribes, or a share of extortion proceeds. For, barring exceptions, they wait about eighty per cent of development funds by enjoying high salaries, while doing little or no work, and obstructing the legitimate activities of law-abiding citizens. Above all, government functionaries have also mastered the fine art of fraudulent withdrawal of funds from government treasuries.

Nevertheless, not to speak of revenues earned by various States in the NER, the investment of New Delhi in the region is so much that it can wipe out poverty and unemployment by developing the immense horticultural, hydrological, and mineral resources, etc. and the like – provided the depredations of the aforesaid quadrangular alliance can be contained. For, approximately, the Union Government's annual allocation per family to the NER stands at three lakhs of rupees. If a drowning person is permitted to catch a straw, one can suggest the imposition of the Union Government's (or the President's) Rule over the entire NER (excepting Sikkim). But for such a drastic step, the widespread operations of the quadrangular alliance cannot be stopped while current administrative boundaries remain, the entire region has to be treated economically as one unit, and normal malpractices by leaders of political parties, factions, ethnic groups, etc. have to be kept under suspension till the NER achieves a high degree of economic progress, banishing or minimizing poverty/unemployment.

If enthusiasts for preservation of ethnic identity and local government are a little disappointed with this suggestion for NER's rejuvenation, let them be reminded that patronage for local government often degenerates into putting local persons without any knowledge of law into judicial positions, and allowing local government leaders, constituting not more than ten to fifteen per cent of the people, to loot development funds. If the drastic remedy of Union or President's Rule, suggested as the unavoidable interim solution to an intractable problem, eventually succeeds (hoping against hope), and a sort of NER economic union emerges, the next step will be to foster economic integration with southwest China and southeast Asia. The Government of India's Look East Policy can facilitate such integration – once again hopefully – endowing centuries-old cultural-economic ties with an appropriate significance in an era of liberalization and globalisation.

Jayanta Kumar Ray

Section I

Political Dynamics of North East India

Looking at Contemporary Governance in North-East India

Abhijit Choudhury

If one examines the map of Asia one may notice the importance of India's North Eastern region on two counts. Geopolitically, it is situated on an international frontier zone predominantly marked by a chain of mountain ranges. Besides, it is a virtual 'cultural' buffer between several civilizational systems of South, Southeast and East Asia. Historically, it has seen population movements accompanied by cultural and social transactions. From the ethno-cultural angle, therefore, it represents a 'plural' entity. This complex mosaic demands special attention from the point of view of 'governance'. The paper attempts a brief study of at least two issues in the context of governance for development with particular reference to the hill people. These are :

a) What is the pattern of governance in this region as we experience it today? What is its historicity or, in other words, is it a product of the Indian experience with the British Colonial practices?
b) To what extent the post-independence Indian State experimented with the mode of governance suitable for this region?

Governance in India is based on the principles of parliamentary democracy. Until the 1990s, the Nehruvian model of 'welfare' state functioned with a large degree of governmental role in the national economy which was 'protectionist' by nature. Developmental processes were directed by the State. However, since 1995 'globalization' started working on this system of governance, beginning with the gradual withdrawal of the State from a virtual 'Command' economy, and with it, from the 'welfare' role. But the full impact of 'globalization' is yet to become visible in the North Eastern region since its economy still remains largely subsidized.

If 'governance' in our present understanding means management of polity and society by way of adjustments of contesting claims and interests of different groups within a heterogeneous structure, then developmental issue would definitely assume centrality in 'political' discourses. How far these discourses are translated into mobilization would depend on actual commitments of the participants. Given the erstwhile 'Third World' matrix[1], within which India has been posited this fact dominated the Indian scenario for long in view of the pulls involving the so-called 'forward' and 'backward' sections of the larger society. One may remember that India has emerged from its colonial past only recently.

As far as the colonial practices in North Eastern India were concerned, examining the primary records, one would find two 'guiding' principles behind its governance. One, to secure the eastern-North Eastern frontiers of the empire from the standpoint of their strategic locations. In fact, one of the records talks about how to build up a special cadre for frontier police duties[2]. Two, to exploit the region's rich resources especially minerals and forest products and expand the British Commercial interests in terms of both internal and external trade[3]. Naturally, the system of governance was not oriented towards wholesale development of the people concerned. The infrastructures like roads, railways, and aerodromes were built to a bare minimum, and with the aim of serving the strategic and commercial requirements. As with the colonial pattern, industrialization was neglected. The sectors which were given importance were plantations and, from the late-nineteenth century, oil, education, health services, and social upliftment were left largely to the Christian missionaries. If it is argued theoretically – unlike Hobson – that 'civilizing mission' was a major (and not secondary) motive for imperialism and its ideological justification[4], then indeed these missionaries did a commendable job in the sphere of 'colonial' modernization. Of course, how far it succeeded in 'de-tribalization' of the so-called 'tribes'—a category that came along with the colonial ethnographic exercises—remains debatable. It appears that the colonial regime used such political expedients as the 'Partially Excluded Areas' and 'Excluded Areas' in order to segregate them from the plainsmen with the ostensible purpose of protecting them from exploitation. The 'non-regulation' status of the administrative apparatus might have helped preserving their 'tribal' identity. But it is actually difficult to comprehend the nature of this 'tribal' identity within modernity. [Because modernity emphasizes reason above impression and passion, one truth and, above all, secular enlightenment[5].] Rather the colonial policies encouraged tribalism. The above said priorities defined the colonial policies.

Since this paper stresses the mode of governance for 'tribal' development, our next problem is : how far the post-colonial Indian State has been marked by any radical departure from the colonial regime. India began with the so-called Nehruvian model, which professed that the tribals of this region should develop "along the lines of their own genius"[6]. Nehru raised the issues of maximum possible autonomy as well as safeguarding the interests of the Nagas in his letter to T. Sakhrie, Secretary of the Naga National Council[7]. This philosophy of Governance was also reflected in his participation in the debates on the Sixth Schedule in the Constituent Assembly. It is possible that this philosophy was a product of the necessity to consolidate the infant Indian State facing tribal assertions for their identity and rights, which Nehru could not have been unaware of[8]. As a result, the Sixth Schedule [Articles 244 (2) and 275 (1)] of the Constitution granted large degree of autonomy for the developmental governance to the tribals of Assam, which was then a composite state. Its purpose was to protect tribal identity, culture, and traditions. However, it was not extended to the hill areas of Manipur, Tripura, and the then NEFA (now Arunachal Pradesh). The Naga Hills were given a separate system under Article 371-A, which established the Village Development Councils. Interestingly, for other tribal areas of India, the Fifth Schedule [Article 244 (1)] was granted, which provided for Tribal Advisory Councils in the Scheduled Areas.

It was only with the reorganization of the North Eastern region in 1971 that District Councils were granted to the Manipur hill areas. But these have so far remained outside the purview of the Sixth Schedule[9]. Later, however, the scope of this Schedule has been extended to Tripura, and to the Bodoland Tribal Council through amendments of the Sixth Schedule (the latter in 2003), while the bill concerning the Gorkha Hill Council in West Bengal is yet to receive the nod from the Lok Sabha. The Sixth Schedule empowered the autonomous District Councils and Regional Councils to administer not only in the sphere of developmental governance, but also in preserving 'tribal' identity, rights, and culture. These Councils were given the rights to manage education, forests, and tribal lands. The tribal customary laws were to be the guiding force in managing forests, lands and rural judicial dispensations. The District Councils by nature are primarily rural bodies of self-governance.

The Sixth Schedule, on the surface of it, appears to have been a departure from the colonial mode of 'paternal' governance. But in reality, the post-colonial state offered a mixed baggage in that it signified the colonial tradition of 'conditional' legislation[10]. On the other hand, in NEFA it retained the 'single line' administration of the colonial era. Under this system the executive, judicial and developmental functions were welded into an ' all-in-one' form, which was managed by a basically Nehruvian bureaucracy. Much later on, the three-tier Panchayati system was introduced. My field experiences there suggest that developmental programmes from the Gaon Panchayat and Anchal Samiti to Zilla Parishad can be successful, provided there is active community participation in governance. The participation of the bureaucracy cannot be done away with since it executes the programmes. But active interaction involves a mechanism for monitoring implementation of the programmes. Community participation in monitoring is a must. It is here that problems lay. A joke was current in Arunachal Pradesh official circle at one time that if one calculated the total area covered by road (including village paths) construction programmes under the various governmental agencies in square kilometers, it would exceed the total geographical area of the state.

There was, of course, a radical departure in that the post-colonial State had done away with the institutional practices of the 'Partially Excluded Areas' and 'Excluded Areas' in order to ensure participation of the tribals in the new political processes. The concept of democracy for development, through the institutionalization of the Sixth Schedule, started functioning with promises for the future. In NEFA, Nehru's tribal policy adviser, Verrier Elwin, guided the developmental processes in spite of his detractors like Ghuriye and others. Like other Nehruvian members of the elite, Suniti Kumar Chatterji and Nirmal Kumar Bose, believed in pluralism. However, in the process, Elwin was accused of devising a state policy, whereby the 'tribal' cultures of NEFA were treated as museum pieces even as 'modernity' might be ushered in with administrative initiatives. Indeed, inspite of good intents of the Nehruvian line, certain contradictions became apparent. Chatterji tried to provide an ideological basis to the Nehruvian polity structured along the theme of 'unity in diversity', through such works as The Place of Assam in the Indian Civilization and Kirata-Jana-Krti. [though he may face criticism for his apparent orientalism]. I have dealt with it elsewhere.[11] All said , however, a fundamental question may appear here. That is: How far these experiments have gone to achieve the goal of the Indian State—development of the hill people.

The conclusions of this paper are as follows. Let us first look at our achievements on the developmental front in the last fifty-five years (taking 1952 as our starting point with 'democratic' processes for development). The UNDP released its Human Development Report (HDR) 2006 on 09 November, 2007. It says India in general has achieved much success in providing equitable distribution of water and sanitation services through community-government partnership wherever access and management rights are transferred to the communities themselves. In the romping Human Development Index (HDI), based on calculation of average life expectancy, educational attainment and adjusted real GDP per capita as its indices, however, India's position is 126 among a total of 177 countries. It has gone up from 0.602 in 2005 to 0.611 in 2006. India's rank on the Human Poverty Index (HPI), is now 55 among a total of 102[12]. The recent NSSO (National Sample Survey Organization) findings state that as in 2004-2005, 22.5 per cent of our population still live in abject poverty[13]. It reveals that while the GDP grew at around 06 per cent between 1999 and 2005, poverty has actually declined by 0.75 per cent, clearly indicating 'mismatch' between growth and distribution[14]. It is known that a large number of villages go without basic sanitation and health facilities. Of our legislators, at central and state levels, 20 per cent have criminal records. More than 40 per cent people are illiterate, and budgetary allocations for education are yet to reach the level of 0.4 per cent[15].

As for the North-Eastern region, the HDI is as follows. Against the national average of around 0.590 this region has recorded a dismal 0.431. Meghalaya's current standing is at 0.393, with Arunachal Pradesh's being the lowest at 0.358. Only Mizoram, Nagaland and Tripura are in a better position by virtue of high literacy rates. Mizoram made progress in health sector. Out of the eight states, these three show conscious policy efforts[16]. In Meghalaya school dropouts are quite large in number. If one looks at the rate of literacy, the Census of 2001 shows that against an all-India average of 55.18 per cent, Arunachal Pradesh has the lowest, 44.71 per cent, while Mizoram (74.44 per cent), Tripura (63.81 per cent), Manipur (59.85 per cent) and Nagaland (57.65 per cent) surpass the all India average. Out of a total of 1,61,722 'problem villages' (where drinking water is not available within a radius of 1.6 km in plain areas and within elevation difference of 100 metres in hilly areas), the NER has 18,592. By 1997-98, this region could cover only 775 of such villages, against an all-India figure of 2,908. While the all-India percentage of surfaced road to total road length is 54.68, for the NER, it stands at 24.96. Total railway network in this region (as on 31 March, 2002) combining all three gauges (broad, metre and narrow) stands at 2,577.94 km. In rural electrification, however, the NER has done generally better than the all-India average of 73.39 per cent[17].

The data above clearly show that except in certain sectors, the performance does not match the fund allocated to this region since 1952. The then Union ministers from L.K. Advani to Shanta Kumar, Kumari Selja and Jairam Ramesh were, therefore, justified in their statements that many of the centrally sponsored schemes remain either under-implemented or unimplemented[18]. In recent times nexus between politicians and underground elements, siphoning off funds allocated for developmental programmes, have been established[19]. What do all these reflect? Well, the developmental governance has not percolated down to the masses in spite of the importance given to the NER in this respect. One has to agree with the historians, Bipan Chandra et.al., that the tribal society 'almost everywhere' has been developing 'class differences', with the tribal elites reaping major gains from developmental processes[20]. This is visible in both the Fifth and the Sixth Schedule areas. Elsewhere, I have dealt with the problems inherent in the Sixth Schedule's functioning with particular reference to Meghalaya[21]. Here, I shall indicate a few. These are: inefficient handling; jurisdictional friction with government departments; governmental obstructions in releasing funds; endemic corruption[22]; the emergence of new types of pressure groups, masquerading as NGOs; and facilitating an alternative haven for those politicians who lose out in state-level politics (and who do not mind to start again as MDCs).

Factionalism in state politics, as it has recently been reflected in the happenings in Meghalaya and Arunachal Pradesh, exposes the fact that developmental governance occupies only a remote corner in the politicians' schemes. It has been seen that the district councils in Meghalaya could not handle primary education, nor manage non-reserved forests[23]. Even an active MDC, Bindo Lanong, admits that there are issues relating to the Sixth Schedule which are controversial[24]. Though the district councils are expected to adjudicate such issues as land, property, inheritance, marriage and divorce, etc., on the basis of customary laws, their actions generated more complications.

In fact, an observer, Valentine Ladia, feels that the existence of two systems of law—state and customary, has created confusion and that the district councils often show a propensity to move towards the state Law. Locality based variations in customary law have, so far, prevented both codification of customary laws and cadastral survey of land in Meghalaya. Emergence of private property in land has compounded the situation[25]. Another observer, Toki Blah, points out that the district councils have failed to set up courts at village and other levels. Most of their courts are manned by people without any judicial background[26]. However, Bindo Lanong thinks that the district councils can handle the customary laws better, since as a 'local indigenous' tribal body it knows "the culture, tradition, local conditions, etc". According to him, the subject is not with the State Government, because in the state administration the officers of the level of, say, Deputy Commissioners "may come from outside with different customs and traditions who know less about the indigenous tribal people"[27].

Yet another observer, J.M. Phira, argues that the modern-day circumstances such as disruption of the close-knit clan and family structures, urban way of life, etc., have made it difficult for rigid enforcement of customary laws. Moreover, no serious work is done as yet on codification of customary laws[28]. Considering the above said issues, therefore, one has to agree with Lt. Gen. Sushil Pillai's observation that the autonomy envisaged in the Sixth Schedule is only "part of the problem and not the solution"[29]. Other observers like H. Ghonglah believe that rampant corruption and "absence of public accountability" have made the district councils redundant[30]. In Meghalaya two phenomena are visible. These are: one, conflict has surfaced between the 'new' leadership emerging through the district councils and the 'traditional' ones in the Syiemships and Doloiships. Two, after the re-organization of the NER in 1971-72, Mizoram has transferred the operation of the Sixth Schedule to the minority tribes—Lai, Mara and Chakma, from the majority Mizo tribes. Whereas Meghalaya appears reluctant in accepting the logic that once a 'tribal' majority state is granted the Sixth Schedule would become redundant. Polarization has appeared on the questions of doing away with the District Councils and restoring the powers of the traditional Chiefs in the context of developmental governance and preservation of tribal customs and identity.

But such issues as well as the State Governments' policies in these directions are holding back the emergence of a 'modern state' in a state like Meghalaya with a truely Civil Society by encouraging excessive 'tribalism' in a now 'heterogeneous' society[31]. Moreover, the very existence of a Ministry of District Council affairs in the State Government nullifies autonomy of these councils as it signifies the continuance of bureaucratic interventions which often lead to friction[32]. In the three-tier polity of Meghalaya – that of the State, the District Councils and the Syiemships, Doloiships, etc., –there appears a system of 'States within a State', which blurs the vision for actual priorities before society. It is viewed that the district councils have become a "training ground for secondary rung politicians who want to enter state politics". This is, however, "not a part of the mandate" of the councils. The state-level politicians feel threatened by these 'new' politicians. Since the state has overwhelming powers over these councils, the state-level politicians have a "hand in preventing the latter from being effective"[33]. Thus it may be observed that a noble principle and experiment as the Sixth Schedule has not only succeeded in creating a new elite among the hill people, but has also been a factor in the feuds within ruling elites of a tribal state like Meghalaya.

Yet many communities kept on demanding 'tribal' status within the Sixth Schedule, such as the Koch-Rajvanshis, Tiwas, Rabhas and others. Among them the Tiwas, Hasongs and Rabhas have already been granted autonomous tribal Councils, but outside the Sixth Schedules. This explains their dissatisfactions. In the case of the hill areas of Manipur, one may see disagreement among the experts (Profs. Meijinglung Kamson and M. Horam, and Dr. B.K. Roy Burman) as to the number (and pattern) of the autonomous District Councils.

However, they agree on one issue. That such Council, whether single or more, would be necessary for the development of the hill areas[34]. On the other hand, the autonomous state demand movement in Assam's Karbi-Anglong perhaps also shows the functioning of the district council there in a negative light[35]. The problem is: how to look at these issues? Do we see in the first case of growing demands for 'tribal' status a genuine cause, since the state could not deliver the goods? Or, is it only mobilization of 'tribal' cause to satisfy the whims and ambitions of a few elites from these communities? And, in the second case (involving autonomous state movement), is it, to borrow from David Hardiman's concept of 'faction',[36] that new political cliques at district levels demand a share in the system of governance? Or, in both these cases, is it a matter connected with getting a share of the spoils of the special constitutional provisions such as reservation, etc. meant for the tribals? In either of these possibilities one may discern political mobilization with tribalism working as its ideological justification that, in reality, brings out the issue of 'otherness' as a consequence of grievances. We need to see deeply whether a social and political psychology that develop from this constant 'othering' is an expression of cultural difference and therefore, whether the subsequent mobilization emerges from a real sense of alienation, or is it a method which mutates into a new materiality of social life[37].

Finally, if the model of developmental governance presented by the Sixth Schedule has failed, then can there be an alternative? It is, indeed, a difficult issue to decide. A section of the Khasi-Pnar intellectuals holds the view that the traditional chiefs should be restored to their powers so that they could fulfill the functions of local governance[38]. In fact, a few years ago, in a public congregation in Shillong this demand was raised. It repeated the 1968 plea of the Syiems to the President of India that Syiemship was an essential condition of preservation of the Khasi way of life and that in accordance with the agreements of the Syiems with the Dominion of India, their rights should be protected[39]. Other intellectuals from Meghalaya think that, in spite, of their weaknesses, the district councils are an agency which has helped the people to participate in them and thereby raise their levels of political awareness. This group believes that the Schedule has given a fair degree of autonomy to the people[40]. Thus Toki Blah thinks that, despite many limitations of the district and regional councils, alternatives to this Schedule cannot be recommended due to its strong political base. A suitable amendment to scrap the overriding powers of the state government would be necessary to restore the autonomy of the district councils[41]. There is a view that these councils have at least done some work. That was why the S.K. Dutta Committee of 1984 recommended that in spite of their weakness they should not be dissolved since there was no alternative to them[42]. Yet another group suggests a synthesis between these councils and Panchayati institutions which are extensively empowered under the 73rd Amendment to the Constitution[43]. It is argued that this Amendment has exposed the "extremely limited power of self-government" conferred under the Sixth Schedule[44]. Assam, Manipur and Arunachal Pradesh have adopted this Amendment. Even the Concept Paper of the National Commission for Reviewing the Working of the Constitution (NCRWC) appears to subscribe to this synthesis, albeit with local variation[45].

Earlier I took a stand that there could be a suitable amendment to the Constitution empowering the traditional institutions of Meghalaya, such as the Raid Dorbars and Village Dorbar Shnong, for the developmental governance by way of such a synthesis[46]. I continue with this stand. It is vindicated by successful experiments in Nagaland since 2002, whereby communitization of elementary education, grass-root health services and electricity management has empowered the people to take initiatives in developmental works. They have formed the village education committees (VEC), village health committees (VHC) and village electricity management boards (VEMB)[47]. However, even here the success would depend on community-government interaction. To end this exercise, I may cite Subrata Mitra's observation that in India, unlike many other 'changing societies', political institutions show a high level of innovativeness and elasticity. Interestingly, he also highlights this elasticity in accommodating the embedded cultural values on the part of the modern institutions as well as in utilizing the 'historical memory' of the traditions of the colonial state in India. Thus, in the spheres of law and governance, the post-independence Indian State has been able to maintain balance between coercion and persuation[48]. While looking into the district and regional councils, there is consensus; there is, however, doubt as to his view about the Indian State's 'orderly conduct' of its affairs. This is in the context of the confusion and multiplicity of claims and counterclaims in the NER. This argument is further corroborated by the very recent admission by Assam government that 'social chaos' might overtake the balance unless help was taken from both the public and the private sectors to generate employment among the tea tribes[49]. It reflects the gap between the avowed aims and purposes of 'governance' and their translation into reality over the decades after independence.

This admission confirms another aspect of our public life: that of our tendency, through more than five decades, to seek solutions to every major problem "by means of administrative apparatus". Nirmal Kumar Bose had already warned us as far back as in 1967.[50] We have seen that such dependence led to corruption in bureaucracy. It is an open secret that the money-game is rampant in certain centrally controlled nodal agencies for developmental funding specifically for the NER. One of them would not mind granting several crores to a private educational institution under dubious bona fides in Meghalaya.[51] It is not understandable as to how corruption and the so-called "orderly conduct" of affairs can go together.

NOTES AND REFERENCES

1. Very recently the Western agencies classified India as a "transforming economy".
2. Records from *Home (Police)* and *Foreign (Political)* departments are extant. For this specific case see *Home Police, September 1873, 55-73(A). Notes* of Home Department *vide Bengal No. 2804 of 24 June 1873*, referring to correspondence from E.B. Baker, District Supdt. Of Police, Champaran. Baker suggested that the European officers for the frontier should be selected from the "most active, energetic and hardy". Such officers should have a "natural liking and ability for military police duty, which to them will be a labour of love". The Foreign Department endorsed this view. Accordingly, Baker was asked to proceed to Assam to do the needful *(No. 55 of 12 June 1873)*. These concerns were reflected earlier too. See *File No. 305 Bengal of 1866 Assam Secretariat Progs.* The subsequent formation of the Chief Commissionership of Assam under the Govt. of India in 1874 has been consequent to this concern among others. See *Foreign Deptt. Secret India 1871 37-39.*
3. See *Foreign FC 11 May 1840 128-129*. Letter from Rev. Miles Bronson to Francis Jenkins, Governor General's Agent on the North East Frontier. See also *Foreign FC 9 November 1840 81-83*, for Bronson's suggestion on the scope of tea and salt-trade on the Naga frontier. See

further *Foreign FC 22 November 1841 124-125. Bronson's* views, endorsed by Jenkins, reflected the general interests of the Colonial State in this regard. Almost all correspondences on the frontier touched this issue.

4. See *Foreign FC 22 November 1841 124-125* for Bronson's proposal for the "civilization of the Nagas". That Jenkins was pursuing this mission for quite sometime, is evident from his *letter* to H.T. Prinsep, Secretary to the Govt. of India in the Secret Deptt *(vide No. 41 of 3 April 1838)*. He wrote that by bringing these hill tribes under "our management" all the frontiers would be tranquilized and the passages through the mountain passes on the frontiers would be *secured*. Jenkins added that with a British officer in charge of the area and with the "means we possess of instructing and *humanizing* the Nagas there seem to be every reason to hope that these *unfortunate* races may be soon raised in the scale of civilization". On the margin of the letter, he noted that with the establishment of a Missionary family (obvious reference to Rev. Bronson) at Jeypore for the instruction of the Nagas, he hoped to increase the Mission and plant it in the hills "were the country in our hands". See *Foreign_PC 16 May 1838 53-58*. Interestingly however, the Foreign Deptt. of the Govt. of India did not openly endorse Bronson's project. But the Govt. of India sanctioned a small grant to the school set up by Bronson. See *India Political Despatch to the Secretary of State No. 71 of 13 November 1840 (Foreign Deptt.)* The records extant reveal, on close examination, that 'civilizing' the "wild, savage" tribes was an *essential* condition for security of the frontiers as well as for commerce (italics within quote are added for emphasis on our point).
5. The colonial records and the monographs prepared by officials used such terms as *Hillmen, barbarians, semi barbarians* and *wild tribes / savages*. The colonial regime never defined as to what was a 'tribe'. It appears that the regime's use of qualified categorizations such as the "savage tribes" would never provide a *space* for these people within the *matrix* of '*modernity*'. The use of certain types of expression as the "criminal tribes", in the larger Indian context, actually placed the so-called 'tribes' as *outsiders* under control of the system. Hence there was no question of modernizing them!
6. See his 'Foreword' to the First edition of Verrier Elwin's work, *A Philosophy for NEFA. Shillong*: NEFA Administration (Research Deptt.), 1957.
7. Nehru's *letter*, dated 1 August 1946. See for details Sajal Nag, *Contesting Marginality. Ethnicity, Insurgency and Sub nationalism in North East India.* New Delhi: Monohar Publishers & Distributors, 2002, pp. 125-127.

8. The Naga National Council demanded independence. The Mizos were divided on the question of whether to join the proposed Indian Dominion or not. Assertions in various forms were articulated by other organizations like the Khasi National Dorbar. The Syiem of Nongstoin, U Wickliffe,opposed joining India and ultimately left to live in East Pakistan.
9. See the *Manipur (Hill Areas) District Councils Act, 1971*. This *Act* provided for division of Hill areas into *not more* than *six* autonomous districts (Section – 3, Chapter – II). These councils are given at least seventeen functions including management of primary schools and dispensaries [Section 29 (iii) & (iv), Chapter-3].
10. The idea of 'conditional' legislation is used here from B.L. Hansaria's work, *Sixth Schedule to the Constitution of India – A Study*. Gauhati: Ashok Publishing House, 1983. 'Conditional', because certain conditions were set for the executive and judicial administration of these tribal areas. Such legislations differentiated the tribal areas from the adjacent 'Regulation' provinces, considered more advanced. In fact, the long series of 'conditional' legislations began with Cleveland's experiments in the Raj Mahal Hills in the 1780s,which inaugurated the system of *non-regulatory* control over the *tribal* areas where the *normal* regulations meant for the *plains* were not applicable. See E.T. Dalton, *Tribal History of Eastern India* Delhi: Cosmo Publication, 1973. See for my analysis of the 'civilizational' mission aspect of *conditional* legislation in Abhijit Choudhury, "The Contextual Dimensions of the Sixth Schedule", in *Contemporary India, Journal of the Nehru Memorial Museum and Library*. New Delhi, 1(4), Oct –Dec. 2002, pp. 1-55.
11. Abhijit Choudhury, "The North Eastern India in the Perception of Suniti Kumar Chatterji" – Paper presented at the *Workshop on Historiography of North East India: Critical Perspective*, Guwahati, (Cotton College; Gauhati University & CENISEAS, OKD Institute of Social Change and Development), 27 February, 2004.
12. *The Mainstream*. 11 Nov. 2006.
13. *The Times of India*, N.E. Edn., 20 Oct 2006.
14. Prof. Tapas Mazumdar, "The Probability Game", in *The Telegraph*, Guwahati Edn., 21 Sept. 2006.
15. *Ibid*. The facts vindicate an *Editorial* titled, "*A Ritual Foretold*" (*The Telegraph*, Guwahati Edn, 17 Aug. 2003) which said, "speeches on ceremonial occasions by the President or the Prime Minister are imbued with more optimism than reality yet warrants."
16. *The Times of India*, Guwahati Edn., 11 Oct. 2006.
17. These data are culled from *The Basic Statistics of NER*. Shillong: The North Eastern Council, 2002.

18. Their interactions with the media during visits to the region including Meghalaya between 2000 and 2007 AD.
19. See media reports, with increasing evidence, since 2000 AD.
20. Bipan Chandra, Mridula Mukherjee & Aditya Mukherjee, *India After Independence, 1947 – 2000*. New Delhi : Penguin Books India (P) Ltd. 2000, p.110. The *implication* of this observation becomes obvious, if one sees what G.K. Pillai has to say. That *90 per cent* of the budget of the Karbi-Anglong ADC are controlled by only 12-14 families. See his essay, "Misgovernance and its Impact on Economic Development in the North Eastern States" in *Dialogue Quarterly*. 4 (1), July – Sept. 2002, New Delhi : Astha Bharati, pp. 75-84.
21. See Abhijit Choudhury, 2002, *Op. cit.*
22. Let us cite a very recent instance. The Jaintia Youth Federation submitted a *memorandum* to the Meghalaya Chief Minister, demanding enquiry into the "incomprehensible disappearance of *Rs. 4.79 crores"* from the Jaintia Hills Autonomous District Council. They alleged that this public money was squandered in paying advances to the MDCs and the JHADC officers. See *The Meghalaya Guardian*, 15 June 2007.
23. See J.M. Phira, *The Autonomous District Councils of Meghalaya under the Sixth Schedule of the Constitution of India*. Shillong: Techno–Quip, 1993; Patricia Mukhim, "of dummy tribals and policies" in *The Telegraph,* Guwahati Edn., 28 Nov. 2002. She suggests that *community* efforts are necessary to break the tentacles of *Timber Mafia.* In fact, a visit to Meghalaya-Bangladesh borders would reveal the truth of her observation on the necessity of such efforts. Toki Blah's *interview* to my students, 2006.
24. Bindo Lanong's *interview* to my students, 2006.
25. See O. Deo Valentine Ladia, *The Administration of Justice in Meghalaya*, Guwahati : Assam Law House, 2006, especially Ch. VI, pp. 151-67. See also Abhijit Choudhury, 2002, *Op.cit.,* for discussion on the *correlation* between inhibitory land laws and development in Meghalaya. In very recent times, tea *plantations* under *private* initiatives of the local tribals have been coming up in certain areas of Meghalaya. But the planters are facing problems regarding acquisition of land under the prevailing customary laws. As a result, the North Eastern Council, has not been able to provide funds to them (interview with the persons concerned on strict condition of anonymity). See further Patricia Mukhim, 2002, *op.cit.* She writes that some areas are so far-removed from the present system of governance that people there follow only traditional land laws. Under comparable circumstances in Nagaland, for instance in the Ao-Naga areas, land ownership pattern has been inhibiting development. See 'Keynote Address' to a seminar by

Alemtemshi Jamir, Development Commissioner, Nagaland, in C.J. Thomas & Gurudas Das, *eds., Dimensions of Development in Nagaland.* New Delhi: Regency publication, 2002, pp. 1-8.

26. Interview with Toki Blah, 2006.
27. Interview with Bindo Lanong, 2006.
28. J.M. Phira, 1993, *Op. cit,* pp. 38-42. All said, however, the district councils in Meghalaya have passed a few *Acts* related to social customs and usages. Some of them have been struck down by the State. See for details Abhijit Choudhury, 2002, *Op.cit.*
29. Lt. Gen. Sushil Pillai, "Three Matryoshkas: Ethnicity, Autonomy and Governance," in KPS Gill & Ajai Sahni, *eds., Faultlines.* Vol. 12. New Delhi: Bulwork Books & ICM, 2002, pp. 28-32.
30. Interface with Dr. H. Ghonglah, a social activist. He believes, without public accountability corruption cannot be checked.
31. Ibid.
32. Interface with Dr. Omarlin Kyndiah and A. Ghosh. In the recent *The Week/C-Voter* nationwide poll on the occasion of the 60th anniversary of Indian independence, *30 per cent* (the highest) of the votes cast have indicted the bureaucracy for being the worst element in our democracy. See *The Week,* 19 August 2007, p. 58. In case of the district and regional councils in the NER, the bureaucrats obstruct the release of funds and processing of legislations. In Tripura, for instance, the Tripura Tribal Autonomous Council demanded a *role* in the State Finance Commission, because of these reasons. See *The Telegraph,* 27 Nov. 2002. However, there are instances where a well-intentioned bureaucrat can contribute towards the enlargement of democratization of developmental processes as in Nagaland. See *Kurukshetra,* 55 (8), June 2007, pp. 40-41.
33. Interview with Toki Blah, 2006. Bindo Lanong (2006), however, thinks that weak executive committees and "too much politics", instead of development, are factors behind the failures of the district councils.
34. See "The 6th Schedule Imbroglio", in *The North East Sun,* 15-30 Nov. 1995. In the context of the debate on whether the Sixth Schedule should be extended to the Manipur Hills, it is *doubtful* if Prof. M. Horam's hope of *narrowing down* ethnic tension between the Nagas and the Kukis, with its extension, will ever be fulfilled. Who knows there would not be ethnic conflict within a 'single' ADC that Horam advocates! In course of an interface, Dr. Robert Tiba (Assam University, Silchar), who hails form Manipur and is a historian, expressed his belief that introduction of District Council(s) in the Hills might ease many of their problems.
35. See *The Asian Age (N.E. Age),* 3 Dec. 2002. The Autonomous State Demand Committee rejected the *ADC* on the ground that it "failed to

fulfill the hopes and aspirations of the people due to its institutional shortcomings.

36. This view is based on ideas derived from reading David Hardiman's critical essay titled, "The Indian 'Faction': A Political Theory Examined", in Ranajit Guha, *ed., Subaltern Studies I*. New Delhi : OUP, 1982, pp. 198-231.
37. Interface with Dr. Rajesh Dev, a Shillong based Political scientist and analyst.
38. See E. Jyrwa, "Critical Assessment of the working of the Khasi Hills Autonomous District Council", in M.N. Karna, L.S. Gassah & C.J. Thomas, *eds., Power to People in Meghalaya (Sixth Schedule and the 73rd Amendment)*. New Delhi : Regency Publications, 1998, pp. 85-100; L.S. Gassah, "A Critical Assessment of the Role and Functions of the Jaintia Hills Autonomous District Council", in *Ibid.*, pp. 116-29.
39. See *The Shillong Times*, 15 Aug. 1971, for a reference to the 1968 plea. The Khasi Chiefs contested the jurisdiction of the district council on the "appointment and succession of chiefs and headmen" on the ground that *Entry 5* of the *Seventh Schedule* placed it as a *concurrent* subject of the Union and the Meghalaya governments over and above the existing authority of the Council in this regard. The Khasi Chiefs regarded the creation of Meghalaya as "a manifestation more of a special kind of *regionalism* than of a 'tribal' *identity*" (Italics within quote are mine)
40. See M.S. Sangma, "Working of the Garo Hills Autonomous District Council (An overall view)", in M.N. Karna *et.al., Op.cit.*, pp. 130-37; & Kshirode Marak, "Critical Assessment of the GHADC", in *Ibid.*,pp. 138–56.
41. Interview with Toki Blah, 2006.
42. Interview with Bindo Lanong, 2006.
43. See Pascal Malngiang, "The Khasi Hills Autonomous District Council and the 73rd Constitutional Amendment", in M.N. Karna, *et.al., op.cit.*,pp. 101-08; & P.M. Passah "The working of the Jaintia Hills Autonomous District Council", in *Ibid.*, pp. 109-15.
    See also B.K. Roy Burman, "Constitutional Framework for Tribal Autonomy with Special Reference to North East India", in M.K. Raha & A.K. Ghosh, *eds., North-East India: The Human Interface*. New Delhi: Gyan Publishing House, 1998, pp. 81-114.
44. B.K. Roy Burman, *Ibid.*
45. See Abhijit Choudhury, 2002, *op.cit.*
46. *Ibid.* Toki Blah, during the interview (2006) with him, pointed out that the district councils have not been able to do much in establishing village councils and town committees, administration of village, public health and sanitation, use of water sources, etc. Moreover, these councils were

autocratic in appointing the headmen, he regretted. On the other hand, Bindo Lanong (Interview, 2006) did not think that Panchayat Raj would be suitable for the hill people. It was suitable for the plains areas since it had been "working there for many years".

47. See R.S. Pandey, "Communitization in Nagaland : A Unique Experiment in Empowering People", in *Kurukshetra,* 55(8), June 2007, pp. 40-41.
48. See for his detailed and interesting interpretation, Subrata Mitra, *The Puzzle of India's Governance: Culture, Context and Comparative Theory.* London: Routledge, 2006.
49. See *The Telegraph,* 27 March 2007
50. Nirmal Kumar Bose, *Problems of National Integration.* Shimla / Calcutta: Indian Institute of Advance Study / Rddhi India, 1988 (first published in 1967), pp. 64-65.
51. Interview with persons concerned on strict condition of anonymity.

Pangs of Proximity

INDIA'S NORTH EAST AND HER EASTERN NEIGHBOURS

Ishani Naskar

India is a large country full of diversity and endless complexities. For all practical purposes we often refer to the various geographical regions of this vast piece of land and relate various research aspects of the concerned regions to serious government policy formulations. India's North East is one such region that has been a subject of serious research and policy debates. However, this essay does not see North East India as only a geographical region but as a system that is unique and conspicuous. This region, along with its geographical neighbours, constitute an encompassing whole. This paper looks at the inseparable role that North East's geographical neighbours, who are also India's *political* neighbours, have in the present state of affairs. It also makes us aware of the fact that the continuous involvement of India's neighbours makes any decent solution for the region a far cry from possibility. Given such a context, it is necessary to relate the challenges of India's foreign-policymaking towards her eastern neighbours with the almost insurmountable challenges in the North East.

The paper presents its arguments in three sections. The first section queries why North East India needs to be established as a different 'systemic whole' set apart from the Indian one. It involves a look at the geographical location, its demographic composition and historical developments that have shaped the contemporary complexities in the region. The second section highlights the inevitable role that India's eastern neighbours have in the complications of the North East. The third section considers the challenges of foreign policymaking that ought to be based on an ideal balance of India's interests towards neighbours and her domestic situations within the North East.

SECTION I

North East as a Distinct System—Geographical Contiguity, Demographic Composition, and Historical Developments

Geographical Contiguity with India's Eastern Neighbours

The geographical position of North East is the least debatable of components that account for its distinctiveness. The integrity of North East to the Indian territory is challenged by geographical exclusiveness from the Indian landmass, and the inclusiveness with her neighbours. As a geographical region, North East covers an area of 2,63,000 square kilometers sharing international borders with more foreign states than any part of India. The region shares highly porous and sensitive borders with China, Myanmar, Bangladesh and Bhutan. Therefore, the region's strategic location is underlined by the fact that it shares a 4,500-kilometer long international border with India's eastern neighbours. The only land-based connection that the region has with India is the Siliguri corridor also known as the 'Chicken's Neck'. It may be added that J.R. Mukherjee makes three geographical divisions of the North East of which only the first division points to the connection with the mainland. The other two divisions reiterate the continuity between the region and our eastern neighbours as much as the self-contained character of the region. The divisions are:

1. Himalayan mountains of Nepal, Sikkim, North Bengal, Bhutan, Arunachal Pradesh and Tibet binding Brahmaputra and the Gangetic Valley plains to the North;
2. Eastern hills that link India and Myanmar to the East, the Meghalaya, Karbi Anglong Plateau, BarakValley and the plains of Bangladesh to the South; and
3. Cachar and North Cachar Hills, the Manipur Valley, the Mizoram and Manipur hills and the piedmont plains of Tripura bound to Barak Valley.[1]

It is important to make a note of the fact that there is no distinct geographical boundary (as between India and Tibet) that separates South Asia from Southeast Asia. Taking this observation further, it would be plausible to look at it this way – the North East Region serves as the crucial landmass-link between South Asia and Southeast Asia. Contiguity of states is not an essential condition for a system by itself. There needs to be some amount of interstate linkages, of which cultural attribute is emphasized as a cardinal attribute.[2] Though, cultural homogeneity is desirable, it is quite difficult to achieve; as Bajpai emphasizes, regions are zones of "cultural affinity and fracture"[3]. Such an observation applies to the North East both as a region and as a system. Cultural cleavages do not impede economic interaction between states of the region; economic interaction only reiterates its systemic character. In this context, one can also refer to Kenichi Ohame's description of the region as natural economic zones. A system analysed in terms of cross-border economic interdependence has been termed by him as a region state. Our conceptualisation of North East as an economic system reiterates the intense linkages and synergies emphasized by Ohame in explaining region states.[4]

It is rather complex to delineate North East as a system in terms of strategic and security concerns. Although North East as a system cannot be ascertained through Buzan's regional security complex logic[5], some other opinions regarding security complexes may be applied to understand the turmoil in the North East where states interact intensely within a given regional security complex for the protection of their various interests; consequently the policy and behaviour of any one state make up a necessary element in the calculation of others.[6] In the case of the North East, complex interdependent relations are established not only between states but also between belligerent ethnic and religious groups. The region also comes close to a serious strategic zone where more than one player, both state and non-state, in character is involved in the struggle for power.[7]

Demographic Composition of the North East

The demographic composition in the North East has been conditioned by two contradictory factors. First, North East constitutes inhospitable terrain comprising a maze of rivers running through mountains cutting deep gorges as it moves on. The hill ranges segregate valleys and plains from each other. Such a segregation of the hills from the valleys, plateaus from the plains, are also responsible for demographic isolation of the tribal and non-tribal populations inhabiting these regions. Cross-tribal interactions have also been conditioned by their geographical surrounding and have remained so over the years. Second, the large-scale migration and population movements that have taken place from the adjacent areas, mainly from India's eastern neighbours, have brought about a significant change in the demographic composition of the region. This has resulted in interactions (not essentially peaceful) between tribal and non-tribal populations across India's borders. A look at the chart below will help highlight the links between the population of the North East and its neighbours:

States	*Approximate Number of Tribes*	*Tribes/Races/ Places of Origin*	*Non-Tribal Population*	*Languages*
Arunachal Pradesh	79 tribes and sub-tribes	i) Tibeto-Mongoloid (known as *kirats*) ii) Indo-Burmese (with affinity to Naga tribes)	Tibetans, Nepalese (associated with Assam Rifles), Chakmas, Bangladeshis (some of them moved from Brahmaputra alley)	Nagamiz
Assam	23 tribes and sub-tribes	i) Ahoms (related to Shans who moved from Yunan to Southeast Asia and were perhaps associated with the *tai* tribe from Thailand) ii) Bodos (sub-tribes include *Karbis, Mikirs, Mishungs, Raj Banshis*) Indo-Burmans/ Tibeto-Mongoloids	Nepalese, Marwaris, Biharis, Bangladeshi and Muslims and Hindus	Assamese, Bengali, Bodo, Karbi, Mising, Rabha.
Manipur	32 tribes and sub-tribes	i) Meiteis/Tibeto-Burmans (linked to *tai).* ii) Kuki-Chins-Mizo (sub-tribes-*Chiru, Chothe, Lamlang, Paite, Hmars*), Indo-Burmans. iii) Nagas(sub-tribes-*Angami, Zeliang, Ma, Tangkuls*)/Mongoloid Burmans.	Muslims called *Pangals* (also known as *Meitei Pangals*) who settled here in the seventeenth century. Also, Nepalese, Marwaris and Bangladeshis.	Meitei. Kuki, Chin dialects like Thado, Hmars.

States	*Approximate Number of Tribes*	*Tribes/Races/ Places of Origin*	*Non-Tribal Population*	*Languages*
Meghalya	17 tribes and sub-tribes	i) Khasis (sub-tribes- *Wars, Khynriams, Nars and Bhois*) and Jayantias(sub-tribes- *Lakers, Mons, Dimsas, Hajongs*) belonging to Mon Khmer affiliated to Asia-Austrics. ii) Garos, also called *Achiks* or hill men (*Awe, Chisak, Matchi-Dual, Matabeng, Ambeng, Ruga-Chibox, Gara-Ganching, Atong* and the *Megam*) belonging to the Bodo family, affiliated to Tibeto-Mongoloid origin).	Bangladeshi and Nepalese	Mon Khmer affiliated dialect, Tibeto-Burmese affiliated Garo
Mizoram	44 tribes and sub-tribes	i) Mizos (*Lushai* tribes)/Mongoloids. ii) Kuki-Chi-Mizos (moved from Chin Hills, Myanmar in the Seventeenth and Eighteenth Century), sub-tribes-*Hmars, Paite, Poi, Lakhers* affiliated to the Indo-Burmans	Bangladeshis, Myanmarese, Nepalese and Biharis	Lushai/ Duhaliya Twang/ Mizo Twang all affiliated to the Tibeto-Burmese family of languages.
Nagaland	17 tribes and sub-tribes	Indo-Mongoloid origins (*kirats*) sub-tribes include, *Angami, Ao, Thangkul Chakseang, chang, Khiamniungan, Kuki, Konyak, Lotha, Phom,Pochury, Rengma, Sumi,Sangtam, Yimchungru, Zeliang*	Bangladeshis, Myanmarese and Chakmas	Nagamese

States	*Approximate Number of Tribes*	*Tribes/Races/ Places of Origin*	*Non-Tribal Population*	*Languages*
Tripura	26 tribes and sub-tribes	i) Tripuris (belonging to the Bodo family i.e. Tibeto-Burmans) ii) *Jamatias, Garos*, (Bodo sub-tribe) iii) Chakmas iv) Chin-Kuki-Mizos v) Jayantias (Austrics)	Bengali Hindus and Bengali Muslims from Bangladesh	Bengali, Kok Barok.

Chart prepared on the basis of readings from Girin Phukan (ed), Inter-Ethnic Conflict in North East India, Kolkata, Maulana Abul Kalam Azad Institute of Asian Studies, 2004; Lt. General J.R. Mukherjee, An Insider's Experience of Insurgency in India's North-East, Anthem Press; Lt. Gen N.S. Narahari, Security Threats to North-East India, The Socio-Ethnic Tensions, Delhi, Manas Publications 2002; Subir Bhaumik, *Insurgent Crossfire: North-East India*, New Delhi, Lancers Publishers, 1996; *Chandra Bhusan, Terrorism and Separation and North-East India, Delhi, Kalpaz Publications, 2004.*

A look at the chart reveals the complexity of the demographic profile of the region. It reveals the predominance of the tribal population over the non-tribal population. The roots of this tribal population of the region can be traced to the countries around the North East as evident from the various tribal groups-Tibeto-Mongoloid, Indo-Burman, Tibeto-Burman being some of these groups. Moreover, a majority of the non-tribal population in the region also comes from the neighbouring countries viz. Bangladesh, Myanmar and Nepal. In comparison, a lesser number of Indians (mainly Biharis, Marwaris and Bengalis) comprise the non-tribal population. Interestingly, Chakmas comprise both tribal and non-tribal populations in separate contexts. For instance in Tripura, they are a part of the tribal population however, in tribe-dominated states like Nagaland and Arunachal Pradesh, Chakmas are part of the non-tribal population from Bangladesh.

Historical Developments in the Colonial Period

A preliminary idea of the history of the region would reveal the continuous struggle between the various tribes still found in this region long before the advent of the British, even before the Aryans and the Mughals. For instance, Bodos fought the Jayantias, the Ahoms fought the Bodos, Nagas fought the Ahoms.[8] Different historical chronicles contain rich accounts of the ancient developments in North East India. Moreover, during the nineteenth century, right up to the years approaching Indian independence, many Europeans traveled across the length and breadth of North East mostly under government patronage and wrote about it[9]. Not discounting the importance of the other states of the region, Assam (Kingdom of *Kamrupa*) has gained consistent importance through all the periods of history from the pre-Aryan times to the British colonial India.[10] The reasons are not far to fathom. A good look at the North East will bring out the central position of Assam in the region; a large and fertile valley makes it attractive for human settlement. Moreover, any physical communication across the length ad breadth of the region would involve traversing through Assam. However, it was the British colonial period that had brought maximum change[11]. The British colony spread to the region in the Nineteenth Century and introduced administrative changes that underlined their divide-and-rule policy. The notorious divide and rule policy resulted in complications that have been carried over to the post-British period. As a consequence, the region remains alienated from the Indian nation.

Ironically, when the British arrived in the region, it was almost a messianic event, because turbulence ruled the region. The Ahoms and the Manipuris were braving the attacks from Myanmar, and the British came to their rescue. The Anglo-Burman war ended with the Treaty of Yandaboo in 1826 and gave the British an entry into the region through Assam. It marked the beginning of the British administration in the North East. However, establishing dominance over the region was not easy for the British and they faced tough resistance from the hill tribes[12]. On realizing their inability to subordinate the ferocious tribal populations of the hills especially of those in the North East Frontier Agency or the NEFA, the Inner Line Regulations were introduced in 1873. By the late nineteenth century they were in substantial control of the region. The British administration had clear-cut priorities towards the North East – the richly endowed plains, and the large tea gardens of the North East (mostly concentrated in Assam province) would serve their mercantile needs. The freedom loving tribes dwelling in the dense forests, up in the mountains and hills, were not initially of any consequence to the British. Soon, however, they realized the importance of these hilly regions. First, these tribes were capable of hindering economic expansion of the British and therefore all forms of hill uprising had to be contained. There were also external threats; Myanmar was an aggressive neighbour, and the Chinese were also interested in some of the hills of the north. Finally, the British realized that tribes were fierce warriors, and would make good soldiers; hence, a number of Nagas were inducted in the British army to serve during the Second World War. Subsequently, the plains of the North East would primarily serve the economic priorities of the British Empire while the hilly frontiers were important for politico-strategic reasons.

The outcome of such prioritization was the conscious and consistent promotion of the plain areas like Assam and the Surma Valley in Manipur as economic power centers in the region; economic power begets political power. British policies towards the tribes were based on administrative pragmatism propelled on non-interference in tribal issues, introduction of Christianity wherever possible, and a plan to bring the tribal areas under the 'Crown Colony'. Alongside, administrative categorization of the provinces of the region ranged from 'Excluded' to 'Partially Excluded' areas[13]. The former fell under the British jurisdiction and the latter were given a limited representative system under the British administrative control. Viewed in this context, the Inner Line Permit can be seen as a complement to this administrative categorization. However the motive behind the Inner Line as an innocuous administrative act needs to be scrutinized. On March 27, 1870, the Pioneer wrote, " Baffled at length by the inveterate savagery of the people and the difficulties of their hills, the Government fell back on a policy of absolute non-interference and defence; the Imperial Dalhousie emphatically pronounced the game not worth the candle. "We had nothing to gain", he said, "by annexing a wild people and their barren hills. So we relegated them to a kind of political 'Coventry'. In the year 1851 our troops withdrew..." The first attempts to open up the Naga territory was made rather in the interest of Manipur than of India, and was due to the fact that Raja Gumbhir Singh was desirous of strengthening his hands against Burma by intimate trade relations with Assam, and it was thought well to encourage him in this policy."[14] It clearly shows British indifference towards the people and is also indicative of their desire to sow seeds of rift between the plains and the hills.

The British did not trust the tribes. A continuous sense of insecurity from these volatile communities haunted their success as rulers. Therefore they set themselves to the task of crafting divisions within the social domain. First they sought to change the demographic composition of vast tracts of the region. Particularly, where the British had economic interest, a substantial non-tribal population from other parts of India were brought in to contribute to the economic activities of that place; such has been the case of Assam. This coupled with segregation between the tribal and non-tribal population, to identities to remain at permanent poles. At the same time, the British were not encouraging strong tribal fraternity for sheer reasons of political insecurity. Subsequently arbitrary policies would prevent creation of any form of tribal identity from being crystallized. For instance, the arbitrary borders through the extreme eastern frontiers of North East along the Patkai Hills dismembered the tribal fraternity of the Indo-Burmese tribes living in that area. On the other hand, forced migration and resettlement of tribes between the British governed areas of the North East and the areas of volatile tribes served two purposes. First, the resettled tribal areas would act as buffers between the British and the aggressive tribes. Second, it would cultivate mutual intolerance between those tribal communities, making it easy for the British to gain control over them. Such was the case of the *Kuki Chin* tribes from Burma, who were forced to settle between the Nagas and the British administered regions of Manipur and Cachar.

The British managed to associate the North East politically with the rest of India[15] . They had at the same time done mischief by sowing a sense of distrust and apathy towards the state administration (predominantly non-tribal administration) dominated once by the sahibs in Assam and Bengal, and in the post independence period taken over by the Indian state at Delhi. Unfortunately, the Indian system has failed to free itself from the colonial mindset. In this context, B.B. Kumar detects a colonial bias among Indian social scientists and academics in general as they fail to free themselves from the strong clutches of the imperialist/colonial disciplines.[16] Baruah correctly observes that at the very outset the transformation of non-state spaces into state-controlled spaces provided the backdrop to North East discontents.[17] It has only structured the feeling of alienation from the Indian mainland. A weak inexperienced leadership with a very inadequate understanding of the complex and confusing demographic matrix and a failure to estimate the needs of the people made it difficult for the government to thwart the rising voices of dissent since independence. Along with that, the wave of communism in the early days of independence in the neighbouring countries of North East India took some of its areas under its influence. The road for external intervention was paved even before it was realized by the Indian administration. Unfortunately, annoyance with the Indian government has hardly receded; even to this day experts of the region voice their frustration with the government, "Most of the armed struggles of the North-east originate from a sense of deep frustration at being repeatedly caricatured as minions of the centre. How did the fiercely independent tribes suddenly become obsequious lackeys of Delhi? This is palpable when national bigwigs arrive at the state capitals to 'help resolve' the internal squabbles among politicians here."[18] Moreover cross border linkages have multiplied over time; solution is a word that is hardly to see the light of the day.

SECTION II
The Gradual Involvement of North East's Geographical Neighbours in the Region

Our perceptions and views relating to the partition of India in 1947 are somehow concentrated on the fate of the millions of hapless Hindus and Muslims who had to undergo the terrible trauma of moving out of India into Pakistan and vice versa. However, there were other issues of no less significance emanating out of the tumultuous politics of the sub-continent during 1930s and the 1940s. For instance, the separation of Burma from India in 1937 and the subsequent creation of East Pakistan in 1947 etched out North East as a distinct unit. One is well aware of this region's close contacts with their immediate neighbours long before colonization took place. A lengthy and consistent trajectory of movements between the hills and plains made it possible for the evolution of a complex social matrix comprising multiple cultures and languages distinct from one another yet within close proximity; this in turn helped inculcate strong cross border ethnic affiliations. On the other hand, some of the arrangements were entirely administrative brought about by the colonizers[19]. Be it for administrative convenience or socio-cultural ties, the pre-independence period links were maintained with the countries of Bangladesh in the west, Burma in the east and Tibet in the North. An analysis of Bhaumik's works on North East helps us understand these close links:

- Khasi Jaintia and Garo Hills maintained close relations with Sylhet, Bangladesh:
- The Mizo Hills with Chittagong Hills Tracts;
- Tripura with Comilla, Noakhali and Sylhet;
- Parts of the Mizo Hills, Manipur and the Naga hills had direct links with Burma and,
- North East Frontier Agency (now Arunachal Pradesh) had close contacts with Tibet and Bhutan.[20]

It may also be added at this point that Assam depended on Rangpur and Syhlet for its communication and trade, and once Partition took away both these options Assam was virtually isolated from mainland India until connectivity in 1950 was established through Siliguri.

Events that followed independence both in the North East as well as in some of the countries around it made it easier for the external intervention. To begin with, the formation of East Pakistan in the 1940s on the basis of religious identity brought amongst other consequences the Pakistani administration breathing over the shoulders of India's North East. Over time, the Chinese occupation of Tibet in the 1950s spelt undesirable consequences for India. First, she lost the buffer between herself and China putting to peril her overall security. Second, the occupation paved the way for Chinese military intervention into the North East, an apprehension that became a reality soon enough. At the same time, beyond the extreme east of the North East, the then Burmese U Nu administration was facing the uphill task of nation building, being challenged both by the Communists as well as various ethnic forces. India was herself concerned with the growing Communist guerrilla activity at home, and a Chinese backed Communist insurrection spreading out of Burma to engulf the whole of India's North East was one of the worst case scenarios tormenting Indian intelligence in the early 1950s. Speaking at the UN General Assembly on 17 April 1953, V.K. Krishna Menon said: 'What hurt Burma would hurt India because of links of friendship, geography and history between the two countries.'[21] The problems only multiplied with the change of regime from a democratic one to one ruled by the army. East Pakistan was ruled by a hostile government mostly dominated by military rulers since the late 1950s. Atrocities on the Bengali Muslims and minorities alike led to a relentless exodus of millions that was to affect the demographic and cultural identity of the region forever. The wars with China and Pakistan in the 1960s coincided with the brewing trouble within the various states of North East like Nagaland, Mizoram, Manipur, and Tripura, Assam voiced its demands a little later. Cross-border affiliations of some of these fighting tribes like the Nagas, the Kukis and the Chins have made it easier for them to make friends across borders with ethnic discordant forces in Myanmar. Subsequently, a symbiotic relationship has developed between the rebellious forces in the North East and the disruptive forces in our neighbourhood.

Political considerations have always determined the way in which India's eastern neighbours have viewed and involved themselves in the insurgency movements of the North East. However, given the geographical location, the easy accessibility into the interiors of the land coupled with tribal brotherhood, it definitely makes it easier for those external powers who wish to create trouble for the Indian state. Again going by Bhaumik's descriptions on the state of insurgency in Tripura and Mizoram which he clubs with the Chittagong region, gives quite a clear impression of the geopolitical significance of the 'triangle'.[22] In another context, he mentions how the Meiteis of Manipur would reach East Pakistan through the Lower Cachar district or via the North district of Tripura where substantial Meiteis resided[23]. There was this great expectation that if Nagas could pick up the traill of the Meiteis to East Pakistan, the Tripuris could follow the Mizos through the large jungle tracts that touch the borders of India and East Pakistan, then it could hardly be a problem for outside forces (viz. Pakistan along with China) to coordinate a massive and long stretched insurgency in various parts of the North East.[24]

On having highlighted the backdrop and events that have not only paved the way but has in a way underlined the inevitability of the involvement of India's Eastern neighbours in fomenting and supporting insurgencies in the North East, it is imperative to probe the kind of roles played by at least two of these neighbours, Bangladesh, and Burma. The role of China will find place contextually in the discussion on these two neighbours.

Bangladesh

More of an India locked country Bangladesh shares 4,094 kilometers of land border on three sides, the fourth side opening towards Bay of Bengal[25]. Bangladesh's significance as a neighbour to India can be studied in a two-phase manner – as East Pakistan and subsequently as Bangladesh. Before its independence its role needs to be seen as that of Pakistan's. There is also evidence that the US was involved in cooking up trouble for North East by trying to materialize a master plan to create a separate state of 'Independent Bengal' that would comprise East Pakistan, West Bengal, Assam, Manipur, Tripura, Sikkim and Nagaland. This plan was first spelt out in none other than a Dacca datelined dispatch circulated by the International Press Agency on December 7, 1963. The separatist leaders are said to have accepted the plot of independent Bengal with its capital in Calcutta. It promised the Nagas and Mizos of 'Greater Nagaland' and 'Greater Mizoram' as autonomous units within the framework of 'Great Bengal'.[26] Pakistan's active support for the insurgents right from the Nagas to the Mizos is a well known fact. Phizo's flight to East Pakistan followed by the training of Naga insurgents has been discussed time and again. Several camps that were established were concentrated in the easily accessible areas of the Chittagong Hill Tracts at Rangamati, Ruma, Bandarban Ukhia and Alikadam[27]. They also received an enormous amount of armaments. The Mizo chief Laldenga was received cordially in East Pakistan in the 60s, they transferred their armaments through Chittagong, Tripura and Cachar. By 1965, they were well prepared to take on the Indian troops, and in 1966, Operation Jericho took the Indian administration by surprise. In the post operation period, the MNF settled their camps in the Chittagong Hill Tracts. The *Sengrak* movement in Tripura began in the second half of the 1960s, and its association with East Pakistan is clearly exemplified in Bhaumik's words: "It marked a clear departure from the tradition of guerilla combat in the violent history of Tripura. For the first time, the state witnessed an insurgency with trans-border bases, willing to look for foreign patrons... A decade after the *Sengrak* died a natural death with the defeat of the Pakistanis in the eastern theatre and the emergence of a friendly Bangladesh...".[28]

In the 1960s, East Pakistan's vicious designs to spell trouble was compounded with the Chinese interests in keeping the pot boiling and keeping the Indian troops busy. However it was almost in the second half of that decade that their liaison gained momentum and a joint Sino-Pakistan strategy was in place to coordinate various forms of assistance to the members of almost all the major North Eastern insurgent groups – Nagas, Meiteis and Kukis. In fact around 1969, an effort as serious as setting up of a small airstrip within the vicinity of Rangamati was also in the agenda. Relatives of a senior Naga insurgent commander Thinoselie went to the extent of comparing Sino-Pakistan efforts towards North East with the Indo-US efforts in Tibet.[29] The role of the Indians in liberating East Pakistan was therefore driven as much by realist considerations as by idealist ones.

Bangladesh got back to its mischief after the demise of *Banga Bandhu* and with advances in Islamisation of Bangladesh. The present role of the Inter Services Intelligence (ISI) from Pakistan is in wide collaboration with the Bangladeshi counterpart, the Directorate General of Forces Intelligence (DGFI) in supporting the disruptive activities in the North East. Insurgent groups like the ULFA, ATTF and the NLFT that were formed in the 1970s and later have also managed to establish links with our neighbour. In this context the relentless concerted efforts by Bangladesh to nourish eternal chaos in the North East is underlined by a number of very alarming developments.

First, Bangladesh continues to house and shelter insurgents. There are a number of training liaison camps and safe houses for underground groups like National Socialist Council of Nagaland (Issac Muvaih), United Liberation Front of Assam, All Tripura Tiger Force, National Democratic Front of Bodoland, Peoples Liberation Army (Manipur), Achik National Volunteer Council, Kanglei Yawol Kanna Lup, Hynniewtrep National Volunteer Council, and Manipur Peoples Liberation Front. Probably there is no unanimity on the exact number of camps in Bangladesh but they certainly run above 150. Presently, the Indo-Bangladesh International Border Survey, 2007 has revealed the startling fact that though many rebel groups of the North-east announced ceasefire with the Centre and some of them are in peace talks with the Government of India, there are as many as 174 camps of North-east rebel groups on Bangladesh soil[30] . In addition, Saikia provides a list of North East Indian muslim fundamentalist organization camps[31], which definitely brings to light the dimension of Islamic fundamentalism in the North East. However, no list is ever exhaustive, and a complete account of the training camps in

Bangladesh is not available only because there is no permanency of the bases and patrons. There is always the provision for moving on to new locations. We are also aware of the number of enclaves on either side of the border.[32] They can serve purposes of camp sites as the governments are not aware of the status of these enclaves.

Second, a number of prominent members of insurgent groups have found shelter in Bangladesh. ULFA being the most important of these groups, their leaders like Anup Chetia and Paresh Barua have entrenched interests in Dhaka, Syhlet and Cox Bazaar. They have Bangladeshi passports. Chetia alias Golap Barua alias John David Salemar alias Jaj William Balot alias Abdul Aziz had been arrested and sent to jail in Bangladesh on January 1, 1998 under Foreigners Act and Passport Act. Babul Sarma was jailed on December 24, 1997 also under the same Acts as was another top ULFA leader Laxme Prosad Gosham. Chetia's term got over in 2005, but 'still is in jail' under the present caretaker government of Bangladesh. The absence of an extradition treaty between India and Bangladesh seems to be the biggest obstacle in his handing over to India, and Bangladesh seems to be in no hurry to sign one.[33] Paresh Barua leads a citizen's life in the heart of Dhaka. Also, Naga leaders possess Bangladeshi passports. Ranjit Deb Barman of the ATTF is also said to have frequented Dhaka. There are many more leaders, and the list being long, recently the Indian government has demanded the handing over of those insurgent leaders.[34] The Indian Daily recently has brought out India's weariness with Bangladeshi nonchalance to India's appeal for assistance[35].

Third, Bangladesh serves as the transit route for arms deals, and ULFA has made the maximum use of this route.ULFA acquires arms from Cambodia and Thailand, and Cox Bazaar is the naval transit for weapons transfer; unmonitored naval ports around the region are used for such arms trade.[36] Bangladesh provides a large transit market for arms trade coming from various parts of Asia, primarily China and neighbouring Southeast Asia The modus operandi is very simple. The consignment comes through sea routes to Cox Baazar and St. Martin's Island. After downloading the goods are transported by road to North East India. On the long journey, the arms carriers rest overnight at camps run by the Jamaat-e-Islami in the Chittagong Hill Tracts.[37] Finances by way of foreign funding are widely available for such arms shopping, and local smugglers and criminals are also involved in networking illegal financial conversions.[38]

Fourth, illegal influx of Bangladeshis has resulted in gradual but very consistent changes in the demographic profile of the North East, threatening the indigenous identity of the land. Assam is the state that has undergone tremendous change affecting the socio-economic as well as politico-strategic stability of the place. Proving Mullen's observations true[39], the Muslim population in Assam has been increasing in geometric proportions. The order of demographic invasion is deteriorating so much by the day that S.K. Sinha, PVSM, one of the Governors of Assam, who sent the report on illegal migration to the President of India in 1998, apprehended the dire consequences of this consistent exodus:

> This silent and invidious demographic invasion of Assam may result in the loss of the geostrategically vital districts of Lower Assam. The influx of these illegal migrants is turning these districts into a Muslim majority region. It will then only be a matter of time when a demand for their merger with Bangladesh may be made. The rapid growth of international Islamic fundamentalism may provide the driving force for this demand. In this context, it is pertinent that Bangladesh has long discarded secularism and has chosen to become an Islamic State. Loss of Lower Assam will sever the entire land mass of the North East, from the rest of India and the rich natural resources of that region will be lost to the Nation.[40]

Moreover he expressed his deep concern over the government's attitude towards the problem:

> There is a tendency to view illegal migration into Assam as a regional matter, affecting only the people of Assam. Its more dangerous if dimension of greatly undermining our national security is ignored. The long cherished design of Greater East Pakistan/Bangladesh, making inroads into the strategic land link of Assam with the rest of the country, can lead to severing the entire land mass of the North East, with all its rich resources, from the rest of the country. This will have disastrous strategic and economic consequences.[41]

The importance of his latter observation must be examined in view of the infamous concept of an Islamic *lebensraum* threatening the internal security of India. If ISI's designs are to be believed, then they have launched Operation Pin Code[42] to pan-Islamise the North East. An estimated fifteen to eighteen million illegal Bangladeshi migrants have found ways into the North East of India, and a large section of them are in Assam. Another three to five million are spread across Bihar and Bengal. In this context, Sekhon points out the designs of the ISI:

Another disquieting development has been the large-scale illegal migration of Bangladesh nationals into the region that has altered the demography of the entire North East. Such steps have been taken by the ISI to create an autonomous Islamic state over there and to ensure that its separatist anti-India agenda is carried out successfully to its logical conclusion.[43]

Fifth, there is an increasing involvement of Islamic forces in North East India, their roots traced back to Bangladesh. Pan-Islamisation plans to raise *jihadi* groups to carve out parts of Muslim dominated areas within the North East, especially areas close to Assam. Therefore, Bangladesh serves as the important link between pan-Islamisation and our restless North East. Since 2001, the resurfacing of the *Jamat-e-Islami,* as the main Islamic party in Bangladesh, signals the resurgence of Islamic forces in Bangladesh[44]. As a member of the erstwhile ruling coalition, violent anti-Hindu activities in Bangladesh have been complemented by serious programmes that are aimed at establishing and expanding links with the Islamic groups that are functioning in the North East. A number of Islamic fundamentalist and terrorist groups operate from Bangladesh – *Harkat-ul-Jihad-al-Islami, Islamic Oikyo Jote, Islami Chatra Shibir,* Arakan Rohingya National Organisation and Rohingya Solidarity Organisation[45]. There are a number of Muslim fundamentalist organizations (MFOs) on this side of the border like the Muslim United Liberation Tigers of Assam (MULTA), *Harkat-ul-Mujahideeni,* Muslim Liberation Front of Assam (MULFA),[46] who are functioning as the counterpart organizations to achieve *Brihot Bangladesh.* Moreover the involvement of Al Qaeda in this part of South Asia has been established. Selig Harrison reports, "A State Department report cited evidence that one of the Jamaat's main allies, the Harkat ul-Jihad-i-Islami, also headquartered in Pakistan, "maintains contact with Al Qaeda in Afghanistan." Bangladesh Harakat leader Fazlul Rahman was one of the six signatories of Osama bin Laden's first declaration of holy war against the United States, on Feb. 23, 1998. Since the October 2002 Bali bombings led to repression of al-Qaeda, some of its Indonesian and Malaysian cells have shifted their operations to Bangladesh[47]. Indoctrination goes on unabated as madrassas and training camps (training North East Indian fundamentalist organizations) have been established on either sides of the border, the latter blooming in Bangladesh.[48] The MFOs in the North East are a little older than a decade; their activities serve the ISI in two ways. First, they sabotage the North East and keep it detached from the Indian mainstream. Second, recruits from such Islamic organizations can also be used for other anti-state activities in other parts of India. The relevance of the Siliguri Corridor as a popular thoroughfare for terrorists between North East and India is known to the Indian administration. The ISI seem to be engaging these elements in their age old strategy of 'proxy war against India'.[49]

Myanmar

Burma, now officially renamed as Myanmar, is a state situated at the intersection of the major geographical landmasses- India, China and Indo-China. This makes Myanmar a strategic focal point of three different geographies, historical trajectories and cultures. It shares its international borders with a number of countries apart from India. The complex, harsh terrain that characterizes the 1,643 km Indo-Myanmar border has not been able to control the mobility and interactions between the tribes. It has encouraged trans-border ethnic kinships. The Nagas, the Chins, and the Kukis are well aware of their ethnic ties across the border making it easy to exploit the land inhabited by their tribal cousins.

To begin with, Nagas inhabit Patkai hills and Chins live in the south, Both are christian tribes constituting a Christianity affiliated cordon across the Indo-Burma border. Again, on the Indian side the Mizos live in the north, and spread into the Chin regions in Myanmar. Kukis also try to exploit their claims of kinship with the Chins[50]. Mizos had made good use of their contiguity with the Chin state of Myanmar, and furthered their connections with the anti-state groups in the Arakans. They had managed to establish an access to the Sagaing division of Myanmar. At the same time an Indian security analyst observes that, "When Chin refugees started flowing into Mizoram following the 1988 military crackdown in Myanmar, the Mizos – themselves emerging from a protracted war with the Indian Union and, more importantly, sharing an ethnic bond with the Chins – played magnanimous hosts"[51]. The most voracious tribes of the North East, the Nagas have made good use of their strategic positions in the Patkai hills and have a natural access into Sagaing and Kachin regions where

Nagas live along the Indo-Burma border; their claims to areas across the international boundary are only too plausible. The Manipur Peoples Liberation Front (MPLF), a coalition consisting of three leading Meitei rebel groups, has a number of bases around the town of Tamu and close to Molcham; other camps are at Namphalong and Khunjao, near the Manipur border.[52]

Insurgency movements and their characters have changed over time. The movement of the Mizos has come to an end but the Nagas have continued. Their movement has become complicated since the formation of the National Socialist Council of Nagaland (NSCN) in the post Shillong Accord period[53] and their breakup into two factions – NSCN (Issac Muvaih) and NSCN (Khaplang). The Khaplang section finds shelter in Burma, and is assisted by the Kachin Independence Army (KIA). The Kachins have a good hold over Stillwell road, and can ensure the continuous supply of essential goods and armaments to keep the movement running. Moreover, this route ensures the connectivity between the North East with China through Burma. It has its own fallouts[54]. The ULFA establishments are of relatively recent times, they have established their own routes through Myanmar. Most of the routes run though Assam, Arunachal and Nagaland.[55] The dense jungles along Assam and Arunachal provide an ideal spot for surreptitious activities.[56] Some of these routes are used by the PLA of Manipur. Going a step further than just establishing training camps, cooperation amongst the various insurgent groups from across the borders has been consolidated through the formation of the Indo-Burmese Revolutionary Front (IBRF) in 1989. It comprises the NSCN(K), ULFA, United Liberation Front of Bodoland, Kuki National Front and Chin National Front (Myanmar).[57]

Second, a steady and constant flow of weapons and drugs from Myanmar have nourished the insurgent groups of the North East. Supply of weapons primarily comes from China. These weapons were found in large amounts in Indo-China during the cold war; once the war ended, these weapons were reaching the insurgents through a large illegal market thriving in Southeast Asia. Myanmar along with Thailand serve as the crucial link in the supply chain from Indo-China to the North East. A number of places within the vicinity of the Andaman and Nicobar islands within Myanmar's waters are used as contact points to collect and supply weapons and other essential equipments.[58] In 1997, the Royal Thai Navy seized an arms shipment for the People's Liberation Army (of Manipur) following a chase in the Andaman Sea off the port of Ranong.[59] These routes are used by the ISI to maintain a steady supply of arms to the various insurgent groups of the North East. Around the 1990s a new trend was noticeable; the rebels of the North East have turned to the Yunnan mafia. By 1999-2000, these mafia groups had become the prime source of weapons for the North East Indian rebels like the ULFA. Bhaumik writes:

"By the end of the 1990s, the rebels of the North East had turned to the Yunnan mafia. In an attempt to turn the state-run ordinance factories into profit centers, Chinese state-run Norinco started selling huge quantities of weapons to even mafia groups based in Yunnan – groups such as the Blackhouse. By 1999-2000, these mafia groups had become the prime source of weapons for the North East Indian rebel groups like the ULFA. A top leader of ULFA, now surrendered, told this writer that the weapons from Yunnan are at least 50 per cent cheaper than those from Thailand".[60]

He also adds that, "In November 2001, the Burmese army raided five Manipuri rebel camps in and around Tamu and recovered 1,600 pieces of weapons including mortars and rocket launchers. Investigations have revealed these weapons have been purchased from the Yunnan mafia".[61] However for the ULFA this connection has been very beneficial for now it has 'been frying fish in its own oil' – buying weapons from the Yunan mafias and selling it to Nepali and the Indian Maoists and even the Islamic jihadis in Bangladesh at a double price good enough to pay for their own acquisitions.[62]

Third, the troubled North East sits on the western corner of Burma's infamous Golden Triangle, one of the two largest opium producing regions in the world. It makes insurgency in the region far more challenging, given the fact that the linkage between drug trafficking and proliferation of small arms is well established. The relation is almost symbiotic and it may not be possible to control the spread of small arms unless there is a corresponding control of drug trafficking. Myanmar has been branded as the producer of opium[63], and is now coupled with amphetamines (produced in the Wa state of Myanmar) which come cheaper than opium. Most insurgent groups in the North East have been involved in drug trade as it means easy money. However there are allegations against the Myanmar junta also.[64] The jungle covered hilly tracts prove a very easy way of transferring drugs along the Indo-Myanmar border, and then ship it through the Kolkata port in India and Chittagong Cox Bazaar. Drug traders have *quid pro quo* arrangements with the insurgent areas; they provide drug money and the groups permit transit rights through their territories as is the case of NSCN (IM).[65]

In recent years, drug refineries have been established along the borders with India's North East, mostly in the Sagaing division and the Chin Hills.[66] Moreh in Manipur and Tamu in Sagaing division in Myanmar are of the points through which drugs enter North East India. Incidentally, one of the reasons for the clashes between the Nagas and the Kukis is over the fight to control the swelling drug trade along this route. There are allegations that border authorities on both sides in this region are also involved in this, making it virtually impossible to eradicate the menace. Subsequently, the unholy nexus between insurgency and drug trade continues to grow at the cost of the youth of the North East.[67]

Fourth, the warm relation between China and Myanmar adds[68] a dimension to Myanmar's involvement in the North East. It is known that Myanmar has been incorporated within China's strategic sphere and will find it not so necessary to get out of it. The Chinese presence in Myanmar will only increase the growth of Chinese interest in the North East. The Chinese have earlier (from the 50s to the mid 80s) supported the Nagas, Mizos and the Communists in Tripura. There is evidence that some of these groups like the Mizos and the Nagas had received training from China. The most popular route ran through the Mon district of Nagaland to Yunan. At present, Chinese enthusiasm to sponsor insurgency in North East has taken the mould of supplying arms to the North East through the Southeast Asian illegal market.[69] Myanmar is the place that is receiving a large amount of military hardware for Myanmar's military regime. China's arms exports to Myanmar since 1990 have been running into billions of dollars. Besides, the Chinese have also reportedly secured radar, refit and refuel (three R's) facilities at three Myanmarese ports-Hyanggi, the Coco Islands, and Mergui. Senior Chinese defence personnel have made several visits to Myanmar that have resulted in a long project towards the modernization of Myanmar's naval bases, some of which were rented to China.[70] A defence ministry report of the '90s admits that the Chinese threat to Indian security, so long seen as a land based one, now had a naval dimension to it. Particularly because, in addition to the North-East, where the Chinese land threat remains, New Delhi seems to be worried about the security of the Andaman and Nicobar Islands, and the country's eastern coastal regions.[71]

SECTION III

Challenges of Foreign Policy Making: Relating Foreign Policy Making towards her Eastern Neighbours with the almost Insurmountable Challenges in the North East

The foreign policy of any state is directed towards the attainment of national interest on the basis of a cost benefit analysis. Of the three neighbours that have an immediate effect on the developments in the North East, China is the only country that India would consider more powerful than herself. However the other two states, though not placed on the same platform with India, have proved their capacity by encouraging low to medium level trouble in the Indian territories adjacent to it. Therefore, India must deal with these countries with due importance. The role of these countries individually or in connivance with each other is largely controlled by one major factor – what they perceive of India. Apparently, their perceptions work at cross purposes but they are certainly harmonious at the functional level. For instance, the Chinese never consider India as an aggressive neighbour but certainly acknowledge her potential to rise to the occasion. Since China projects itself as a powerful country in Asia and the leader of the region, it will not wish that India acquires the status of a predominant Asian power. At best, China would rather see India as a South Asian player. On the contrary, both Bangladesh and Burma, who belong to the Indian subcontinent, would never be happy with India as a South Asian power centre. Therefore, the three countries have varying perceptions but they meet at a common point – the need to contain India and the strategy is to pin her down using her own weaknesses against her. The Chinese see sense in encouraging those countries and elements that would keep India busy in within her region. The neighbours see sense in encouraging those dissenting groups within India and are constantly looking for external support for 'India bashing'. Given the geographical location of the three countries North East India has become the core area of activity. The region is a constant factor in their foreign policy formulations towards India. The question then is how India reciprocates, and formulates her foreign policy keeping in mind this reality about her North East and her eastern neighbours.

India's perception of three eastern neighbours is placed on three different platforms. First, China has been our weakness ever since our position was exposed in the Sino-India war in the beginning of the 1960s. Most of our problems concerning foreign policy towards that country, and our inability to solve them, arise from the fact that this is a relation between unequals and both are aware of this fact. Second, in the case of Bangladesh, it was considered a foreign policy success. Subsequently for sometime we held almost a similar attitude towards Bangladesh as China expressed towards us. A triumphant India soon realized that this nascent state has engaged herself in various anti-Indian modalities. Moreover, problems within Indo-Bangladesh relations are complex and hard to solve, particularly because in the case of the latter, the dialectics between nation state and political state have become increasingly blatant. Third is Burma where our realistic estimates of foreign policy had gone wrong as India failed to prioritize between region and neighbour. Apparently, Myanmar's junta administration that began in the 1960s led to the gradual de-prioritization of Indo-Myanmar relations, especially from the late 1970s to late 1980s.[72] However, there were other reasons explaining such erratic behaviour. First, Burma is not politically a part of South Asia, and therefore was not on the high priority list of the Indian administration. Second, Cold War absorbed South Asia, especially Pakistan and India, and therefore, we were busy playing the games of Cold War. Since Burma was free from super power influence, Indian administration was not paying all that attention to our immediate eastern neighbour.

The significant role that these countries play in the North East of our country makes it necessary that India pursue an active and vigorous foreign policy towards these countries. It means that a number of issues need be thrashed out and fences mended. We now look at the present state of relationships with these countries.

China

The tension between India and China was never a war of ideas or ideology that was a characteristic of Cold War. Rather, with China it has been a realistic contention of two primary issues. First, the race for influence and leadership in Asia, and second, claims and counterclaims over territories and borders. The Sino-Indian war need to be understood in the light of the above two observations. In the case of North East, China's changing position has been mentioned, but what adds to the problem is the dimension of territorial dispute. The dimension of complexity is the unresolved dispute over the North East involving Arunachal Pradesh and its international border with China. The proximity of the Chinese to the North East would increase if the Chinese realize the claims they make over Arunachal Pradesh. Three rounds of encounters with the Chinese People's Liberation Army are already in the official records of the Government of India– 1962, 1967 and 1986. What adds to the problem is that the once peaceful Arunachal Pradesh is being gradually taken over by insurgency (Lohit, East Kameng)[73] it increases the vulnerability of India's North East to Chinese claims.

Chinese also have a natural leverage over us as the upper section of Brahmaputra known as Tsang Po lies in China-occupied Tibet. It gives the Chinese the bargaining chip against India (also against Bangladesh). If records are right then in 2000 Arunachal Pradesh faced the worst floods due to a dam breach in Tibet, and it was kept a hush-hush by both the sides until satellite pictures brought out the reality[74]. A major dam is being constructed on Tsang Po at the Great Bend, Yarlung Tsangpo as a "strategy to divert water from rivers in the south and west to drought-stricken northern areas".[75] China's bastion in Myanmar and its implications on Indian security have been discussed previously. We may now remind ourselves that Bay of Bengal will become one of the future regions of concern for Indian security as China has given enough proof of the fact that China has long term designs on parts of the sea. Of no lesser concern is the Sino-Indian relation is the nuclear factor. India's nuclear explosions, particularly the second one, had created ripples in the international society. However, India's nuclear policy is certainly controlled by her external security concerns in her immediate neighbourhood. Apart from the constant concerns with Pakistan, the Sino-Pakistani nexus continues to guide Indian nuclear policies. A brief by the Indian embassy in Washington D.C. read, "Pakistan's nuclear weapons programme predated ours and was built after years of clandestine acquisition. While we are mentioning the Pakistan factor, there is no obsession with Pakistan. Our security concerns go far beyond Pakistan and South Asia."[76] The statement, further, clearly hints at China when it emphasizes the worsening regional security since the '60s.[77] The Sino-Pakistan nexus has added another dimension to India's concerns.

After India's nuclear explosion in May 1998, the Chinese were assisting the Pakistanis.[78] The fact of the matter is that China has described Pakistan as its Israel[79] who needs to be well armed to take on adversaries if any, in the Indian subcontinent. Unfortunately, India remains at the receiving end of security complications in the region.

In the light of the above observations, it is imperative that our moves towards China be proactive. From the visit of the late Prime Minister Rajiv Gandhi in 1988 to the visit by Chinese Premier Wen Jiabao in April 2005, India's relation with China has begun to bear some fruits for India. There are three plausible avenues of India-China relationship—bilateral, multilateral and the countering and containment method. At the bilateral level, the rate of progress seems to be the lowest because this is where the contentious border issues are discussed. The Chinese are yet to provide to the Indian side all maps on the disputed Line of Control. Besides, very humble progress has been made in resolving border disputes. As the Indian External Affairs Minister of State reported at the Parliament, "The Eighth Round of talks between the Special Representatives of India and China, Shri M.K. Narayanan, National Security Adviser and Mr. Dai Bingguo, Executive Vice Foreign Minister respectively, on the India-China Boundary Question was held in Xi'an and Beijing in China from June 25 to June 27, 2006. The Special Representatives continued their discussions on an agreed framework for a boundary settlement on the basis of the "Agreement on Political Parameters and Guiding Principles for Settlement of India-China Boundary Question, which was signed on April 11, 2005. Talks were held in a friendly, cooperative and constructive atmosphere."[80] However he had previously mentioned that, "No time frame has been fixed for the final settlement of the boundary question."[81] Moreover, there is difference in the way the two countries wish to see solutions come about. For instance, India's Prime Minister Manmohan Singh spoke to Chinese President Hu Jintao on the sidelines of the East Asia Summit in Kuala Lumpur in December 2005 about a fast track border resolution mechanism, and also emphasized the need for moving simultaneously on all three disputed sectors. The Chinese, on the other hand, favour a sectoral, also called as 'step by step' approach, but the PM told Hu that this was slackening the pace and delaying a solution. Officials said that though the Chinese President agreed to speed up the process, he still felt a final solution would take 'long'.[82] Over and above, the provisions under the guidelines are of significance, and it is hoped that these will yield the fruitful results.

At the bilateral level, defence cooperation has begun between the two countries. China and India have signed a Memorandum of Understanding (MOU) on their defence cooperation. The MOU was signed during Indian Defence Minister Pranab Mukherjee's visit to China on May 29, 2006.[83] The 2005 Protocol includes, among others, border meeting points at Kibithu-Damai in the Eastern Sector and Lipulekh Pass in the Middle Sector; exchanges between the relevant Military Regions of China and Army Commands of India; and exchanges between institutions of training, sports and culture of the two armed forces. In 2006, such activities have gained momentum. Both sides held joint naval exercise in December 2005 off the Kochi coast in the Arabian Sea.[84] Meanwhile, Chinese views on the Indo-US nuclear deal have also turned flexible, and they have expressed their confidence in India's commitment to the peaceful use of nuclear resources.[85] Bilateral defence initiatives are being complemented by bilateral trade that is increasing rapidly. The trade turnover between India and China during the financial year 2005-06 amounted to US$ 17.46 billion.[86] The Nathu La reopening is expected to facilitate trade. Under the mutual duty-free trade agreement, signed in 2003, Indian exports can now bring in 29 commodities to China through Nathu La Pass. They include carpets, cigarettes, tea and barley, while Chinese traders can export 15 types of goods, including goat and sheepskin, wool and herbs, through the Pass. However, Indian should not ignore the fact that the Chinese still have the capacity to run a parallel market in the North East.

At the multilateral level, interactions are possible where India and China are common members of multilateral forums. In fact, from China's vehement position in Bandung Conference, both countries have come a long way in showing keen interest in making the best of the Kunming Initiative that revolves around four countries – Bangladesh, Myanmar, China and India. To encourage trade amongst these countries an elaborate network of roads have been planned, of which the famous Stillwell Road would connect Ledo in Arunachal Pradesh with Kunming in Yunnan through Mytkyina in Myanmar. Yunnan administration has shown much enthusiasm in this initiative as that land locked region of China will get access to the vast markets of North East India and parts of the Indian subcontinent. The Ledo route in turn will be connected to the Silk Route. There are future proposals of connecting these routes to New Delhi through North East. Another stretch would connect the Burma Roads through Myanmar to Rangoon Port. Volumes have been written on the kind of benefits that they would usher for the North East[87], but it needs to be focused that roadways can also be a source of insecurity.[88] Moreover, with the boost in economic activities in the North East, the kind of money that will flow into the region may get appropriated for the wrong reasons and insurgency activities may soon stop depending on external funding. Irrespective of that, the North Eastern states are overwhelmingly in favour of reopening the Stillwell Road. North Eastern academics, top-level state and national politicians, as well as large corporate interests have all expressed the view that reconstruction of the Road is the ideal vehicle for advancing vital economic ties between the North East, ASEAN partner countries and China Leading that charge has been Pradyut Bordoloi, Assam's Minister of Environment and Forests, in whose constituency the Road begins. In 2002, Bordoloi participated in the Dhaka meet of the Kunming Initiative – an unusually forthright action for a minister; in so doing, Bordoloi essentially bypassed New Delhi, taking his concerns directly to the international delegates.[89]

The third way is what would perhaps be appropriately termed as the 'counter and contain' China, in which India has been trying to make sincere efforts at countering Chinese influence on her Eastern neighbours, especially southeast Asian countries. It involves a two pronged strategy- multilateral activism and bilateral relations. At the multilateral level, India has gained success in becoming summit level partner with Asean and its politico security affiliate Asean Regional Forum (ARF), and is actively engaged in the Mekong-Ganga Cooperation, the BIMST-EC, in establishing the India-ASEAN FTA and the newly formed East Asia Summit. The ASEAN is the major stage on which the Indian economy seeks integration into the Asia-Pacific. However, there is also a foreign policy and strategic dimension. Tim Huxley stressed on the significant strategic niche that India has carved for itself in Southeast Asia and contended that this is a consequence of its Look East Policy and the widening horizons of its navy. He strongly advocates India's involvement in institutions connecting Southeast Asian governments on security matters.[90] Perhaps in the distant future, India may also be interested in expanding the ASEAN+3 model to the ASEAN+4 model and find for herself a place.

At the bilateral level, the active cultivation of bilateral relations with East Asian, particularly Southeast Asian countries, has received priority in recent Indian foreign policy considerations. The fact is that India does not have similar levels of relationships with each of the ten Southeast Asian states. At the practical level, India seems to have given priority to those Southeast Asian nations that have traditionally close relations with India such as Singapore, Thailand and Malaysia. Yet, Myanmar is of particular interest to India because the state is geographically the closest to India and is of immense consequence to India, particularly to her North East. Most of the countries have responded well to India's initiatives and ties are gradually strengthening.[91] At the same time, Indian experts feel that Indian interests cannot be limited to the Indian Ocean only, and that South China Sea and West Pacific must be a necessary extension, where India will have increasing interests to defend. Accordingly India has been sending naval troops for exercises in South China Sea and the navy has made exchanges on defence matters with Vietnam.[92] In spite of all this, India's attempts at earning a prominent role in the region will largely depend on how better China has fared in the same.

Myanmar

Myanmar's importance to India was never more prominent than in the late 1980s when the Myanmar army dismissed democracy and sooner took over the administration in 1990. A phase of dissidence or insurgency sponsorship followed on either side of the border. India's open support for pro-democracy students, the offer to provide them asylum and the opening of refugee camps along the Indo-Myanmar border was reciprocated by the junta's tacit support for the NSCN, the PLA, the UNLF and the ULFA. The Myanmar army had also penetrated Indian borders in the North East time and again in 1991.[93] The Indian government, annoyed with the junta, were supporting the ethnic groups in their struggle-the Chins, the Kachins, the latter in particular. Thus in the early nineties, India and Myanmar were encouraging cross border insurgency.

A change took place around 1993, when Indian diplomats initiated the diplomatic model of 'Constructive Engagement Policy' a volte-face in formulating policies towards Myanmar.[94] Subsequently, Indo-

Myanmar relation had begun to gain strength; soon India accepted the official name of Myanmar, and issued a declaration in 1996 that democratic movements in Myanmar are an internal aspect of Myanmar, and that India does wish to be associated with it.[95] Cooperation between the states covers various aspects but the two crucial issues are: first the problems of trans-border linkages used by insurgents in the North East,and second, the predominant influence of the Chinese in that country. Trans-border linkages have been exploited particularly for illegal economic interactions[96] between insurgents and smugglers on either side of the border. The enhancement of official trade between the two countries would not only put a check on parallel trade until eliminated, but will also benefit the North Eastern part of India as it is the closest to this neighbour. Not only India, Myanmar shall also benefit economically from increasing trade, and at present, it is the fifth largest trade partner with India.[97] Insurgency issues are seen with utmost seriousness, and closer defence links are seen as a way to deal with insurgent activities on both sides of the border. However, in practice, joint endeavours in combating insurgency have not given the desired results. In 1995, the joint expedition against the North Eastern insurgents holed in Myanmar was called off as India conferred the Nehru award on Aung San Syu Kyi. Since 2000 high level army dialogues have taken place in order to understand the ground realities which are necessary to conduct joint endeavours against insurgency in the North East. Yet in 2001 military expeditions met with failure.[98] Joint expeditions have their own complexities and have to be dealt on an issue to issue basis. India must remember that Myanmar administration will not throw itself into the arms of the Indian administration. We must remember that North East is our problem and not Myanmar's. More importantly, Myanmar has the choice of selecting between India and China, we have no such choice.

India's sincere attempts at wooing our eastern neighbour include not only trade relations but also establishing suitable connectivity to ensure a smooth flow of trade. India has constructed the 160 kilometer Tamu-Kalewa-Kalemyo road called the India-Myanmar Friendship Road. According to the 2005-2006 report of the Ministry of External Affairs, India seeks greater cooperation and development towards the integration of North East India with Western Myanmar by building infrastructural facilities like building of roads that would connect North

East with Myanmar.[99] Of particular importance is the Kalandan Multimodal Transport facility that will establish links between Myanmar, the North East and the Bay of Bengal. In 2002, India, Myanmar and Thailand announced the landmark international highway project, a 1400 kilometer long highway aimed at completion by two years. Establishing rail links between India and Myanmar through the North East is also in the stage of proposal.[100] However, the feasibility of integrating such regions cannot be detached from security concerns; Routray for instance very crisply identifies some of these concerns – the misuse of such connectivity by insurgent groups, the increase in illegal trade and the constant concern over the increasing influence of the Chinese over Myanmar authorities.[101]

India also needs to make good use of the Bay of Bengal area in order to counter the Chinese presence in the region. She has updated her naval air base in the Andamans.[102] India has been conducting joint naval exercises with some of the Southeast Asian countries around the Malacca Straits. Most of the countries of that region are not comfortable with the idea of a strong Chinese naval presence in the way towards the Malacca Straits. India has also offered to construct a port at the Arakan coast as the Chinese have a naval base there. Chinese will perhaps not respond positively to India's proximity to their naval base.

Bangladesh

The development of Indo-Bangladesh relations is seldom based on strong friendship. On the contrary, the fact is that India-Bangladesh relations often highlight the importance of geographical realities in depicting Bangladesh's security dilemma vis-à-vis India. Geographical realities often result in a stereo-typed vision about the Indian threat, which hinders beneficial cooperative ventures with India. Sharing common borders also creates a scope for generating a horde of disputed issues like illegal migration, cross-border criminal and terrorist activities and so on. This is particularly true in the context of North East India.

On the Indian side, the issue of unresolved borders continues to put the Indian side in perpetual disadvantage. While sharing 4,096 kilometers of land border, only 6.5 kilometers of land along the Comilla-Tripura border is considered as officially disputed by the governments of both the countries, but the border disputes between

Bangladesh and India is by no means confined to the demarcation problems only. Rather, it is intrinsically linked with the issues of illegal movement of people and goods and cross-border criminal activities which often leads to skirmishes between the border security forces of the two countries. Bangladesh inherited disputed border relations with India as a legacy of the partition of the subcontinent in 1947. The border between Pakistan and India was drawn within six weeks only by Sir Cyril Radcliffe on the basis of the Two Nation Theory. The arbitrary division resulted in India's control over 112 enclaves and Bangladesh's control over 32 enclaves based on the religious identities of the inhabitants of those areas.[103] In April 2001 the boundary dispute between Bangladesh and India acquired a serious dimension. Border skirmishes occurred around the village of Padua (known as Pyrdiwah in India), adjoining the Meghalaya state of India and Tamabil area of Sylhet district in Bangladesh. The Bangladesh government claimed that India held illegal possession of the area since 1971. As the Indian forces attempted to construct a footpath to Meghalaya from an outpost in Padua across a disputed territory some 300 meters wide, the Bangladesh authorities drew attention to the disputed status of the area. The refusal of the Indian forces to withdraw resulted in the Bangladesh military initiating an offensive that lasted from 16th to 19th April, 2001, and claimed the lives of 16 Indians[104] and three Bangladeshi soldiers. An estimated 10,000 people on the Bangladesh side and 1,000 people on the Indian side were forced to flee from the disputed area as a result of the on-going tension. The intensity of the border tension started to normalize as the Bangladesh military withdrew from the area to restore the status quo.[105] Though the Indian press raised the issue of Indian soldiers' bodies being severely mutilated, the Indian government sought to downplay the magnitude of the claim as the Bangladeshi Prime Minister regretted the sudden turn of events. However, the killing at the border areas certainly reflected tensions between two countries. A Bangladeshi human rights organization *Odhikar* reported in January 2004 that in the period from 2001-2003, India's Border Security Forces have committed a number of atrocities that includes abductions, detentions, assistance in acts of robbery.[106]

The issue of demarcating territorial waters has led to serious differences between the two countries. The issue of ownership of a new-born island in the estuary of Haribhanga River on the border of the two countries has been a source of contention since the 1970s. This new-born island known as South Talpatty Island to Bangladesh and New Moore/ Purbasha to India was picked up in a satellite picture in 1975 and led both countries to lay competing claims on the island. While Bangladesh proposed sending a joint Indo-Bangladesh team to determine the flow of channels of the river on the basis of existing international river-laws to resolve the ownership of the island, the Indian authorities sent forces to establish claims by stationing naval troops in that island.[107] Developments reported by the media around 2004 show a renewal of tensions since the Indian Border Security Forces (BSF) have established a base on that island, which is regularly visited by the Indian navy.[108] The recent activities have been viewed with suspicion by Bangladesh as the sovereignty over the island is yet to be determined.[109] We must not loose sight of the fact that any maritime dispute among the littoral nations of the Bay of Bengal might distract our focus away from trade and development and pull the region toward a nagging geopolitical rivalry.

Illegal immigration is a constant irritant in Indo-Bangladesh relations. It is related to the problem of porous and ill defined borders. Illegal immigration involves militants, smugglers and thugs. This has been the case with Assam and Tripura. To stop illegal immigration, India has started fencing the international border. Bangladesh has protested against the Indian move as a violation of International Law.[110] The JBWG was established in June 2001 to implement the Land Boundary Agreement of 1974 but their activities are not of great help. For instance, even as late as July 2006, the officials of the JBWG met for the second time in four years to deliberate on the longstanding issues of border demarcation and exchange of enclaves and territories presently in the possession of the other side. The two-day meeting ended inconclusively with a decision to meet once a year. It is no wonder that fencing the border with Bangladesh has progressed at a slow pace. Under Phase-I, which commenced in 1986, 854 kilometers of fencing were erected. According to the Ministry of Home Affairs, the 854 kilometers fence had been built in Phase-I, however, large stretches of it have already been damaged due to bad construction and bad weather and have consequently ceased to be effective in controlling illegal cross border activities. Under Phase-II, an additional 2429.5 km of fence was sanctioned and by the end of 2006, 1,601.05 kilometers has been completed,[111] The stiff resistance by the BDR especially during early 2005 has been responsible for slow progress of the work.[112] The Ministry planned to start replacing the damaged fencing during 2006-07. A Pilot project for flood lighting 277 km of the Indo-Bangladesh border has been completed.[113]

In order to thwart the pressure of illegal immigration successive governments (especially the BJP-led government) have been trying to pick up Bangladeshi Muslims, and sending them back to Bangladesh. In course of *Operation Push Back* Bangladesh has refused to accept the people being pushed back by India, claiming that they were not Bangladeshis at all. As a result, many hapless men were stuck in no-man's land on the edge of the border desperate to get to the Indian side by bribing soldiers and officials.[114] The Indian government continued pushing back such illegal residents in the same year, at least 60 times on record.[115]

In this context, erstwhile Bangladesh Prime Minister Begum Khaleda Zia's visit in 2006 saw some attempts at salvaging Indo-Bangladesh relations. Apart from the decision to maintain high level political dialogues between the two countries, at a concrete level, two Agreements were signed during the visit of the Bangladesh Prime Minister. These were the Revised Trade Agreement and the Agreement for Mutual Cooperation for Preventing Illicit Trafficking in Narcotic Drugs and Psychotropic Substances and Related Matters. While the Revised Trade Agreement is expected to provide a framework for expansion of bilateral trade, the other agreement signals the joint determination of the two Governments to combat drug trafficking. Begum Zia pointed at the hot and cold state of relations between India and Bangladesh: "It is only natural that there would be scope for differences on various issues between our two countries. But this need not stand in the way of honest efforts by our two countries to address them. I believe we owe it to ourselves to do our best to narrow these differences".[116] Following her visit, a four-day interaction at the Secretary level took place at Dhaka in August 2006 where substantial decisions were taken that would help reduce issues of differences and tensions between both the countries.[117]

Yet there are still more unresolved issues like Bangladesh's position on India's river linking project. Bangladesh thinks that the Farakka Barrage has already caused irreversible damage to the country. An additional 10-20 per cent water withdrawal by the current project could turn much of the areas to arid lands. This issue has been raised by the Bangladesh representatives at the Joint Rivers Commission.[118] For instance, at the September 2003 water talks between India and Bangladesh concluded with no major breakthrough, though India assured Bangladesh that there would be no water diversion from the Ganges and Brahmaputra under its River-Linking Project (RLP). In comparison, the 36th meeting of Indo-Bangladesh Joint Rivers Commission held at Dhaka has created a new era of goodwill and trust between both the sides. Bangladesh and India agreed on a joint inspection by their water ministers of the border areas affected by erosion near trans-boundary rivers in January 2006. Bangladesh is nonetheless skeptical. According to Bangladesh representative Dr Ainun Nishat, an expert on water and member of the Joint Rivers Commission, "We did not see positive activities from our counter-side as they are not still disclosing the facts, including both the technical and financial feasibility studies."[119] Reiterating Bangladesh's resentment M. Ferowz Ahmed, member of BAPA, comments that, "The withdrawal of the Ganges water at Farakka is already a sore point in Indo-Bangladesh relationship. The relationship may drop further if IRLP is implemented, which is likely to exacerbate the regional conflicting relationship that India has with Bangladesh and Nepal over river-sharing issues."[120]

Trade relations between India and Bangladesh are not at a comfortable state either. The geographic proximity is the major factor that has made India Bangladesh's biggest trading partner. Bangladesh had a staggering trade deficit that ballooned to a record $ 2,003 million in 2003-04.One of the problems in this regard has been that Bangladesh has little to offer to India, while the latter has a comparative advantage on a wide range of commodities. However, of late, there has been a noticeable increase in the exports of Bangladesh to India. It has risen by 68 per cent, amounting to $ 241.96 million in fiscal year 2005-06. This increase has largely been due to exports to India's North Eastern states. On the other hand, Bangladesh's imports from India dropped in the last financial year by around 8 per cent, totaling $ 1,868 million. Subsequently, Bangladesh trade deficit has come down to $ 1,882 million in FY 2004-05 and $ 1,626 million in FY 05-06.[121] However, there is a large informal trade carried out through the porous border between the two countries, that adds to the loss of legitimate customs revenues, a realistic estimate of the trade deficit. To avoid trade imbalances, Bangladesh has long been demanding reduction or abolition of trade barriers between the two countries, which is yet to be considered by India. The issue of trade deficit is not confined within the economic sphere. Due to the nature of troubled political relations, trade deficit has been yet another issue of contention between India and Bangladesh. Along with this issue, the issues of trans-shipment, transit and export of natural gas figure as other contentious issues in Indo-Bangladesh trade relations. Having said that, it is also true that the trade relationship between Bangladesh and India is currently of special interest in both countries, particularly in the context of discussions on a potential bilateral free trade agreement (FTA). However, very little research has been done on FTA. FTA is beneficial for both countries as most of Bangladesh's imports are necessary goods that add value to the domestic industries, and trade with Bangladesh is seen as an important way of reducing the economic isolation of the eight Indian eastern and north eastern states. In addition, lowering or eliminating tariffs between the two countries and the harmonization of customs procedures and documentation could also yield benefits. Under an FTA between India and Bangladesh, Bangladeshi exporters would have duty free access to the Indian market, and the most obvious apparent opportunity would be in the exports of readymade garments. However, an FTA would not eliminate many of the existing Non-Tariff Barriers, and the workshop needs not only to study the possibility of an FTA, but also other barriers to trade, whether Para-Tariff or Non-Tariff. While the business community sometimes showed positive response to these issues, political considerations generally override Bangladesh's intention of settling these debatable issues.

The tri-nation Myanmar-Bangladesh-India pipeline is also full of doubts because of Bangladesh's attitude. The joint statement after a trilateral meeting between the Minister of Energy of Myanmar, the State Minister for Energy and Mineral Resources of Bangladesh and the Minister of Petroleum and Natural Gas of India, held at Yangon on January12, 2005, reads: "The Government of Myanmar agrees to export natural gas to India by pipeline through the territory of Bangladesh and India to be operated by an international consortium as may be agreed upon by the parties concerned, based upon technical and commercial feasibility. *The Government of Bangladesh and India reserve the right to access the pipeline as and when this regard will be worked out on the basis of commercial agreements.*[122] This route would be determined by mutual agreement of the three Governments with a view to ensuring adequate access, maximum security and optimal economic utilization. Bangladesh has said that it will consider allowing a similar pipeline originating from Myanmar provided India allows Dhaka a free trade corridor to Nepal and accompanying trade benefits. It also asked India to remove barriers that exist in trade between the two countries. A section in Bangladesh also wants India to allow purchase of cheap hydropower from Bhutan and Nepal so that the gas reserves of Bangladesh could be conserved. These new conditions have further complicated the negotiation over the laying of pipeline, as any free transnational movement through the sensitive 'Siliguri Corridor' may not be acceptable to India. Bangladesh is fully aware of this situation.[123] The matter of fact is that any bilateral (even trilateral) contract/agreement with India continues to come under opposition attack, being portrayed as selling Bangladesh's interests to India. Adding to this argument, M.K. Dhar, a former Indian intelligence officer opines that Islamist forces in Bangladesh – wary of India's intentions – are against any policy, especially of an economic nature, that would benefit India. He argues, Bangladeshi policy-makers will not grant India rights of passage for a transnational pipeline because such a decision/policy will be blocked by Jamaat-influenced senior military and political officials.[124] In any case, in 2006, India lost a potential tri-national deal when Myanmar declined gas supply to the Myanmar-Bangladesh-India pipeline. Instead, Yangon (the then capital of Myanmar) signed an agreement with the Hong Kong-listed Petrochina, under which Myanmar's Ministry of Energy agreed to sell 6.5 tcf from A-1 block (Rakhine coastline) reserve via an overland pipeline to China for a period of 30 years.[125] India finds excuse for its failure to acquire the gas from Myanmar by pointing fingers at Bangladesh, because of unreasonable demands from Bangladesh, Myanmar opted to sell its gas to China instead. When the Indian Foreign Minister during his visit in January 2007 raised the pipeline issue, Myanmar reiterated its promise to supply provided India and Bangladesh thrash out their differences. Thus, India's blame on Bangladesh is substantiated. However on May 1, 2007, Bangladesh Foreign Affairs adviser, Iftekhar Ahmed Chowdhury re-launched the project stating that his country "agreed to negotiate for allowing the pipeline if Myanmar sells gas and India agrees to buy."[126] The pipeline would cost US$ 1 billion, and it is estimated that India would pay

Bangladesh US$ 100-120 million to allow right of passage. It is a very expensive project. In case the length of the pipeline has to be increased, the price will rise and if India fails to pay, Myanmar will easily get other energy hungry customers, China primarily, also South Korea, Japan, even Thailand.[127]

At present, the caretaker government in Bangladesh, seems to have shown some interest in improving relations with India. For instance, a small territorial dispute involving the Feni river at Tripura has been resolved, thanks to the cooperative gesture of the new government in Bangladesh.[128] Moreover, India and Bangladesh seem to be eager to work cooperatively on a number of non-contentious issues like improving connectivity, Inland Water Transit and dealing with the power shortage, especially for Bangladesh. Besides, Dhaka is also keen to see that the tri-nation gas pipeline from Myanmar to India through Bangladesh is implemented. Bangladesh now thinks that this will provide scope for it to take Myanmar gas as and when such necessity arises. With this objective, Dhaka is showing flexibility to alter its earlier conditions.[129] With the reduced hostility in Indo-Bangladesh relations, it has created a congenial atmosphere during the BSF-BDR biennial meet that was held in New Delhi in 2006 where both sides have shown interest in border management which includes a serious effort at undoing the irritant issues involved.[130] Yet Bangladesh's response to sponsoring terrorism has not been particularly applaudable; though the Bangladesh intelligence chief has been changed[131], it remains to be seen what positive results will accrue to India.

Conclusion

North East India undoubtedly poses one of the most intriguing areas so far as successful policy formulation and implementation is concerned. The Indian state has been juggling with various policy ideas so as to find a suitable solution to the seemingly insurmountable problems of the region. The primary problem seems to originate from the poverty of ideas that pervade government policy formulations; for years the post colonial state and its authoritative bodies have formulated ideas that are directed towards what I would like to describe as state driven integrationist orientation. This involved earnest attempts towards minimisation of pluralism heterogeneity so characteristic to the North East. A very sketchy, somehow distorted idea of nation building has been doing the rounds of the Delhi corridors that have failed to understand the basics of the North East. Subsequently, various experimental approaches have been put to use to integrate the region starting from exotic and the exclusive, to the politico-security approach taken over by the socio-economic developmental approach. A predominant view that India needs to fold in the North East into 'her mainstream' (which itself remains ill-defined) further reinforces the basic contention that North East is a region by itself more at parlance with its neighbours than with India. It is no wonder that experts on North East consider Indian government's gestures towards the region as a self-defeating exercise[132]. There is enough skepticism that the prism of security through which Indian policy-makers view the North East is likely to remain a major factor inhibiting serious investment of resources – intellectual, political and material.[133] On the other hand, more radical views would go further to insist that state driven development merely galvanises internal colonialism.[134] As time has passed, the situation has turned out to be more complex and the government's grand project of State driven integrationist approach is being challenged by 'nations from below' phenomenon.[135]

It is in this context that the Government's enthusiasm for Look East Policy needs to be estimated. A fairly rich amount of literature has been written on India's Look East Policy, but what is of relevance is how to relate the future of North East with the interest that India has shown with its eastern neighbours especially its southeastern neighbours. Here it becomes most necessary to make the best use of the positive forces unleashed by the market forces in the age of globalization. It particularly encourages transnational networks to facilitate cross border interactions. It is in harmony with the needs of globalization that the Look East Policy reinforces the fact that North East India and her southeastern Asian neighbours constitute a region state. Perhaps for the first time the Indian government is giving a serious thought at trying out a regional approach to a national problem by encouraging transnational interactions. It is a mere effort at undoing some very expensive mistakes of the postcolonial modern political state system in India. Even Jairam Ramesh, Honorable Minister of State, Commerce and Industry emphasies: "The political integration model with India and the economic integration model with the rest of Asia is one direction that certainly holds much promise. For this to happen, mindsets in India have to change as well, not just mindsets in the North East because we have traditionally been very suspicious of sub-regional cooperation. The word sub-regional is a 'no, no' in the lexicon of 'mainstream' India. We look upon India as a single entity cooperating with other countries. But clearly a time has come when it is in the interest of individual units of this entity to develop economic cooperation with neighbouring countries in the interest of the larger entity."[136] It is almost a total reversal of the Indian approach of looking at the North East as a discordant periphery to one that envisages the North East region as the centre of a thriving and integrated economic space linking two dynamic regions with a network of highways, railways, pipelines, transmission lines crisscrossing the region.[137] Subsequently, it involves a gradual transition from the shepherd-folk-game strategy to a more humanitarian approach based on a bio-power game.[138]

At a practical level the picture may not be as rosy as it seems. The fundamental challenge comes from the need to maintain the precarious balance between the transnational trends of encouraging cross border contacts and the need to reiterate the identity of the region with that of the Indian nation. Look East Policy is a foreign policy of an independent state towards its eastern neighbours,[139] and need not be misinterpreted as a compromising gesture towards its sovereignty and territorial integrity. On the contrary, Look East Policy serves Indian national interests in more than one way. First, it is a launching pad for successful relationship with the eastern neighbours, and ultimately dissuades them from encouraging anti-Indian elements; simultaneously it seems to be a stepping stone towards gaining respect in Asian politics. Second, it is a soft containment strategy for rising Chinese influence and ambitions in India's eastern neighbours. Third, it has helped focus attention on the immense potential of North East India as a hub of economic activity and has managed to wean some of the attention from the Chinese province of Yunan; on the contrary it has encouraged joint economic enterprise between these two regions, yet another example of a region-state approach that will ultimately help roll out differences between states. Fourth, but not the least, the trickle down effect of such cross border economic invigoration is expected to benefit the North East and give a facelift to India's goodwill towards the region. Subsequently, security challenges arising from anti-state disruptive activities will be in the wane.

For these goals to be achieved, India must take both its foreign policy and its North East as an extreme by serious business. A simple but well coordinated effort at building confidence at both the external and domestic levels is very essential. At confidence building with its neighbours, India seems to be in earnest, but that ought to be complemented with building confidence about the Indian state within the people of the North East. At the domestic level, a consistent police state image amongst the masses of the North East has had its fallouts, mostly negative. It has encouraged what Roy calls 'folk politics' hijacked by ethno classes.[140] It is time to look at the North East beyond the 'law and order problem prism' and what better way than by subtly accepting it as a region distinct from the rest of India. Look East Policy only supplements this change in outlook by simply acknowledging the inclusiveness of India's eastern neighours in this sub-regional development and cooperation paradigm. Going a step further, Indian policy seems to have come of age where she has managed to make a practical concoction of her politico-security priorities arising from her geo-strategic realities with the need of a developmental and welfare approach towards the North East. At present it may not be yielding miracles but a sustained effort should deliver positive results.

NOTES AND REFERENCES

1. Lt. General J.R. Mukherjee, A*n Insider's Experience of Insurgency in India's North-East*, Anthem Press, London, 2005, p. 3.
2. For instance Raimo Varyrynen delineates regional sub-systems on the basis of various components that would underline interstate linkages but most important for him is the cultural affinity. See, Raimo Vayrynen, "Regional Conflict Formation: An Intractable Problem of International Relations", *Journal of Peace Research*, vol, 21, no.4, 1984, p. 340.
3. Kanti Bajpai, "Introduction: International Theory, International Society, Regional Politics, and Foreign Policy", in Kanti P. Bajpai and Harish C. Shukla (eds), *Interpreting World Politics: Essays for A.P. Rana,* New Delhi, Sage Publications, 1995, pp. 30-31.
4. See, Kenichi Ohame, "The Rise of the Region State", *Foreign Affairs*, vol. 172, no. 2, 78-87.
5. See, Barry Buzan, *People, States and Fear: The National Security problems in International Relations,* New Delhi, Transasia Publishers, 1983, p.106.
6. See, Hedley Bull, *The Anarchical Society: A Study of Order in World Politics*, New York, Columbia University Press, 1977, p.10.

7. Bajpai, no.3, pp. 31-32.
8. For a concise idea on the ancient tribal conflicts see, Chapter 1, Chandra Bhusan, *Terrorism and Separation in North-East India*, Delhi, Kalpaz Publications, 2004. Also see, Girin Phukan (ed), *Inter-Ethnic Conflict in North East India*, Kolkata, Maulana Abul Kalam Azad Institute of Asian Studies, 2004; Lt. Gen N.S. Narahari, *Security Threats to North-East India, The Socio-Ethnic Tensions*, Delhi, Manas Publications 2002.
9. A vast and diverse literature of European accounts of the North East is available. Whereas Verrier Elwin had provided very basic descriptive details of the tribes, other narratives would portray the tribals as an insubordinate lot obstinate in nature. Johri refers to Major John Butler's writings where he speaks of the *Khamptis,* the *Singhpos,* the *Abors,* the *Mishmis* and the *Nagas* as a non-suppressible category. See, Major John Butler, *Sketch of Assam*, London, Smith, Elder & Co. 1847, also his other narrative, *Travels and Adventure in the Province of Assam*, Bombay, Smith, Taylor & Co. 1855.
10. For an account of the history of Assam, see N.N. Acharya, *Historical Documents of Assam and the Neighbouring States*, New Delhi, Omsons Publications, 1983.
11. H. K. Barpujari, *Assam in the Days of the Company1826-1858: A Critical and Comprehensive History of Assam During the Rule of East India Company From 1826-1858*, Guwhati, North-Eastern Hill University Publications, 1996 (new edition). Also see Kanak Sen Deka, *Assam Crisis: Myth and Reality*, New Delhi, Mittal Publications, 1993.
12. For instance, Sitaram Johri writes of continuous conflicts in the early nineteenth century between the British and the adamant tribal chiefs of the *Khamptis, Daflas* and the *Akas*. See the introductory pages in Major Sitaram Johri, *Where India, China and Burma Meet*, Calcutta, Thacker Spink & Co. 1933.
13. The excluded areas were North East Frontier District, Naga Hills District, Lushai Hills District and North Cachar Hills Sub division. The partially excluded areas were Garo Hills District, Khasi and Jaintia Hills district except Shillong and Mikir Hills district.
14. Cited in Johri, 1933, p. 61.
15. Lalsangkima Pachuau cites the work of F.H. Downs on how the process had taken place but he points out that this so called political integration of the North East with the rest of India was done without the consent of the contemporary political leaders most of whom the British talked of as uncivilized 'tribal' leaders. In fact, Pachuau, in his article goes on to argue how the term tribe and tribal have been used by the British in a very derogatory sense and independent Indian administration also uses these words reiterating the same psyche. See, Lalsangkima Pachuau,

"Tribal"[1] Identity and Ethnic Conflicts in North-East India: A Christian Response, *article published by Henry Martin Centre*, February 2000. For the study by Downs, see, F. S. Downs, *History of Christianity in India*, Volume 5, Part 5, *North East India in the Nineteenth and Twentieth Centuries* Bangalore: The Church History Association of India, 1992, p. 6.

16. Kumar while criticizing the British administration traces the ancient connections between the North East and the mainland through ancient historical narratives and ancient geographical routes. His arguments try to portray that the whole thing of the North East about being 'non-Indian' is much ado about nothing and labels the problems of the North East as one of historical misgivings and misperceptions. B.B. Kumar, "North East India: Crisis of Perception & Credible Action", *Dialogue*, (Quarterly), vol. 1, no. 2, Oct-Dec 1999.
17. Sanjib Baruah, "Postfrontier Blues: Toward a New Policy Framework for North East India", *Policy Studies 33*, Washington East West Centre, 2007, p. vi. A comprehensive idea of integration of various regions of India including North East in the post independence period can be acquired from V.P. Menon, *The Story of Integration of the Indian States*, London, Longman Greens, 1956.
18. Patricia Mukhim, "Voices from the periphery", *The Statesman*, July 30, 2007.
19. After the great Indian revolt of 1857, British rule over the North East gathered pace and the North East was tossed about by colonial policy. Expansion of the area under control and administrative rearrangements were among this policy's characteristics. For example, Assam was ruled as a part of Bengal Province until 1874, when it became Assam Province governed by a Chief Commissioner who was subordinate to the Lieutenant Governor of Bengal Province. Between 1905 and 1921, Assam Province was merged with Bengal Province to become East Bengal and Assam Province, a unit that was again divided into two in 1921 following strong protests against the merger. Under the new arrangements, Assam was named Assam Province, and was directly administered by the Governor-General of Assam Province. Even so, Assam's independence as a province must be taken with a pinch of salt. For example, Sanjib Baruah emphasises that throughout their rule, the British had seen the border of Assam as that of Bengal. See, Sanjib Baruah, author of *India Against Itself: Assam and the Politics of Nationality* Philadelphia, University of Pennsylvania Press, 1999 pp. 38-39. For an idea on the formation of states in the North East see, Kyoko Inoue, "Integration of the North East", in Mayumi Murayama, Kyoko Inoue and Sanjoy Hazarika (eds), *Sub-Regional Relation in Eastern*

South Asia: With special Focus on India's North-Eastern Region, Research Paper, Institute of Developing Economies & Japan External Trade Organisation, 2005.

20. Read, Subir Bhaumik, *Insurgent Crossfire: North-East India*, New Delhi, Lancers Publishers, 1996.
21. Official Records of the UN General Assembly, 7th Session, April 1953 cited by S. Bhaumik in "Guns, Drugs and Rebels", published in *Arakan Information Website*, 03.04.2007.
22. See Bhaumik, Op cit. 20, pp. 22-65.
23. Ibid, pp. 131-132.
24. Ibid. pp. 132-133.
25. This term had been used by Barrister Harun ur Rashid who is a former Bangladesh Ambassador to the UN, Geneva in his article entitled, "Bangladesh and north-eastern Indian States" in BNEIT Quarterly Newsletter - Issue - 3, Bangladesh-North East India Trade Facilitation Centre, June, 2005.
26. V.I.K. Sarin, *India's North–East in Flames*, New Delhi, Vikas Publishing House Pvt. Ltd., 1980, pp. 24 cited in Dinesh Kotwal, "The Naga Insurgency: The Past and the Future", *Strategic Analysis* vol. xxiv, no. 4, July/ 2000, p. 764.
27. Krishna Gopal, "Islamic Fundamentalism in Bangladesh and Its Role in North-East Insurgency", in Dipankar Sengupta and Sudhir Kumar Singh (eds), *Insurgency in the North East: The Role of Bangladesh*, New Delhi, Authors Press, 2004, pp.181.At present the number and expanse of such training camps have increased. The exact number differs but runs well over 150.
28. Bhaumik, Op, cit. no. 20. p. 134
29. Cited by S. Bhaumik, based on his interview with the Naga commander Thinsolie Medon Keyho, ibid, p. 48.
30. *Sentinel*, July 13, 2007. Also, Jaideep Saikia has provided a detailed list of such camps, their location and the nature of their activities. See Appendix XVII in Jaideep Saikia, *Terror Sans Frontier: Islamist Militancy in NorthEast India*, New Delhi, Vision Books, 2004
31. Ibid, Appendix XII.
32. There are 111 Indian enclaves (locally known as Chits) in Bangladesh territory covering 17,258.24 acres. On the other side, there are 51 Bangladesh enclaves in Indian Territory, measuring 7,083.72 acres. Of these disputed enclaves, 65 are along the West Bengal-Bangladesh border (35 Indian enclaves in Bangladesh territory and 31 in reverse)
33. In May 2007, a newspaper report provided news of Anup Chetia conducting ULFA operations from jail which was reported by his co-inmate Shahriar Kabir, a prominent Bangladeshi writer, filmmaker and

civil rights activist. He was quoted that Chetia has "access to a mobile telephone and runs ULFA's operations from the jail, where he is kept in royal style." Report by Nilova Roy Chowdhury, *Hindustan Times* New Delhi, May 21, 2007.

34. Other insurgents demanded by India from Bangladesh include Bendage Wati, Chooba alias Maden, Tusi, Champa alias Chaoba, Kaning Aum (all of ULFA), Sohan Deb Barma and Ghanta Deb Barma of ATTF, Saul Borok, Dhingro Deb Barma, Makshod Borok, Saybam Deb Barma and Kumon Deb Barma. Source: "India seeks the closure of 155 ISI camps in Bangladesh", *News Story*, in Zambian News Agency, internet source, http://www.zana.gov.zm/news/viewnews.cgi?category=9&id=1052671990.
35. The report titled, 'The Secret Nexus of Pakistan, China and Bangladesh that keeps ULFA leaders captive in Bangladesh and causes havoc in India', reads that, "Indian intelligence is now getting clear signal of what really happened in Assam. The secret nexus of Pakistan, China and Bangladesh that keeps ULFA leaders captive in Bangladesh and cause havoc in India is getting exposed slowly. Talking tough, the government today said it would pursue the ULFA in a manner it had avoided so far as the banned militant group from Assam was possibly acting at the dictates of a 'foreign power'.". *India Daily*, Jan. 13, 2007.
36. Anil Khamboj, "Bangladesh Factor Affecting insurgency in the North East", *Peace and Conflict*, vol. 8, no. 6, June 2005, p. 25. Also see a very well researched article by William van Schendel on the Burma-Bangladesh border trade activities, that gives a substantial idea of the kind of activities related to illegal border trade (including arms) across the Naf river between Teknaf and Maungdaw, "Guns and Gas in Southeast Asia: Transnational Flow in the Burma-Bangladesh Borderland", *Kyoto Review of Southeast Asia*, vol 43, no. 4, August 2006, pp. 1-18.
37. Krishnan Gopal, "Islamic Fundamentalism in Bangladesh and Its Role in North-East Insurgency", in Sengupta and Singh (Ed), Op.cit. no. 27, p. 189.
38. Imtiaz Ahmed provides a precursory idea of arms deals which he discusses in the context of 'subaltern globalization and the arming of the non-state'. Imtiaz Ahmed, "Small Arms in South Asia", *South Asia Journal*, 2004.
39. S.C. Mullen Census Superintendent had commented in the 1931 Census Report, where he had said that, invasion by a vast horde of land hungry Bengali immigrants; mostly Muslims from the district of East Bengal" is going to change the province (Assam), its culture and civilization than any other previous historical event. S.C. Mullen, ICS, Census

Superintendent of Assam in 1931 Census Report- Assam Part I, quoted in the Assam Governor's report to the President of India on *Illegal Migration into Assam*, November 8, 1998, cited in Saikia, Op.cit. no. 30, p.44.

40. "Illegal Migration into Assam" R*eport on Illegal Migration in Assam*, report submitted by The Governor of Assam, to the President of India, November 8, 1998, posted at http://www.satp.org/satporgtp/countries/india/states/assam/documents/papers/illegal_migration_in_assam.htm.
41. Ibid.
42. Operation Pin Code is a recent master plan (designed in late 2004) to Islamise the North East. A report on this was published in The Pioneer describing its intents and activities to be undertaken to materalise the plan. *The Pioneer*, January 15, 2005.
43. Harider Sekhon," Pakistan's Inter Services Intelligence in North East India", *SSPC Paper 1,* March 2005, p. 2.
44. For a detailed idea on the origins and activities of the Jaamat e Islami in Bangladesh read Hiranmay Karlekar, *Bangladesh? The Next Afghanistan*, New Delhi, Sage Publications, 2005. Also see the website of Jaamat to learn about their aims and objectives at www. jaamat-e-islami.org.
45. For a very basic idea of such groups see Appendix XIII, in Saikia, Op.cit. no. 30. pp. 190-191.
46. See, Appendix I, Saikia, Op.cit, pp. 163-177.
47. Selig S. Harrison "A New Hub for Terrorism", posted at Bangladesh Awami League website, http://www.albd.org/autoalbd/index2.php?option= com_content&do_pdf=1&id=30. Also see report by A.B. Mahapatra, "Another Pakistan, Salafi terrorism has come to Bangladesh, but it is going unchallenged", *News Insight*, electronic version at http://www.newsinsight.net/archivefeatures/nat2.asp?recno=72&ctg=Defence. There is also an early report by *Time* reporter saying Ayman al-Zawahiri is hiding in the Chittagong tracts in 2002. Alex Perry, "Deadly Cargo", *Time*, October 14, 2002.
48. See Appendix XII, Saikia, Op.cit. no. 30. pp. 188-189.
49. Read the editorial by Subhash Kapila, "Bangladesh: New Base of Terror?" *The Kashmir Telegraph*, May, 2004.
50. For a concise idea on tribes along Indo-Myanmar border areas see, S. N. Barua, *Tribes of Indo-Burman Border,* New Delhi, Mittal Publications, 1991. A very detailed presentation of these tribes is available in Gertrude M. Godden, "Naga and Other Frontier Tribes of North-East India", *The Journal of the Anthropological Institute of Great Britain and Ireland*, Vol. 26, 1897 (1897), pp. 161-201.
51. Bibhu Prasad Routray, "Belated Adventures", *South Asia Intelligence*

Review, Volume 4, No. 9, September 12, 2005

52. Subir Bhaumik, "Guns, Drugs and Rebels" available at http://www.india-seminar.com/2005/550/550%20subir%20bhaumik.htm. A couple of these camps were raided during joint Indo-Burma operations in the first half of 1990s but many still exist. See Dr Udai Bhanu Singh, "Perspective on Myanmar-India Relations", *Dialogue*, January - March, 2004, Volume 5, No. 3. Also for a preliminary on Myanmar's role in Insurgency in North East, see Renaud Egreteau, *Wooing the Generals, India's New Burma Policy*, New Delhi, Author's Press, 2003.
53. The Shillong Accord was signed on November 11, 1975, between the Government of India and representatives of Naga National Council and the underground federal Government of Nagaland, in which the groups agreed to accept the Constitution of India and lay down their arms.
54. For the strategic implications of the opening of Stillwell Road read, Section III titled 'Political' in D. Nath (Ed), *Reopening of the Stillwell Road, Prospects and Problems*, Kolkata, Maulana Abul Kalam Azad Institute of Asian Studies, 2004.
55. The three major routes have been provided by Bibhu Prasad Routray. First, through the upper districts of Assam- Sibsagar, Tinsukia and Dibrugarh to their bases in Nania-Nisha, Chunumu, Tamlu Kachintala. Second, the Mon district of Nagaland which is at the same time an NSCN(K) stronghold. The route runs through Sonari in Sibsagar through Nyasa in Mon district and passes through Hoyet to the camps at Kachintala. The third option is the route through Tirap and Changlang of Arunachal Pradesh. Bibhu Prasad Routray, "Assam: ULFA's Routes of Terror", *SAIR*, Volume 1, No. 8, September 9, 2002.
56. In September 2005, the Indian army had launched operations to flush out ULFA insurgents from the jungles of the Dibru-Saikhowa National Park along the easternmost part of Assam bordering Arunachal Pradesh. This was followed by another operation at Dehing-Patkai to flush out the rebels and a 350-member group of the United Liberation Front of Assam's (ULFA) 28th battalion who had entered Assam from Burma three months earlier. Army feared that about 250 stayed in Dibru-Saikhowa, the remainder are likely to have taken shelter at the Dehing-Patkai Wildlife Sanctuary, which also falls in Tinsukia district, not far from the Arunachal border. See "Indian insurgent bases in Burma", *Mizzima News*, Tuesday 27, 2005.
57. In fact an editorial observes that IBRF was created as part of the greater Naga conflict between the Khaplang and the Issac-Muvaih faction. It reads that, "Khaplang had been instrumental in trying to unite the insurgent outfits of India's North East and Burma under the banner of

the Indo-Burmese Revolutionary Front (IBRF) at Mukpa in West Burma on May 22, 1991. The IBRF defined 'Indo-Burma' as "the region between India and Burma comprising the so-called north-eastern region of India and the present north-western part of Burma," adding that it "is one of the few regions in world which remains to be liberated from colonial rule." On the other hand, the Isaac Muivah group of the NSCN roped in the Bodo Security Force (now the National Democratic Front of Bodoland), the National Liberation Front of Tripura, and some smaller tribal insurgent groups into an informal alliance. Editorial by Sashinungla, "Nagaland: Insurgency and Factional Intransigence" *Manipur Online*, Tuesday, July 26, 2006.

58. Egreteau speaks of extensive Indo-Burmese networks also used by the LTTE to maintain a steady flow of arms. He particularly mentions "two islets of the deserted Indian islands – Landfall Island and St. Martin's Island – between the Burmese Coco Islands and the other major transit point to the Ocean, although the Indian authorities in Port Blair are now keeping a close eye on them and patrolling the sector relentlessly". Egreteau, Op.cit. no. 50, pp. 67-68.
59. Vijay Sakhuja "Indian Ocean and the Safety of Sea Lines of Communication" *Strategic Analysis*, vol. XXV, no.5, August 2001, electronic version.
60. Bhaumik, Op.cit, no. 50.
61. Ibid.
62. Ibid.
63. Shakuja traces back the roots of drugs and arms in Myanmar, where this linkage started in the 1950s. During that period it was the United States that supplied the nationalist Chinese of the Kuomintang (KMT) with weapons and drugs to fight against the Communists in Mainland China. By 1953, the opium industry had been well established to fund the movement. Later the Khun Sa emerged as the heroin drug lord. Opium is easily supplied to Bangladesh also through very porous borders. Shakuja, op. cit. no. 57.
64. See,Clive Parker, "Irrawaddy: Burmese drugs still hurting North Eastern India", *Burma Net News*, Wed 24 May 2006, electronic version at, http://www.burmanet.org/news/2006/05/24/irrawaddy-burmese-drugs-still-hurting-northeastern-india-clive-parker/.
65. NSCN(IM) apparently went about instituting a twenty per cent tax on all drugs trafficking on its territory in the late 1990s. Egreteau, Op.cit. no.50, p.72.
66. Bhaumik, Op.cit. no. 50.
67. There have been serious allegations that the Indian government had encouraged the influx of drugs into the North East in order to weaken

the tribal youth who could turn potential rebels. However the unabated flow of drugs not only has given some form of a lifeline to insurgency movements in the North East, but has also added to social woes in the form of HIV/AIDS as a result of intravenous intake of drugs.

68. For a concise idea of the evolution of Sino-Myanmar relations read Ch 4. in Egreteau, Op. cit. no.50, pp. 73-101.
69. At present there is evidence that Chinese intelligence has renewed its contacts with some of the insurgent groups in the North East especially the NSCN-Muvaih faction, and the ULFA after the Bhutan expedition in 2003. However, the Chinese have kept it a low profile affair, and still continues to supply large caches of armaments to the insurgent outfits just mentioned. See, Renaud Egreteau, "Instability at the Gate: India's Troubled North East and its External Connections", *CSH Occasional Paper*, No. 16, 2006, pp. 99-118.
70. The main ports along the Myanmar coast were Sittwe (on Arakan Rakhine state coast near Bangladesh), Bassein (now known as Pathein, in the Irrawaddy delta along with the Hyanggi, Seikkyi facilities near to the coast)Monkey Point (South of Yangon), Moulmein (Mawlamyine, with the tip of Kyaikkami, at the mouth of the Salween) Mergui and Kawthung (extreme south of Tenasserim Division at the Thai border). Ibid, pp. 91-92.
71. Annual Defence Ministry Report 1996,p, 11 cited in S. Bhaumik, "Insurgency in the North East", *Bharat Rakshak Monitor*, Volume 5(2) September-October 2002, electronic version at http://www.bharat-rakshak.com/MONITOR/ISSUE5-2/bhaumik.html#_ednref10.
72. A good idea of the evolution of Indo-Myanmar relations can be obtained from, Thin Thin Aung & Soe Myint "India – Burma relations", in David Arnott et.al (Eds), *Challenges to democratization in Burma: Perspectives on multilateral and bilateral* responses, Stockholm, IDEA, December, 2001. http://www.idea.int/asia_pacific/burma/upload/chap4.pdf.
73. A number of insurgent groups are functioning in these districts in addition to two other districts particularly Tirap and Changlang. They were a hub of insurgent activities since long given their proximity to Myanmar. They have also witnessed the clash between the two factions of NSCN In Lohit and East Kameng, other active groups include United Liberation Front of Assam (ULFA) and the National Democratic Front of Bodoland (NDFB). It has led to some cases of social tension between the local people and insurgent groups. See Bibhu Prasad Routray, "Growing Tentacles of Insurgency in Arunachal Pradesh", *IPCS Armed group Database*, Article no. 783, July 3, 2002.
74. See, "Breach in Tibet Dam Caused Arunachal Floods," *Times of India*, (July 8, 2000); "India Blames Flash Floods on Chinese Dam," *Agence*

France Presse, (July 10, 2000); "Arunachal floods—dam breach in Tibet, China 'hushed' it up," *Indian Express,* (July 10, 2000).

75. Tashi Tsering, *Hydrologic: Water for Human Development, An analysis of China's Water Management and Politics*, Tibet Justice Centre, 2002, pp. 21-22, available at http://www.tibetjustice.org/reports/hydrologic.pdf.
76. "Global Disarmament or Equal and Legitimate Security for All", *Brief on India's Nuclear Tests* produced by the Indian Embassy, Washington D.C. on behalf of Ministry of External Affairs, Disarmament & International Security Affairs Division.
77. Ibid.
78. According to ministry of External Affairs, Government of India, a Chinese ship carrying materials for A.Q. Khan Research Laboratories was sighted in 1998. Again on August 6, 2001; The Washington Times reported that "a US spy satellite detected the latest shipment as it arrived by truck at the mountainous China-Pakistani border on May1". Quoting the US intelligence agencies the report stated that the China National Machinery and Equipment Import and Export Corp. (CMEC) supplied the missile components for Pakistan's Shaheen-1 and Shaheen-2 missile programmes. See, *Ministry of External Affairs Spokesperson's response to a question on the Washington Times June 4, 1998 report regarding a Chinese ship carrying material for A.Q. Khan Labs, June* 5, 1998. Regarding the report by Washington Times,, Dr. Rajesh Kumar Mishra, "Indian Nuclear Doctrine and Indian Security", *Dialogue*, vol. 4, no. 4, June 2003, electronic version.
79. Ibid.
80. Response by External Affairs Minister of State, Government of India, Shri E. Ahmed in response to question by M.P. Shri K. Subbarayan, *Lok Sabha Unstarred Question Number 3167*, 23/08/2006.
81. Response by External Affairs Minister of State, Government of India, Shri E. Ahmed in response to *Lok Sabha Unstarred Question Number2780*, 10/05/2006.
82. Dr. Bhartendu Kumar Singh, "Sino-Indian Relations: Recent Developments", *IPCS Special Report 18, May 2006*, pp.11-12.
83. The original MoU can be viewed at http://www.indianembassy.org.cn.
84. For more activities related to Sino-Indian bilateral defense cooperation, see Singh, Op.cit. no. 80, pp. 10-11.
85. Chinese objections to the nuclear deal in the past hinged on two aspects: India should first sign the Nuclear Non-proliferation Treaty and Comprehensive Test Ban Treaty before it can reap the fruits of the nuclear deal, and that the nuke deal would alter the strategic balance in the region and fuel an arms race. However, of late, the Chinese Foreign

Minister has gone on record saying that, "China believes that countries can develop cooperation on the peaceful use of nuclear energy abiding by their respective international obligations." Report from Anil K Joseph in Beijing, "China softens stance on Indo-US N-deal" *PTI News*, posted on *Rediff News*, August 07, 2007, 17:33 IST.

86. Op.cit. no. 78.
87. For instance see, Carin I Fischer, "The Stillwell Road: Straight Ahead", *Himal South Asian*, September 2005.
88. Vast tracts of the Ledo Road are dense jungle making it easier for clandestine trading by the Indian, Burmese and even Chinese smugglers as much as by insurgents of North East India particularly for supply and stocking of weapons and ammunitions. It is apprehended that upgrading of the roads that are currently being used for such unholy purposes, would hardly be able to put a stop to such activities, but on the contrary would encourage influx of illegal migrants and insurgents. Moreover some stretches of this road is too much in the north (close to the Paungsaw Pass, East of Arunachal Pradesh) to be kept under Indian security vigilance. Therefore Indian government's enthusiasm to revive this road link must be taken with a pinch of salt. See, Egreteau, Op.cit. no. 50. pp. 170-171.
89. *Himal South Asian*, Op. Cit, no.85.
90. Opinions in his presentation entitled, "India's Defence and Strategic Relations with Southeast Asia" P*aper at the* 9th *Asian Security Conference on Security Dynamics in Southeast Asia: Emerging Threats and Responses* at New Delhi, Institute of Defence Studies & Analysis, 9-10 February, 2007.
91. In a recent speech by the Indian Minister for External Affairs Minister at a function in Indonesia, a synoptic idea of the state of bilateral relations between India and the Southeast Asian states can be acquired. However, he does not make any mention of Indo-Myanmar relations. See Address by the External Affairs Minister Shri Pranab Mukherjee, at a function jointly organized by the Embassy of India in Jakarta and the Indonesian Council for World Affairs "India's Growing Engagement with East Asia", *Press Information Bureau, Government of India Press Release*, electronic version at http://pib.nic.in/release/release.asp?relid=28704.
92. On July 6, Vietnam and India issued a joint declaration on strategic partnership in New Delhi following the talks between Prime Minister Nguyen Tan Dung and Prime Minister Manmohan Singh that agreed to establish a Strategic Dialogue at the level of Vice Ministers in the Foreign Office. The two leaders agreed that contacts and exchanges of visits between the Defence and Security establishments of the two countries should be further enhanced.

93. Egreteau cites the Survey of India to show that between 1971 and 1981 the Burmese government had changed the delineation of frontiers between Sagaing Division and Manipur, taking 29 sq. km. from the latter. Comparatively, Indian actions were less. Egreteau, Op.cit. no. 50. pp.130-131.
94. The official visit by the then foreign secretary, J.N. Dixit, to Yangon marked the turn around in Indian policy perspective towards Myanmar. India thereon decided to cautiously engage junta, dropping its isolationist strategy.
95. Egreteau, Op.cit. no. 50. pp. 133.
96. Egreteau provides a detail of the flourishing narcotic trade in the Indo-Myanmar borders as also about the various insurgent groups involved in this trade on either side of the border. Renaud Egreteau, "Instability at the Gate: India's Troubled North East and Its External Connections", *CSH Occasional Paper*, no. 16, 2006, pp. 133-136.
97. Jurgen Haacke, opines that Myanmar will benefit enormously from Indo-Myanmar trade and in turn good relations with India will help Myanmar improve political image and legitimacy. Jurgen Haacke, "Myanmar's Foreign Policy, domestic influences and international implications", *Adelphi Papers*, June 2006, pp.35-49.
98. Egreteau, Op. cit. no. 94, p. 140.
99. *Annual Report Ministry of External Affairs 2005-2006*, p. ii.
100. There is a proposal being considered by India and Myanmar to construct the Jiribam-Imphal-Moreh line in India, and the Tamu (Moreh) - Kalay - Segyi line Myanmar, along with rehabilitation of the existing Segyi-Chaungu Myohaung line in Myanmar. [8/07] RITES is conducting a feasibility study on this link. See data put by the Indian Railways Fan Club in response to question on possibility of rail links both with China and Myanmar respectively. Source: http://irfca.org/faq/faq-inter.html.
101. Bibhu Prasad Routray, "The Indo-Myanmar-Thai Highway: Impact on Insurgency in India's North East", *Bharat Rakshak*, Vol. 5 (3), November-December 2002.
102. See "India set for Military Expansion in Andamans", *The Jang*, March 17, 2006.
103. Lailufar Yasmin, "Bangladesh-India Tussles", *South Asian* Journal, July-September 2004, online version at http://www.southasianmedia.net/magazine/journal/bangladeshindia_tussels.htm.
104. The Indian army claims that the number of deaths is much less than what is claimed by Bangladesh. However in response to questions at the Indian Parliament the government put the number of deaths at 45. See, "Lok Sabha Starred Question number 31 on Border Disputes with Bangladesh", on 24. 07.2001.

105. For a detailed description of this border incident, see, "2001 Indian-Bangladesh Border Conflict", at http://en.wikipedia.org/wiki/2001_Indian-Bangladeshi_border_conflict.
106. Sharier Khan, "Indian, Bangladesh Pledge to End Border Bickering", *One World South Asia*, January 7, 2004, online version at http://southasia.oneworld.net/article/view/76271/1/.
107. Ishtiaq Hossain, 'Bangladesh-India Relations: Issues and Problems,' in Emajuddin Ahamad (ed.), Foreign Policy of Bangladesh: A Small State's Imperative, Dhaka, Bangladesh: The University Press Limited, 1984, p. 47.
108. Yasmin, Op.cit. No. 101.
109. To understand Bangladesh's claims and position on Talpatty islands, read the detailed explanation on sea baselines by Mahmud Nazmul Haque, "The Legal and Scientific Assessment of Bangladesh's Baseline in the Context of Article 76 of the United Nations Convention on the Laws of the Sea", *Report sponsored by the United Nations, National University of Ireland and the Nippon Foundation*, 2006. p. 106. Also see, "Defence Committee Orders the Navy to Achieve the Unachievable", *The Daily Star*, October 2, 2003.
110. India and Bangladesh had entered into a Boundary Accord in 1974, which is commonly known as the Mujib-Indira Treaty. This bilateral treaty stipulates that no defence works can be built within 150 meters of the no man's land. Bangladesh says that the planned fence is a violation of a bilateral treaty. It says the fence that India is trying to construct falls within the no-build zone. But the fence is only meant to prevent illegal infiltration and possibly cross-border movement of rebels active in Indian territory. Hence, it cannot be considered a defence work. Though India has tried to maintain the distance of 150 meters wherever possible, in certain areas it is difficult to construct fences so far away from zero line because of difficult terrain and dense population.
111. Annexure V of the *Report of the Ministry of Home Affairs, Government of India, 2006-2007.*
112. For details on the events of 2005 see, Anand Kumar, "Bangladesh: Fighting Over Fence", *South Asia Analysis Group No. 1330*, April 8, 2005.
113. Op.cit., no. 110. p. 37.
114. In January 2003, the former Deputy Prime Minister of India, L.K. Advani, announced the deportation of some three million Bangladeshis who were staying illegally in India. Bangladesh condemned the Indian accusation as completely baseless. The Indian authorities finally deported some 213 Bengali-speaking people of disputed nationality terming them 'illegal migrants' near Satgachi under Mathabhanga police station in

Cooch Bihar district, West Bengal, on 31 January. The group of people — consisting of 68 women and 80 children — were left in the no man's land for six days as the security forces of both Bangladesh and India refused their admission on the basis of contested nationality. This issue of 'push-out and push-back' took India-Bangladesh relations to their lowest point. See, Yasmin Op. cit., No. 101.

115. See, Khan, Op. cit., No. 105.

116. Speech by Her Excellency Begum Khaleda Zia, Hon'ble Prime Minister of the People's Republic of Bangladesh at the Banquet hosted by H.E. Prime Minister of India Dr. Manmohan Singh in New Delhi, 21 March 2006, published by the Ministry of Foreign Affairs, Government of the People's Republic of Bangladesh.

117. According to the joint press statement, both the countries have agreed to jointly visit the enclaves and territories in adverse possession at an "early date" without prejudice to each other's positions. Further, the two countries renewed commitment to full implementation of 1974 Land Boundary Agreement and exercise utmost restraint along the 4, 200-km common border to avoid an untoward incident. The two countries also agreed to "examine the possibility" of quickly instituting a bilateral mechanism to combat terrorism and organized crime. The Indian side put forward the drafts of three deals on Extradition Treaty, Agreement on Mutual Legal Assistance in Criminal Matters and Bilateral Agreement on Combating International Terrorism, Organized Crime and Illicit Drug Trafficking. In response, Bangladesh side said it would revert at an early date. On peaceful border management, the statement said the two sides agreed on sensitizing their border forces, populace along the border and the media to maintain peace and tranquility along the India-Bangladesh border. The two sides agreed to hold regular meetings between the border forces and exercise "utmost restraint" along the Bangladesh- India border to avoid any untoward incident and avail of the existing institutional mechanism to resolve situation arising out of such incidents. The meeting also called for greater vigilance and cooperation between the two countries to prevent illegal movement of goods, people, illicit drugs, narcotics and explosives across the border and tackle the smuggling of fake currencies. Information gathered from, *Xinhua*, August, 28, 2006. posted on *People's Online Daily*, at http://english.peopledaily.com.cn/200608/28/eng20060828_297297.html.

118. Diverting just 10 to 20 per cent of water of the Brahmaputra River in India could cause 100 Bangladeshi rivers to dry, estimate scientists who are working on transboundary issues in Bangladesh. The Indian plan seeks to divert up to 40 per cent of the flow from some major rivers, according to Bangladesh Paribesh Andolan or BAPA research.

119. Sultana Rahman, "India's Ambitious River-Linking Project Irks Bangladesh", available at *Asia Water Wire*, 2003 online version at, http://www.asiawaterwire.net/node/84.
120. Ibid.
121. Data taken from Anand Kumar, "Changing Dynamics of Indo-Bangladesh Economic Relations", *South Asia Analysis Group Paper No.1992*, October 16, 2006.
122. Siddharth Varadarajan, "India, Bangladesh and Myanmar agree to lay pipeline", *The Hindu*, January 14, 2005.
123. Anand Kumar, "India-Myanmar Gas pipeline Through Bangladesh-*Pipe Dream*?" *South Asia Analysis Group Paper No. 1216*, January 1, 2005.
124. Based on an interview with M.K. Dhar, by Srinjoy Bose, "Energy Politics, India- Bangladesh Relations", *IPCS Special Report No. 45*, July 2007, p.2.
125. Anand Kumar, "Myanmar-Petrochina Agreement: A Setback to India's Quest for Energy Security". *South Asia Analysis Group Paper No. 1681*, January 19, 2006.
126. "Dhaka to resume talks on tri-nation gas pipeline," New Age, May 1, 2007, at, http://www.newagebd.com/2007/may/01/front.html.
127. Bose, Op.cit, no. 123, p. 4.
128. In the bordering areas of Tripura, Feni river had eroded some land 36 years ago. This land was disputed due to absence of border pillars on the zero line. This issue at times created a tense situation between the people of the two countries near the border. However, this issue was resolved by the joint survey teams of both the countries. These teams visited the Bangladesh portion of the area on May 6 and subsequently border areas in Sabrum, Udaypur and Chitabari in South Tripura in India on May 7. These 35 acres of land on Koilermuk-Ramgarh border in Feni were given to Bangladesh. A bilateral accord giving effect to the border demarcation and setting up of new pillars was signed at Udaipur Circuit House in India. Work has also started for setting up of 28 sub-pillars and three 'reference pillars' on the border and to draw the zero line afresh. Anand Kumar, "Indo-Bangladesh Relations Under the Caretaker Government", *South Asia Analysis Group Paper No. 2266*, June 11, 2007.
129. Ibid.
130. Ibid.
131. The present Director General of DGFI is Major General Golam Mohammad, who replaced Major General Sadiq Hasan Rumy.
132. Some of the most vocal critics like Patricia Mukhim and Rajesh Dev have written a number of articles that have identified the various faults and fissures in governance and policy initiatives undertaken by the

government. For example see the features under North East section in the daily, *The Statesman*. Particularly, see Rajesh Dev, "Autonomy Regimes and Inter-Ethnic Conflicts", *The Statesman*, August 13, 2007.

133. Sanjib Baruah, Introductory Chapter, "The Problem", *Seminar*, vol. 550, June 2005.
134. For instance, popular scribe Pudaite contends that India's development is associated with her interest in the resources of North East. Therefore, state led development strategies are the least associated with the genuine needs and wishes of the region. This is coupled with cultural apathy towards the region. See, Izzy Pudiate, "North East India The Forgotten Region", available at *Kangla Online*, Monday, October 22, 2007.
135. A very enriching idea of the tension created by the centrifugal tendencies released by the nations from below phenomenon is provided by Sanjay K. Roy, "Conflicting Nations in the North East", *Manipur Online*, Thursday, May 11, 2006.
136. Jairam Ramesh, "North East India in a New Asia", *Seminar*, vol. 550, June 2005.
137. Such a view had been expressed by Rajiv Sikri, the erstwhile Secretary East of the Ministry of External Affairs, cited by Sudha Menon, "North East India and Globalisation: The Way Ahead", *Working Paper of the Digital Library of the Commons*, January 1, 2007, available at http://dlc.dlib.indiana.edu/archive/00002194/01/North East_the_way_ahead.pdf.
138. According to Foucault, a shepherd-folk game involves the uncensored use of force on the subjects to attain discipline and loyalty amongst subjects as much as to punish the anti-state elements. A bio-power game approach on the other hand is a more human liberal approach to dealing with problems of loyalty by attending to the day to day needs of the subjects and is definitely concomitant to development. For further understanding read, Michel Foucault, 'The Subject and Power' in Kete Nash (Ed), Readings in Contemporary Political Sociology, Blackwell, UK, 2000, pp 8-26.
139. Hon'ble Union Minister of DoNER has been persistently harping on improving relations with Bangladesh also as much as with Nepal. See, "Help North East Benefit from Look-East Policy: Aiyar", *The Hindu*, October 10, 2007.
140. Roy, Op.cit. no. 130.

North East India Planning in the Winds of Change

Toki Blah

When one speaks of the Geo-Political and Strategic factors that influenced India's domestic and foreign policy vis a vis its North Eastern Region, it can safely be claimed that history played a major role in the determination of such policies. To the South, partition of the subcontinent set up man-made barriers between a traditionally populous market in the plains and its natural hinterland in the hills. Suspicion, hatred and clandestine relations replaced a once carefree life style for a region and its people. The eventual liberation of East Pakistan and Indian assistance in the setting up of the independent Republic of Bangladesh has done little to restore the good old days. The North East still has to find ways and means on how to get along with its southern neighbour.

To the North, the High Himalayas provided the North East of India with a psychological sense of security even if this natural barrier was impudently breached by the Chinese in 1962. The invasion forever changed Delhi's attitude to the region. From an awkward territorial appendage inherited from the partition, the North East overnight became a valuable piece of real estate, strategic in blocking Chinese ambitions of access to the Bay of Bengal. The Chinese betrayal is an issue that continues to impinge upon mindsets in South Block and mainland India still has to make up its mind about the new North East role in coping with emerging challenges in South East Asian relationships, SAARC and ASEAN.

The North East Region also has borders with other sovereign nations such as Bhutan and Nepal to its North and North West and Myanmar to its East. Relationship of Independent India with Nepal and Bhutan has maintained an even keel in the last sixty years, and there is no reason why this status quo need be upset, regardless of Maoism in Nepal. To the East stands enigmatic Myanmar, a country with which India has been able to maintain the best of relations despite chronic domestic problems that haunt either side of the border.

It is within the constraints of these historical geo-political factors that the North East region will have to design its curriculum of interfacing amidst change with the rest of the World in the 21st Century.

Globalisation and its Impact

(a) The Northern Problem

As mentioned above, the trauma of 1962 is still vivid in Indian minds, and Indo-Chinese relations continue to oscillate on the vexed border dispute along the acrimonious Macmohan line. But as of today, both China and India have become major forerunners for the economic leadership of not only Asia but perhaps of the world. The stakes need no longer be limited to small wretched strips of disputed territory, They have gone beyond that. Sustainable foreign relations, with immediate neighbours as well as distant nations, now depend more on the ability to penetrate and outsource foreign markets than seizing territory. Both countries recognize the rationale of economic competition against each other, rather than engage in open hostility over nuclear sights. The practicality of the first overshadows the suicidal absurdity of the other. Mutual past mistrust is for the backburner, while both countries forge ahead with their new found economic roadmaps.

For both, peace is a prerequisite that will dominate future bilateral relations between the two Asian giants. The shift from military confrontation to economic competition brings in new challenges and calls for appropriate strategies to meet these challenges. West and South West China still need outlets to the nearest sea routes. A route through Nathula, Sikkim–Assam–Meghalaya–Bangladesh to the Bay of Bengal is the most ideal. For India, an international overland trade route through its territory brings in prestige, while the move will also ensure that North East goods also get transit rights through Bangladesh to the sea. Nepal and Bhutan also benefit. It is an international economic networking system that the North East desperately needs in a globalised scenario. It is an undertaking most compatible with SAFTA and ASEAN. For the Bangladeshis, it would mean not only economic remunerations but the enviable goodwill of two Asian giants who are expected to invest heavily in such a tie up. It is a win win situation for everyone. The North East needs to sell the idea to New Delhi. The times demand and require a paradigm change on how we relate with our neighbours. Its time we address this paradigm change from the perspective of the future than from the viewpoint of history!

(b) The Southern Problem

Indo-Bangla relations are somewhat paradoxical. Bilateral friendship is espoused but offset by mutual suspicion. We regularly charge and counter-charge each other with sins of commission and omission on matters of trade and sharing of inland rivers. From the Indian perspective the threat of illegal Bangladeshi immigration into the North East with all its demographic implications is real and factual. India also has complains regarding Bangladeshi connivance in sheltering North East militants. The Bangladeshis on their part have never hesitated in voicing their resentment over what they see as Indian attempts at hegemony in the bilateral relations between the two. As usual, the truth lies somewhere in between.

Politics on both sides of the border has been the prime cause for perpetuating suspicion and misunderstanding. Bangla bashing is a popular vote catcher in the North East, and India baiting is as popular in Bangladesh. But the time has come for politics to take a back seat and for economic considerations to come forward and shape the course of future relationships. There is now urgent need to come up with a new diplomatic approach regarding our attitude to Bangladesh. The basic concepts of a globalised economy should guide such a strategy. Bangladesh has attractive transit facilities and markets for North East products. North East tourism on the other hand has potentials for Bangladeshis. The Look East Policy calls for some serious introspection on how to win friends in the region. The erection of a barbed wire fence along the entire border may look good as an anti-infiltration mechanism, but viewed from across the border, it can hardly be seen as a friendly neighbourly act.

(c) The Eastern Problem

North East India's gateway to the markets and technology of South East Asia lies through Myanmar. The problem lies in that country's political instability and its weak infrastructure, both of which may not be capable of carrying India's Eastward trade ambitions. Illicit drugs that flow into the North East from the golden triangle, pose a clear and present danger to the social fabric of the region. Our economic concern vis a vis Myanmar emanates from the brittle political situation prevailing in that country. A revolt against the present junta is just a question of time, and the overflow of such a revolt into Indian territory worries us. Socio-political instability in Mynamar will adversely impact on the Look East Policy and Indian ambitions for a greater role in South East Asian affairs. Unfortunately the physical road East for the region has to pass through Myanmar. That is the problem. In the long run, however, irrespective of the internal politics in Myanmar, India's long term interests will lie in continuing to concretize its image as Mynamar's friend, well wisher and patron.

Strategy for North East Development

Globalisation, the Look East Policy and India's future relations with its North East neighbours have been discussed. What needs serious analysis is the impact these will have on the people and the region. A Delhi-centric top down development approach has for too long been accepted as the panacea for North East development. This paradigm has failed. North East development exhibits an unusually high element of unsustainability and this is mainly due to an absence of peoples' understanding and sense of ownership over developmental initiatives. People see Government efforts at development as insensitive, unimaginative and as target- driven. A regional political mindset that seeks power for power's sake has only helped in perpetuating this belief through poor governance. Continuing with this failed approach will therefore be foolish.

A new development paradigm, custom-made for the North East to fit in with the North East challenges of the 21st Century, is urgently needed. If enhanced socio-economic changes are the future expectations of the region, then we cannot allow our rural masses to remain indifferent to, and untouched by, such transformations. Liberalization cannot afford to leave people behind. We cannot have sections who will remain excluded from the benefits of science and technology; from the fruits of a vibrant economy; nor can we allow people to remain trapped within the paralyzing tentacles of poverty, illiteracy and fear. Force can no longer be a State option for ensuring

North East integration with the rest of the country. Ways and means now exist on how to win hearts and minds, and for communities of the region to associate their own survival with that of a strong India. Economics must chart our political roadmaps not the other way round. In this context the following core issues need articulation.

a. People's involvement in Development

People's participation in all future North East development programmes has now become mandatory. The indigenous communities of the region need to be brought onboard the developmental band wagon. North East communities no longer need to perceive change as divisive, intimidating or as a threat to their Tribal Identity. An integrated Regional Development Plan, one that is inclusive and that cuts across artificial political divides, has to come up. Stand-alone developmental initiatives by individual states may no longer be viable. A conglomerate of North East states aiming at mutual economic benefits holds vast promise. The North Eastern Council and DONER need to review their role from fund dispensers to that of regional policy facilitators. Sustainable Livelihoods should be the regional mantra to be ably backed by robust environmental concerns. A Development Paradigm designed to carry the people along is urgently called for.

b. Agriculture and Tourism

The primary sector that engages 80 per cent of the region's population has to be actively engaged in any future development plan of the region. Aside from food security, focus on value addition and marketing, especially for organic products, is the key. This is a strategy to involve people in activities they are comfortable with, and through which they can see a rapid improvement in their quality of life. The feasibility of rural enterprises based on a federal business structure offers vast attractions.

The North East will also have to create a tourism brand of its own. The region is strong in Traditional Health Care and in English. Basic HRD infrastructure for the two already exist. Health tourism based on alternate health care systems, and Educative Tourism based on imparting good English to students from Non English speaking nations has potentials. Computer based Information Technology that services a global economic network system has made it mandatory for such countries to tone up their English skills. Can we therefore have a policy where the North East is the one-stop-destination for such toning up requirements in the English language.

c. Global Warming

Global Warming and Climate Change have now reached alarming proportions. As some said, "Technology has allowed man to play God, but saving what God has created is now a problem. Its solution may very well determine mankind's continued existence on Planet Earth." The Koyoto Protocol, the recent EU resolutions on the subject are indicative of the crisis in our hands. It shall not be long before a reluctant USA will follow suit. Carbon emission will be discouraged, while Carbon sequestering will be the order of the day.

How does one mitigate Green House gas emissions? Obviously by sequestering them through Carbon sinks that are basically composed of large number of trees and foliage. Huge bio-sphere reserves is the answer, and the North East forms one of the most viable and robust bio-sphere reserves in the world. Interestingly most of this bio-wealth is community owned and managed on technology and skills that are inherited, sustainable and traditional in character.

Of further interest is the existence of an alarmed global humanity that is now willing to pay for services rendered towards Carbon Sequestering through the continued upkeep and preservation of biosphere reserves. The North East has to recognize this potential and ready itself on how it can economically exploit the situation. A Policy and Approach Strategy on how we manage and market this unique community owned technology and skill in natural resource management is now urgently required.

d. The Fresh Water Prospects

It is an accepted historical fact that most of the major conflicts of the 20th Century have been over attempts to gain access to and control over a vital natural resource—oil. For the 21st Century predictions have already been made that Fresh Water shall be the most precious and sought after resource. Some have even gone to the extent of predicting that future wars will be fought over its control and management.

The North East of India receives the highest precipitation in the entire world. The total quantity and volume of fresh water, in the form of rain, in any single monsoon is enough to slake the thirst of the entire world thrice over. Is it possible to bring about a participatory water management programme where communities can start earning from conservation of fresh water? Secondly one of the mightiest of all river systems, the Brahmaputra and its numerous tributaries, flow through the region and its adjacent neighbours. There is no reason why China, India and Bangaldesh cannot come together in joint partnership aimed at preservation, harvesting, management and marketing of the fresh water from this mighty river system.

Conclusion

The essay is a world view from a North East perspective. If India is to grow into a world economic power; if it is to grow at the projected rate of 9-10 per cent annually, it can hardly do so by allowing the North East to lag behind. The views of the region will have to be taken into consideration. The region has to be enabled, capacitated and coaxed into becoming a viable contributing unit in this economic enterprise of the Nation. The gap between the haves and the have-nots has to close and close rapidly. This can only take place through the establishment of a Road Map that is based on a long term vision for the Region. Such a Road Map will necessitate incorporating the views of Ministry of Commerce, Ministry of External Affairs, Ministry for Forest and Environment, Ministry of Defence, Home Ministry, Economic Affairs and DONER. It shall require the vision of statesmen to design the framework of such an enterprise. The Look East Policy may become redundant. It may need perhaps to be replaced by a Doctrine—A specific Development Doctrine for the North East of India.

Section II

North East India's Economy: Development Bottlenecks

Challenges of Natural Disasters

Shyamananda Bhattacharjee

The role of natural disaster in history is significant and can in no way be ignored[1]. There is no denying the fact that natural disasters like earthquake, flood as well as landslide have been playing their disastrous role in North-East India since antiquity. It is also common knowledge that if not earthquake the other two are there in the region in quick succession almost in a regular order to affect a large segment of human settlement as well as the other bodies, both living and non living. It is also true that their occurrences are almost unavoidable in the region due to its location and characteristic geophysical formation. If not for anything else, North East India is known globally for being one of the most seismic zones of the world. In a Workshop held at Honolulu in 1978, the region has been identified as one of the six most earthquake prone zones in the contemporary world. It may be worth mentioning here that the region has experienced two of the largest known earthquakes of the globe causing immense long and short-term damages to its lives and properties in the year 1897 and 1950.

The young geological formation coupled with the heavy rainfall has made the region very prone to landslide. If not destruction of human habitation, substantial disruption of surface communications due to landslide along a number of national highways have become a part of the regular living process here in the region during the rainy season every year.

The region, having the highest rainfall in the world, is also known for the inundation of its vast area due to devastating floods almost at a regular interval, primarily due to its two big rivers—*Brahmaputra* and *Barak*. The initial wandering days of *Ahoms* here in the region, endangered by the dreadful presence of river *Brahmaputra* are well documented in the *Ahom Buranjis*—a well known historical text of the *Ahom* rule in Assam. The devastating impact of the mighty *Brahmaputra* has compelled the Government to constitute a separate body called Brahmaputra Board to specifically look after the river. The periodic devastations of *Barak* in southern Assam are also no less.

Earthquakes

Although calamities like flood, diseases have been more reported as associated with the history of North East India, earthquake has been no less a devastating force for the region. Conventional history has tended to ignore this aspect even though wars and battles have had less profound impact on the social history of the region[2].

Recent statistics show that in between 1900 and 1976 the total persons killed as a result of earthquake over the globe is 26,62,165 and the number of persons rendered homeless is 2,88,94,657. Compared to this, other calamities like volcanic eruption killed 1,28,058 persons and left 3,37,931 homeless, floods caused death of 12,67,845 and rendered homeless 17,52,20,220, land slides killed 3,006 and made homeless 44,673, cyclones 4,34,894 dead and 1,76,48,463 homeless, hurricane 18,513 dead and 11,97,353 homeless, avalanches 3,059 dead 150 homeless, typhoons. 34,103 dead and 54,57,054 homeless, storms 7,110 dead and 34,32,641 homeless and tornadoes 1,175 killed and 3,42,459 homeless.[3] Total human lives lost due to earthquake during the first eighty years (1901-1980) of the 20th century in India numbers 70,000, which means 900 lives per year. The corresponding global average is about 1,800 lives per year.[4] In Tokyo's earthquake of 1st September 1923, the city was virtually destroyed and the people killed numbered 1,00,000 and millions were rendered homeless Thus, earthquake has always been one of the most dreadful natural calamities known to mankind and man is continually reminded of its ruinous power virtually without warning.[5]

Earthquake being a dreadful natural calamity, and its cause being unknown till the other day, became part of myths in many of human recordings long before historical recording came into existence in North East India. Although there are very few studies done on this aspect of the region, most of the chronicles, gazetteers, memoirs, accounts, reports available here mention earthquakes prominently.

Pre-Colonial Period

In the pre-colonial period a number of earthquakes were recorded in the *Burunjis,* the royal chronicle of Assam. A compiler of Ahom royal chronicle, Lila Gogoi puts it this way:

> As Assam is lying in the earthquake zone she had faced a number of devastating earthquakes during the six hundred years. The *Burunjis* recorded information relating to such earthquakes. There were a few tremors which not only caused collapse of buildings but also water, sand, fish had been found thrown up from below. The earthquakes of 1548, 1594, 1607, 1649, 1696 are noteworthy.[6]

The History of Assam: 1681-1826 AD (Tungkhungia Buranji), comp., Tr. and Ed. By S.K. Bhuyan, OUP, 1933, records an earthquake event in a very distinct manner:

> In the month of Puh, 1618, Bandar Phukan of the Chetia family constructed a fort at Pungdang under the orders of the king which took two months. In the same year there was an earthquake which continued for six months in an abortive fashion from Phagun to Saon of the following year. The earth was rent asunder at Sadiya, and magur and kawai fish appeared in the breaches. As sands and water appeared at that place the sides of the hills crumbled down.

A brief list of earthquakes of the North Eastern Region for the period of 1548-1962 has also been prepared by H.K. Gupta[7].

Records of earthquakes of the region are available in more methodical order since the Nineteenth century, i.e., the colonial period. First recorded earthquake of this period was of 1st April, 1810. Similar tremors were felt during 12th to 15th May, 1816. Further records of tremors were found in 1825, 1828, 1830, 1834, 1839, 1840, 1841, 1842. In 1843, the region was again rocked quite a number of times due to a series of earthquakes. Thereafter shocks were felt again in each of the years from 1845 to 1852. There was also a prominent shock in the year 1860. After a gap of a few years earthquake records of the region are available again from the Cachar earthquake of January, 1869.[8]

Colonial Period

*The Cachar Earthquake of 10*th *January, 1869*

The Cachar earthquake of 10th January, 1869 made huge destruction in Cachar and Manipur Valley and a detailed report of which was prepared by the Geological Survey of India for the first time.[9]

The earthquake virtually ruined the town of Silchar particularly its bazaar area. As the noting goes:

> The bazar itself presented one almost unbroken scene of ruin. It had been chiefly composed of bamboo and mat structures, which in other places, had remained undisturbed, yielding sufficiently to the wave by their elasticity, and quickly recovering themselves. With these there were a few pucka or masonry structure – some with flat-terraced roofs. But here all were in ruins. The views I have given, all taken from Mr Pearson's photographs and therefore accurate and detailed representations of the facts, will convey a much better idea of the place than the most detailed description.[10]

The inspection bungalow at *Panchgram* was thrown down. At *Sealtec Bazar* houses sank.

After Cachar, it was Manipur Valley where the shock was fatal. Robert Brown, the British Political Agent, in Manipur had recorded his feelings about the onset of this event there at Imphal in a vivid manner :

> ...the vibrations increasing however, I made at once for the door of exit. I experienced some difficulty in making my way through the front room. The ground at this time was undulating so strongly that walking was a difficult matter. Arrived at the outside of the house, the ground was in such a violent motion, that I found it impossible to proceed more than a few paces, when I either was thrown down or sank down involuntarily, my face turned towards the house and on my hands and knees. At this time the motion of the ground was most remarkable; it seemed to rise and fall in waves of about three feet in height. A very short experience of this worry motion sufficed to settle the fate of my house, after swaying about, and cracking and groaning for a brief span the upper storey, built of wood and bamboo, settle down with a crash on the lower walls which fortunately although much fissured and well out of the perpendicular, withstood the pressure.[11]

Records of quite a good number of shocks felt in the region are also there for the period between May, 1874 to December, 1877.[12] Two earthquakes of 1876 and 1885 of the region deserve special mention.

The Great Shillong earthquake of 12th June, 1897

The Great Shillong Earthquake of 1897 brought in an unbelievable massacre to the lives and property of the region. Loss of lives was reported from many places of the region. Total loss of lives due to this great shock from many places of the region was recorded as 1542[13]. Damage to pucca constructions and roads were almost universal between Nowgang in the east and Goalpara in the west, Darrang in the north and Sylhet in the south. Even considerable damage was done to the road between Dimapur and Golaghat. Though shock was felt but Manipur Valley and Aizawl remained almost unhurt[14].

A brief on the district-wise damages to infrastructure as available in the government record would be able to portray the gravity of the situation in clear terms. Shillong being nearest to the seat of that earthquake exhibited a scene of complete destruction. In Khasi and

Table 1: Impact in Khasi and Jaintia Hills District due to 1897 Earthquake

Place/ Town	*Stone Buildings/ Pucca Houses*	*Mission Buildings etc.*	*Ekra Building*	*Plank Building*	*Water Supply Network.*
Shillong	Totally collapsed	Completely collapsed	Suffered heavily but not like stone buildings	Those un-attached to the ground suffered least	Completely destroyed; no water for many days.
Jowai	Court building, military block houses and police line collapsed entirely.	chapel/ bungalow/ dispensary all collapsed. buildings at Shangpung, Raliang N.E. of Jowai were damaged			
Cherra-punjee	All pucca houses destroyed	Hospital, school, Missionary houses destroyed			
Sohiong, Mairang, Normai, Nongkhlaw, and the adjecent villages, 40-50 miles west and north west of Shillong		Damage done to roads, bridges and pucca houses in these villages were great. Mission, station and churches at Mawphlang and Mairang were destroyed. All the Rest Houses along Mawphlang-Nongkhlaw and Nongstoin were also destroyed			

Source: Report of DC, K&J Hills in Gait's Report (compilation in the tabular form is by the author)

Jaintia (K & J) hills the number of people killed was 916. Loss of Government property in K & J hills district was enormous (Table 1). The loss incurred by only Welsh Mission in the K & J hills was estimated at Rs. 10,000- 11,000 at that time.[15]

The next district which suffered most from this calamity, was the erstwhile Sylhet district (now in Bangladesh) where death count was

Table 2: Impact in Kamrup District due to 1897 Earthquake (In Kamrup Death toll were 29)

Place/Town	*Stone Buildings/Pucca Houses*	*Ekra Building*	*Remarks*
Gauhati	All European Bungalows destroyed; jail wall was completely demolished and government structure collapsed in general	The building with strong wooden or bamboo posts with *ekra* walls escaped without injury	Homeless European took shelter in the mail streams over *Bramhaputra.*
Kamakhya Hill	Its spire with golden kalsi fell; nat mandir cracked; Bhubaneswari Temple on the hill top collapsed completely & other minor temples cracked but remained erect.		
River Island close to Gauhati	The temple built by Ahom King in saka 1616 cracked; its spire fell but remained erect when it's surrounding wall was destroyed.		
Aswaklanta on the North Bank of Gauhati	One temple with two buildings completely demolished; other building lower down cracked and it's spire fell.		
Patidarang tahasil	A stone bridge of historical importance made by Baktiar Khilji in 1203 was ruined		
Barpeta			Loss of private property of worth Rs. 50,000 was reported.

Source: Report of the Kamrup Deputy Commissioner P.R.T. Gordon in Gait's Report

545. In the town of Sylhet the death toll was 55, which was caused mostly by the fall of buildings. In the district of Kamrup, particularly at Guwahati, there were a general collapse of government buildings and regarding the failure of structure, Guwahati faced almost the same fate as that of K & J Hills (Table 2).

Table 3: Impact in Garo Hills District due to 1897 Earthquake (Death toll at Garo hills were 27 and the loss of infrastructure was also quite large)

Place/Town	*Stone Buildings/ Pucca Houses*	*Mission Buildings etc.*	*Ekra/mat/reed Building*	*Remarks*
Tura (hill portion of Garo Hills)	Govt. construction in general suffered – DC's, DSP's, Forest Officer's, Sub-Engg.'s bungalows as well as IB & Cutcherry mainly suffered.	American Baptist Mission Building could with-stand the shock with comparative immunity.	Among the III type construction with mud floor-timber or bamboo frames, mat or reed walls lightly plastered having roof of thatch or corrugated iron were reduced to ruins.	The tradi-tional Garo houses with raised floor and built entirely of wood, bamboo, cane and thatch had escaped any damage.
	The house of Civil Surgeon, Dispensary, post office, Treasury & some shops in the market having stone and cement plinth cracked and broken up.		The police barrack, clerk's quarters and the majority houses in bajar belong-ing to this type of construction could withstand the shock.	
The down plain portion			Many houses sank into the ground badly only roof being visible.	several village remained submerged for a consi-derable period.

Source: Report of the DC Garo Hills in Gait's Report

Table 4 : Other affected Districts of Assam due to 1897 Earthquake

Dist/ Units	*Goalpara (Dhubri)*	*Darrang (Tezpur)*	*Nowgong*	*Cachar (Silchar)*
Cutcherry	Standing with injured walls; at *Goalpara* fell flat	Damaged	Complete wreck	Slight crack in several places
DC/Asstt Comm.'s Bungalow	At *Goalpara* Asstt. Comm's one entirely fallen	DC's bung-alow, planter's club damaged severely	DC's one was complete wreck	
SDO's Bungalow	At Goalpara was in complete ruin	Destroyed at *Mangaldai*		At *Hailakandi & Halflong* ruined
Circuit House	Walls injured	Was dilapidated at Mangaldai		At Halflong wrecked completely
Post & Telegraph Office	Post office at Goalpara, both P&T office buildings thrown down		Damaged slightly	
Treasury	Suffered severly; destroyed at Goalpara	Damaged		
Jail	Thrown down	Damaged	Complete wreck	
Hospital/ Dispensary	Walls injured	Considerable injury to the hospital at Magaldai		
Church/ Temple/ Masjid	Church & Temple flattened, Masjid was dilapated	Church damaged	Masjid behind the Dak Bung-alow fell.	
Private Building	seven newly built houses on dispens-ary ground flattened; Zamindar's pucca buildings at Gouri-pur suffered very badly;	Two Nos damaged; public build-ings suffered more seriously at Mangaldai	Several Masonry shops, store houses collapsed	

Dist/ Units	*Goalpara (Dhubri)*	*Darrang (Tezpur)*	*Nowgong*	*Cachar (Silchar)*
Kutcha House		Kutcha building had escaped altogether		
School	Thrown down			
Remarks	*Goalpara, Gosaigaon, Gauripur, Sukhchar, Mankachar, Bijni* all places were virtually wrecked		All the wells were choked with mud and several tanks were also filled with mud.	108 houses were thrown to the river and 649 houses were thrown to the ground

Source: Reports of respective Deputy Commissioners in Gait's Report

Table 5: Disruption of Surface Communication in the District of K & J Hills due to 1897 Earthquake

Name of the Road	*Type of the Road*	*Disruption due to*			*Remarks*
		Subsidence/ Cracks etc	*Land-slides*	*Failure of Bridges*	
Shillong-Cherra-Theriaghat-Sylhet Road	Partly Car road partly cart		At 6th & portions 17-24th & 29-32nd miles slipped down	Except one at 10th mile all collapsed	Suffered heavily upto *Theriaghat*, then 10 mile bridle portion in between Cherra and Theriaghat completely destroyed.
Shillong–Guwahati Road (63 miles)	Cart Road	Extensive Fissures	Random landslips in between *Nongpoh & Shillong*	Other than *Burnihat* and *Barapani* bridges rest all collapsed	
Shillong-Jawai-Jaintiapur-Sylhet	Bridle path upto Jaintiapur via Jowai				Considerably damaged

Name of the Road	*Type of the Road*	*Disruption due to Subsidence/ Cracks etc*	*Land-slides*	*Failure of Bridges*	*Remarks*
The old Cherra road via Maoflang			Collapsed badly on both sides of Shella river		
Shillong to Nongstoin/ Nongklaw via Mairang	Bridle path		path was obstructed by the mud out of land slides		

Source : Gait's Report(compilation in tabular form by the author)

Table 6: Disruption of Communication in a number of Districts of Assam due to 1897 Earthquake

Name of District/ Road name		*Road Type*	*Disruption due to Land slides/ subsidence/ fissures etc*	*Failure of bridges etc*	*Remarks*
Kamrup	a) Trunk Road South of Brahmaputra	Car Road	Cracked and sank at many places		
	b) Trunk Road North of Brahmaputra	Do			Considerably damaged
	c) At Gauhati	Do	Cracked through-out the town; Strand Road sub-sided in several places		
	d) Barpeta town	All			surface com-munication completely shattered
Garo Hills	a) Tura town		One sank and another one remained covered by land slides		
	b) Dalu-Mankachar Road	Cart Road	Blocked due to land slips up to Tura for several weeks; in hills slips were many.	At 22nd mile a timber bridge 80 ft long was raised by 8 ft above its level.	Movement became impossible for several weeks

Name of District/ Road name		*Road Type*	*Disruption due to* *Land slides/ subsidence/ fissures etc*	*Failure of bridges etc*	*Remarks*
Goalpara	Trunck road beyond Goalpara sub-division	Car Road		All bridges including one of 80 ft, two of 60 ft and other two of 22 ft span around 74th mile destroyed.	The road had been breached at many places. P&T communications were also snapped.
Darrang	a) *Tezpur-Balipara* Tram way	On rails	At *Rangapara* Upheaval and lateral throw underneath could successfully destroy the way		Mangaldai *sub*-division was worst sufferer; banks along with trees fell in rivers affecting boat traffic.
	b) *Patharughat Sonapur(Siali kuchi Road)*		Road on a bund, portion of which subsided disrupting communication.		
Now-gang	a) Strand Road	Car Road	Roads disappeared in parts, in general fissured, sunken etc.		Telegraphic links snapped.

Source: Gait's Report (compilation in tabular form by the author)

Impact on Railways

The portions of the railway lines, which were most seriously affected by the earthquake of 1897 were the Guwahati Branch and the line through South Sylhet and its branch to Silchar.

The Guwahati branch line was functional for all classes of traffic upto Jamunamukh till the earthquake had disrupted this railway communication by destroying a number of bridges. The Titamari bridge—a high bridge with a span of 100 feet, two other bridge of 40 feet span over a navigable channel and the Kopili bridge of 3 spans—100 feet, 18 feet and 60 feet span, as well as, all other minor bridges and culverts on the line were destroyed. All the station buildings and staff quarters along the whole of 75 miles railway line were razed to the grounds. The damage was so much that the railway authority had to express their inability to restore the situation to its former condition until the next working season.[16]

Srimangal Earthquake of 8th July, 1918

The epicentral zone happened to be the worst sufferer of this shock and Srimangal (located in the erstwhile Sylhet District of Assam presently in Bangladesh) being the centre of that zone bore the brunt to its maximum (the names of places, valley, river, mauza, thana etc. are retained as they were at the time of the shock). In the Balisera Valley and Part of Doloi Valley, the effect was most severe.[17]

> With few exceptions all brick buildings were found to be destroyed within this area. Coolie lines on the tea estates, built mostly of sundried mud, and thatched roofs, were levelled to the ground. The usual type of planters bungalow built of poorly burnt bricks and very thick, exceedingly heavy thatched roofs, also collapsed in almost every case. Tea factories and certain bungalows having steel girders frames were left standing, but the brick work in them was either thrown down or left in a shattered and tottering condition in almost every case. The tea estates visited by me in the Balisera Valley were the *Phulchera, Kalighat, Lakhichera, Kajurichera, Rajghat, Putticherra* and *Sisal Baria*. At the *Phulchera* estate the Manager's bungalow was levelled to the ground, practically every leaf house was down. The Assistant Manager's bungalow had only one shattered room standing, and the factory, which had a steel girder frame, was left in a tottering condition. The factory boiler shifted, owing to the fracturing of its brickwork foundations, and two of the heavy drying machines were loosened from their beds. The general direction of fall was towards the south…area.[18]

Dhubri Earthquake of 3rd July 1930

At Dhubri, very few brick masonry i.e one and two storey buildings could escape the shock of 3rd July 1930 undamaged. Majority of them were badly cracked and partially collapsed, while at least in one instance almost total collapse of the structure took place immediately following the main shock. Of the semi-pucca buildings, a number of them were more or less badly affected, though in the case of a few well built houses, constructed in recent past including the Girls' High School situated on a more stable ground, practically no damage was visible. Of the other two types of structures—(i) structures of split bamboo or ekra, covered with mud plasters, and supported on a wooden frame with parts driven into the masonry plinth or alluvial foundations and (ii) structures like semi-pucca or the ekra with mud plasters type with framework merely resting on a masonry plinth so that the structure was free to move as a whole, in most instances, where the supporting posts had been carried down into the plinth or into the ground, the structures were severely effected, whereas in the case of a few buildings in which the wooden frameworks merely rested on the plinth were undamaged, with the exception of slight cracks on plaster.[19]

Post Colonial Period

*The Great Assam Earthquake of 15*th *August, 1950*

Within a gap of 53 years following that of 1897 North Eastern India was once again rocked by another great shock and to be precise, there were hardly two shocks larger than that of the 15th August shock of Assam, that occurred on the globe between 1856 to 1956 as per the list revised and published by Gutenberg in 1956.[20] Once more the damage caused was of dimension without a parallel. About this the famous seismologist C.F. Richter remarked: "This shock was more damaging in Assam, in terms of property loss, than the earthquake of 1897".[21] A trapped Botanist working in the area very close to the epicentre records his feelings at the commencement of the great shock:

> Suddenly a most extraordinary rumbling noise broke out, and the earth began to shudder violently. Shattering the dead silence of the night in that remote mountain retreat, the ominous rumble swelled to a deafening roar. It was as though the Keystone had fallen out of the universe and the arches of the sky were collapsing.[22]

At Dibrugarh heavy damages were caused to the court buildings, jail, Assistant Commissioner's residence, hospital building, PWD godown, Executive Engineer's residence, and out of these, the Court building and the Executive Engineer's residence became unsafe for occupation. Several other government buildings suffered minor damages. Practically all pucca buildings, private or Government, in the town suffered damages and in some cases very badly. The *thana* at Doom Dooma was very severely damaged and was unsafe for occupation. At Sadiya proper, many buildings were severely damaged. Part of Saikhowa bazaar including one rice mill subsided. The dispensary, the doctor's house and inspection bungalow were all severely damaged. 35 Military Barracks were very badly damaged demanding reconstruction. Several tube wells in the bazaar were reported to have been cleaned-out at a depth of about 20 ft. below the ground[23] . In the town of Sibsagar, jail buildings, high school buildings and police lock-up suffered heavy damage. The town was under water for 3 to 4 days due to a breach in the right bund of Dikhu just below the bazaar. At Jorhat some of the residential and office buildings suffered damages but not of very high magnitude. But a large number of private buildings in the town and some surrounding villages were completely destroyed, some badly damaged. A large number of tanks and ponds were filled up with sand, causing difficulty in supply of drinking water. North Lakhimpur town was affected where the PWD office godown, overseer's quarters, *thana* and a portion of the jail compound suffered damages. Private buildings in the whole town were hit badly. Due to subsidence of the ground many people were rendered homeless[24] .

In *Abor* Hills at *Pashighat* practically all new and old central and state government buildings were more or less damaged. Even temporary sheds completely collapsed. Main military buildings, school and boarding houses were very badly damaged, Assistant Political Officer's bungalow was washed away by flood, Commandant's Bungalow and Inspection Bungalow were threatened by erosion.[25]

The total recorded death due to this great earthquake was 1526. This figure was however doubted as much lower than the actual.[26] Oil and Tea companies suffered a huge loss in terms of property. Estimated loss of the Oil company was Rs. 11,00,000/-[27] , of the Tea companies £ 1,84,000/-, and the loss incurred by whole of Assam was estimated at £ 20 million.[28]

The Great Assam Earthquake of 1950 had also severely disrupted the surface communication of the region. The worst affected part of the Assam Trunk Road was in Sadiya between Dholla and Sessinighat via Saikhowaghat. All bridges collapsed, the roads cracked and subsided at several places. The entire extent of 3 miles length between Saikhowa and Sessinighat was completely destroyed.[29]

Impact on Railways

Railways also suffered to a great extent in the concerned areas:

> Immediately after the earthquake, four sectors of the Assam Railways were suspended. (1) Mariani and Duklingia on the Jorhat Section, (2) Simulguri and Tinsukia, (3) Margherita and Ledo and (4) Makum Junction and Saikhoaghat. Excepting the last one where the damage was extensive, the remaining communications were restored within a very short time. Besides damages to Dihing and Tingrai bridges over the

Tinsukia – Simulguri section, most of the railway bridges from Makum Junction to Saikhoaghat were badly damaged. The naturalist E P Gee puts it this way: "The Assam Railway form Mariani eastwards suffered greatly, rail tracks being torn up and twisted into snake-like patterns".[30]

Land Slide

A land slide defined in most simple terms is an upward and downward movement of material in which detachment from the parent mass along a plane of separation is a must. The young and hilly topography (70 per cent) of the North Eastern Region of India provides this opportunity in abundance.[31]

Though earthquake induced landslides have done enough damage to the region, that was not all. Landslides as an independent ongoing process here in the region have all along been a great barrier to its surface communications. The connecting link between Meghalaya and Barak Valley via NH 44 happens to be a perennial victim to these occurrences. The Sonapur landslide on this road, which occurred on 7th July, 1988 following heavy rainfall reported to have dragged a truck down into the river and subsequently buried it below the slipped mass. The failed slope covered an area of about 0.44 sq km, and the progressive failure of the slide continued till 30th September, 1988. The road could be cleared by deploying three bulldozers, two compressors and 150 labourers working round the clock for twenty days.[32]

The 17th and 18th May, 1995 witnessed another heavy landslide in Mizoram in which vast tracts of land areas covering two townships of Sahia and Lawngtlai of Chimptuipui districts including a major section of road – life line for the population of the area – and a vast forest were severely affected. Apart from damages to land and property, 39 people were killed and around 24 suffered various degrees of injuries.[33] It may further be noted that:

> It was subjected to heavy cloud burst on 16th, 17th and 18th May, 1995 which resulted in the area was also effected by mild earthquake of intensity 3.5–4.0 on Richter Scale which aggravated the situation by coupling the landslides which had already started as slump failure culminating into debris and mud flows.[34]

Landslide occurred on 9th August, 1992 at a place 7 Km away from the capital town of Aizawl, and killed 66 persons and destroyed 17 houses. Investigation revealed that the houses were located on the toe of a deep slope of Calcareous sandstone, siltstone and thinly laminated claystone, a quarry site located above the village along a road removed the toe support. This may be treated as a typical case of planning failure. In this case also it was reported that there were heavy rainfall for 2-3 days prior to the land failure[35].

There was one more earthquake induced land slide known as Tulli Paper Mill Slide, which occurred in Nagaland following an Indo-Burma earthquake on 6th August, 1992. The damage caused to the paper mill due to this was such that the mill remained closed for about six months. It involved replacement of several machines and the losses in terms of cost ran into crores[36].

Hundung Cement Plant at Ukhrul, Manipur as well as Gumti Hydro electric Project at Tripura suffered quite extensively due to landslides. Other than being a part of young geologic formations and a zone of extreme rainfall, the prevailing jhum cultivation in the region also adds to the devastating ongoing denuding process of the hills in a great way, and this denudation in turn has an accelerating impact on the landslide of the region[37].

The unstable condition under water saturation used to constitute the major cause for slope failure along the rail alignment in Limbding–Badarpur section, Lalabazar-Bhairavi section, Badarpur-Dharmanagar section and Dharmanagar-Kumarghat section.

The old landslide forms flat ground at places and those are often been utilised for development purposes. Hunding cement plant at Manipur and Mawnynmkhong village in Meghalaya are good illustrations of this, which developed extensive creep after construction resulting in ground distress. Remedial measures for those were however, suggested after serious study.

Flood

The region with highest rainfall and holding a mighty river like Brahmaputra in a bowl like structural set up cannot just avoid being a place of disastrous flood. It is known that as the Brahmaputra rolls down the Assam Valley from east to west for a distance of 640 Km with its 38 tributaries – 26 of which joining from the north and the other 12 from the south bank[38] virtually carrying the entire share of the Brahmaputra valley rainfall for about few months beginning with the onset of monsoon in the first week of May, has all the potentials of flooding the valley almost every year.

The Barak, another very important river of southern Assam, equally vulnerable for flood due to very heavy rainfall in the area, used to cause heavy damage all along its course in the Barak Valley region at a regular interval.

Assam being affected not merely by the tributaries but mainly by both Brahmaputra and Barak with a cumulative increase in their level of disaster has been asking for support from the State's coffer since long back. The Table 7 would in short space spell out in clear terms the amount of loss that the region had incurred over a long period during its post independence era.

Table 7: Flood Damage Statement of Assam during 1953 to 1995[39]

Year	*Area affected*	*Croped area affected*	*Lives lost*	*Total Damages Crops, Houses & Pub. Utilituies*	*Total Damages Crops, Houses & Pub. Utilituies*
	Million Ha	Million Ha	Nos	Million Ha	Million Ha
1	2	3	4	5	6
1953	0.08	NEG	4	2.66	55.71
1954	3.15	0.27	32	15.77	355.19
1955	1.41	0.09	Nil	3.71	92.53
1956	0.60	0.08	19	3.27	71.25
1957	0.40	0.02	5	4.51	91.84
1958	1.25	0.07	4	2.71	53.89
1959	1.04	0.19	20	8.40	160.53
1960	0.47	0.22	14	7.76	140.17
1961	0.19	0.02	3	0.57	10.11
1962	1.62	0.38	115	20.33	363.05
1963	0.58	0.08	13	2.05	35.41
1964	0.76	0.15	10	2.46	36.32
1965	0.60	0.02	5	0.69	8.98
1966	1.78	0.40	57	22.52	262.03
1967	0.26	0.07	3	2.44	24.50
1968	0.41	0.13	19	8.36	86.64
1969	0.81	0.10	12	8.47	76.63
1970	0.72	0.20	37	10.43	97.07
1971	0.36	0.11	1	5.63	51.63
1972	1.10	0.38	116	24.15	209.06
1973	2.75	0.29	19	16.49	114.17
1974	1.12	0.26	40	19.25	103.49
1975	0.01	0.01	4	0.34	1.88

(*Contd...*)

1	2	3	4	5	6
1976	0.57	0.11	67	11.98	72.74
1977	1.10	0.45	76	31.09	164.16
1978	0.31	0.08	2	4.26	22.49
1979	0.67	0.24	28	28.15	139.68
1980	1.16	0.29	57	39.80	178.10
1981	0.46	0.07	21	7.40	28.97
1982	0.61	0.10	16	21.89	82.98
1983	0.73	0.14	22	56.18	187.09
1984	1.52	0.49	90	50.82	154.09
1985	0.65	0.08	57	54.73	162.96
1986	0.43	0.32	15	204.59	575.11
1987	1.53	0.99	127	346.60	838.23
1988	3.82	1.13	232	663.84	1511.79
1989	0.72	0.37	34	308.62	692.97
1990	0.49	0.21	28	74.54	152.69
1991	1.00	0.33	108	202.05	394.25
1992	0.21	0.04	12	33.12	33.12
1993	1.25	0.21	72	92.72	133.90
1994	0.05	0.03	7	9.48	12.62
1995	1.14	0.56	74	473.82	573.32
Total	39.89	9.78	1697		8613.00
Average	Nil	0.23	39		200.31
Max	3.82	1.13	232	663.84	1511.79
Year	(1988)	(1988)	(1988)	(1988)	(1988)

As in the case of landslide, the impact of seismicity also has its role in further worsening the situation of flood in the region "After the earthquake of 1950, the erosive activity of the river increased resulting in Sadfiya town at the confluence of Dibang and the Lohit disappearing in 1953'[40].

Alternative to Fight Back

Thus the challenges that these natural disasters do pose to the region are multidimensional and are of a very great magnitude. However difficult those challenges may be, the region cannot just ignore them any more. So, no sustainable development work can be done here in the region without paying due attention to this very important aspect. It is therefore very essential that a Master Plan for Integrated Regional Disaster Mitigation Programme be prepared for the region with all seriousness without any delay rather within a given time frame. The task being extremely complex demanding integration of very high order, the desired international input/experience/expertise in this respect should be taken into consideration to incorporate the latest technical know-how to make it not only viable but also effective for the region.

Possible Approach

Since the tectonic set up responsible for seismic activity, the rainfall and the geologic formation responsible for flood and landslide are there to stay in the region, so, the goal here should necessarily be to minimise their disastrous impact on the people, society and the environment of the region as far as possible if not exactly like those of other developed countries. This in brief means:

In case of Earthquakes

a) The buildings, the hydro-electric power generation units, embankments, industrial units, the mines and the habitats in general available in the region may be allowed to shake but should in no way be allowed to collapse;
b) Communications may be disrupted but should be repaired immediately and intra-regional best possible cost affective alignments will have to be found out on analysis of cloud free satellite imageries of the region to establish multiple communication channels both through surface and water bodies of the region to act as much-desired all-weather alternatives;
c) The minimum ensured services, such as electricity, drinking water, drainage, supply of essential food items and medicines, security, etc. though may be disrupted due to earthquakes should be restored or alternate arrangements be there to meet the challenge in no time;
d) Loss of property as well as injury to individuals, resulting from an earthquake, should be taken care of out of the insured fund received from the available mandatory disaster mitigation insurance of the region for each and every family.

In Case of Flood

e) Bramaputra and Barak will have to be restricted within its own limited width i.e not only the embankments are to be made more powerful, scientific and location specific but rain waters are also to be harvested at different levels by all concerned and means to restrict the rain water run-off to the major rivers;

f) To ensure better absorption by the top soil, afforestation of the region should be enhanced under strict surveillance and be made a part of the mandatory activities of all the existing institutions/organisations;

g) Affordable mechanical units for preparing one's own drinking water, fire-place and food has to be developed and distributed at the individual family level here in the region, particularly in the flood affected areas;

h) Flood essentially disrupts both the surface and water communications for the public and so communication through air-fields at strategic locations of the region, as well as effective satellite communication, will have to be there in the region.

In Case of Landslide

i) Road alignments are to be redefined and rectified, wherever necessary in the region, in consonance with those of the latest satellite imageries of the region;

j) Because of increasing pressure of population, risks due to landslide in the newly extended urban settlements of the region should be minimised through proper technical support and due awareness;

k) Failure of hill-slope, due to landslide induced by earthquake or heavy down pour in the region, has to be avoided through continuous surveillance;

l) Loss of top soil due to landslide has to be minimised, as otherwise those loose land masses not only raise the river beds of the region, there-by enhancing the flood risk to a great degree, but also take away the precious top soil there by menacingly enhancing the deforestation in a cumulative manner, taking it to its climax – Cherrapunji, the wet desert, a case in hand for ready reference.

The region being truly a victim of natural disasters, demands an active humane support from all concerned, and particularly from the development planners. Without proper scientific guidance and due awareness and a firm political will, no sustainable development seems possible here in the region in the true sense of the term.

NOTES AND REFERENCES

1. Rezanov, I.A., *Catastrophes in the Earth's History*, Moscow, 1980, p. 7.
2. Bhattacharjee, S., Unpublished Ph.D thesis on 'Man, Calamities and History: A Study of the History of Earthquakes and its impact on North East India [1228-1960], The Deptt. Of History, Assam University, Silchar, 2002.
3. Despande, B.G., *Earthquake Animal and Man.*
4. Arya, A.S., 'Earthquakes are Avoidable Disasters', paper presented at a seminar on Earthquake Engg., Roorke University, 1978.
5. Helmut, Tributsch, *When the Snakes Awake; Animals and Earthquake Prediction*, Cambridge, 1943, p. 185.
6. Gogoi, Lila, *The Buranjis: Historical Literature of Assam*, 1986, p. 232.
7. Gupta, H.K., *et al.*, 'Seismicity of North East India Region Part 1 : The Database' *Journal of Geological Society of India,* vol. 28, November, 1986, p. 354-365.
8. Oldham, T., *Catalogue of Indian Earthquake*, Geological Survey of India, Calcuttal, 1869.
9. Oldham, R.D. (ed.), *Memoirs of Geological Survey of India*, vol. 19, Calcutta, 1883.
10. Ibid., p. 13.
11. Ibid, pp. 28-29.
12. Keatinge, R.H., Chief Commissioner, 'XI-Record of the Occurrence of Earthquakes in Assam during the years 1874, 1875, 1876', *Journal of Asiatic Society*, No. 3, Calcutta, 1877, pp. 296-297 and 306-09.
13. Gait, E.A., Report on the Earthquake of the 12th June, 1897, Proceedings of the Chief Commissioner of Assam, Home, March, 1898 (herein after referred to as Gait's Report).
14. Nightingale, W.H., 'Report of Superintending Engineer ' in Gait's Report
15. Gait, E.A., *Op.cit*
16. Mr Way, quoted in *Gait's Report*, p. 7.
17. Stuart, M., 'The Srimangal Earthquake of 8th July, 1918', *Memoirs of Geological Survey of India*, vol. 46, p. 7.
18. Ibid., p. 9.
19. Gee, E.R., 'The Dhubri Earthquake of 3rd July, 1930', *Memoir's of Geological Survey of India*, vol. 65, pp. 8-9.
20. Richter, C.F., *Elementary Seismology*, pp. 709-715.
21. Ibid., p. 63.
22. Kingdon-Ward, F., 'Caught in the Assam-Tibet Earthquake', *National Geographic.*
23. Garg, G.R., 'Earthquake of August 15th and its effect on the topography, the regimes of the rivers in North-East Assam and damage to roads',

Rao's Compilation on 1950 Earthquake, pp.69-70.

24. Dutta, G.N., 'Damage caused by the Earthquake of the 15th August 1950 in Assam', *Rao's Compilation on 1950 Assam Earthquake0,* p.72-75
25. Ibid., p. 74.
26. Poddar, M.C., 'A short note on the Assam Earthquake of 15th August, 1950', A compilation of papers on the Assam Earthquake of August 15, 1950 by M B Ramchandra Rao, The Central Board of Geophysics, pub. No. 1, Calcutta, 1953, p. 42.
27. Corps, E.V., 'Assam Earthquake of 15th August, 1950, as experienced at Digboi, upper Assam', M B Ramchandra Rao (compiled) A Compilation of Papers on the Assam Earthquake of August 15, 1950, The Central Board of Geophysics, pub. No. 1, Calcutta, 1953, p. 14. (hereinafter referred as Ramchandra Rao's compilation).
28. Tillotson, E.; 'The Great Assam Earthquake of August 15, 1950', Nature, January 27, 1951, no. 167, p. 130.
29. Dutta, G.N., *op. cit.*, pp. 73-74.
30. Gee, E.P., 'The Assam Earthquake of 1950', *Journal of Bombay Natural History Society*, vol. 50, no. 3, p. 630.
31. Avasthy, R.K., 'Incidence of Landslides : A basic input for the disaster management in North East India', *Status of Landslides in North East India and Natural Disaster Management,* Assam University, Silchar, 1998, p. 1
32. Ibid. p. 2
33. Ibid., p. 5
34. Ibid.
35. Ibid., p. 7
36. Ibid.
37. Ibid.
38. Mohile, A.D., '*Flood Management in Brahmaputra Valley - constraints and prospects*', proceedings of International Conference on Disaster Management, 23-26 April, 1998,Guwahati, Assam, Org. by Tezpur University, Assam.
39. Ibid.
40. Ibid.

Development of Infrastructure in Mizoram

PROBLEMS AND PROSPECTS

James L.T. Thanga

The role of infrastructure in economic development is well recognized and it is well known to be the backbone of economic development. India has made significant progress in the last ten years in infrastructure development, and private investments have been magnetized in telecommunications, ports and roads and other individual projects.

Broadly speaking, infrastructure means the stock of fixed capital (inclusive of equipments) in an economy, viz, factories, roads, etc., considered as determinants of economic growth. Unlike other inputs of production whose magnitude vary with the magnitude of outputs and thus they are accounted for in the variable cost, infrastructure does not, by and large, vary with the magnitude of production unless the scale of production changes or the technology of production is altered. Infrastructure facilities are broadly classified into economic infrastructure and social infrastructure. Economic infrastructure includes power, transport, communication, banking and insurance, etc., while social infrastructure indicates health, hygiene and education facilities, etc. This essay would try to highlight the development of infrastructure facilities such as transport and communication, power and electricity and financial infrastructure in Mizoram.

Development of Transport and Communication Infrastructure

Transport and communications include railways, roads, shipping, civil aviation, posts and telegraphs, telephones, telecommunications, etc. Of these facilities, the roads, posts and telegraphs and telecommunications are more relevant in the context of Mizoram than others.

Roads

Road transport occupies the most important means of transport in Mizoram as the contribution of other means of transport is very small. Road construction in the state started during the 5th Five Year Plan (1974–79) and is mainly undertaken by the State PWD and the Border Road Organization (BRO). The length of all types of road was 3735.68 km in 1998–99 with a road density of 17.72 per 100 sq km, and it was increased to 5948.15 on 31 March 2006 with a road density of 28.22 per sq km. The road density of Mizoram was much below the national average, which was 73 in 1995-96. During the 9th Plan Rs. 202.22 crores had been approved for road construction and it was raised to Rs. 231.22 crores during the 10th Plan (including the approved annual plan outlay of Rs. 29.17 crores for 2002-03). The achievement of project targets during the 8th and 9th Plans and the physical target of 10th Plan are summarized in Table 1.

Table 1: Road Development during 8th and 9th Plan and Target of 10th Plan

Sl No	*Activities*	*8th Plan Achievement*	*9th Plan Achievement*	*10th Plan Target*
1	Formation and Cutting (Km)	335.67	108	79.50
2	Improvement & widening (Km)	422.93	149	-
3	Culvert Construction (Nos)	1333	876	687
4	Retaining Wall (Rm)	11302.40	9262	6915
5	Soling (Km)	489.73	213	-
6	Metalling (Km)	502.08	537	-
7	Blacktopping (Km)	629.21	262	-
8	Resurfacing (Km)	81.90	128	1093.50
9	Side drain (Km)	-	-	70
10	Bridges	-	-	5

Source: Draft Tenth Five Year Plan (2002-07), Draft Ninth Five Year Plan (1997-2002) & Annual Plan(1997-98), Govt. of Mizoram

During the 10th Plan period the Mizoram State Road Project, funded by the World Bank with an estimated cost of Rs. 312 crores (15 per cent to be shared by the State Government), intended to execute road improvements (187 Kms) and Road Maintenance (520.62 kms). Besides the World Bank Project, there are projects funded by NABARD (an estimated cost of Rs. 26.144 crores) and PMGSY (an estimated cost of Rs. 711.32 crores) meant for construction and maintenance of roads in the State.

The state road network is classified into National High Way, State High Way, Major District Roads, Other District Roads, Village Roads, Town Roads and Satellite Town and Village Roads. As on 31st March 2006, surfaced roads accounted for 59.29 per cent of the total road length. The percentage of surfaced road is quite high, compared with the national average of 55.38 per cent in 1995-95. In 2006, National High Way maintained by the BRO and State PWD constituted 30.73 per cent, followed by Major District Roads constituting 25.26 per cent.

Communication

The network of Post Offices, Telephone Exchange and telephone connections are the major infrastructures for communication. Mizoram witnessed a good progress in postal services since independence. In 2005-06, there are 359 Post Offices with the population per post office of 2475 (Based on 2001 Census). At the same time, the area served by PO per sq km in Mizoram is 58.7. The figure of Mizoram in respect of area per post office is much larger than the all India average (21.42 per sq km in 1998-99). However, the population per PO is much lower in Mizoram than the all India average (5502 persons in 1998-99). This is due to the sparse location of settlements and low density of population (42 per sq km in 2001 Census), which raised a number of problems in the development of transport and communications infrastructure in the State.

Telecommunication is now accepted as basic infrastructure along with power and transport for growth and development of the economy (*Vanlalchhawna;*MIPAA, 2002, pp.199). In India, the story of telecommunication in many ways epitomizes the new India. The total number of telephones (Basic and Mobile) rose from 22.8 millions in 1999 to more than 125 millions at the end of 2005. As on 31 March 1999, there were 45 telephone exchanges in Mizoram and the number increased to 76 with 782 PCOs in 2006. As on 31 March 2006, the number of telephone connections (basic and mobile) in Mizoram was 89,177, indicating that one-tenth of the population has telephone facilities. The figure would be much higher if we include the connections provided by private operators (i.e. Airtel, Reliance, etc), which started operations since 2006. The number of internet connections in 2000–01 in Mizoram was 499. Considering the recent development in IT, the number of internet connections would significantly increase in the near future. Mizoram has become one of the global villages nowadays.

Development of Power Generation Infrastructure

Power infrastructure in the region is important for improving the quality of life as well as the productive capacity. With economic development in the country, per capita electricity consumption is bound to increase. The Government of India has taken significant policy initiatives to improve conditions for attracting private investment and FDI in the power sector. Broadly, 100 per cent foreign equity participation is allowed under automatic approval route in all the segments of the industry.

The per capita consumption of electricity in Mizoram during 2005-06 has increased by 66.6 per cent to 151.64 kwh, compared to 91 kwh during 1992-93. However, the per capita power consumption in Mizoram is still much lower than the all India average, which was 335.42 kwh during 1995-96. Up to March 2006, out of 671 villages, 570 were electrified indicating that more than 84 per cent of villages in the state have been electrified. The category-wise consumption during 2003-04 reveals that consumption of electricity was the highest in the case of domestic use, which accounted for more than 67 per cent, followed by public water works (15.3 per cent). The capacities of power station installed, and generation of power in Mizoram are shown in Table 2. It can be observed that the installed capacity of the state is increasing, but the generation is decreasing, revealing that the state's dependence on import of electricity is increasing every year.

Table 2: Development of Installed Generation Capacity (in MW)

Sl No	*Source*	*Installed Generations*					
		1996-97		2000-01		2005-06	
1	Diesel Power	25.36	14.16	26.15	5.87	9.92	*
2	Hydel	5.27	4.01	8.20	6.58	14.25	8,65
3	Thermal	-	-	-	-	22.92	2.4
4	Total	30.63	18.17	34.35	12.45	47.09	11.05

* Generation of electricity by diesel has been discontinued.

Source: *Socio-Economic Review of Mizoram (2000-01) and Statistical Handbook of Mizoram (2006),* Directorate of Economic and Statistics, Govt. of Mizoram.

The ongoing projects targeted to be commissioned during the 10th Plan were Tuipanglui (3MW), Kau-Tlabung (3MW), Maicham Stage-II (3MW), Serlui B (12MW), Bairabi (80MW) etc. Besides these, Bairabi Thermal Power Project (20MW) has been commissioned recently, but the power generation is yet to be started. Even though the State has a vast hydro-electric potential (it is estimated to be 3100 MW), its dependence on outside sources is still increasing.

Financial Infrastructure Development

The existing level of financial institutions, financial markets and financial instruments and services, which facilitate transfer of funds, constitute the financial infrastructure in the economy. The service provided by these agents is the key factor for the development of agriculture and industries, mobilization of resources and capital accumulation in the economy.

The financial system of Mizoram largely revolves around the State Bank of India, and its group and cooperative banks. Though there are some developmental banking institutions working in the state, the activities of the financial institutions are examined in the present paper. The development of banking activities is shown in Table 3.

Table 3: Development of Banking Activities in Mizoram

Sl No	*Name of Banks*	*31.3.2001*			*31.3.2006*		
		No. of Branches	*Total Deposit (Rs.in Crore)*	*C-D Ratio (%)*	*No. of Branches*	*Total Deposit (Rs.in Crore)*	*C-D Ratio (%)*
1	SBI	24	251.87	27.52	24	581.26	55.59
2	UCO Bank	1	11.16	10.44	1	30.03	14.69
3	Vijaya Bank	1	51.02	13.37	1	177.55	32.73
4	MC Apex Bank	10	79.40	31.94	10	159.18	60.27
5	MRB	54	68.34	23.67	54	166.02	65.38
6	Total	90	461.79	21.39	90	1114.04	45.73

Source: Statistical Handbook of Mizoram 2002 & 2006, Directorate of Economic and Statistics, Govt. of Mizoram.

Regional Rural Banks dominate the banking sector in the State. They have achieved commendable success in extending branches in rural areas. At the same time, Mizoram Cooperative Apex Bank has also done a good job in strengthening the cooperative movement in the state. However, the role played by the UCO Bank and Vijaya Bank are negligible in respect of branch expansion, loan and advances.

The performance of these banks in the State is not satisfactory, regarding the Credit-Deposit Ratio. The CD Ratio of all banks taken together has increased from 21.39 per cent in 2001 to 45.73 per cent in 2006. The increase of CD Ratio is quite commendable. However, if we look at what is happening in other parts of the country, it is far from satisfactory. CD Ratio at all India level was 66.51 per cent in 2005 and it was increased from 55.6 per cent in 1995. There may be genuine problems in advancing loans by these commercial banks in the State. But one of the main causes of low CD ratio in the state is the complexity of loaning activities. The problems faced by the poor people in getting loans and advances are mostly in connection with collateral security, which is being demanded while applying for loan. The situation is worst in the rural areas especially for workers in the unorganized sector.

Conclusion and Suggestions

Looking at the development of transport and communication infrastructure, electric power generation infrastructure and financial infrastructure, the State's performance is commendable. However, the data we have presented above reveals that the present position of the state in the development of these infrastructure facilities is still lower than the national average. It can be said that the state's performance in the development of infrastructure is far from satisfactory.

In respect of road development, the road density of Mizoram is still much lower than the national average, but we should not overlook the geographical structure of Mizoram. In the hilly terrain region of Mizoram, construction and maintenance of roads is not an easy task. With the deficiency of funds in the State, the state should try to maximize the utilization of centrally sponsored projects (like PMGSY) and the World Bank Project in the construction and maintenance of roads simultaneously the people themselves who reside in the area must feel that whatever roads are constructed by the Government or any organization are for their own facilities, and they must co-operate in construction and in the maintenance of it.

In the power sector, the dependence of the state on outside is increasing every year. The vast potential of hydro-electric power in the state is still untapped. To utilize these untapped resources the state's financial resources may not be sufficient. The state government has to try to attract (with requisite Central approach) private investment from within and abroad for the construction of hydro-electric power project. In this period of globalization, we cannot remain isolated from the rest of the world.

Since the activities of financial institutions are important factors for the development of agriculture and industries, the constraints for the expansion of banking activities in the state must be removed. It is not difficult to get loans and advances for those who are working in the government sector, while these facilities are still beyond the reach of more than one-third of the rural population. As mentioned above the main problem faced by rural population is the collateral demand by banks. In this connection, the state government has to look into the matter seriously to find out practical solutions.

NOTES AND REFERENCES

1. Directorate of Census Operation, Mizoram: *Census Report – 2001.*
2. Government of Mizoram: *Statistical Handbook, 2002,2004 &2006.* Directorate of Economics and Statistics.
3. Government of Mizoram: *Draft Ninth Five Year Plan & Draft Tenth Five Year Plan.* Planning & Programme Implementation Department.
4. Govt. of India: *Economic Survey 2005-06.* Ministry of Finance.
5. MIPAA (2002): *Mizoram at A Cross-Roads.*
6. NEC Secretariat: *Basic Statistic for North Eastern Region, 2000.*

The Dynamics of Economic Change and Good Governance

ISSUES OF DEVELOPMENT

T.C. Nunga

An overview of economic change in the North Eastern Region of India (NER) reveals that the development that has taken place is an isolated phenomenon, which promotes isolated pockets of affluence, while the masses are left untouched. It is the exploitation of the government machinery by the powerful and the rich, which causes extreme imbalances in economic power leading to social tensions, deterioration of moral values and social order. The Indian government, which has provided extreme freedom, sliding to the level of licentiousness, is primarily responsible for this state of affairs.[1] The proliferation of messy business dealing, that permeates the society, has fueled a get-rich-at-any-price mentality. Owing to the prevalence of this mindset, the remark that, '*the most frustrated man in India, next to the poor man, is the honest man*', applies more aptly to the people of North-East states.

It is apparent from the provisions of our Constitution that the economic system exists for the welfare of the common people. It exists to provide a means, without excessive waste or loss, whereby those who live under it may enjoy a reasonable standard of living. Its important function is to provide food, shelter, clothing and comforts in as dependable and adequate quantities as natural resources and the state of technical arts permit.[2] From the functional point of view, it must be remembered that an economic system is greatly sensitive to mishandling. Order, discipline, the consciousness of a definite social aim are needed to ensure a dependable flow of goods from the earth to the ultimate consumer.

This study is essentially in the area of consistency rather than of evaluation. For instance, there is a close association between individualism and development in western capitalistic society because men recognize fewer social obligations than they do in most other societies. This may not be true of semi-feudal and backward societies of the North-east. But in the problem of consistency, one encounters a difficult task of explaining why people hold the beliefs they do. Here we are dealing with the interaction between people and resources and try to offer an answer to the question, 'why the people with the same endowment of natural factors achieve success quite unequal'.

The various ways in which people react to changes in economic opportunities do not admit of easy explanation. It belongs to the realm of unsolved mysteries. Frustrated over their attempt to reduce the gap between poor and rich countries during the last half of the 20th century, the World Bank officials pointed out that "there is no accepted theory of poverty that establishes a hierarchy of causes, nor is there any widely adopted empirical model that might serve the same purpose" (White and Killick 2003). There are various factors to which scholars attribute a differing achievement in economic development, such as culture, religion, climate, natural resources, etc. Now, the evidences from many empirical studies appear to have pointed to effective public administration (or good governance) as the prime cause of development.

Arthur Lewis concluded, after an elaborate study of development history, that the most plausible explanation of high national achievement lies with the quality of leadership. If a community is fortunate to have a good leader, born at a crucial time in its history, who catches the imagination of his people and guides them through a formative experience, he will create traditions and legend and standards which weave themselves into the thinking of his people, and govern their behaviour through many centuries.[3]

A study of national development history over the different continents conclusively proved that the presence of effective public administration is what makes the difference. In this regard, three points need to be emphasized.[4]

First, the existence of extensive natural and human resources does not make much difference. Countries such as the Democratic Republic of the Congo and Angola are fabulously rich in resources but overwhelmed by poverty. Until about 1980, Hong Kong with fewer than 5 million people earned more from its exports and had more public telephones than the whole of India (with then about 700 million people).

Second, foreign aid does not do much good by itself. Egypt, for example, received $ 52 per capita per year during 1987-'96, more than twice that of other large countries with similar income levels. Similarly, Tanzania received more foreign aid than any other country during the '70s without escaping extreme poverty. Egypt continued to show a poor record of performance.

Third (perhaps the saddest point of all), because of poor governance, more money goes from poor to rich countries than the poor receive in foreign aid. In undermining their own financial institutions, leaders of poor countries encourage capital flight (including money laundering), amounting to more than $ 1 trillion a year, equivalent to 3 per cent to 5 per cent of gross world product, according to an estimate in the Economist (April 14, 2001).

Lack of resources is aften ascribed to be the cause of poverty of the poor countries. That is not the case with the poor in Africa or Asia who are wallowing in poverty in the midst of plenty. Since their problem is elusive, it is as difficult to help them as the vagrants in urban centres. In as much as many vagrants suffer from various forms of mental illness or social pathology, it is impossible to help them become self-supporting without getting deep into their psychological and social problems.[5] Most of the poor countries suffer, from what may be called 'political illness' (similar to mental illness such as alcoholism or drug addiction), which manifests itself in improper policies, weak bureaucracies, inadequate supervision, the illegitimacy of laws and regulations, and the lack of independent spheres of power. It is because governance is far weaker in the poor countries than in the rich countries that the poor countries remain poor or backward.

Comparative Case Study

It is not unusual in development studies to take case studies of different countries for the purpose of understanding relevant propositions. Our central proposition here is that governance rather than natural resources is the primary reason for the wealth and poverty of nations. We have selected Jamaica and Singapore for comparison, because the two countries have many similarities and these two island nations were freed from colonial rule at the same time. In the early 1960s both the countries had a population of about 1.6 million and a per capita gross domestic product of $ 400.

To all appearances, Jamaica had a better future despite problems arising from colonial rule, racial tension, and the danger of hurricanes and earthquakes (Horris 1962). In 1960, Jamaica was the world's primary source of bauxite and alumina. It had a blooming industrial operation with 30 factories and more than 300 manufactured items. Its agricultural exports consisted not only of such plantation products as sugar, bananas, citrus, and coconuts but also various exotic fruits and spices, suitable for small plantation holder production. The beautiful landscape and salubrious climate gave it a tremendous potential to attract tourists. Its geographical proximity to North America also gave it a remarkable potential for export-led growth. In contrast, Singapore had no natural resources and was suffering from severe racial, religious and political turmoil, intensified by its 1965 separation from Malaysia (Yew 2000). It could be described as "a somnolent, swampy fishing village" (Neher, 1999).

In 2003, it was evident that there was a great disparity in the achievement of the two countries : the per capita income of Singapore was nearly $ 30,000 (with 6.5 per cent annual growth), and Jamaica less than $ 2,500 (with negative growth for most of the previous 25 yrs.). It is the effectiveness in governance that made a difference. The government of Singapore managed to eliminate persistent poverty, unemployment, and crime, whereas Jamaica's government was unable to break the link between high teenage pregnancy rates (40 per cent), female-headed households (40 per cent), school drop-out and failure rates (one-third of those from poor households), poverty (1/3 of the population), and extremely high rates of ordinary and violent crimes (Human and Social Development Group 1997). Whereas Singapore had been able to undertake some of the World's best programmes in public housing, public transportation, urban planning, public health and public education, Jamaica's efforts largely failed. Though it may not be possible to imitate Lee Kwan Yew's virtual authoritarian form of democracy, the leaders in free democratic states can do much better if at all there is a political will.

Pragmatic Approach to North East Problem

The North East is rife with political turmoil ignited by insurgency, communal violence and corruption. In spite of the flow of enormous financial assistance from the Centre, the region remains one of the least developed parts of the country. What causes the region to lag behind others is the weak governance. For effective implementation of development policies, the government should be able to establish acceptable goals, hire qualified personnel, delegate responsibility, promote legitimacy or protect an independent sphere of authority. Singapore's capacity to reform its culture has depended on the government's ability to effect "Cultural change" within the bureaucracy, recruiting the best and the brightest, improving salaries and working conditions, reducing staffing, discouraging corruption, and changing the values of civil servants (Quah 1994).

In developed countries they have stable institutions which provide offsetting factors to corruption. These factors include the high quality and integrity of the civil service, the emphasis on consensus and harmony; the role of whistle-blowers, investigative journalists, official auditors, and public prosecutors, the active role of local governments and interest groups, and the public intolerance of dishonesty within the public bureaucracy (Johnson 1995). In respect of integrity, the civil service is as deplorable as the politics itself in the North East. What is expected of the civil service is professionalism that goes beyond income or even family. Far from being so, the reigning motive of the civil servant is to serve his political master and to please him and him alone.

As special category states, the N.E. region survives on plan assistance from the central government. In this situation, the bulk of expenditure is made by the government, as the size of the private sector is extremely small. It is thus inevitable that most of the wealth-creating activity flows from government contractorship, and to a great extent, contracts are given out by the government for patronage purposes. Among the rich are counted the politicians who receive a kickback and the clients who receive their favour. In so far as there are few evaluations, either inside or outside the government, of how well it performs, contracts tend to be mismanaged and handled corruptly. In addition to this, the refusal to reform civil service, legal, judicial, tax administration, and financial management, has aggravated the problem. In our analysis, other factors such as geography, history and culture do not figure in the explanation of the wealth and poverty of nations, even though they have a definite role to play. Ultimately, we learn from historical evidence that the most successful cures for poverty come from within, and the most effective empowerment is self-empowerment.

NOTES AND REFERENCES

1. *Facts for you*, April 1992, Vol. 13. No. 10, p. 31.
2. Chase, Stuart, *A New Deal*; The MacMillan Company, New York, 1932, p. 22.
3. Lewis, W.A., *Theory of Economic Growth*, George Allen and Unwin Ltd. 1954, p. 55.
4. Werlin, Herbert H., *Public Administration Review*, May/June 2003.
5. Werlin, Herbert, *Public Administration Review*. May/June 2003, Vol. 63, No. 3.
6. Johnson, Chalmers, *Japan : Who Governs*? New York, W.W. Norton, 1995
7. Human and Social Development Group 1997. Violence and Urban Poverty in Jamaica, Breaking the cycle. Washington D.C., World Bank
8. Neher, Clark D., *The Case for Singapore. In the Singapore Puzzle*, edited by Michael Haas, 39-54. Westport, CT : Praeger 1999.
9. Norris, Katrin, Jamaica, *The Search for an Identity*, London, Oxford Univ. Press.
10. Quah, Jon S.T., Cultural Change in the Singapore Civil Service, Washington D.C. World Bank 1994.
    Yew, lee Kwan, *From Third World to First: The Singapore Story, 1965-2000*, N.Y. Harper Collins 2000.

Regional Structure: Income and Growth in India's North East

Rakhee Bhattacharya

India's North East presently has become a hub for our policy makers, academicians, researchers and journalists for its multi dimensional issues, problems and also the prospects. There has emerged a plethora of perspectives to deal with such manifold and multifaceted issues in the domain of the political, economic, strategic and security aspects. The region, which was 'alienated' and economically truncated for several decades, and is primarily sustaining on central assistance, has suddenly reverberated with numerous economic possibilities and prospects. The prospects of South Asian and Southeast Asian economic cooperation and integration to a large extent depend on the stability of the North East India corridor. The reason is that the eight North Eastern states, though small in size, share more than 90 per cent of the border with the neighbours like Bangladesh, Bhutan, Myanmar and China. Scholars and policy makers therefore feel that India's 'Look East Policy' can very well make a platform in this region to make a gainful economic integration with its neighbours by extending transnational trade and other economic activities through this passage. This is well positioned to take advantage of the opportunities by opening up the Asian market in order to diversify the risk. It has thus attracted the attention of our social scientists to make studies for this region on a cluster of issues. It is in this perspective, important to look at the present economic status of North East India and to compare it with that of other states of the country to see how different are this group of states from the rest in terms of their income and growth. Whether this part of India is ready to take the opportunities of future economic prospects and openness, and whether it is ready to accept the challenges of transnational economic cooperation and trade? How volatile will be the growth of this region, once the trade openness is encouraged? India's eight states are clubbed together in North Eastern region, which share merely 8.74 per cent of the total land area and around 4 per cent of total population. Given such small shares, the states are categorised as 'small states' of India[1], where the area of each state is less than 35,000 sq. km. and population less than 5 million each. Given this threshold, all the states except Assam fall under 'small category states'.

There are a number of theoretical justifications given by various authors to say that small states are vulnerable due to their size, which prevents them from diversifying economic activities, and also from realizing an increasing return to scale[2]. Some small states also suffer additionally from locational disadvantages (as in the case of North East India) of remoteness and isolation. On the other hand, authors like Easterly and Kraay[3] say that, "if small state is a disadvantage, then these states must suffer with a vengeance", and shows that controlling for location and other range of factors, small states can have higher per capita GDP than other states. This income advantage is largely due to a productivity advantage. Small states also do not have different per capita growth rates due to various factors. One of such factors is, as shown by Easterly and Kraay[4], due to their greater volatility of terms of trade shocks. But the authors also highlighted that small states are no different from large states, and should receive the same policy advice that large states do. According to T.N. Srinivasan[5], "Smallness is neither a necessary nor a sufficient condition for slow economic development". Kuznets[6] had mentioned long ago that a small state sometimes has comparative advantage as a reservoir of rich natural resources (as can be seen in North Eastern states) and small and more cohesive population, allowing them to adapt better to change. Keeping such polarized views in mind, the objective of this paper is to find out the satus of small North Eastern states in India, their economic performance, and to see whether they suffer from any low level of income and growth rates and how different are they from the larger states of India also, whether North Eastern states showed any sign of convergence in the growth performance over the last decade.

Income Level: Small vs. Large

To look at the economic status of North Eastern states of India, this paper has considered a cross section of 19 states, divided into four groups for which at least 10 years of annual data on net state domestic product and per capita net state domestic product are incorporated. The paper relied upon the data of Estimates of State Domestic Products, Central Statistical Organisation. The comparison is being done amongst the following broad groups.

1. Seven North Eastern states (The NSDP data at constant price is not available for Mizoram).
2. Three other small states.
3. Four BIMARU states.
4. Five large/prosperous counterparts (Punjab, Himachal Pradesh, Gujrat, Kerala and West Bengal. These states are chosen at random to represent each corner of India).

Thus the regions/states with same range of income are clustered together to trace the trajectory of regional dynamics and distribution pattern of income over time. This to a possible extent can capture the degree of dispersion across the regions and states in the country.

Table 1 shows that except Assam, rest of the North Eastern states have the output shares of less than 1 per cent, and the same is the case of population share. Similar is the situation for other two small states like Goa and Pondichery, though Delhi shares 5.54 per cent and 7.33 per cent of total output with population shares of 1.98 per cent and 2.28 per cent respectively for the years 1993-94 and 2003-04. Other large prosperous states like Gujrat and Punjab share more domestic product than the total population. On the contrary, Bihar and Uttar Pradesh share more of population than the domestic product. Looking at the population and NSDP shares for all these four groups, one can see the disparity, where the shares of domestic products are much higher in other small states and large prosperous states than the population shares but reverse is the situation for North Eastern region and BIMARU states.

While looking at the per capita income of these 19 states for the years 1993-94 and 2003-04 in the last two columns of table 1, it is highly amazing to find the gap in income between two small states. They are Goa with per capita income as high as Rs. 30,506 (2003-04) and Manipur with per capita income as low as Rs. 8,751 in the same year. Rest of the states in North East region except Assam (Rs. 6,466 in 2003-04) do not have a very low per capita income compared to other parts of country with Sikkim having a very high income of

Table 1: Regional Variation in Size and Income of Indian Economy

States/Regions	*Population Share*		*NSDP Share*		*Per capita Income (Rs)*	
	1993-94	*2003-04*	*1993-94*	*2003-04*	*1993-94*	*2003-04*
Assam	4.47	4.27	3.93	2.99	5715	6466
Arunachal Pradesh	0.17	0.17	0.24	0.18	8733	9678
Manipur	0.38	0.37	0.33	0.36	5841	8751
Meghalaya	0.36	0.37	0.38	0.43	6893	10795
Nagaland	0.27	0.34	0.37	0.46	9129	12292
Tripura	0.55	0.94	0.47	0.57	5534	9969
Sikkim	0.08	0.94	0.10	0.12	8402	22062
Delhi	1.97	2.28	5.54	7.33	18166	51664
Goa	0.23	0.21	0.58	0.69	16558	30506
Pondichery	0.91	1.50	0.24	0.48	9781	37926
Bihar	12.95	13.35	6.07	5.21	3037	3557
Madhya Pradesh	9.75	9.75	9.91	8.86	6584	8284
Rajasthan	8.88	9.02	8.46	9.70	6182	9685
Uttar Pradesh	26.52	27.41	20.71	16.78	5066	6138
Himachal Pradesh	1.02	0.98	1.24	1.32	7870	12765
Kerala	5.66	5.01	6.96	6.77	7983	12328
Gujarat	8.24	8.08	12.43	14.89	9796	16779
Punjab	4.03	3.74	7.90	6.65	12710	15308
West Bengal	13.56	12.56	14.13	16.20	6756	10951*
North Eastern Region	6.27	6.11	5.82	5.12	7174	11430
Other Small states	3.11	4.00	6.36	8.50	14835	40032
All Small States	9.38	10.11	8.25	10.63	9475	20011
BIMARU States	58.11	59.53	45.15	40.54	5217	6916
Larger Counterparts	32.52	30.36	42.66	45.83	9023	13626

Source: Population, NSDP and PCI figures at 1993-94 prices are taken from CSO reports, GOI. Shares are estimated from total NSDP and total population of 19 states. 2003-04 PCI for WB is not available, so the figure represents 2002-03. North Eastern region consists here Assam, Arunachal Pradesh, Manipur, Meghalaya, Nagaland, Tripura and Sikkim Other small states are Delhi, Goa and Pondichery. BIMARU is Bihar, Madhya Pradesh, Rajasthan and UP. Larger Counterparts are Himachal Pradesh, Kerala, Gujarat and Punjab.

Rs. 22,062. A large state like Gujarat has per capita income of Rs. 16,779 whereas Bihar has Rs. 3,557 in the same year. Thus, looking at the four groups together, it can be seen that the position of the North Eastern Region is not very gloomy with its average income of Rs. 11,430, whereas its larger counterparts have an average income little higher with Rs. 13,626 for the year 2003-04. But the other group

Table 2: Growth Rates of NSDP and Per Capita NSDP (1993-94 prices): 1993-94 to 2003-04

States/Regions	*Growth Rates of NSDP*	*Growth rates of PCNSDP*	*Rank (93-94) PCNSDP*	*Rank (2003-04) PCNSDP*
Assam	2.53	1.08	16	17
Arunachal Pradesh	2.92	0.93	7	14
Manipur	6.42	4.28	15	15
Meghalaya	7.16	4.73	11	11
Nagaland	7.86	2.77	6	9
Tripura	8.50	7.39	17	12
Sikkim	8.31	5.72	10	7
Delhi	8.33	4.71	1	1
Goa	7.77	6.14	2	2
Pondichery	13.52	11.65	5	3
Bihar	4.69	1.33	19	19
Madhya Pradesh	3.88	1.77	13	16
Rajasthan	5.47	3.02	14	13
Uttar Pradesh	3.15	0.89	18	18
Himachal Pradesh	6.04	4.35	9	8
Kerala	4.88	5.39	8	4
Gujarat	5.57	3.26	4	6
Punjab	3.93	2.29	3	5
West Bengal	6.18	5.42	12	10

Source: NSDP and Per Capita NSDP data are taken from CSO reports, GOI. Growth rates are estimated by fitting log linear trend to NSDP and PCNSDP and are tested at 5 per cent and 1 per cent level of significance.

of small states is showing excellent performance with the average income of Rs. 40,032 in the year 2003-04. This shows that the small states can enjoy higher per capita income than their larger counterparts[7].

While looking at the growth rates of NSDP for the last decade in Table 2, one can say that most of the small North Eastern states like Meghalaya, Nagaland, Tripura and Sikkim have performed very well. Growth rate of NSDP in Manipur is also reasonably well, despite the fact that these states are extremely disturbance prone with the problems of internal conflicts and insurgency. Pondichery has the highest growth rate of 13.52 per cent, followed by Goa and Delhi. Thus one can say that small states in India are not suffering from any growth rate disadvantage, rather are performing better than the larger counterparts.

States like Assam and Arunachal Pradesh have the lowest growth rates of around 3 per cent. In case of per capita NSDP similarly, North Eastern states are almost at per with other progressive states of India except Assam and Arunachal Pradesh, whose figures are as low as Bihar and Uttar Pradesh. Thus it can be seen that small states in India do not have different per capita NSDP growth rates than their larger and prosperous counterparts. Some of the North Eastern states like Sikkim, Tripura, Meghalaya and Manipur have experienced very satisfactory growth rates. While ranking their per capita NSDP there is not much change in the position of North Eastern states from the year 1993-94 to 2003-04. In 2003-04, Delhi, Goa and Pondichery are topping the list, followed by Kerala, Punjab and Gujarat. States like Sikkim and Nagaland are within top 10.

Sectoral Composition of NSDP: Small vs. Large

Coming to the sectoral disaggregation of net state domestic product, let us find out the performance of North Eastern states as compared to other Indian states. Sectoral compositions of SDP are given in tables 3 and 4 respectively for the years 1993-94 and 2003-04. There may not be very sharp distinction in the shares of primary and secondary sectors in these two points of time, that is 1993-94 and 2003-04, especially for the industrial and prosperous states, as they both represent the post globalised period. But for North Eastern state, one can see significant differences in shares in these two points of time. A reduction in the contribution of the primary sector is noticeable for these small states. The tertiary sector is gaining shares even in these states, showing a sign of progress.

Thus in this sectoral breakup of NSDP, one can see that the tertiary sector has been growing faster than other sectors throughout the post-globalised period of Indian economy. States, which are showing more economic openness, are naturally fast growing states in the service sector. State-wise sectoral growth rates study, to a large extent, also can verify the economic buoyancy of the prosperous states, and at the same time it can point out the economic failure of weaker states, as also the cause of widening disparity across these states in India. The study takes up the nine major components of SDP. These are agriculture, forestry and logging, manufacturing, construction, trade-hotel-restaurant, banking and insurance, real estate, transport-communication and public service. Forestry and logging may not be

Table 3: Sectoral Composition of NSDP (%): 1993-94

	Agriculture	*Forestry*	*Manufacturing*	*Construction*	*Transport*	*Trade*	*Banking*	*Real Estate*	*Pub A*
Assam	45.67	2.80	11.66	4.37	2.97	18.01	4.24	3.60	6.68
Arunachal Pradesh	48.33	5.57	2.93	15.10	4.56	8.23	1.60	2.53	12.16
Manipur	42.90	2.63	7.52	0.18	4.87	14.44	3.02	5.03	19.41
Meghalya	30.58	1.72	3.02	8.86	3.89	17.29	2.61	16.05	15.97
Nagaland	22.87	5.07	3.29	8.88	18.11	6.76	1.48	13.62	19.91
Tripura	38.31	3.25	3.72	7.73	5.54	19.44	3.63	2.61	15.77
Sikkim	39.66	2.38	6.42	15.38	1.51	8.54	1.51	9.57	15.04
Delhi	6.67	0.01	17.24	9.39	9.63	39.65	2.93	9.18	5.30
Goa	11.82	0.06	26.38	8.88	11.85	20.71	7.31	7.78	5.20
Pondichery	5.29	0.89	34.23	4.47	1.34	31.90	5.95	10.64	5.29
Bihar	47.08	2.72	6.68	3.81	4.26	19.87	4.04	3.07	8.47
Madhya Pradesh	46.47	3.06	12.88	5.33	4.78	13.45	3.05	6.53	4.45
Rajasthan	32.30	2.00	14.39	14.53	4.07	19.55	3.22	6.10	3.83
Uttar Pradesh	42.67	1.47	14.82	6.02	4.73	16.45	2.97	6.37	4.51
Himachal Pradesh	27.05	8.23	12.99	17.41	11.61	2.08	5.39	6.39	8.84
Kerala	27.61	4.32	12.39	10.46	6.43	22.09	4.84	6.28	5.58
Gujarat	24.74	1.05	29.76	5.73	13.43	6.06	8.65	6.91	3.68
Punjab	49.54	0.18	13.15	6.85	2.60	14.37	4.65	4.54	4.12
West Bengal	34.42	1.07	17.84	5.02	6.85	14.84	7.51	7.04	5.40

Table 4: Sectoral Composition of NSDP (%): 2003-04

	Agriculture	*Forestry*	*Manufacturing*	*Construction*	*Transport*	*Trade*	*Banking*	*Real Estate*	*Pub A*
Assam	37.44	2.26	9.17	5.74	5.36	20.67	7.19	4.18	8.00
Arunachal Pradesh	31.69	4.31	2.88	20.68	8.27	5.57	3.38	2.67	20.55
Manipur	31.60	2.76	12.80	0.20	6.05	14.97	2.35	4.46	24.81
Meghalya	27.77	1.28	3.22	13.89	6.13	18.59	4.19	10.77	14.16
Nagaland	36.59	2.64	0.69	11.49	19.02	5.73	1.32	9.75	12.76
Tripura	36.16	2.61	4.11	30.46	7.03	22.20	4.46	2.91	18.85
Sikkim	22.00	1.19	3.19	17.87	3.99	4.95	3.42	13.43	29.66
Delhi	1.17	0.00	10.24	10.68	11.99	24.60	25.77	10.61	4.95
Goa	8.69	0.30	33.92	8.39	12.42	12.20	10.04	8.55	5.48
Pondichery	2.15	0.20	51.75	1.53	4.91	11.15	2.71	20.64	4.95
Bihar	44.57	2.19	2.47	5.78	6.65	17.38	5.86	3.76	11.34
Madhya Pradesh	34.30	2.38	15.29	10.33	8.09	12.36	5.14	6.76	5.36
Rajasthan	34.37	1.62	13.32	9.32	7.31	18.44	5.03	6.16	4.42
Uttar Pradesh	37.18	1.70	13.13	7.27	8.77	14.89	6.06	5.31	5.70
Himachal Pradesh	20.35	4.47	26.07	16.48	9.46	3.83	6.50	3.96	8.88
Kerala	15.67	2.52	9.33	10.63	16.07	24.42	9.43	5.16	6.76
Gujarat	23.97	0.58	30.23	4.44	15.76	8.54	7.51	5.90	3.08
Punjab	40.57	0.14	14.55	7.25	7.41	14.21	7.06	3.38	5.44
West Bengal	24.22	0.65	15.24	4.82	7.57	16.12	16.79	9.43	5.17

All the results are estimated from the sectoral break up of NSDP figures (constant prices) compiled by the CSO, Govt. of India.

a very good reflector for other states in India, but is an important sector for the North Eastern region. These should by and large reflect the performance of three broad categories of primary, secondary and tertiary sectors of SDP. The states like Delhi, Goa and Pondichery are fast growing in services like banking and insurance, trade and real estate, as their shares have gone very high from the year 1993-94 to 2003-04. Percentage shares for secondary sector (manufacturing and construction) also have gone high for these small states. In the North Eastern states, the growth of tertiary sector is mainly reflected in the increasing shares of public administration from 1993-94 to 2003-04. One may also note that 'if income grows faster than employment in services like public administration, then it does not imply corresponding growth of real volume of services it merely implies that the existing employed persons are generating higher income from the same real volume of services'[8].

The sectoral shares of NSDP show that in all the North Eastern states except Nagaland, the share of agriculture has followed the declining trend like the rest of India. The shares of real estate, which were the highest in Meghalaya (16.05 per cent) and Nagaland (13.62 per cent) in 1993-94, have gone down in 2003-04. Rest of the states in North East also have shown a marginal increase in the share of real estate, except Sikkim whose share has gone high from 9.57 per cent to 13.43 per cent during this period. Better social and physical infrastructure, political stability and economic prosperity can actually give a boost to the shares of real estate in this beautiful region of the country. Compared to this in Pondichery, the share of real estate has just doubled from 10.64 per cent to 20.64 per cent during the same period. Another component that has gained sizeable increase in its share in this region is transport in the tertiary sector. All the seven states uniformly show an increase in shares from 1993-94 to 2003-04. This sign of improvement in transport and communication in this region is very crucial. This boost in infrastructure can actually generate growth and diversity in this hilly terrain of North East region. The shares of transport in other states also have increased over this decade. In the case of trade, four North Eastern states like Assam, Meghalaya, Tripura and Manipur have gained a substantial share in NSDP over the decade. These states have wide potentialities of border trade with the neighbouring nations and through policies and initiatives that have taken place in this decade to improve the trade of North East India with the bordering nations, probably have added increasing shares in the trade for these states. Though the trade and transport are gaining shares in the service sector, the other vital sector for economic prosperity, that is banking and insurance, is one of the very poorly performing sectors in North East India, compared to other states. Thus in Delhi and Goa the shares of banking and insurance have gone high to 25.77 per cent and 10.04 per cent respectively in the year 2003-04 from a sheer 2 per cent and 7 per cent in 1993-94, whereas, for North Eastern states, the trade sector is improving. In Assam, the shares were dwindling around 3 per cent in both the years. This reflects a poor performance of the financial sector in the region. Thus secondary sector is also week in this region. Manufacturing, which has gained tremendous shares in Goa and Pondichery, has very little shares in all North Eastern states. Construction is rather a better sector in this region, which is contributing more in their NSDPs. Thus one can say that a few components of the tertiary sector like banking and insurance, along with the secondary sector, are poorly performing sectors in North East India, and the primary sector still predominates here.

On the contrary, in the other small states, the service sector is taking off at a galloping rate, followed by manufacturing/construction sector, and thcn with a thin share of primary sector. Table 4 shows that the percentage share of trade and banking in these states have gone high many folds over these 10 years of time. In Delhi, both these sectors together shares around 50 per cent of NSDP. Manufacturing and construction also are performing well in these states. On the contrary, the other weaker group, i.e. BIMARU states, sadly reflects a very poor performance. Here in all the four states, the share of agriculture is the highest, though the trend is declining in the post reforms period, and the shares in the service sector are improving. Except Bihar, the manufacturing sector has improved in the rest of the three states in the post reforms period. In the tertiary sector, the share of trade has declined in all these four states over the decade, whereas the banking share has marginally improved. The shares of real estate are at a low level here, and the share of public administration has gone high.

Coming to the group of large prosperous states, it can be seen that during the last 10 years, the percentage share of agriculture has declined in all these states, including Punjab and West Bengal, though in these two states the shares are still around 40 per cent and 24 per

Figure 1 : Shares in Primary Sector (per cent)

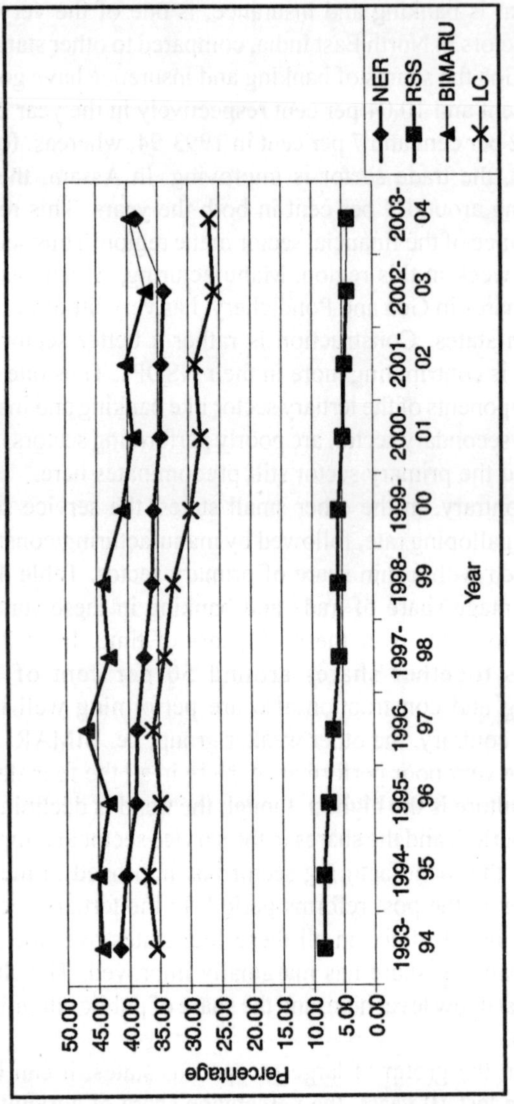

Figure 2 : Shares in Secondary Sector (per cent)

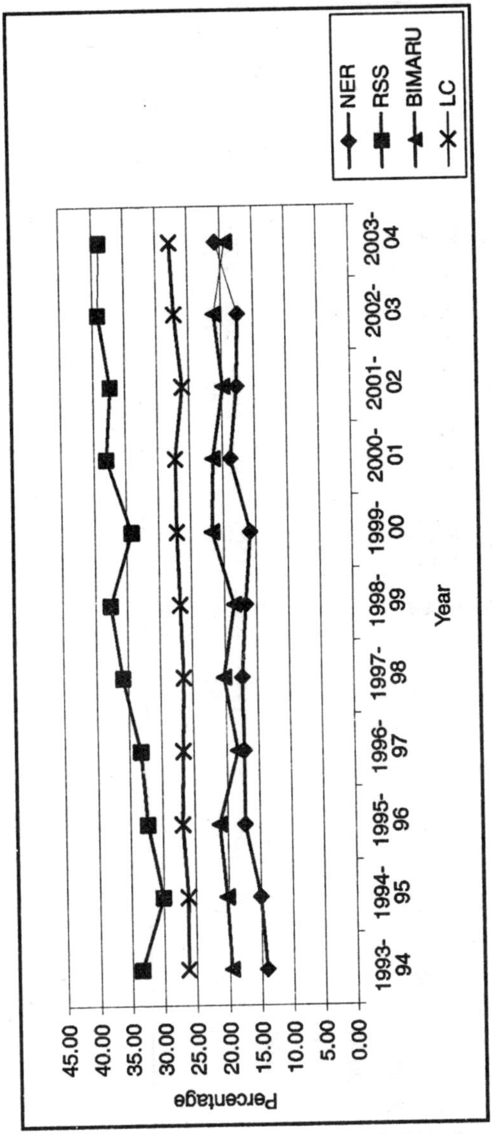

Figure 3 : Shares in Tertiary Sector (per cent)

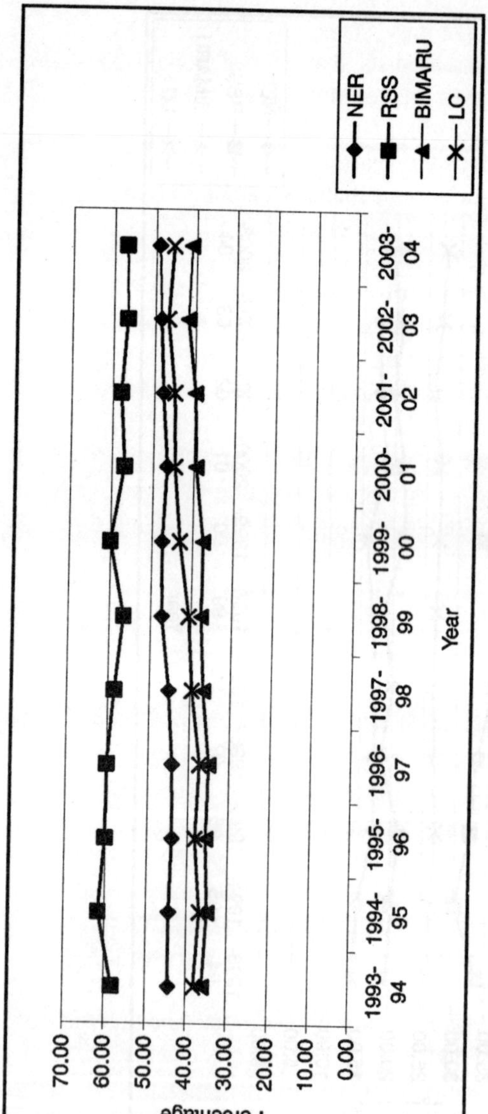

cent respectively. As mentioned by Kurain[9], for some of the Indian states the share in agriculture is far above the level in the developed nations, whose shares are normally less than 10 per cent. The tertiary sector is accelerating in these states, except in real estate, where only West Bengal has increased its share. West Bengal has witnessed a decline in its shares in secondary sector proving a sign of deindustrialization (this finding is similar to the findings of Kurain[10].

To further look at the share of primary, secondary and tertiary sectors of the four sub-groups that are taken in this study, it is clearly seen from Figure 1 that the primary sector still dominates most of the Indian states, though the trend is declining over the years. BIMARU and North Eastern region are on the top but for other small states the trend line is much lower than the others. But for the secondary sector (Figure 2), the trend is just the reverse, with the North Eastern region at the bottom and other small states at the top. BIMARU states are lying marginally above North Eastern states, and other large prosperous states are much above these two groups. Coming to the tertiary sector (Figure 3), one can see that all the four groups are above the minimum range, though BIMARU is lying at the bottom. The North Eastern region is below the other small groups, and the gap between them is narrowing down over the years. Thus it can be said that the smaller counterparts in India are also performing remarkably well in the tertiary sector in the post reforms period, and they are not really vulnerable in the economic sense. We find that small states of North Eastern region along with other states have similar income levels. But this is not to say that these small states are free of economic problems. These problems need to get attention to make them self-sustainable in the long run.

The growth rates of NSDP at 1993-94 prices for different sectors during the period from 1993-94 to 2003-04 are shown in Table 5. One thing can be noticed that on an average the growth rates in all the components of service sectors are higher than the overall NSDP growth rates during the same period, except for some sectors like trade and real estate for some states in North East India. The commodity sector has not shown such high growth rates in this decade.

Thus for all the states, the decadal growth rate in the tertiary sector has remained much higher than the primary and secondary sectors, clearly reflecting that the growth of Indian economy is primarily for a buoyant tertiary sector. The process of development has witnessed

Table 5: Sectoral Growth Rates of NSDP: 1993-94 to 2003-04

	Agriculture	*Forestry*	*Manufacturing*	*Construction*	*Transport*	*Trade*	*Banking*	*Real Estate*	*Pub A*
Assam	0.92	1.08	-0.35	2.94	8.53	4.18	7.83	4.81	5.65
Arunachal Pradesh	0.61	0.49	2.94	6.32	11.56	-0.42	11.95	5.12	10.28
Manipur	3.24	4.20	10.86	1.91	8.88	4.92	5.04	5.05	8.47
Meghalaya	6.13	-0.18	5.08	12.48	11.44	7.04	11.46	2.68	6.08
Nagaland	14.95	1.68	-15.57	10.74	9.21	6.80	7.51	4.32	3.64
Tripura	4.34	2.42	7.34	18.09	10.77	5.08	5.82	11.12	10.30
Sikkim	0.21	3.52	0.84	8.42	16.13	1.34	16.77	12.39	15.26
Delhi	1.69	6.15	8.12	16.30	15.24	8.89	22.92	8.41	13.61
Goa	4.45	1.91	11.78	8.98	7.81	3.19	7.72	8.62	8.88
Pondechery	0.74	-3.80	16.87	1.25	25.78	6.84	4.84	19.45	12.84
Bihar	4.47	2.53	-5.98	9.78	9.21	4.11	6.80	6.14	7.61
Madhya Pradesh	-1.13	1.42	5.15	12.08	9.52	1.76	8.32	4.79	5.38
Rajasthan	1.34	3.15	2.76	0.90	11.24	4.58	9.12	5.34	7.09
Uttar Pradesh	2.08	9.95	0.97	6.18	9.52	2.56	9.40	1.50	6.62
Himachal Pradesh	3.61	0.16	11.09	6.16	5.89	14.88	8.58	2.26	8.95
Kerala	-1.62	-0.64	1.90	5.58	14.30	6.46	12.45	2.81	8.15
Gujarat	1.08	1.23	5.64	5.52	7.76	11.24	5.68	6.20	7.13
Punjab	2.20	2.32	5.14	4.35	14.60	4.26	7.82	1.03	7.42
West Bengal	2.88	1.88	5.23	6.95	8.27	7.74	14.41	10.23	7.73

Growth Rates are estimated with loglin model and have been tested with 5 per cent and 1 per cent level of significance.

a shift from agriculture towards manufacturing and then to the service sector. Thus this analysis of growth performance and structural change in the components of domestic product of Indian states in the last decade reveals that there is a sharp switch off from agriculture. For North Eastern states, except for the secondary sector, rest of the sectors are growing almost at the same level with other states, despite the fact that most of these states are afflicted by underground militancy and insurgency problems. More initiatives and restoration of peace and security can positively improve the economy in the region, and the dream to make South and Southeast Asian integration through this passage may come true in future. Thus a state like Sikkim is performing exceedingly well compared to other states of this region. This small state has proved that though remote, it has progressed very well with its economic initiatives, right political dynamism and social safety. Now with the opening of Nathu La, the state will achieve even more in the coming decades. Thus this small state of Sikkim in North East India can be compared with the small state of Goa in west India.

Conclusion

Though North Eastern states with their immense potentialities could have achieved much more than what is reflected in this paper, yet the overall performance in terms of state domestic products has remained satisfactory. Goa can be taken as a model state for all the members of the small groups of states in India, which has grown tremendously due to tapping up of right kind of economic activities like tourism. North Eastern states also with their enormous potentialities, virgin nature, vibrant and multiple culture, can perform no less than the state of Goa. Goa has proved that, it is not only the size that actually matters but a competitive economic environment along with good governance, sound social and physical infrastructure and a dynamic culture, which can, to a large extend, improve its economic performance. North East India being such highly enriched region with its natural endowments can definitely be an economically viable region if the issues of insurgencies and other problems are resolved. Also a greater financial openness may insure this group of small states against any volatility, may provide a valuable means to them to diversify their economy in the long run. As Kurain[11] has mentioned, the forward states are characterized by a better demographic and social development along with higher per capita income and more developed economies, lower levels of poverty, higher levels of revenue receipts and planned and non-planned expenditure, higher per capita resource flows and private investments and significantly better infrastructural facilities. The eight North Eastern states are clustered in one group within the same geographical region of the country, but in reality the region reflects the least integration in the country. Greater integration among this small group of states can probably generate better performance along several dimensions. It is also essential to manage the conflicts within the region and across the borders, so that cross country trade and other economic integration can be widened. Once such problems are removed from this region, it can be one of the most vibrant economic zones of the country.

NOTES AND REFERENCES

1. Debroy and Bhandari, 2005, As cited in R. Saran, "The Best States to Live in" *India Today*, Special Issue, 15 August, 2005
2. Paul M. Romer "Increasing Return and Long Run Growth" *Journal of Political Economy*, 94: 1002-37, 1986 Barro, R. and Xavier Sala-I-Martin "Economic Growth" McGrow Hill, New York, 1995
3. W. Easterly, and A. Kraay, "Small States, Small Problems? Income, Growth and Volatility in Small States" World Bank, 1999
4. Ibid.
5. T.N. Srinivasan, "The Cost and Benefits of Being a Small,Remote, Island, Landlocked or Ministate Economy." *World Bank Research Observer*, 1(2): 205-218, 1986
6. S. Kuznets, "Economic Growth of Small Nations. In *The Economic Consequences of the Size of the Nations*, ed. E.A.G. Robinson, Proceedings of a Conference Held by the International Economic Association, McMillan, Toronto, 1960
7. W. Easterly, and A. Kraay, "Small States, Small Problems? Income, Growth and Volatility in Small States" World Bank, 1999
8. B.B. Bhattacharya, and A. Mitra, "Excess Growth of Tertiary Sector in Indian Economy: Issues and Implications", *Economic and Political Weekly*, Nov. 31, 1990, pp 2445-2450
9. N.J. Kurian, 'Widening Regional Inequalities in India: Some Indicators', *Economic and Political Weekly*, 35(7), pp 538–550. 2000
10. Ibid
11. Ibid
12. Samir Amin, *Unequal Development: An Essay on the Social Formation of Peripheral Capitalism*, Oxford, Delhi, 1979

13. R.E. Baldwin, *Economic Development and Growth*, Wiley Eastern Pvt. Ltd., New Delhi, 1971
14. N. Banerjee, and Marjit, S. (ed), *Development, Displacement and Disparity: India in the Last Quarter of 20th Century*, Orient Longman Pvt. Ltd., New Delhi, 2005
15. J.B. Bhattacharjee, *Sequence in Development in North East India* (ed), Omsons Pubs, New Delhi, 1989
16. B.J. Deb (ed), *Development Priorities in North East India*, Concept, New Delhi, 2000
17. K. Deb, *Development and Disparities: Experience from Southern India*, Rawat Pub. Jaipur, 2001
18. Jean. Dreze, *Indian Development: Selected Regional Perspective*, OUP, Delhi, 1997
19. T.B. Lahiri, *Balanced Regional Development*, Oxford and IBH Pub Co., Calcutta, 1972.
20. Baidyanath Mishra & R. Meher, *Economic Liberalisation and Regional Disparities in India* (ed), A.P.H. Publishing Corporation, New Delhi, 2000
21. R.P. Misra (ed) "Regional Development" *Maruzen Asia*, 1982
22. Planning Commission "Regional Dimension of India's Economic Development" GOI New Delhi, 1983
23. A. Shaban "Regional Structure, Growth and Convergence of Income in Maharashtra" *Economic and Political Weekly*, May 6, pp 1803-1816, 2006.

Section III

North East India's Economy: Revival Strategy

Rethinking Development Paradigms

ISSUES AND PERSPECTIVES

Vanlalchhawna

The North Eastern Region of India including Sikkim, has, over the years, attracted the attention of policy-makers, media and even civil society groups, because of its strategic location, bountiful natural endowment and varied linguistic and cultural life of different ethnic groups inhabiting the region. Despite liberal provision of development fund by the Central government, the region continues to remain one of the most backward regions in the country, which is a clear testimony to the fact that development strategies adopted by Central and State governments so far have limited impact on regional development. This paper is an attempt to highlight the major issues involved in the development dynamics of the region. First, it deals with the evolution of state formations in the North East, which is followed by a brief overview of the resources and structure of regional economy. The evolution of Central government's development policy towards the North East is given in the third section. The last section presents the major issues and perspectives that must be considered in order to put the region on a new development path.

Dynamics of State Formations in the North East

The North Eastern States, which presently consist of Arunachal Pradesh, Assam, Meghalaya, Mizoram, Nagaland, Sikkim and Tripura, underwent different stages of political and administrative changes through their evolution over time. The Ahom or Tai-Ahom rulers of Assam, progenitor of the present Assamese culture, were Shans who came to Assam in the thirteenth century, and established a state that survived for six hundred years. Other states like Nagaland, Meghalaya,

Mizoram, Tripura, etc have their own tribal state formations in the pre-colonization period. The period starting from the Treaty of Yandaboo (1826), which passed the Ahom Kingdom to British hands, until independence in 1947, was the history of the expansion of British rule. The hill kingdoms such as Khasi, Lushai (Mizo) hills and Naga hills were also merged into Assam subsequently. In the early colonial period, Assam formed a part of Bengal Province until it became a separate province in 1874. Assam was administered by the Governor General. Separation and isolation formed the core of British policy towards the North East[1] . The colonial administration introduced a number of laws to administer the areas. The Scheduled District Acts of 1874 and the Frontier Tract Regulation Act of 1880 excluded the hill areas from the operation of the Codes of Civil and Criminal procedures, property and transfer rules etc. Another law, the Bengal Eastern Frontier Regulation of 1873, introduced 'Inner Line' by which the minority indigenous ethnic groups living in the hills were protected against infiltration by the plain tribes/outsiders. Outsiders were not allowed entry, business activities, land transactions and settlement. In 1935, the hill areas were demarcated into 'excluded' and 'partially excluded' areas in which the former fell under direct British jurisdiction and the latter were given a limited representative system under British administrative control. Under colonial regime, the process of modernization of the region also began to take shape. Tea and oil industry were established in Assam, attracting large immigrants from outside the region. Meanwhile, Christianity and the spread of education, started by western missionaries, had also a deep impact on the cultural transformation of the hill people. For instance, the entire Mizo tribal community was converted into Christianity within a short span of forty years during the colonial period.

India's Independence saw a new development in the process of state formation in the region. The regional formation at the time of independence consisted of the Assam plains, the hills districts, North Eastern Frontier Tract (NEFT), and the princely states of Manipur and Tripura that merged with India in 1949. The Indian Constitution, which came into effect in 1950, established Assam into a full state and provided the Sixth Schedule, which consisted of part A—autonomous district councils, and part B-administered by the Governor of Assam acting as agent of the President of India, within Assam. The Autonomous District Councils were the United Khasi and Jaintia Hills, the Garo Hills, the Lushai Hills, the Naga Hills, the North Cachar Hills and the Mikir Hills. They were given autonomy to administer themselves according to their own traditions and customs. The Governor of Assam administered them. The North East Frontier Tract, the Balipara Frontier Tract, the Tirap Frontier Tract, the Abor Hills and Mishmi Hills Districts came into Part B, which were administered by the Governor of Assam, acting as Agent of the President of India. Tripura and Manipur were constituted as special administrative areas under the central government. NEFT also became NEFA—North Eastern Frontier Agency.

The process of state reorganization took place in 1956. Accordingly, Manipur became Union Territorry in 1956. Naga hills was made into a central government administrative area in1957 and later in 1963, a full-fledged state. In 1963, Tripura was made into a Union territory. A sub-state called Meghalaya Autonomous State was created in 1970. Following the North East Areas Reorganization Act 1971, Meghalaya was formed into a full-fledged state, and NEFA which was renamed as Arunachal Pradesh and the Mizo Hills district, christened as Mizoram became UT and Tripura a state. In 1975, Sikkim, the protectorate of India, merged with India. Arunachal Pradesh and Mizoram became full-fledged states in 1987. Today, along with these eight states, autonomous tribal areas were created in the North East; six in Manipur, three each in Assam, Mizoram, Meghalaya, and one in Tripura. Since most of the states were created on ethnic lines, ethn-political movements demanding separate statehood, autonomous district, separate homelands etc., continue to afflict the region till today. The region has presently more than 15 major insurgent groups operating in different states[2] .

Resources and Structure of North East Economy

The North Eastern Region is home to a large number of different tribes and communities. Culturally and linguistically, it is one of the most diverse regions in India. Around 200 ethnic groups are found in the region. Besides indigenous tribal religions, the region has the followers of all the four of world's major religions—Christianity, Hinduism, Islam and Buddhism. The region which covers 2,62,179 sq. km has a total population of 39 million in 2001 Census; constituting 3.8 per cent of the population and 8.5 per cent of the geographical area of the country. The region is rich in natural resources, primarily in water and forests. There are about 60,000 MW of economically viable hydropower potential, of which only 6 per cent is developed or is under construction. Hydro is a prime asset to Arunachal Pradesh. The total generation potential (in megawatt) in different North East states are:

Arunachal Pradesh: 50,328, Meghalya: 2,394, Mizoram: 2,196, Manipur: 1,784, Nagland: 1,574, Assam: 680, Tripura: 15, and Sikkim: 4,286.

The region has vast forest reserves covering 64.6 per cent of the total area of the region, as against 20.6 per cent for all-India. The North East is the confluence of three biodiversity regions and has been declared as one of world's biodiversity hotspots. Natural resources are partly managed by the state and partly by the community.

Table 1: Socio-Economic Indicators of North Eastern Region including Sikkim

State	*Area (Sq.Km)*	*Population (in thousand) 2001*	*Literacy rate (in per cent) 2001*	*Per capita NSDP (at current prices 1999-00 (New Series)*	*HDI 1991 (New Series Rank)*	*Infrastructure Index*
Arunachal Pradesh	83743	1091	54.74	13352	29	69.71
Assam	78438	26638	64.28	9720	26	77.72
Manipur	22327	2389	68.87	12721	9	75.39
Meghalaya	22429	2306	63.31	12083	24	75.49
Mizoram	21081	891	88.49	14909	7	82.13
Nagaland	16579	1989	67.11	12594	11	76.14
Sikkim	7096	540	69.68	14751	18	108.99
Tripura	10492	3191	73.66	13195	22	74.87
All India	3287263	1027015	65.38	15626	-	100

Sources:

1. Government of India, Economic Survey 2002-2003, Ministry of Finance & Company Affairs
2. Census of India, Mizoram, Provisional Totals, 2001.
3. Government of India, Report of Eleventh Finance Commission (For 2000-2005), June 2000. Ministry of Finance, Department of Economic Affairs.
4. Government of India, India 2004 (A Reference Manual), Publications Division, Ministry of Information and Broadcasting.

The economy of the region is dominated by agriculture and allied activities, with a small industrial base and a highly inflated tertiary sector. All states are classed as special category states whose development plans are financed on the basis of 90 per cent grants and 10 per cent loans. The industrial sector has grown mainly around tea and timber in Assam; mining, saw mills, plywood factories, handicrafts and handloom in other parts of the region. The tertiary sector is emerging as the most important sector in the regional economy.

Some of the states made remarkable achievements in social sector development over the years. As given in Table 1, the human development index (HDI) ranked Mizoram at 7th position out of 32 states/UTs, followed by Manipur (9th) and Sikkim (11th). Arunachal Pradesh, the lowest amongst the North East states was placed at the 29th position. Availability of infrastructure facilities is an important factor determining the attractiveness of investment in the state and a critical means to enhance the welfare of the people. The Social and Economic Infrastructure Index adopted by the Eleventh Finance Commission put all the states in the region, except Sikkim, below the national average of 100 points. Sikkim got the highest points (108.99), while Arunachal Pradesh the lowest (69.71).

Based on the available resources, North Eastern Development Finance Corporation (NEDFC) identified several industries as investment potentials for both public and private sectors in the North East. These include mineral based industries, horticulture and food processing industries, plantation industries - tea, coffee, etc., rubber based industries, medicinal and aromatic plants and bamboo-based industries, dairy farming, tourism, border trade, health care, etc.

Evolution of Development Policy for the North East

During the past five decades of planned economic development, a number of development schemes and policy initiatives had been implemented in the region[3]. The major initiatives may be described as follows:

Special Category States: All the North-eastern states are placed under Special Category states in the scheme of plan financing. The criteria for distribution of normal Central Assistance for State Plans provide for a built-in preferential treatment in favour of the Special Category States. The criteria under Gadgil formula that gives large weightage to population (1971 census) and the incidence of poverty does not apply to North Eastern States. If these criteria were to be applied strictly, North east states would get small allocations because of their small population and also because of lesser incidence of poverty in these states compared to the more populous states of Bihar, UP, Madhya Pradesh, Rajasthan and Andhra Pradesh. The National Development Council provided that out of the total plan assistance available for State Plan assistance in any particular year, the requirement for funding the externally aided projects, and special areas programme is deducted as the first charge. Of the balance, 30 per cent is earmarked for Special Category States leaving 70 per cent for distribution among the non-special category states according to the Gadgil formula. The inter se distribution of this earmarked fund among the Special Category States is determined in the light of previous Plan size and special problems, needs and priorities of each state. The terms and conditions of Plan assistance for the special category states are far more favourable than those applicable to other states. Special category states receive 90 per cent central assistance as grants and 10 per cent as loans as against 30 per cent grants and 70 per cent loan for non-category states.

Formation of North Eastern Council (NEC): The Fifth Five Year Plan (1974-1979) was a watershed for planned development for the North East. The states in the North Eastern Region were reorganized in 1972 under the North East Areas Reorganisation Act, 1971. Three new states, Meghalaya, Tripura and Manipur, were created, while Arunachal Pradesh and Mizoram were upgraded into Union Territorry, having their own Legislative Assemblies. The North Eastern Council (NEC) was also set up in 1972 under the NEC Act, 1971 for regional planning and development. NEC is envisioned to act as an advisory body and empowered to discuss the matters of common interest to the Union and the North Eastern states, and recommend to the Centre/State governments any matter of common interest, inter alia, in the fields of economic and social planning, inter-State transport and communications, power and flood control. Broadly speaking, the functions of the NEC can be grouped into three categories: Regional Planning, Zonal Council and Security. The NEC has been focusing largely on its role as a regional planning body and a zonal council.

During the Tenth Plan (2002-2007), the total outlay for NEC has been fixed at Rs. 3,500 crore. The strategy for the development of the region is to put more thrust on completion of on-going priority works, initiation of a few major projects to have a better impact on areas of intervention, instead of taking up a large number of smaller projects, consolidation of schemes, better monitoring, and improvement in project implementation. Balanced development of the region is the primary responsibility of the organisation, and emphasis would be given on financing of projects with a regional approach.

***New Initiatives for North Eastern Region**:* The then Prime Minister of India announced several new initiatives for rapid socio-economic development of the North Eastern Region on October 27,1996. These include the followings:

(*i*) Commission to determine gaps in infrastructure and backlog in Basic Minimum Services,
(*ii*) Priority for creation of Employment Opportunities for educated unemployed,
(*iii*) North East Sub-Plan in all Central Ministries/Departments,
(*iv*) Visits and intensive monitoring by Central Ministers/ Secretaries,
(*v*) Full funding of the on-going projects,
(*vi*) Comprehensive water management and flood control measures,
(*vi*) Full coverage through Employment Assurance Scheme,
(*vii*) Extension of Border Roads/BADP Programme,
(*viii*) Full coverage of North East through Telecommunication and Electronic Media,
(*ix*) Improved credit flow to North East,
(*x*) New Industrial Policy,
(*xi*) Decentralization at the district and sub-district levels,
(*xii*) Strengthening of Central Agencies,
(*xiii*) Export Policy,
(*xiv*) Measures for control of Narcotics and AIDS,
(*xv*) Improvement in Railway Services.

Besides, the Prime Minister was committed to implement several state-specific important projects worth several crores of rupees. On January 2000, the Prime Minister announced again an agenda for Socio-Economic Development in the North-East and Sikkim worth Rs. 10,271 crore. The agenda covered 18 items like banking, commerce, border trade, health, education, security related expenditure, Peace Bonus for Mizoram, New India Reserve Battalion, border fencing and border roads, streamlining the procedure for selection of projects to be funded under Central Non-lapsable Pool of Resources (NLCPR), power, Civil Aviation Policy, roads sector, information technology, excise concession to Numaligarh Refinery in Assam, flood control, a technology mission for horticulture, and development of Bodo areas.

NE Industrial Policy 1997: This policy was designed for promoting rapid industrialization of the region. The policy provides for various fiscal incentives such as income tax holiday, central excise exemption and various subsidies such as capital investment subsidy, transport subsidy, working capital interest subsidy, insurance subsidy, relaxation of PMRY norms, development of industrial infrastructure, development of village and small industries (VSI) sectors. The North Eastern Development Financial Corporation Ltd (NEDFi), which has done an impact evaluation study of the Policy, found that it had a positive impact on the industrialisation programme of the North Eastern Region[4].

Non-lapsable Central Pool of Resources (NLCPR): The North East sub-plan was created in each of the Central Ministries/Department by earmarking 10 per cent of their plan fund for North Eastern states following the new initiatives for the North East announced by the Prime Minister in 1996. Under this initiative, a total of more than Rs. 5,000 crore is expected to be budgeted annually by various ministries for the region. The Planning Commission created Non-Lapsable Central Pool of Resources out of the unspent amount of stipulated 10 per cent, allocated for North East sub-plan for infrastructure development projects in the North East. The Central Pool of Resources became effective from 1998-99. The broad objective is to ensure speedy development of infrastructure in the region by increasing the flow of budgetary financing for new infrastructure projects in the region. The infrastructure sectors for financing include both physical and social sectors with projects in physical infrastructure receiving priority. Both State sector and Central sector projects could be financed from the pool fund. Institutional arrangement to administer the NLCPR funds has also been created. Details regarding project formulation, appraisal of project proposals, cost escalation, release of fund, monitoring and evaluation, including transparency and publicity of information, are provided in the guidelines.

Due to this arrangement, the plan expenditure of the Central Ministries in the North East has increased from 6.25 per cent in 1999-2000 to 7.28 per cent in 2001-02. The percentage flow is expected to improve further during the Tenth Plan. Between 1998-99 and 2001-02, state-wise release of funds from the pool increased from Rs. 121.95 crore to Rs. 491.81 crore.

The Shukla Commission 1997: In pursuance of the Prime Minister's announcement of New Initiatives for the North-Eastern Region made at Guwahati on October 27, 1996, the Planning Commission of India appointed a High Level Commission under the chairmanship of Shri S.P.Shukla, Member, Planning Commission to critically examine the backlog in respect of Basic Minimum Services and the gaps in infrastructure sectors for development of States of North-Eastern Region. This Commission, the first ever constituted by the Government of India to examine the problems of North East India, had made a number of wide-ranging recommendations for rapid socio-economic development of the region on the following issues: (i) Basic Minimum Services, (ii) Farm Sector, (iii) Horticulture and Plantations, (iv) Fisheries and Animal Husbandry, (v) Irrigation, (vi) Floods, (vii) Forests, (viii) Environment, (ix) Railways, (x) Highways, (xi) Civil Aviation, (xii) Inland Water Transport, (xiii) Transport Policy, (xiv) Telecommunications, (xv) Broadcasting, (xvi) Hydrocarbon Sector, (xvii) Coal, (xviii) Power, (xix) Industry, Handloom and Handicrafts, (xx) Urbanisation and Spatial Planning, (xxi) Trade and Transit, (xxii) Tourism, (xxiii) Monitoring and Implementation, (xxxiv) Banking and Finance, (xxxv) Additional Resource Mobilisation, (xxxvi) North Eastern Development Council, (xxxvii) Political Infrastructure[5].

Creation of a separate Ministry for the North East in the Central Ministry: The Ministry of Development of North Eastern Region was created in 2001 as one of the ministries at the Central Government. The role of the Ministry is to create synergy and ensure convergence of programmes by coordinating the efforts of both Central agencies and the State Governments. It acts as a catalyst in stimulating the development process and focus on increasing opportunities for productive employment, strengthening infrastructure, particularly connectivity and communication, together with ensuring accountability in the implementation of projects. The Ministry is also responsible for ensuring the implementation of the various components of PM's Package, which had been announced from time to time since 1995.

India's Look East Policy and Border Trade: India's Look East Policy, initiated in the early 1990s, was basically conceived to increase economic interactions with Asian countries, more particularly with those of the so called Asian tigers like Thailand, Singapore, Taiwan, etc. India's market-driven economic reforms and its increasing economic integration with the global economy have given a new impetus to external trade, giving rise to the articulation of Look East Policy (Sarma, 2005). In order to enhance its economic and political co-operation including deepening of trade, investment and cultural relationships with Asian countries, India has made a number of bilateral and multilateral agreements as well as participated in some summit level initiatives. To provide physical connectivity, India has already signed Trans-Asian Highway projects, initiated by United Nations Economic and Social Commission for Asia Pacific (UNESCAP). On the political fronts, India has, in recent years, made attempts to improve better understanding with neighbouring countries, especially with China, Myanmar and Bangladesh. The major components of India's Look East Policy may be enumerated as follows:

(*i*) India is now one of the four summit level partners of ASEAN, the other three being China, Japan and Korea.

(*ii*) Bangladesh-India-Myanmar-Sri Lanka-Thailand Economic Cooperation (BIMST-EC) has been launched recently. The grouping is expected to provide a vital link between ASEAN and SAARC countries. Initiated by Thailand in 1994, BIMST-EC tries to explore economic co-operation on a sub regional basis involving contiguous countries of South East and South Asia grouped around the Bay of Bengal. Nepal and Bhutan had already joined this grouping.

(*iii*) Other important initiatives include Bangladesh-China-India-Myanmar (BCIM) Forum for Regional Co-operation (popularly known as Kunming Initiative), Mekong-Ganga Cooperation (MGC) and South Asia Growth Quadrangle (SAGQ) involving Bangladesh, Bhutan, Nepal and North East India (NEI).

(*iv*) The Agreement on South Asian Free Trade Area (SAFTA) was signed during the Twelfth SAARC Summit held in Islamabad, Pakistan on 4-6 January 2004, which was to be effective from January, 2006. Under SAFTA, a phased Trade Liberalisation Programme (TLP) is envisaged, under which Non Least Developed Contracting States (India, Pakistan and Sri Lanka) would reduce their existing tariffs to 0-5 per cent for other NLDCS within a time frame of seven years from coming into force of the Agreement. NLDCS shall do the same for Least Developed Contracting States (Bangladesh, Bhutan, Maldives and Nepal). The LDCS would reduce their existing tariff to 0-5 per cent within a time frame of ten years from the date of enforcing the Agreement.

(*v*) India has already signed Free Trade Agreements (FTA) with Thailand and Singapore. The Framework Agreement for establishing a Free Trade Area between Thailand and India was signed on 9th October, 2003 in Bangkok. The agreement covered FTA in Goods and Services, and Areas of Economic Cooperation. The modalities for the first phase of the FTA between India and Thailand, involving the reduction of tariff on 82 agreed items in three years, had already been finalised. To be implemented in a phased manner, the two countries will have a fully free trade regime by 2010. There are also plans to implement FTAs with other ASEAN countries like Indonesia, Malaysia and Brunei by 2011, and with the Phillipines, Cambodia, Laos, Myanmar and Vietnam by 2016. India has suggested the formation of Asian Economic Community including ASEAN, China, Japan, Korea and India.

(*vi*) On January 1994, India and Myanmar formally signed a Border Trade Agreement to exchange goods produced locally by people living along both sides of the border as well as to create mechanisms to deal with the foreign trade transactions. Both the governments agreed to open border trade through the following points: (a) Moreh (Manipur) in India and Tamu in Myanmar (b) Champhai/Zokhawthar (Mizoram) in India and Ri in Myanmar. Effort is also under way to open border trade between Bangladesh and Mizoram. The states of Assam, Meghalaya and Tripura had already operated border trade relations with Bangladesh. Sino-Indo Border trade is expected to grow up in a big way in the North East, following the reopening of the historic Nathula Pass in Sikkim.

(*vii*) Physical connectivity through Trans-Asian Highways, Indo-Myanmar-Thailand Superhighway Project, Kaladan Multi-modal Project, etc. have also been pursued.

Linking North East India with dynamic Asia promised vast economic opportunities and benefits including deepening of social and cultural ties between the people of North East and its neighbouring areas. North East India became an isolated region after Independence. Partition disrupted rail and road transport network between mainland India and the North East, and eliminated the region's trade, commerce and other linkages with neighbouring countries like Burma (now Myanmar), East Pakistan (now Bangladesh) and China. Geographical isolation has greatly retarded the region's development and prosperity that existed in the pre-independence period. Furthermore, weakness in the country's foreign policy that ignored Southeast Asia for a long time compounded the region's problems. The North East region was not only cut off from its natural economic partners but also encircled by unfriendly countries. Market integration of the land-locked North Eastern region with Southeast and East Asian countries would boost trade while the North East served as the gateway. Trade would thus serve as a driver of rapid economic development of the region (Sarma,2005).

Towards a New Development Strategy

The region, even after sixty years of Independence, continues to remain one of the most backward regions of the country. Because of shifting cultivation in many of the hilly states and single crop traditional farming in the plain areas, the region is not able to produce adequate food grains to feed its population. The resource bases of the states are also very weak due to low economic activities, especially industrial activities. Since they are not able to develop their own financial resources, all the states are dependent on resource transfers increasingly from the centre. The present financial situation of many of the North East states is not sustainable even in the medium run. Moreover, in the post-liberalisation period during the nineties, while the national economy is growing fast after initial contraction, overall North Eastern economy has slowed down. As a result, the gap between national growth rates and regional growth rates has further widened. The North East economy is in a critical state[6] . Shukla Commisison Report 1997 identified four deficits in the North East: a basic needs deficit; an infrastructure deficit; a resource deficit; and a two-way deficit of understanding with the rest of the country, which compounds the others. Other constraints upon development include lack of skilled manpower, lack of entrepreneurship, low level of savings and investments, high freight cost, limited linkage with national economy, uncontrolled migration from neighbouring countries, unstable law and order condition, inadequate marketing initiatives, etc. The following broad issues in the development discourse of the North East Region may be considered:

(i) ***Private sector development*:** The North Eastern Region has a number of potentials for development. Private sector development through a better investment climate is the key to development of the region. Over time, it will be the private sector, not the state government, that creates jobs and promotes economic growth. The private sector needs skilled manpower and also the support of infrastructure facilities like sound credit institutions, good roads, adequate power supply, etc. Modification of existing land and labour policy along with improvements in infrastructure facilities are some of the critical measures for attracting private capital, both national and foreign. The existing business associations like the chambers of commerce, industrial and traders associations, need to be strengthened by the state government. They should be encouraged to interact with national level business associations. Developing entrepreneurship should be another key component for private sector initiative. In short, a market oriented approach, that concentrates on economic factors and less on political and cultural factors, and that addresses barriers to market entry, need to be instituted[7].

(ii) ***Redefining the role of the state government and other agencies*:** Besides effective provision for public goods like maintenance of law and order, infrastructure facilities, governments both at the Central and State level need to promote good governance and institution building. Transparent administration, simplicity of rules, encouraging people's participation in government through decentralization, civil service reform, improving the efficiency of public sector units including administration, enhancing public security, combating corruption and encouraging civil society

participation in development projects, are some of the critical elements for good governance.

(iii) ***Common Market Approach in natural resources management:*** The eight states of the region have their own strengths and weaknesses in terms of resources. Each depends on the other in various ways. This mutual economic dependence should be converted into strength through the creation of a regional market. Take for instance, the water resources of the region. There are about 60,000 MW of economically viable hydro potential, of which about 6 per cent is developed or under construction. The abundant water resources have primarily imposed costs on the region because of the recurring flooding events. As could be expected, there are conflicting objectives of states like Arunachal and Assam in harnessing the water resources. Assam is having a significant interest in flood management, while Arunachal's interest is to develop its hydropower primarily for income and job generation. In order to ensure optimal use of the scarce resources of the region for development, certain institutional framework, where the stakeholders could have free exchange, need to be developed. In this regard, creation of a formal body like NER Economic Co-operation Council may be envisaged.

(iv) ***Human resource development:*** Human resource development is fundamental to sustainable development. Health and education are the key elements in human resource development. Though the region had made significant progress in literacy level and improving health facilities since the 1970s, their services are far from satisfactory; their delivery system remains virtually inefficient and inadequate. Steps must be taken to increase the involvement of communities in the planning, monitoring and financing of health and education, and make efforts to upgrade private education and health services.

Conclusion

The North Eastern Region of India, including Sikkim, has a huge potential for sustainable development and building a self-reliant regional economy based on its own resources. However, the Region remains highly underdeveloped, though a large sum of public resources has been injected into the Region over the years. Public investment through central agencies and state governments has failed to generate a growth momentum for the Region. The people of the North East, especially politicians, bureaucrats, academia and other social leaders need to reassess the level of development achieved in the region over the last five and a half decades of planned development in the country. It is high time to realise that the region's development must come through the wisdom, hard work and sincerity of the people and active involvement of the people in the development process, not from the Central government. The quality of governance and participatory planning process, the fundamental ingredients for development, need to be instituted to address effectively the problem of underdevelopment of the Region.

NOTES AND REFERENCES

1. Inoue, Kyoko, 2005, 'Integration of the North East: The State Formation Process' in Mayumi Murayame, Kyoko Inoue and Sanjay Hazarika (eds) *Sub-Regional Relations in the Eastern South Asia: With Special Focus on India's North Eastern Region*, Tokyo, Japan.
2. Government of India, 2003, Ministry of Home Affairs, '*Annual Report 2006-07*', New Delhi.
3. Sachdeva, Gulsan, 2006, 'Rethinking Development Strategy for North East' Working Paper presented at the National Seminar on *Rethinking Paradigms of Development for the North East India,* March 24-25, 2006, Gangtok.
4. Government of India, 2003, Ministry of Home Affairs 'Impact of North East Industrial Policy on Industrialisation of NE Region' *NE Newsletter* (A monthly Newsletter on the North Eastern Region of India) Vol. 5, No. 02, February.
5. Government of India, 1992, Planning Commission, *'Transforming the North East (Tackling Backlogs in Basic Minimum Services and Infrastructural Needs)*-High Level Commision Report to the Prime Minister-popularly known as Shukla Commission Report, New Delhi.
6. Sachdeva, Gulsan, 2006, 'Rethinking Development Strategy for North East' Working Paper presented at the National Seminar on *Rethinking Paradigms of Development for the North East India,* March 24-25, 2006, Gangtok.
7. Sachdeva, Gulsan, 2006, 'Rethinking Development Strategy for North

East' Working Paper presented at the National Seminar on *Rethinking Paradigms of Development for the North East India,* March 24-25, 2006, Gangtok.

8. Government of India, 2002, Ministry of Development of North Eastern Region, '*Guidelines for Administration of Non-lapsable Central Pool of Resources*' New Delhi.
9. ——, 1997, Ministry of Industry, *New Industrial Policy for North Eastern Region*, Department of Industrial Policy and Promotion, New Delhi.
10. ——, 1996, Ministry of Information and Broadcasting, *New Initiatives for North Eastern Region*, Directorate of Advertising and Visual Publicity, New Delhi.
11. ——, Planning Commission, *Tenth Five Year Plan 2002-2007 Vol III State Plans, Trends, Concerns and Strategies,* New Delhi.
12. North Eastern Development Finance Corporation Ltd (NEDFi), *Resources & Investment Potential in North Eastern Region* (Highlights) Guwahati, Assam, India.
13. Singh, E Bijoykumar, 2006, 'India's North East Economic Policy:Evolution and Emerging Trends. Paper presented at the National Seminar on *Rethinking Paradigms of Development for the North East India,* March 24-25, 2006, Gangtok.
14. Vanlalchhawna, 2007, 'India's Look East Policy: Challenges and Opportunities for North East India. *Proceeding of the Eighth Annual Conference of North Eastern Economic Association*, 16-17 November.

Towards a Professional Identity

SOCCER AS CAREER OPTION IN CONTEMPORARY MANIPUR

Kausik Bandyapadhaya

Arguably, for *development* from within, a state or a group of states need, along with governmental support, peoples' urge to develop by appropriating and utilizing the available natural and human resources in the best possible way. A dispassionate look at the contemporary political, social and economic situation in the North Eastern states of India suggests, however, that the North East has internalized over the years a state of political insurgency, economic dependence and cultural isolation not conducive to integrated development strategies at all. In the age of globalization, commercialism and professionalism are the two most crucial weapons by which the underdeveloped states of the region could cope with political instability (insurgency and counter-insurgency), economic backwardness (infrastructural debilities and unemployment) and social anomalies (drug abuse and spread of AIDS). It is in this context that sports like soccer can be looked upon as a lucrative career option generating new avenues of employment as well as sources of livelihood to the youth of the region. The present paper takes up the case of Manipur, where soccer has done wonders to provide the young generation with a viable professional alternative to political instability and social maladies. Women's soccer in Manipur, on the other hand, creates a powerful space for gender empowerment[1], although this has been left out of the purview of the present discussion.

Manipur: A turbulent sports-loving society

Problems facing the Manipuri Society

Since its merger with India in 1949 and even after its attainment of state status in 1972, Manipur remained a hotbed of ethnic clashes and insurgent activities.[2] Sanjoy Hazarika explains the roots of ethnic clashes in Manipur in the following terms:

> Manipur's slide into anarchy has been sure and steady. The hills of the state, where a majority of Nagas live, are dominated by one faction or another of the National Socialist Council of Nagaland (NSCN). Other groups active there include the Kuki National Army. In the plains—essentially, the small and fertile Imphal valley—live the majority community, the Meiteis. For all purposes, the Meiteis are hemmed in on all sides by the hill groups. But here, too, ethnic disparities are reflected in the insurgencies as well: the Meiteis have their own fighting groups which demand independence, including the United National Libertaion Front (UNLF) and the People's Liberation Army (PLA). The dominant Naga group accuses the UNLF of trying to intimidate Nagas and apparently has its own Meitei front which has targeted supporters of the UNLF. Unending ethnic divisions and bitter rivalries have brought Manipur to the brink of unmitigated disaster. The longstanding feuds between the Kukis and Tangkhul Nagas resulted in killings and counter killings in the early Nineties, with the active participation of militants from both sides.[3]

The state also faced the imposition of the draconian Armed Forces Special Power Act (AFSPA)[4] in 1958 by the Government of India in a desperate attempt to curb the unrest. The fierce combat between the insurgents and armed forces saw thousands of youths falling victims to the bloody turmoil. At the height of the turbulence in the 1980s and early 1990s, the Manipuri society felt crippled by unrest, frustration and uncertainty. As increase in population was not complemented by a comparable increase in the number of jobs, unemployment became the order of the day, breeding a deep sense of despair and insecurity among the Manipuri youths, who were left with two vicious options—either to take up guns or to fall prey to the menace of drug abuse. As one writer elaborates: 'Thousands of jaded youth joined insurgent groups and a few more thousands sought 'heaven' in opium, heroine and LSD.'[5] Subtly describing the appalling pervasiveness of Manipur being an oasis of drug abuse, another commentator stated:

> Brothers acquainting you with opium, a peddler aunt giving you a treat of heroin, or access to heroin that your father peddles to other youngsters, a habit that your husband shares with you, quick money your neighbourhood unemployed uncle makes—whoever your source, howsoever your induction, the bottom line here is neglect.[6]

While analysing the crux of the problem, she argued:

> The neglect of the north-eastern states by the Centre has manifested in Manipur as a drug problem, thanks to easy access to the "high stuff" through the porous border with Myanmar. A fairly literate population, high unemployment and social unrest have resulted in the Manipuris resorting to substance abuse, and more specifically intravenous heroin addiction.[7]

Related to this evil is the spread of AIDS. This deadly disease began to flex its muscle since the 1980s. Sharing of syringes among addicts is the most common reason for the spread of this disease. While the pattern of HIV-infection through sexual transmission route is as high as 86 per cent in other regions in India, in Manipur about 72 per cent of HIV infection is through sharing of needles and syringes by drug addicts.[8] At present Manipur has one of the highest per capita HIV positive patients in India.

Thus Manipuri society is infested with a plethora of political, social and economic problems: armed insurgency and ethnic clashes, long-term unemployment and economic insecurity, drug abuse and HIV infection. The masses of the state have become weary of this situation for quite some time now. Given such perilous social situation, most of the families in Manipur, who can afford, prefer to send away their sons and daughters to other states. For the majority, who cannot afford to do so, one way out to save their young children from social as well as political ills has been to encourage them to embrace different sports much more dearly than ever.

Sporting Traditions of Manipur

Incidentally, Manipuris are sports-loving people to the core and the state enjoys one of the most glorious sporting traditions and heritages in the world. Since the ancient days numerous indigenous sports and games originated in the state. In fact, the game of polo originated in this state a few centuries back as it was conceptualised and incepted in Manipur as *Sagol Kangjei* in the ancient times. The game on the horseback, which embodies regal gallantry, later on, underwent changes in rule under the British regiment officers posted in that area in the 19th century, who were readily enticed by the game and transplanted it to the international sporting commune as Polo. As Peter Parkes points out, 'the curious story of polo's imperial reinvention and metropolitan reprocessing, its raw retrieval from Manipur to

Hurlingham and its re-export as a finished product to the subcontinent, offers an instructive paradigm for the historical anthropology of other colonially appropriated sports.'[9]

Apart from *Sagol Kangjei*, there are a few other indigenous sports like *Thang Ta and Sarit Sarak* (Manipuri Martial Arts), *Khong Kangjei* (Manipuri Hockey), *Yubi Lakpi* (Manipuri Style Rugby), *Hiyang Tanaba* (Boat Race), *Mukna* (Manipuri Wrestling) and *Kang*. All these sports originated in Manipur and were widely played in the state, which thus manifested the local people's profound passion and love for sports and games. The people of Manipur comprised 29 communities, which predominantly include three distinct groups of people with different cultural, social and religious backgrounds, namely, *Meiteis*,[10] *Kukis*[11] and *Nagas*.[12] These three tribes with their mongoloid warrior lineage inherently perform and excel in various martial arts and endurance sports with their physical fitness and acrobatic skills.

The Government of India, in its drive to normalise the ongoing grim situation, initiated several welfare activities in Manipur. In that process, Sports Authority of India (SAI), the nodal sports promotion body of India, came to play an important role in the rehabilitation of the youth energy in Manipur, as it once again rekindled the passion for sports among the Manipuri youths. In the 1980s, the SAI started conducting several sports development programmes, especially among the youths and the schoolchildren. This ushered a new era in Manipuri sports as the small state for the first time started making foray into the apex league of Indian sport, and the sportspersons started carving niche for themselves in the national sporting arena.

Inspirational Role of Sportspersons from Hockey to Football

In the early 1980s, it was P. Neelkamal, the prolific hockey goalkeeper, who became a trendsetter of a sort for the 'golden generation of Manipuri sportspersons'[13]. With his acrobatic penalty save in the 1984 Los Angeles Olympics, Neelkamal became a household name in the panic-stricken state and acquired an iconic status among the youngsters. Neelkamal's success at the international level triggered off a new beginning as thousands of youngsters charged up to fulfil their dream to represent the country in the sports. Within a couple of years, Indian hockey witnessed the meteoric rise of two of the most gifted hockey stars from Manipur—Brojen Singh and Thoiba Singh.

The late 1990s marked a watershed in the history of modern sports in Manipur as several sportspersons in different sporting fields came into prominence in the national and international sporting arena. It was in the 6th National Games, held at Imphal, the capital of Manipur in 1999, that Manipur emerged as the over-all team champion, surpassing the giants like Punjab or Kerala. The success of Manipuri sportspersons could be attributed to the dedication, devotion and above all, obsession with sports among the people. Since the late 1990s, Manipur had the distinction of producing international and national level sportspersons in various sports. The illustrious list of internationally successful Manipuri sportspersons include women weightlifters N. Kunjarani Devi[14] and Sanamacha Chhanu; prolific boxer N. Dingko Singh[15] and a couple of mainstays of national women's hockey team like ace gamemaker Suraj Lata Devi[16] and bustling forward Sangai Chhanu.[17] The prominence of such internationally successful sportsmen and women was complemented by a steady rise of Manipuri footballers at the national level. The list included Somatai Saiza, Renedy Singh, Bijen Singh, Manitombi Singh, Tomba Singh, Surkumar Singh, Dharamjit Singh, Rajesh Meetei, Raju Singh, Ratan Singh, Shanta Singh, Bungo Singh, Lolendro Singh, Santosh Singh, Samson Singh, Tiken Singh, James Singh, Gourmangi Singh, Momocha Singh, Napoleon Singh, Akbar Singh and many others. Thus Manipur has become a nursery of most sports (sans cricket) in India. In the words of a journalist: 'These days it seems all a Manipuri has to do is to kick a ball, lift a baseball, shoot an arrow, throw a punch and he/she will win a medal.'[18]

Soccer as Sources of Livelihood and a New Professional Identity

New Powerhouse of Indian Soccer

Amidst the changing balance of power in contemporary Indian football, new forces are clearly on the ascendancy. If the lead in this regard initially came from Goa, Manipur—a rather young entrant from the North East into the national football theatre—has most successfully followed it up. Manipur won the 34th National Championship for the Santosh Trophy in 2002, displacing the traditional bastions of Indian soccer, signaling the arrival of a new soccer power-centre in India, viz. the North East. The victory of Manipur, so long considered to be a minnow in Indian football, opened up possibilities for the game to flourish in the region. Moreover, the successful hosting of the tournament by the All Manipur Football Association (AMFA) pointed to its professional approach towards the game,[19] lacking in many other state units of AIFF.

It is a bit surprising that Manipur has taken so long a time to strike at the National Championship. For the past one decade or so, the state provided a steady stream of classy players like Gunbir Singh, Kiran Khongsai, Renedy Singh, Bijen Singh, Khemtang Paite, James Singh, Lolendra Singh, Manitomba Singh, Tomba Singh and Dharamjit Singh both to national as well as to club sides. It is now common to find Manipuri players in almost all the leading club teams of the country. As Animul Islam writes:

> Browse through the names of the national squad, Manipur have representatives in the senior, junior and sub-junior teams. There is no denying the fact that Kolkata and Goa have the best of clubs at their disposal but Manipur possess the players. Today, most club officials make the trek to the North-East state to hire their footballers. ... After Manipur's historic win (in the last edition of the Santosh Trophy), Bengal cannot claim to be the sole bastion of Indian soccer. Except a few of their home grown players, club officials in Kolkata rely on outstation players; the Singhs have outpaced the Chatterjees and Banerjees...[20]

It is interesting to understand how Manipur came all the way to confirm its new status as a soccer force in India. Renedy Singh, a key member of the national squad and a member of the victorious Manipur team of 2002, noted: 'There are no academies or institutions that can nurture talent. There's nobody to guide us, yet we have done it. It is a story of hard work and dedication.'[21] Manitomba, another rising Manipuri footballer, explains overwhelming Manipuri presence in clubs of other states: 'There is no money in Manipur. The leagues are not very popular, unlike those in Bengal or Goa. So naturally players like us would always want to move to a better place where we can earn a better living.'[22] In nourishing the talent of Manipuri footballers, Tata Football Academy of Jamshedpur and Sports Authority of India's (SAI) Special Area Games Program have played a fruitful part.[23]

Lack of exposure, scarcity of talent-hunters, recruiters and ethno-cultural differences with the other parts of India caused hindrances to the Manipuri soccer players, and kept them confined to the state, while mainstream India remained unaware of their soccer skills. Way back in the early-nineties, it was one self-made individual who broke all the shackles to catapult Manipuri soccer to the national level. Former

Indian midfielder Kiron Khongsai – a *Kuki* by descent – surpassed all odds to move out of the state and pursued soccer as a profession as he started playing for East Bengal Club of Kolkata, one of the top soccer clubs of India. Sooner, a few more players such as Gunabir Singh, Gumpe Rime and Khemtang Paite, from *Paitei* community,[24] too joined the fray, joining respectively East Bengal, Salgaonkar Sports Club and Air India.

Till the late 1990s, thanks to various initiatives of the Sports Authority of India (SAI) and the All Manipur Football Association (AMFA), Manipur registered some landmark performances in several all-India sub-junior and junior tournaments, but the state failed to transmit that to the senior level. Social instability and financial insecurity prevented them from pursuing a career in soccer. The emergence of Khongsai, Gunabir and Paite into national soccer actually propelled Manipuri soccer to the Indian soccer horizon as a diligent band of bustling soccer players who followed the trend to make it to the highest level of Indian soccer. The success of the troika had also generated a massive interest in soccer in the state. More importantly, the successful Manipuri soccer players set a trend of acting as recruiters cum promoters for the budding soccer stars from the home state. Except for the Tata Football Academy (TFA)[25] products, who are readily promoted by the academy itself after passing out, nearly all the present and former Manipuri soccer stars were brought to their respective clubs by their state predecessors or seniors. For example, former Air India player Khambiton Singh played a crucial role to rope in three of the talented players Tomba Singh, Manitombi Singh and Bungo Singh for his club.[26]

Nevertheless, it was Somatai Saiza, more popularly known as 'Soso' by his teammates and fans, who became the first Manipuri star of Indian soccer. While Soso flourished in the national soccer, other players from Manipur such as Ratan Singh, Khambiton Singh and Sanaton Singh also made themselves quite indispensable to their respectable club sides.

The Tata Football Academy played a crucial role in bringing this 'golden generation of Manipuri soccer stars into the limelight. With its policy of spotting and picking of some of the raw and young soccer talents in the remote parts of the country and subsequently nurturing them for the highest level of national soccer, the TFA made a significant contribution to the sudden surge of Manipuri players as it endorsed and then brought into focus a list of star players like Renedy Singh, Lolendra Singh and L James Singh to the national level. This band of players has played a pivotal role in the giant leap, the state's soccer has made in recent times. The number of Manipuris in the cadets of TFA has registered a significant leap since 2002. The percentage of Manipuri footballers in the outgoing cadets from TFA increased from 16 per cent in 2002 to 42 per cent in 2006 (Figure 1).

Figure 1 : Ratio of Manipuri Cadets in Tata Football Academy

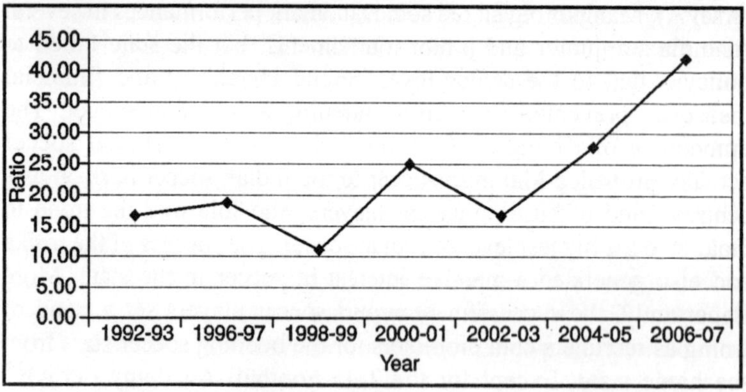

Source: http://www.tatafootballacademy.com/ex_cadets_batch.asp

Alongside Renedy, it was Bijen Singh, who also gave a boost to Manipur's young generation to absorb soccer as a career. However, unlike Renedy, Bijen was a homegrown player as he began his soccer career with the National Sports Talent Contest, a national scheme of Sports Authority of India (SAI) to spot young talent in various sports. After representing his home state and subsequently the country in the junior level tournaments, he joined East Bengal in 1997.[27] Another most exciting Manipuri player was Tomba Singh, who earned the rare honour of the 'Best Player of the Year 2003' by AIFF by dint of his stellar performance in the National Football League.

Despite establishing themselves as one of the supreme powers at the national stage throughout the nineties, players from Manipur had failed to win the elusive title of Santosh Trophy[28], which could have strengthened the state's position as the most powerful in Indian soccer. Interestingly, before 1999 Manipur had never even reached the quarterfinals of the inter-state championship, mostly dominated by

Bengal and on a few occasions by Kerala and Goa. In 1999 in Ooty in Tamil Nadu, Manipur made it to the quarterfinals before losing to formidable Bengal, and thus had registered their best ever performance till that time.[29] But three years later, Manipuri soccer reached its pinnacle as the state, fancied with all its star players in its rank for the first time ever, won its maiden Santosh Trophy crown in front of its own people at Imphal. Incidentally, for the first time in the heydays of the state's soccer, the state witnessed the combined participation of all their prolific soccer exports together, proudly donning the state's jersey in the senior level. For this historic first, as Suvam Pal argues, 'one must appreciate that the ever-idiosyncratic AIFF's creditable policy of passing the recent resolution of ensuring every state to call their outstation players for the prestigious Santosh Trophy as it bore immediate fruit.'[30]

This historic triumph consolidated Manipur's status as the power centre of Indian soccer, signaling the end of monopoly of Bengal and Goa. In the past few years, the success of Goa, Mumbai and Bengal soccer giants like Dempo Sports Club, Mahindra United, Mohun Bagan and East Bengal, can be attributed to the stellar role of players from other states among which Manipur figures prominently, not to speak of the foreign recruits.

The All Manipur Football Association (AMFA) was established in 1976 under the aegis of the Government of Manipur. Earlier, the All Manipur Sports Association (AMSA) was in charge of football in the state. It was with the directive of the All India Football Federation (AIFF), and on the principle of one game one Association, that the AMFA got separated from AMSA. Till 1992, AMFA was directly responsible for all activities including inter-club leagues, inter-districts, state/national championships, preparation of state teams and other soccer development programmes. However realising the necessity of propagating the game in the state with great potential, the AMFA directly assigned the inter club leagues to the district associations—which were divided into 12 district units, namely, Imphal West District Football Association; Imphal East District Football Association; District Sports Association, Bishnupur District Sports Association, Kakching District Sports Association; Churachandpur District Sports Association; Sadar Hills District Sports Association, Ukhrul District. Senapati District Sports Association, Tamenglong District Sports Association, Chandel District Football Association and Thoubal and

All Jiribam Sports Association. All these District Associations have boasted of a few good number of local clubs, divided into four categories—Super Division, 1st Division, 2nd Division and 3rd Division. However, unlike most of the sporting organizations of India, with all its handicaps, AMFA played a decent role in the upliftment of the game of soccer, at least at the junior level. Manipur's glittering track record of producing as many as 200 internationals in both men and women category is quite largely attributed to the modus operandi of the nodal organisation, which tried its best for a holistic development. Though Manipur is located in the extreme North Eastern part of the country, the AIFF, giving due recognition to its recent performances, has been trying to entrust a good number of National Championships to the Association every year. In fact, the Association has now emerged as one of the most successful and well-organized state level sports organizations in the North East with its fully computerized office, permanent staff and other modern amenities. Word about the Association's achievements have reached such proportions that FIFA, the World's Governing Body in football and the International Olympic Committee had listed the Honourary Secy. of the Association in the list of volunteers honoured in connection with the commemoration of the International Year of Volunteers.[31]

Even after the initiation of a tangible process of professionalization and commercialization in the domestic circuit, Indian football with its attractive paraphernalia of mass spectatorship is far away from adapting to the contemporary trends of the game's global culture[32]. When India as a footballing power of some worth flexes its muscle at the international scene, it is again a particular club and not a national side, which gives us a toast of national victory and instills a sense of national pride.[33] India needs more Manipurs to attain the status of a developing footballing nation because Manipur does not represent club syndromes, but provides a viable pool of young promising footballers who can serve the national team. The number of new registrations of Manipuri footballers in National League teams since 2002 reiterates this point. The number increased from 3 in 2002-03 to 14 in 2006-07 (Figure 2).

In the inter-state transfers' list of All India Football Federation in 2006, out of 452 transfers, 103 players (about 23 per cent) came from the North Eastern states, of which 65 (about 14 per cent) were Manipuris. On the other hand, among the players from the North East,

Figure 2 : No. of Players Registered in National League Teams: Manipur

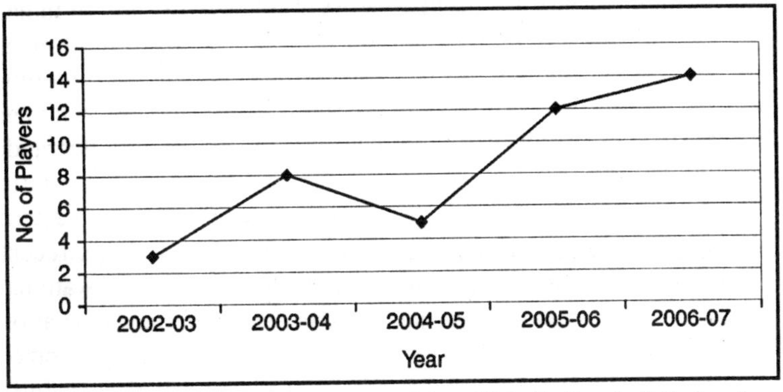

Source: National League Registration Files, All India Football Federation

Manipuris represented 63 per cent.[34] More importantly, The 20-member Indian senior national soccer squad that took part in the Doha Asian Games 2006 comprised as many as 7 players (35 per cent) from the North East, including 4 Manipuris. More importantly, the 22-men Under-20 Indian team that participated in the AFC Championship 2006 had 14 players (63 per cent) from the North East in their rank.[35]

Soccer as career option and exodus of Manipuri footballers

Thus, men's soccer in the state has attained such a standard in the last one-decade, thanks mostly to the efforts of All Manipur Football Association (AMFA) and the Sports Authority of India (SAI), that young football players from Manipur have opted for playing outside Manipur in different club teams throughout India, thereby creating for themselves alternative career options and earning a decent living. Tomba Singh described football to be 'our passport to success in life'.[36] The veteran Rennedy Singh puts the prospect on a high pitch: 'Watch out for some more names [in the national squad] in the next couple of years. Soon, Manipur will become the all and end-all for Indian football.'[37]

Instead of destroying their ethnic identity by any means, this has given wider recognition to their professional expertise and enhanced the prestige and status of their community at the national stage. Dingko

Singh, who sparked off a sporting revolution by winning the Asian Games gold medal in boxing in 1998, neatly sums up the essence of the situation: 'There's nothing else for youngsters to do here; no money, no business. So they get hooked onto some sport because that's the only way they'll find a job.'[38] In case of football, this became apparent at the turn of the century. Bijen Singh talked about the prospect of carving out an independent career in one of his interviews a few years back:

> Now Manipur has a lot of good footballers. Why now, even in the past, when I was young, Manipur had good crop of footballers. But Manipur does not have clubs of the stature of East Bengal and Mohun Bagan. So, for survival, we have to go outside. There are so many players from Manipur who are playing for the top clubs across the country. We cannot go back and play for Manipur at senior level. If one considers all these players, then Manipur will be a very strong side in the senior level, at par with the best. Even the junior players who win the BC Roy Trophy for the second consecutive year, will now move outside Manipur to enhance their career.[39]

The young Manipuri cadets of the Tata Football Academy also think that playing the game in right earnest can give them a tangible option of earning a decent and respectable living outside Manipur thereby putting an end to the increasing anxiety of their parents and families in the state.[40] However, it is important that the AMFA should utilize the experience and support of these soccer stars to boost up the infrastructure and quality of football in the home state.

Vision India and Manipur: Soccer as employment opportunity within the state

In 2000 Manipuri soccer star Somatai Saiza lamented that 'there are not enough scopes for the Manipuris to show their talent to the outside world.'[41] He also noted that no one could think of making football as his career while living in Manipur at that time. He attributed this state of affairs to lack of infrastructure and apathy of the officials towards football. And to put an end to all these possibilities, he was determined to start his academy after his retirement.[42] Things, however, began to change radically particularly since 2002, after AMFA's successful hosting of the Santosh Trophy as well as Manipur's victory in the tournament. Still, there was not much scope for the young Manipuri footballers either to find a job through sport or to take up the game as a profession within the state itself. This was mainly because no leagues like Kolkata or Goa or no major tournaments were staged in Manipur to make the players economically viable for the Manipuri clubs.

Manipur finally got an opportunity to mine out its incredible talent pool in a systematic and organised way when Manipur along with Delhi was taken under the *Vision India* project, an ambitious project under the aegis of the grand *Vision Asia*[43] project of Asian Football Confederation (AFC), envisaging the fulfilment of AFC's latest motto *The Future is Asia*[44]—a holistic approach towards the development of Asian soccer. The *Vision India* was launched by Dato Peter Velappan, general secretary of AFC on 26 April 2004. Manipur and Delhi were chosen the two sites for the implementation of the pilot projects of *Vision India* project in the initial stage. In AIFF general secretary Alberto Colaso's words:

> For a while Manipur has become a powerhouse of Indian football as they have already produced some of the finest players in the present Indian soccer. Football has a great mass appeal in the state. But unlike West Bengal, Goa and Kerala, absence of any premier soccer club has been a hindrance to the upliftment of soccer in the state. Through Vision India, AIFF hopes that soccer in Manipur will receive a big impetus, as they will restructure the entire soccer system in the state apart from conducting a thorough-professional talent hunt scheme and evolving out a good club soccer system.[45]

More importantly, Velappan, along with his fellow *Vision Asia* officials, later visited Manipur to have a first hand assessment of the soccer infrastructure in the state. Pleased with the enthusiastic approach of the AMFA, he declared that the AFC would put Manipur 'on the fast track of development.'[46] After discussions on 'Project Manipur', it was decided to start the Manipur district school league as well as the State League in 12 months' time with 12 strong clubs, which would have proper administration and other key facilities. It was also decided to intensify the grassroots and youth development programme in schools, including a competition structure for girls, since Manipur is a stronghold of women's football in India. The AMFA studied *Vision Asia*'s proposals, came up with their own action plan forming a task force, and began implementation with the appointment of representatives responsible for coaches and referees' education.[47]

As part of the *Vision India* plan, two workshops were held in Imphal in May and July 2006 respectively in preparation for the launch of a Districts' Schools League and for the development of the 12 clubs[48] that would figure in the State League.[49] The School League, the first step in implementation of AFC's *Vision Asia* – Project Manipur was launched in September 2006. This was followed by the launch of the state League on November 2, 2006. Velappan, General Secretary of AFC, and Priya Ranjan Dasmunsi, President, AIFF, attended the latter event. Dasmunsi, in his message, praised Manipur for its coordinated approach to the project:

> It is a great joy for all of us that Manipur shall be figuring in the history of Indian football, to be the first state to implement Vision India Programme in line with Vision Asia, in due time. After several visits of AFC Vision delegation and with the hardwork of All Manipur Football Association in cooperation with the Government, they found it possible to maintain this time schedule of this programme. I thank the great people of Manipur and Football fans for making this effort a great success. I also thank All Manipur Football Association and the Government of Manipur for their total cohesion in this matter. I am confident the future of India will have a great, great support in the field of football from the State of Manipur.[50]

Although the Manipur Project did not have any viable outside sponsor from the beginning, the AMFA could implement it successfully with the constant and emphatic support from the State Government.[51] The AFC President Mohamed Bin Hammam's note of appreciation on Manipur's road to success seems to be more relevant here:

> Manipur was selected by AIFF in 2005 as a pilot project for Vision India because of its enthusiasm for football, passion, leadership and commitment to progress and change. In a short span of just one and a half years, Manipur has made huge strides towards strengthening its core football activities: administration and management, clubs and competitions, grassroots and youth programmes, coaches and referees education. The most important element and key focus of Vision India Project Manipur is the Manipur State League, a League which provides a high-performance platform for the players, clubs, coaches, referees and officials. I am confident that this League will work as a catalyst towards football development in North East India. I urge other states in India to follow the lead of Manipur in embracing the Vision India programme, and thereby commit the goal of making India a formidable force in international football.[52]

Manipur's progress under the Project assumes more significance in the context of Delhi's lamentable performance in the same even with much better infrastructural and resource prowess. As Brandon Menton, AFC Director of National Association and Clubs Development, rightly argued: "Delhi don't have to look too far for inspiration. Manipur would be a great example for them to follow. The sense of purpose and the professional manner in which Manipur conduct their events is really heart warming.'[53] If Velappan's prophetic vision is to be believed then 'The future is Asia' and 'India is the sleeping giant of Asian soccer who will one day wake up to become the spearhead of Asian football.'[54] But Velappan also warned: 'This is the last chance for India. If India does not take advantage of Vision India project, then God help Indian football.'[55] If India at all wakes up from its football slumber to catch up with the international standards, then it will certainly be the state of Manipur, complemented by its neighbours Mizoram and Meghalaya, which will lead the road to that renaissance.

The introduction of the State League under *Vision India* should have far-reaching implications for Manipuri society and economy. Apart from providing a high-performance platform for the players, clubs, coaches, referees and officials, the League would definitely help transform football as a viable economic force in Manipur. The young footballers would now be able to pursue football as career living. With a tangible process of professionalization already set in the AMFA and the clubs, paid jobs as support stuff should open up another option for employment. Besides generating employment opportunities, once the League and the clubs begin to attract sponsors, Manipur might be able to host major national/international tournaments, thereby giving fillip to its tourism prospects and raising its economic infrastructure. And if the state could succeed in sending one or two club teams to the professional National League, scheduled to start from the next season (2008-09), football might thrive as an industry in Manipur. The example of Manipur quite naturally should inspire other states of the North East to realize the sport's potential as an economic force.

Soccer as a Social Opiate: Sport, Youth and Socio-political Stability in the North East

As Manipur has been under the shadow of insurgency and counter-insurgency for decades now, the viability of both is being questioned from different quarters. For the insurgents, their desired goal, i.e. secession and independence come first and peace and development second, while the Govt. of India justifies counter-insurgency in terms of restoration of peace and development in society. However, it might not be too impressionistic to argue that the common people of the state too are becoming tired of this stream of insurgent/counter-insurgent activities as well as ethnic clashes.[56] In view of this tendency, restoration of peace and stability can be the prime requisite to lead the society and economy of Manipur into a road to development.[57] With the Manipuri youth in large numbers being attracted to football in the last one decade, the game can play a positive role in this process of socio-political stabilization.

A new tinge of colour may be added here to understand the ground realities of the sports situation in Manipur. Sports like football in the last decade or so have become more than a mere pastime for on-field entertainment in this state of North Eastern India. Rather, in the turbulent North Eastern states like Manipur, continually struck by insurgency and terrorism, sport assumes the dimension of a partial opiate. As Animul Islam observes: 'Deprived of creature comforts and saddled with insurgency, drugs and AIDS, they turned to the one thing they knew best: sport'[58]. In fact, sport can be one powerful medium through which the restless energies of the North-Eastern youth can be appropriated to serve their respective states and the nation. Manipur has started developing a sports policy, 'which aims to win younger people away from the pursuit of insurgency and the frustration of searching for government jobs or opting, at least for those who can afford it, paying out at all levels to capture contracts and assignments and become wealthy and well-known'[59]. But, to implement this policy fruitfully, the government and the concerned authorities should consult and listen to the trained sportspersons including players and professionals in the field. As one commentator argued, 'they know better than others what is needed to make sports an attractive avenue of channeling the energies of the young and a real alternative for employment'[60].

Stan Rayan wrote about football in 'Contemporary Manipur': 'Football is now fast becoming a way of life for the Manipuris. With insurgency, drugs and AIDS turning many lives into nightmare, and with many young falling prey, parents heave a big sigh of relief when their children take to sport'[61]. That is why even continuous socio-political unrest could hardly hinder the progress of the game. As one young Manipuri cadet of the TFA says:

> We want to play the game as it provides us an opportunity to become professionals. Our parents have taken the pain of sending us to this training centre in the hope that we would do well to earn our living. It's our turn to fulfil their dreams and make them happy by becoming self-sufficient. Both the young generation and their guardians in Manipur have the belief that football can achieve this end.[62]

Another Manipuri cadet of the same academy argues:

> Sports like football can certainly be one way out of the political turmoil and social instability in contemporary Manipur. Since the game has become a profession by itself, it has become synonymous with employment. Moreover, by showing *our* worth as good footballers and contributing to the success of the *national* team, we wish to raise the status of our state and rebuild its image in the eyes of Indian public.[63]

At times, the game has been used as therapy for drug addicts. For example, an NGO called 'Sahara' runs a treatment centre for HIV positives in New Delhi, where football has been used in this way with great success. As one of its programme managers commented, 'The game helps our inmates not only to gain fitness but also acts as an instrument of empowerment. It has helped them boost their morale and lead a healthy life.'[64] Most players on the Sahara teams come from North Eastern India in general and Manipur in particular and many of them have made it to Delhi's A Division League.[65] One such player, Diosiam, remarked: 'I was fed up with life but could not get out of drugs. During rehabilitation, football gave me a zest for life and I now play in Delhi's A Division League'[66].

Conclusions

Broadly speaking, this study intends to put emphasis on two objectives: first to devise peaceful cultural means and constructive social strategies to provide the youth in the region with wider and diversified economic opportunities in order to overcome political instability and social anomalies, and second, to explore, locate and earmark the fruitful areas of professional expertise of the North Eastern people, so that the outcome might be useful in utilizing both the specialized skill and professional expertise for the development of the region from within as well as relocating such skilled human resources of the region to other states of India where such expertise may be meaningfully deployed. As I have tried to show, soccer can be fruitfully appropriated as a novel cultural means to realize this double strategy of generating alternative employment opportunities and achieving socio-political stabilization. However, this could be successful only if the central and state governments, state and central level soccer associations, the media and the people of the North East appreciate the importance of an integrated developmental approach and move together to fulfil that purpose. I will wind up with another excerpt from the Prime Minister's speech I began with:

> I have already said we want to improve Manipur's connectivity to the region around. We would like to invest in the creation of modern infrastructure to enable this. However, for this to happen, we need peace, security and political stability. If we can work together to bring normalcy back I can assure you that Manipur will become the Jewel of India.[67]

There are definitely government-earmarked areas where Manipur could make a lot of progress. The Government of India has started to take small steps in the right direction[68] in order to regain the confidence of the population, which is no easy task. However, creating viable employment opportunities would be a more effective way in making the state a worthy contributor to the nation's progress as a fast developing economy. With soccer Manipur has the great potential to achieve this end, as it has already become a jewel in the crown of Indian soccer.

NOTES AND REFERENCES

1. One interesting essay that deals with this theme, albeit in a somewhat misconstrued way, is: James Mills, 'Nupilal': Women's War, Football and the History of Modern Manipur', in James Mills, ed. *Subaltern Sports: Politics and Sport in South Asia*, London: Anthem, 2005.
2. For wider historical discussion on the roots, evolution and discourses of insurgency movements in Manipur, see S.C. Sharma, *Insurgency, or, Ethnic Conflict: With reference to Manipur*, Magnum Business Associates, 2000. Also see: G. Kabui et al., *Modern Manipur*, Imphal: Modern Book, 1991; P. Roy Choudhury, *The North East: Roots of Insurgency*, Calcutta: Firma KLM, 1986; Sajal Nag, *Contesting Marginality: Ethnicity, Insurgency and Subnationalism in North-East India*, New Delhi: Manohar, 2002; N, Sanjaoba, *Manipur: Past and*

Present, Delhi: Mittal, 1990; K.M. Singh, *Hijam Irabat Singh and Political Movement in Manipur*, Delhi: B.R. Publishing, 1989; N.J. Singh, *Social Movements in Manipur*, Delhi: Mittal, 1992; *Colonialism to Democracy: A history of Manipur 1819-1972*, Delhi: Spectrum, 1992; Lokendra N. Singh, *Unquiet Valley: Society, Economy and Politics in Manipur 1891-1950*, Delhi: Mittal, 1998; B. Ahluwalia and S. Ahluwalia, eds. *Social Change in Manipur*, Delhi: Cultural Publishing House, 1984; G. Phukon, *Ethnicization of Politics in North East India*, Delhi: South Asian, 2003; L. Zehol, *Ethnicity in Manipur: Experiences, issues and perspectives*, New Delhi: Regency. 1998; P. Tarapot, *Bleeding Manipur*, New Delhi: Har-Anand, 2003.

3. Sanjay Hazarika, 'Manipur Lost', in 'A Route Map to the North East', *The Asian Age*, 10 January 2001.
4. The Armed Forces (Special Powers) Act (AFSPA), 1958, was first imposed on some parts of the state as it was hit by the Naga rebellion. Later in 1980 the act was imposed on the entire state towards the height of insurgency in North East.
5. Suvam Pal, 'Guts, Grits and Glory: The Manipur Soccer Story', unpublished paper, 2005.
6. Vani Saraswathi, 'Educated and jobless, youth here seek "heaven" in heroin', *Indian Express*, 17 November 1998.
7. Ibid.
8. Rasheeda Bhagat, 'HIV/AIDS in Manipur: In the "state" of despair', *The Hindu Business Line*, 7 October 2002.
9. Peter Parkes, 'Indigenous Polo in Northern Pakistan: Game and Power on the Periphery', in James Mills, ed. *Subaltern Sports: Politics and Sport in South Asia* (London: Anthem Press, 2005).
10. *Meiteis*, who inhabit in the plains of Manipur, comprise 70 per cent of the total population of the state. They have a grand history as Meitei kings were rulers of Manipur state till the British took over its administration towards the end of the 19th century. Meiteis are Vaishnavite (who worships Vishnu) Hindus. For further details, see V.P. Kaur, 'The Manipur Minefield', *Indian Express*, 26 June 2001.
11. The *Kukis* are Christians, but quite distinct from *Nagas*, and reside primarily in Southern hills of Manipur. *Kukis* have a significant place in the history of Manipur as they initiated the historic Kuki rebellion against the British in (1917-19) Manipur.
12. Though Manipur have a significant *Naga* population the majority of the *Nagas* are inhabitants of Manipur's neighbouring state Nagaland. The *Nagas* are overwhelmingly Christians and live in the surrounding hills in the west, north and east of Manipur.
13. Suvam Pal has used this phrase in his paper.

14. She won medals in various international competitions, including Commonwealth Games and Asian Games, apart from finding a place in the hall of fame of top 100 international weightlifting legends of the century.
15. He won a gold in boxing in the 2002 Busan Asian Games.
16. Prolific hockey midfielder Suraj Lata have so far led the Indian team to two of its most memorable triumphs till date- Commonwealth Games gold at Manchester in 2002 and Asia Cup triumph in New Delhi in 2004.
17. Chhanu was the top-scorer for India in their Asia Cup victory in 2004.
18. Animul Islam, 'Jewel in the crown', *Indian Express*, 10 October 2002.
19. The tournament's successful hosting bears witness to AMFA's long-term commercial and professional planning. The title sponsor of the tournament was LG India. More importantly, the Association launched its official website on the occasion of its hosting the tournament.
20. Islam, 'Jewel in the Crown'.
21. Quoted in Ibid.
22. Ibid.
23. While Manipuri players have always made their presence felt among the top string of TFA graduates since the mid 1990s, SAI offered its sponsorship to a few institutions like the Army Boys School, thereby helping a great deal to locate and nourish budding talent.
24. *Paiteis*, an ethnic clan of Mizo origin, comprise a meagre portion of Manipur's population.
25. Tata Football Academy (TFA) is a venture solely undertaken by the Indian corporate giant Tata Group of Companies for the upliftment of Indian soccer. The soccer academy, situated at Jamshedpur, has already produced a long list of soccer players who have been successfully playing for various top-level clubs of the country, apart from representing the national team.
26. Islam, 'Jewel in the Crown'.
27. Incidentally, Bijen was also the youngest ever captain of East Bengal Club at the age of 21 years in the 87-year old history of the glamour outfit.
28. Santosh Trophy is the apex and most prestigious inter-state soccer championships in India and was started by the All India Football Federation in 1941.
29. Islam, 'Jewel in the Crown'.
30. Pal, 'Guts, Grits and Glory'.
31. I have collected these pieces of information on the AMFA from the official website of the Santosh Trophy 2002. For details, see *www.santoshtrophy2002.nic.in/news.htm.*

32. For football's changing global dimension through the ages, see Richard Giulianotti, *Football: A Sociology of the Global Game,* (Cambridge: Polity Press, 1999). For considerations on the variegated pattern of contemporary global culture of football, see Gerry T. Finn and Richard Giulianotti (eds.), *Football Culture: Local Contests, Global Visions* (London & Portland. OR: Frank Cass, 2000).
33. For example, East Bengal Club's victory (July 2003) in the ASEAN Cup at Jakarta, Indonesia by beating the top club teams from Southeast Asia was perceived as an emblem of national spirit.
34. All India Football Federation Inter State Transfers 2006 available at *www.the-aiff.com/interstate.php*, accessed on 10 April 2007.
35. All India Football Federation National Team Profile available at *www.the-aiff.com/Team.php*, accessed on 10 April 2007.
36. Stan Rayan, 'Football, a way of life for Manipuris', *The Hindu*, 15 November 2005.
37. Ibid.
38. Quoted in Islam, 'Jewel in the Crown'.
39. 'Bijen Singh: A Whiff of Fresh Air', *www.calonline.com/cal/alaap/bijensingh.html*, n.d.
40. The author had a discussion with two of the Manipuri footballers of the present group of Tata Football Academy cadets, Henry Gangte and Jibon Singh. Both expressed this view in confidence.
41. 'Sosho wants to start football academy in Manipur', *Oriental Times*, Vol.3, No.27-28 (22 November-6 December 2000).
42. Ibid.
43. *Vision Asia* is the AFC's grand plan for a continent-wide programme to raise the standards of Asian football at all levels, be it on the field of play, administration or sports science. This is the brainchild of AFC President Mohamed Bin Hammam, who launched the programme in January 2003. Nine months later, after much fine-tuning, Hammam unveiled Vision Asia as a well-defined blueprint to international delegates and VIPs during the FIFA Congress in Doha, Qatar. The President firmly believes that Asia, with its 3.7 billion population, has the potential to produce many world-class footballing nations. His ultimate goal is for an Asian team to one day win the FIFA World Cup. Hammam has identified 11 disciplines - akin to 11 players on the football field - that Vision Asia must address if Asian countries are to catch up with their counterparts in Europe and the rest of the world. They are: National Associations (goalkeeper); Marketing, Grassroots, Coach Education, Referees, Sports Medicine (defenders); Men's Competitions, Women's Competitions, Futsal (midfielders); Media, Fans (forwards). AFC has already recruited experts with specialist skills in each discipline.

These consultants are being assisted by development officers, one for each of the four zones - West Asia, Central/South Asia, South East Asia and East Asia. (Gathered from *www.the-aiff.com/vision_India.php*).

44. FIFA president Sepp Blatter initially coined the slogan 'The future is Asia'. The AFC, since then, adopted the phrase as its motto.
45. Colaso revealed this in a personal communication to Suvam Pal, then a sports journalist with the *Sahara Time*. For details, see Pal, 'Guts, Grits and Glory'.
46. 'Development of Manipur to be fast-tracked', 22 July 2005, available at *www.the-afc.com*, accessed on 21 September 2006. Incidentally the AFC delegation could find to their surprise as many as 200 fields and 296 club in Manipur.
47. Ibid.
48. These 12 clubs are: SAIRC, NEROCA, TRAU, Eastern Sporting Union, MPSC, Southern Sporting Union, YMC (all from Imphal), RACC (Churachandpur), Kakching FC (Kakching), AMOFA (Moirang), PYC (Thoubal) and YWO (Bishnupur).
49. 'Successful workshop held in Manipur to prepare the ground for schools league', 28 May 2006; 'Club development workshop held in Manipur', 11 July 2006, available at *www.the-afc.com*, accessed on 21 September 2006.
50. Available at *www.the-aiff.com/news_details*, posted on 28 October 2006.
51. Shaji Prabhakaran, Director of *Vision India*, admitted this in 'Delhi to launch school football league Wednesday', available at *www.indianmuslims.info*, 2 September 2006.
52. 'India could become major football power: Bin Hammam', available at *www.the-afc.com*, 3 November 2006.
53. 'Delhi "Vision India" project slower than expected', available at *http://footballdynamicsasia.blogspot.com/search/label/Vision%20Asia.*, accessed on 10 April 2007.
54. Velappan reiterated during the launch to the media. Pal, 'Guts, Grits and Glory'.
55. '"Vision India" goes practical', *Times of India*, 21 July 2006.
56. That the people of the North East could even compromise with the ultimate goal of independence in lieu of autonomy for the sake of peace is amply illustrated by the case of Nagaland. As Sajal Nag rightly points out, 'The event (the granting of statehood by the Indian Government to the Naga Hills) was all the more meaningful because it signified the polarization of the mass base. The moderates had control over a large section of these polarized masses who, caught between the violence of the Indian Army and the faction-ridden underground insurgents and traumatized by the bloodshed and harassment, were willing to settle for

little less than complete freedom for the sake of peace.' Nag, *Contesting Marginality*, p.313.

57. This is probably one of the reasons why the Government and the National Socialist Council of Nagaland (Nagalim) (NSCN-IM) are going to considerable lengths to accommodate each other. As Hiranmay Karlekar has argued, 'The latter, as well as the NSCN (K) are under tremendous pressure in Nagaland where ceasefire has not only made the demand for peace to snowball but has also enabled the emergence of a civil society – comprising church, tribal and clan leaders, educationists and so on – which is articulating it vigorously.' Hiranmay Karlekar, 'Nagaland: Intimations of Peace?', *The Pioneer*, 6 May 2007.
58. Animul Islam, 'Jewel in the Crown'.
59. Namaram Kishalaya, 'Beyond Santosh Trophy: Big Bucks Must Back Manipur Sports', *Manipuronline.com/Opinions*, 13 September 2002, accessed on 21 September 2006.
60. Ibid.
61. Rayan, 'Football, a way of life for Manipuris' (emphasis added).
62. Interview with Henry Gangte, 2 May 2007.
63. Interview with Jibon Singh, 2 May 2007.
64. *www.breitbart.com/news/na/060729052913.1q9deia7.html*. Accessed on 21 September 2006.
65. Ibid.
66. Ibid.
67. PM's speech on 20 November 2004 at the handing over of the Kangla Fort to the Government of Manipur, http://pmindia.nic.in/speech/content.asp?id=50, accessed on 21 September 2006.
68. Such steps include handing over the Kangla Fort to the State Government of Manipur, upgradation of the Manipur University into a central university or the new Jiribam-Imphal rail project.

An Exploration into the Possibility of Economic Development through India's Look East Policy

A MIZO PERSPECTIVE

L. H. Rawsea

For many years, India hardly regarded the countries of ASEAN[1] and South Pacific as priority areas despite their cultural, political, economic and strategic significance. With the participation of India in the East Asian Summit and from the level of interaction in the 4th India-ASEAN Summit, both held at Kuala Lumpur from 12-14 December 2005, this dark period of India's relations with the ASEAN countries and South Pacific was brought to an end following the reshaping and reorientation of India's Foreign Policy, manifest in the vigorous pursuits of 'Look East' policy since the last decade of the 20th century.[2] It is a fact that the Look East policy is being pursued aggressively and has started yielding results on the economic and political fields.[3] Hence, the time has come for the North East Region to become a corridor to the east for the whole nation. At this juncture, it is imperative to consider how the North East Region could benefit economically through this policy.

This paper is an attempt to explore economic development for North East India through the Look East policy from a perspective of people living in Mizoram. First of all, we shall highlight some essentials of India's Look East policy and then we shall see the problems of economic development in the North East from its socio-cultural and political context; and finally, we shall identify certain sectors which need to be regenerated in the context of this new economic venture.

Dynamics of India's Look East Policy

The Look East policy was launched in 1992 just after the end of the Cold War, following the collapse of the Soviet Union.[4] After the start of liberalization, it was a very strategic policy decision taken by the Central government in its foreign policy. To quote Prime Minister Manmohan Singh, "It was also a strategic shift in India's vision of the world and India's place in the evolving global economy."[5] The policy was given an initial thrust with the then Prime Minister Narasimha Rao visiting China, Japan, South Korea, Vietnam and Singapore and India becoming a summit level partner of ASEAN and getting involved in some regional initiatives (e.g. BIMSTEC, *Ganga Mekong* Cooperation), and lately becoming a member of the East Asia Summit (EAS) in December, 2005.

(a) Geo-political[6] Trends in South Asia

In order to fully grasp the dynamics of the Look East policy and understand why it entails strategic elements, one has to observe the geopolitical trends in South Asia. The geopolitical environment of a country or region changes from time to time. Since the beginning of the 1990s with the end of the Cold War and the disintegration of the Soviet Union, the global bipolar geopolitical structure has disappeared, changing the geopolitical structure of the Asia-Pacific region. The War on Terror has again reshaped the structure with the military dominance of the USA. Geopolitically speaking, Asia has become very important after the September 11, 2001.[7]

India's interaction with ASEAN in the Cold War era was very limited. India declined to get associated with ASEAN in the 1960s when full membership was offered even before the grouping was formed. With fast changing geopolitical trends in Asia and the formulation of the Look East policy, India had started giving this region due importance in her foreign policy.

(b) Indo-ASEAN Relations

India became a sectoral dialogue partner with ASEAN in 1992, a full dialogue partner in 1995, a member of the ASEAN Regional Forum (ARF) in 1996, and a summit level partner on par with China, Japan and Korea in 2002. The first India-ASEAN Business Summit was held at New Delhi in October 2002. The then Prime Minister A.B. Vajpayee addressed this meet and since then this business summit has become an annual feature before the India-ASEAN Summits, as a forum for networking and exchange of business experiences between policy makers and business leaders from ASEAN and India.[8]

(c) India's Agreement with ASEAN

Four India-ASEAN summits, first in 2002 at Phnom Penh (Cambodia), second in 2003 at Bali (Indonesia), third in 2004 at Vientiane (Laos) and fourth in 2005 at Kuala Lumpur (Malaysia) have taken place till date. According to Nityanand Deva, the following agreements have been entered into with ASEAN:[9]

(*i*) A Framework Agreement on Comprehensive Economic Cooperation (for establishing an FTA in a time frame of 10 years) was concluded in Bali in 2003.

(*ii*) An ASEAN-India Joint Declaration for Cooperation to Combat International Terrorism has been adopted.

(*iii*) India has acceded to the Treaty of Amity and Cooperation (TAC) in 2003, on which ASEAN was formed initially (in 1967).

(*iv*) Agreement on "India-ASEAN Partnership for Peace, Progress and Shared Prosperity" was signed at the 3rd ASEAN-India Summit in Nov 2004.

(*v*) Setting up of Entrepreneurship Development Centres in ASEAN member states – Cambodia, Myanmar, Laos and Vietnam. (The one in Laos is already functional).

(d) India's Proposals

The following proposals were announced by the Prime Minister at the 4th ASEAN-India Summit:[10]

(*i*) Setting up centres for English Language Training (ELT) in Cambodia, Laos, Myanmar and Vietnam.

(*ii*) Setting up a tele-medicine and tele-education network for Cambodia, Myanmar, Laos and Vietnam.

(*iii*) Organising special training courses for diplomats from ASEAN countries.

(*iv*) Organising an India-ASEAN Technology Summit in 2006.

(*v*) Organising education fairs and road shows in ASEAN countries.

(*vi*) Conducting an India-ASEAN IT Ministerial and Industry Forum in 2006.

The ASEAN region has an abundance of natural resources and significant technological skills. These provide a natural base for the integration between ASEAN and India both in trade and investment. The present level of bilateral trade with ASEAN of nearly US $ 18 billion is reportedly increasing by about 25 per cent per year. India had hoped to reach the level of US $ 30 billion by 2007. India is also improving its relations with the help of other policy decisions, like offers of lines of credit, better connectivity through air (open skies policy) and rail and road links.[11]

Problems of Economic Development in North East India
(With special reference to the tribal people)

North East India comprises of seven states, often known as the "Seven Sisters" of the Indian Republic. They are Assam, Meghalaya, Arunachal Pradesh, Nagaland, Manipur, Mizoram and Tripura. The region has an area of 2,45,993 square kilometers. Many tribes and ethnic groups with diverse cultures, traditions and languages, inhabit the region. According to Wati Longchar, about four hundred tribes live in North East India, speaking hundreds of different languages and dialects.[12] Racially they all belong to the Mongoloid stock and are estimated to have arrived in the region during the past three or four hundered years.[13] Most of the hill tribals are Christians excepting the tribes in Arunachal Pradesh who have been protected from Christian missionaries for many decades. The tribal people of North East India have experienced a state of alienation throughout their history. They suffered from the British invaders, and they continue to suffer at the hands of the dominant communities of India today. A number of factors, most of them products of the attitudes and policies of the dominant groups, have contributed to the tribals' alienation.

(a) Geographical and Political Isolation

The whole of the North East is geographically isolated from the rest of the country. It is linked to mainland India through a narrow passage in North Bengal of about thirty kilometers breadth, popularly known as the 'chicken's neck'. North East India has a long international boundary approximately 5,000 kilometers long. To the north are—China, Tibet, and Bhutan; Myanmar is in the east and south, and Bangladesh in the west. Because of its geographical location, North East India is politically a very sensitive region. It has been one of the most strategic regions of India. In terms of racial identity, the tribal people of North East India are isolated from mainland India.

The inclusion and merging of the whole North Eastern Region with the rest of the country, politically speaking, is quite recent, notwithstanding the fact that India has hardly seen political unification in her 3,000 years of existence as a civilization. Apart form Assam, which was included at the time of Independence, the states of Nagaland, Mizoram and Meghalaya were rarely part of mainland India for most of their history. Manipur and Tripura which had been princely states were rarely a part of political India. Arunachal Pradesh was beyond the outer line of British India at the beginning of the 20th century, and Sikkim too was not a part of political India. These areas were then made a part of India during the British rule when British colonial authorities annexed traditionally separate border countries into the Indian Territory to form a buffer between their colony and external powers. After independence in 1947, extension of the Indian state and political apparatus has been a challenge. The North East Region became increasingly isolated.

The isolation of the North Eastern States had begun earlier as a result of British imperialism, when the region was cut off from its traditional trading partners (Bhutan, Myanmar and Indo-China). Soon it became a captive market for mainstream Asia. Today, the North Eastern States are represented by a meagre 25 seats out of a total of 543 seats in the Indian Parliament (Lok Sabha) which is, by any standard, politically insignificant. This has kept the region politically and culturally separate from the rest of India. As for religion, a majority of the population follow Hinduism, although the region is primarily a stronghold of Christianity in India.

It is the general opinion that due to such factors, discontent followed by demands for independence have characterized much of the region for many decades, and are still being raised by disparate groups including the Nagas in Nagaland, and the ULFA and Bodos in Assam. The increasing rise of insurgency in the region especially after the Sino-Indian war of 1962, came to be a major security concern for the Indian government.

(b) Assimilation

It comes as no surprise that the tribes of the North East have become victims of assimilation of varied kinds. This may be social, economic, religious, cultural and likewise. The British had adopted a policy whereby the hill areas were protected from outside interference. The policy prevented non-tribals from interference in the affairs of the tribes, and separated the tribal areas from the purview of normal administration.[14] As a result, the tribal people remained cut off from the rest of the population.[15]

(c) Insurgencies

What accounts for the frequent unrest and insurrections that are led by armed and organized groups in the North East then and now is largely attributed to the failure of the Government of India to address their agony and ambition. The tribal people became exceedingly discontented, and developed a sense of mistrust and doubt towards the dominant communities and the government they represented. All these factors with their apprehension about losing their land and identity have contributed to the tendency for tribals to take up arms and struggle for political separation. In the case of Mizoram, it was the miserable experience of hunger following the *mautam* famine, and the government failed to respond to their problem.[16]

Some contextual thinkers among Mizos argue that it was revolutionary movements that turned the North East of India into one of the most troubled and disturbed areas of the country.[17] The government acted to maintain law and order in this situation by deploying thousands of para-military and armed forces in the region. Armed encounters between the Indian army and the undergrounds brought immense suffering to the people of the North East. The people who suffer the most were the innocent villagers, women, and children. In most cases, it was the passion for liberation from their impoverished condition of life that compelled the tribals of the North East to take up arms and demand political separation. This clearly indicates that in the context of the region, economic problems have been the root cause behind violent movements. As K. Thanzauva suggests, economic transformation must become the primary agenda for both the churches and the state governments in North East India.[18]

(d) Issue of Economic Development

The Constitution of India makes several provisions for the development of the tribals. However, the tribal people in North East India have been neglected. As L.H. Lalpekhlua rightly says, though the country's Five Year Plan began in 1951, it was not until the Fourth Five Year Plan was implemented (1966-71) that any substantial effort was made to elevate the economic status of the tribal people of North East India.[19] The tribal-inhabited hill states of the North East are now receiving from the central government funds for both planned and non-planned expenditures. Besides these, the states of the North East have also received a number of centrally financed schemes meant for rural development and others. In spite of improvement in certain sectors, however, a majority of the tribal people of North East India are still economically very backward and dependent.

As already mentioned, the present system of development programmes for tribal areas in North East India are sponsored by the central government. In this system, planning is done under an elaborate structure of central guidelines and approvals, and the government controls all the planning and development administration. To put in K. Thanzauva'a phrase, "people become objects or recipients, not the subject of development."[20] L.H. Lalpekhlua also comments thus:

> Exclusion of the people from participation in the development process has had very negative consequences within the implementation process, often leading to misappropriation of developments funds. When government officials control the whole direction and administration of the development schemes, the poor villagers lack both knowledge about the details of development programmes and an institutional forum in which to express their views and inspiration. By taking the advantage of their absence, development officials, together with the local politicians and the rural rich, often monopolize the whole development process. As a result, millions of rupees expended on rural development benefit mainly those charged with delivery of policies and the rural rich.[21]

Furthermore, in most states of North East India, development activities are highly politicized and huge amounts of money granted for the economic development of the people are drained off for political purposes. Politicians in power, in their bid to survive in electoral politics, often misappropriate development funds to further their political ambitions. Such politicization of development schemes not only cripples development work, but also fosters corruption in the region.[22]

The North East Region is known for its unique culture, handicrafts, martial arts, and scenic beauty. It has major problems including unemployment, drug addiction, corruption, HIV/AIDS and lack of infrastructure. Since the beginning of the economic liberalisation and privatisation in the early 1990s, studies have shown that this region is lagging behind the other states in terms of development. The North East Region is officially recognized as a part of special category of states. Therefore, some agencies or forums have been established to take care of their socio-economic cultural problems. The North East Council (NEC) was constituted in 1971 as the nodal agency for the economic and social development of the North Eastern States, including Sikkim. The North Eastern Development Finance Corporation Ltd was incorporated on August 9, 1995 and the Ministry of Development of North Eastern Region (DONER) was set up in September 2001.

Economic Development through Look East Policy: A Mizo Perspective

All the countries in the world experience the process of globalisation, including the state of Mizoram.[23] It has envisaged the Look East Policy to be its turning point in the field of economic development.[24] As the second phase of India's Look East Policy has a new dimension for the development of India's remote North East, Mizoram and the other states in the region will facilitate economic development by increasing their connectivity to the outside word. Instead of trying to isolate the North East from external influences, as it had done in the past, the central government is also now recognizing the importance of opening it up for commercial linkages with south-east Asia. Therefore, the Look East Policy has many things to perform for the upliftment of economic situation of the people in the area. Thus, in his address to the 10th Session of the Fifth Mizoram Legislative Assembly (on March 13, 2007), Governor M.M. Lakhera confidently said:

> Mizoram which is presently a peripheral state of the country, devoid of any reliable transport linkage, shall be transformed into a corridor to the east. In ardent pursuance to the "Look East Policy" the Government of India has agreed to take up two major projects which will transform the economy of Mizoram.[25]

This is a great promise to the people of Mizoram that it would be transformed into a 'corridor to the east'. Keeping in mind this great speech, we shall analyse some steps needed to be taken towards its realization.

(a) Agriculture and Allied Sector

Despite its low yields and the acceleration in deforestation, jhum cultivation continues to be the major practice of the people in Mizoram. There should be special programmes in transfer of appropriate technology from the laboratory to the field. As per 1991 Census, a majority of the population, *i.e.* 61.37 per cent are cultivators who are engaged in agricultural activities.[26] A plan should be evolved for transforming the agriculture landscape from a homestead to plantation mode preferably through the cluster method. Government or non-governmental agencies should support production, marketing and certification of organic products.

Value addition facilities at strategic locations could be set up. Marketing tie-ups may be arranged and subsidy may even be released for making products competitive at the initial stages. Bamboo resources of the region are one example, which could be harnessed using this approach. The following programmes, recommended by the NEC 11th Plan Working Group, could be considered for tapping the opportunity.[27]

(*a*) Tissue Culture Laboratories need further support both for agriculture and horticulture crops.

(*b*) Improvement of traditional method of cultivation and sustainable crop production technology.

(*c*) Organized marketing system.

(*d*) Setting up agro-based industries in the region.

(*e*) Improvement of post-harvest technology.

(*f*) Integrated agriculture programme has to be taken-up for enhancement of food production.

(*g*) Selected crops of short duration with high return have to be encouraged for plantation on cluster basis.

(*h*) Farmers and officers of North East States should be imparted training with latest technologies.

(*i*) Livestock and dairy development, control of diseases and production of livestock feed.

(*j*) Integrated fish farming (fish combined with livestock) can generate more income to the farmers.

(*k*) NEC to support innovative and exotic products and related technology.

(b) Forest and Environment

The type of forest found in Mizoram comprises mainly tropical wet evergreen forest, semi-evergreen forest, moist deciduous forests and sub-mountain forests. The forests support a variety of flora and fauna with rich gene pool, few species of which are endemic in origin. More than 400 medicinal plants have been reported from Mizoram of which 62 are recorded as new medicinal plants and 64 are categorized as threatened species. Over 22 species of Bamboo have been reported from the state, and 14 per cent of the growing stock in the country is available in Mizoram.[28] And 9 species of cane have also been recorded from the forests of Mizoram.[29] While the state has very rich forest and natural resources, the productivity of the resources is quite low. There has been very little research to evolve technologies and practices suiting local conditions to increase productivity. The NEC could be approached to commission an inventory of bio-resources including taxonomic and ecological studies on flora and fauna. The NEC could also extend support for production and marketing of exotic and medicinal plants and jatropha. The degradation of the environment caused by unregulated and haphazard mining and mineral extraction will need to be tackled.[30]

(c) Humanpower Development Sector

The outlay for this sector needs to be enhanced as it has vast potential for regional programmes. For example, capacity building will need to be done for specific areas such as biotechnology, organic farming, veterinary science, patent awareness,[31] sports which will complement and tap the core competencies of the region. Capacity building for firming and strengthening the cluster approach development can be supported. The existing cooperative societies' mechanism should be strengthened to further improve its efficacy and influence in each of the states.[32] Institutes of excellence within and outside the region can be identified for training deserving students in job-oriented courses. In the handloom and handicraft sector, courses for fashion design and fabric value addition could be set up in some of the state capitals. To further deepen the impact and widen the scope, existing universities and colleges could be financially supported to include these subjects in their curriculum.[33]

A policy under the aegis of NEREC could be evolved for channeling academically underperforming students from conventional courses to vocational schools. The Industrial Training Institute (ITI) needs to be strengthened and its curriculum needs to be revised.[34] This should be coordinated with a long-term industrial policy, which will generate employment opportunities at the appropriate time. The state may facilitate the setting up of engineering and medical colleges in the region. Teaching departments on bio-resource development, tourism, cultural and peace studies, languages of neighboring countries, could be set up in the university.

(d) Science and Technology

Information Technology is yet another area which has a tremendous scope in the region due to the absence of spatial constraints. A dedicated bandwidth through an independent Internet gateway could be considered. Updated and valid socio-economic database banks should be created for use by the state as a tool for developmental planning of the region. In this connection, a GIS resource map could be prepared for the entire region with NEC funding. NESAC could be mandated as the coordinator to help obviate duplication and to ensure synergies amongst all states. IT assistance and computer education programmes at school and college levels should be intensified. NEC could facilitate provision of OFC backbone to cover all the states. The hardware and software facilities could be updated and modernized through NEC assistance.

(e) Tourism, Industries and Banking

Tourism[35]

A regional plan could also be evolved for the Tourism Sector where existing tourism activities and tourists arrivals can be enhanced by assisting genuine and creditable tourism operators and hotel owners. The state government can also create selective infrastructure and help in promotion and capacity building. Circuit development possesses ample scope for regional cooperation and in the Eleventh Plan tourist products evolved and supported through NEC funding should be compatible with the objectives for producing world-class circuits. Publicity costs for promotion of specific destinations and circuits could be borne either by the Mizoram state or NEC. The State must support participation in domestic and international fairs. Sponsoring appropriate curriculum in the Mizoram University could ensure capacity building and skills transmission. Through NEC, the Mizoram state could contemplate assisting the development of heritage and cultural circuits. Tourism could be declared as an industry to gain access to subsidies.

Industries

Outlays for this sector should be appropriately increased. Mizoram could enter into a tie up with agencies like ILandFS (Infrastructure Leasing and Financial Services Ltd.) for product development and forming of Special Purpose Vehicles that the state could utilize for attracting external investment. The SPINE schemes should be continued albeit with improved guidelines to plug loopholes, increase opportunities for generating local employment, and expedite industrialization of the region. Financing of value addition projects and technological assistance for ginger or grape growers would be a catalyst for industrializing rural areas. The handloom and handicraft sector, hitherto neglected, should be identified as a thrust area in the 11th Plan. Existing sericulture and seed farms languishing due to resource constraints of the state governments, could be reviewd from NEC funds.[36]

In the context of Look East Policy, it would be imperative for the NEC to support and supplement ongoing Central Government schemes such as ASIDE (Assistance to States for Development of Export Infrastructure and other Activities) and EDF (Export Development Fund). To achieve fast results, the mission mode for promoting industrial activities needs to be encouraged. A formal patent regime should be activated for the region to protect ethnic and traditional design and fabric. Infrastructure along existing and potential trade routes to neighboring foreign countries should be funded to activate border trade.[37]

Banking

Micro-credit mechanism would need to be improved particularly in under-banked and rural areas. The state, with NEC funding, could manage coordination between financial institutions based in the region so that overlapping and duplication are avoided. In view of the traditional land tenure system prevailing in most of the hill states, it would be necessary to involve the landowners as stakeholders and partners in projects. Project design and capacity building particularly in accounts and book keeping, should be mandatory requirements before funding is recommended for any project to ensure return on investment and build investor and creditor confidence.[38]

(f) Transport and Communication

The partition of India severely affected the traditional trade link and economy of the people in North East India. Before the partition, Mizoram had established a certain sort of trade relations in small quantities with the people of Chittagong hill tracts and the Chittagong district. They used to sell their products—such as rice, cotton, oranges, and chilies; and in exchange they imported consumption articles like food items other than rice, and kerosene, clothing, utensils, and agricultural goods. But when the Chittagong hill tracts and the Chittagong district went to East Pakistan (*now Bangladesh*) at the time of the partition of the country, the main traditional trade route was practically closed. This had an adverse effect on the economy of the Mizo people.[39]

After the partition, the only trade links Mizo enjoyed was with the Cachar District of Assam in the north. The people had to depend upon commodities that came through the Silchar-Aizawl road link with high prices. As Animesh Ray notes, after partition, prices of commodities, which Mizoram obtained from the pre-independence Chittagong side increased six to ten times, whereas the prices of their exported commodities fell appreciably.[40] While Mizoram is producing large quantities of ginger, bananas, orange, squash, chilies, owing to lack of trade links, these articles were left to rot every year.

Lack of infrastructure in communication, transport and market access has severely hindered the economic growth of Mizoram. The whole of North East India is falling far behind the rest of the country in infrastructure facilities. This is not a mistake, but an act of negligence on the part of the Government of India. In pursuance of Look East policy, the Kaldan Transport project with a fund allocation of Rs. 7,459 million has been launched to a link up the North East Region with Sittwe port in Myanmar providing a much needed access to the sea for this region. The other project coming up is Triangular Project which will connect Mizoram with eastern and northern Myanmar through roads connecting Rih village on the Mizoram-Myanmar border to Falam and Tiddim. The upgradation of the roads inside Myanmar will be financed by the Government of India, for which Border Road Organisation (BRO) has submitted a detailed project report to the tune of Rs. 711.47 crores.[41]

Funding of important roads could be supplemented through BOT (Build-Own–Transfer System), BOL (Build-Own-Lease), etc even in neighbouring countries such as Myanmar to link strategic markets across the borders. Railway links nearest to the state capital and beyond to international borders could be contemplated. The South Asia Free Trade Agreement (SAFTA) should be unitized to formalize the existing informal trade between the North East states and Myanmar and Bangladesh.

(e) Strengthening Civil Society

The crisis of economic liberalisation is linked with the crisis of meaning we face today in Mizoram. We must be aware that globalization, which is a market process survives because of its ability to convert all realities into commodities. Therefore, as K.C. Abraham says, in a market society, people, land, knowledge, faith, religion and politics are measured by values on the scale of money.[42] This means that those realities which refuse to assume or submit themselves to be valued in monetary terms as commonalities have no place in society. The concepts of freedom, equality, compassion, *tlawmngaihna*, and other Mizo moral and cultural values have lost their legitimacy and spiritual strength within the prevailing market principle.

In the context of the Look East policy, the significance of civil society should be seen and redefined against the process of commodification and curtailment of meaning systems. Chuauthuama, in his editorial note, entitled "Church's Look East Policy," warns his readers not to blindly welcome the policy on account of its material blessings to flow in from markets of Asian metropolitan cities. Even he cautions them not to build another Siliguri and Nepal in the state![43] Moreover, as the Look East policy brings global networks and generate new culture, it challenges us to live by the plurality of culture, demanding justice as a pre-requisite for meaningful human solidarity. Above all, the pressing need of the hour is to strengthen civil society and to preserve democratic values.

Conclusion

In conclusion, the study clearly indicates that there is a great possibility of economic development through India's Look East Policy for the whole of the North Eastern Region. The siege mentality prevalent in most of the inhabitants of the region, because of its geographical isolation, should change with the opening of windows towards various directions. In spite of all the benefits to flow in terms of economic progress, prosperity, and development, all the North Eastern States, particularly Mizoram, must keep their eyes open to see the dangers of being opened up. K. Thanzauva rightly observes that among various sections of people in our country tribals are the most unprepared group for globalisation.[44] As the state is one of the youngest and which is under special protection since the British colonial era, it has many things to do in order to compete with stronger global partners. Therefore, if the policy is to be fully implemented sooner or later, unless there is tremendous economic development in all aspects, the people in North East, and Mizoram in particular, would have no other option but to throw themselves on the bigger platform of exploitation by outsiders.

NOTES AND REFERENCES

1. Association of South-East Asian Nations (ASEAN) was formed on August 8, 1967 by Indonesia, Thailand, Philippines, Malaysia and Singapore to promote active collaboration and mutual assistance in matters of common interest in the economic, social, cultural, technical, scientific and administrative fields. Brunei joined in 1984. Vietnam was admitted as the seventh member in 1995 followed by Laos and Myanmar in 1997. Cambodia whose membership was held in abeyance because of internal strife for power was finally admitted to ASEAN on April 30, 1999. India attended the annual ASEAN meeting held in Jakarta in July 1996 for the first time with the status of a "Dialogue Partner".
2. K. Raja Reddy (ed.), *India and ASEAN: Foreign Policy Dimensions for the Twenty-First Century* (New Delhi: New Century, 2005).
3. Nityanand Deva, "India's Look-East Policy" in *IndianMBA.Com*, 1.
4. For the background reading, see Biplab Dasgupta, *Globalisation: India's Adjustment Experience* (New Delhi: Sage Publication, 2005).
5. As quoted by Nityanand Deva, "India's Look-East Policy," 2.
6. Geopolitics means the social and political relationships formed among the people or countries which live or are located in the same region or geopolitical environment. For a country, geopolitics means the international relationship between or among countries that are located in the same region, such as the inter-relationship of politics, economy, military, culture, religion and so on among those countries and people.

For more details, see Ninan Koshy, "Geo-Political Trends in South Asia" in National Council of Churches Review CXXIV/8 (September 2004): 583-589.

7. *Ibid.* 583-584.
8. The former Prime Minister A.B. Vajpayee's South-east Asian tour to participate in the ASEAN summit in Bali (Indonesia) in October 2003 marks the success of a decade-long shift in Look East policy. For more information on the PM's tour, see Sultan Shahin, "India's 'Look East' Policy Pays Off", in *Asia Times* (October 11, 2003). See also C.S. Batra, *Globalisation of Financial Markets* (New Delhi: Deep & Deep Publications, 2004).
9. Nityanand Deva, "India's look-East Policy", 2.
10. As cited by Nityanand Deva, Ibid.
11. Ibid., 5.
12. Wati Longchar, *An Emerging Asian Theology: Tribal Theology - Issues, Method and Perspective* (Jorhat: Tribal Study Centre, ETC, 2000), 14.
13. Frederick S. Downs, *History of Christianity in India (Volume V, part 5): North East India in the Nineteenth and Twentieth Centuries* (Bangalore: Church History Association, 1992), 1.
14. Lalsangkima Pachuau, *Ethnic Identity and Christianity: A Socio-Historical and Missiological Study of Christianity in North East India With Special Reference to Mizoram* (Frankfurt am Main: Peter Lang, 2002)
15. K. Thanzauva, *Theology of Community*, 18.
16. L.H. Lalpekhlua, *Contextual Theology: A Tribal Perspective* (Delhi: ISPCK, 2007), 59-60. On October 30, 1965, the MNF, formerly *MNFF* (Mizo National Famine Front) submitted a Memorandum to the Prime Minister of India demanding "the creation of MIZORAM, a free and sovereign state". The MNF declared the independence of Mizoram and began an armed revolt on the midnight of February 28, 1966, taking all major towns except for the army (Assam Rifles) headquarters at the capital. See, Lalsangkima Pachuau, *Ethnic Identity and Christianity*, 52. For a wider reading, Rashmi Akhoury, "Poverty Eradication: A Challenge in India", in *Poverty and Sustainable Development: Third World Perspectives* Vol. II (Delhi: Abhijeet Publications, 2005), 525-541.
17. L.H. Lalpekhlua, *Contextual Theology*, 59.
18. Lalsangkima Pachuau, *Ethnic Identity and Christianity*,33
19. L.H. Lalpekhlua, *Contextual Theology*, 63.
20. K. Thanzauva, *Theology of Community*, 39.
21. Ibid., 65.
22. Ibid., 66.
23. Priyanka Priadarshini Behera, "Globalizing Tribal Economy", in *Globalization: Myth and Reality* (New Delhi: Concept Publishing

Company, 2004), 224.

24. For more refer V.S. Lalrinawma, *Mizo Ethos: Changes and Challenges* (Aizawl: Mizoram Publication Board, 2005).
25. Mizoram to become "Corridor to the East" in *Newslink* (March 14, 2007, Aizawl).
26. *Socio-Economic Review Mizoram 2000-'01* (Aizawl: Directorate of Economics & Statistics), 31.
27. See *Report of Working Group on North Eastern Council and related issues for the Eleventh Five Year Plan* (August 10, 2006), 4.
28. *Cf.* P.A. Koli, *Economic Development and Environment Issues* (New Delhi: Serials Publication, 2005).
29. *Socio-Economic Review Mizoram 2000-'01*, 47. See also R. Rozika, *Medicinal Plants* (Aizawl: Medicinal Plants Board, 2005).
30. *Report of Working Group on North Eastern Council*, 4.
31. To understand significance of patents, see D. Samuel Jesupatham, "Capitalism, Recent Economic Policies, Poverty and Working Class Struggle in India", in *Christianity, Wealth and Poverty: Indian Perspective* (Delhi: NCCI/ISPCK, 2004),120-121.
32. Ibid., 5.
33. *Cf.* Ishwar C. Dhingra, *The Indian Economy: Environment and Policy* (New Delhi: Sultan Chand & Sons, 2006), 116-142.
34. Ibid. At present there is one ITI in Mizoram managed by the State Government with a total intake Capacity of 300. The Institute offered training courses in 14 different trades of which 11 are Engineering trades and 3 are non-engineering trades with an objective of raising the quantity and quality of industrial production and creating employment opportunities for the educated youths. *Socio-Economic Review Mizoram 2000-'01*, 83.
35. For more details regarding development, prospect, and problems of tourism in Mizoram, see Lianzela, *Economy of Mizoram* (Aizawl: Mizoram Publication Board, 1998), 132-140.
36. *Report of Working Group on North Eastern Council*, 6-7.
37. Ibid.
38. Ibid.
39. Lalpekhlua, *Contextual Theology*, 69.
40. Animesh Ray, *Mizoram Dynamics of Change* (Calcutta: Pearl Publishers, 1982), 189.
41. *Newslink* (March 14, 2007, Aizawl).
42. K.C. Abraham, "Towards a New Political Culture in India", in *National Council of Churches Review* CXXIV/4 (April 2004): 265.
43. Chuauthuama, "Kohhran 'Look East Policy' " in *Didakhe* XXXVI/2 (March-April, 2007): 2.
44. K. Thanzauva, *Transforming Theology: A Theological Basis for Social Transformation* (Bangalore: Asian Trading Corporation, 2002), 144.

Section IV

Conflicts in North East India: Hindering Development

Conflict and Insurgency Historical Perspective

THREAT TO SECURITY AND DEVELOPMENT

Lt. Gen. J. R. Mukherjee

This paper seeks to examine insurgency as a threat to security and development in the North East India (NEI) from a historical perspective, and to arrive at the possibilities of problem resolution. Seventy per cent of the region is mountains/hills covered with forests dissected by major rivers, segregating valleys, such that ethnic groups lived in isolation, retaining their primordial value systems of 'tribe-land-autonomy'. The Brahmaputra valley forms the core of this extremely rich region, attracting migrating hordes, making it a melting pot for cultures, being a transitional area between high Asia, Indo-China and the Gangetic—Brahmaputra plains. It has a multitude of ethnic groups who are now competing for resources, leading to inter ethnic conflict. The region's history shows that conflicts and insurgency have been prevalent frequently due to these reasons, and they include the conflict between tradition and modernity.

Sources indicate the earliest inhabitants to be of Austric stock, and a limited Dravidian and Negrito presence. From the BC period till date, there were waves of Mongoloid migrations who established control over the east. Their descendants are the Bodo group of tribes found all over the north east. The Bodos established the Kingdom of Kamrupa, with the capital at Pragjyotishpura, extending over the east. Aryan migrations then spilled east and overwhelmed local groups in the region. The Bodos, however, managed to retain control over parts of the region.

Between the 12th and 14th century Kamrupa disintegrated, with Kamtapur, the Mech and Chutiya Kingdoms coming into being.

Manipur and Tripura had also become independent. The Turk-Afghan Sultanate conquered Bihar and Bengal, and they repeatedly tried to conquer Kamrupa but were defeated–yet many of the invading Muslims settled in lower Assam and parts of Cooch Behar. There were also further Mongoloid migrations through Myanmar into present day Mizoram, Manipur and Tripura by the Kuki-Chin group of tribes from Chin Hills in Myanmar. The Ahoms, a Myanmar Shan tribe, originally from China, also migrated into upper Assam, gained control and came into conflict with the Bodo groups. In the 16th and 17th centuries lower Assam was invaded by the Mughals from Bengal—they gained control of parts of Assam, till their ouster by the Ahoms. Groups of them, however, settled in lower Assam in the existing Muslim pockets. The Ahoms gained control over most of Assam with the exception of certain Bodo pockets and the hill tribes, who frequently raided Ahom and Bodo areas. They were kept under check through non-interference in their affairs and punitive expeditions.

By the 18th century, due to continuous strife, the population of the NE was denuded, agriculture adversely affected and heavy taxation led to a great deal of discontent. Further, the Ahom rulers persecuted the locals who had turned to Vaishnavism. The people launched a large-scale insurrection, which was most powerful in Tinsukia, Dibrugarh and Sibsagar districts. The Ahoms appealed to the Myanmar King for help. He responded promptly, assisted in quelling the rebellion with extreme ruthlessness, and left Assam with many thousands dead, and took large numbers of slavers. The 18th and 19th centuries were also periods of misrule and civil war amongst the Ahoms on matters of succession. This resulted in the Myanmarese again being invited to settle disputes with consequent mass killing. Some Ahom chronicles indicate that from the 16th to the 19th century Assam was depopulated extensively. The Myanmarese occupied Assam for two years and was also at war with the Manipuris around the same time. Areas of internal strife in Assam then were the same as today - Tinsukia, Dibrugarh and Sibsagar with support and sanctuary being offered by the Nagas and tribes in Myanmar Naga Hills. This remains the hotbed of ULFA activity today as the Marans and Muttocks, who were the core of the Moamaria rebellions, also form the core of the ULFA cadres.

In the 19th century the British entered Assam to help the Ahoms quell the civil war/insurgency, and then for pushing out the

Myanmarese. After defeating the Myanmarese in 1824, the British progressively took control of the region. They imposed an administration that supported imperial priorities and objectives of mercantile capitalism to extract raw materials and wealth out of the colony. They developed rail, road and river infrastructure accordingiy towards Chittagong and Calcutta. Tea plantations, coal, iron, other minerals and oil extraction were started. As Assam had been depopulated, labour was imported from Bengal, Bihar and Uttar Pradesh, clerical/lower supervisory staff from Bengal, and migration encouraged for cultivating land.

As the hill tribes were considered heathens, fierce warriors and potential threats and they frequently raided British facilities, the British attempted to subjugate them but found the process too costly, and so gave them partial autonomy and set about to civilise them through conversion to Christianity. To prevent depredations, they inducted Kuki-Chin tribals from Chin Hills in Burma, and settled them as a buffer between the Nagas/Mizos and their colonies in Cachar and Manipur, thereby creating animosity between the tribes. To isolate the hill tribes from the politics of the plains, learnt bitterly from the experience of the 1857 uprising, they debarred migration of the plains' people into the hills and imposed what is today called the 'Inner Line', which ran along the base of the hills. Having brought in the Kuki-Chin tribes, they drew up the administrative boundaries on the principle of 'divide and rule', as a result of which communities were segregated by boundaries.

By the 18th century, Nepal's warring clans had come together under one rule. The Nepalese then attempted to colonise Kumaon, Garhwal, Sikkim and a part of Tibet. A number of their soldiers and followers then migrated and settled in these areas in large numbers. These were then almost of British protectorate status. This led to conflict and subjugation of the Nepalese by the British. The British were so impressed by their bravery that they started recruiting them in large numbers, and then used them as the primary force to subdue the NE. This involved stationing Nepalese troops all over, and their ultimately settling down in these areas.

The British, due to a perceived Russian and Chinese threat, adopted a forward deployment policy in the 19th and 20th centuries, and accordingly subjugated Tibet, Nepal, Bhutan, Sikkim and declared them protectorates to create a buffer zone. As Arunachal bordered

Tibet, they subjugated Arunachal. They gave these tribes limited autonomy as well and an 'Inner Line' was imposed.

Migration of population, thereby engineering serious demographic change, is an issue of concern. In the early 20th century, when Bengal was partitioned and Assam was included in East Bengal, the majority of East Bengal migrants were Muslims. After the grant of provincial autonomy in 1935, the Muslim League was favoured by the British, and with Siadullah as the Chief Minister of Assam, immigration of Muslims into Assam, from East Bengal, was encouraged. This was all the more so because the Muslim League prior to Partition had demanded that undivided Assam be included in East Pakistan. Unfortunately, after Independence, this trend was allowed to continue, with the majority of migration being from the then East Pakistan. In 1971, again, there was a major refugee exodus from East Pakistan into eastern India, the majority of whom never returned, which ultimately led to the 1971 Indo-Pak war. Thereafter, consequent to major agitations, particularly in Assam, immigration reduced but did not stop, primarily due to vote bank politics, wherein politicians for political gain encouraged this illegal migration. The effects of this migration are that Tripura, which had a tribal majority is now a tribal minority state with a consequent long drawn insurgent movement by the tribals; Sikkim which earlier had a Lepcha and Bhutia majority now has a Nepalese majority; Assam today, has at least 30 per cent of its population who are Bangladeshi immigrants, with another 8-10 per cent from Bengal, Bihar, UP and Rajasthan, which has changed its demographic profile and given birth to the Assam (ULFA), Bodo (NDFB and BLT), Karbi and Dimasa insurgencies. Assam now also has a minority Islamic fundamentalist movement; in North Bengal it gave rise to the Naxalite (Left extremist), Gurkha (GNLF) and Kamtapuri (KLO) movements; in Meghalaya it gave birth to the Khasi (HNLC) movement and the anti-non Khasi agitations; and in other hill states harsh anti-immigration policies.

The partition of eastern India, with long existing infrastructure passing through the then East Pakistan, disrupted traditional and British era trading patterns. East Pakistan being hostile, no routes were available except through the Siliguri corridor to the rest of India. With extremely indifferent communications, Chittagong was no longer available and Calcutta, the trade hub, was out on a limb, it became uneconomical to trade either with the rest of India or with the outside world through Calcutta. Consequently, both Calcutta's industry (which lost the East Bengal raw material and market) and Assam's (then comprising the entire North-East less Arunachal, Manipur, Tripura, Sikkim and North Bengal) fell into decay. Artificial boundaries created between India and Burma split the Naga, Kuki-Chin-Mizo tribes and the Meities (Manipuris), coupled with pitting ethnic groups against each other, and segregation of the hill people from the plainsmen, resulted in present day problems of Naga, Mizo and Meitei demands for uniting their homelands and sowed the seeds of ethnic sub-nationalism and strife.

The freedom struggle, partition, political changes, including the two World Wars and participation of people from the north-east in the same, the initial British defeat in World War II by the Japanese diluting the myth of British invincibility; the conjoint effort to defeat the Japanese, and promises of Indian independence, all played a significant role in shaping political views of the opinion makers in India and the NE region. Politically aware hill tribes, scared of assimilation into either the Hindu or Muslim homeland for fear of being overwhelmed, demanded freedom from the British and strengthened their determination to fight for it, if necessary. Independence, with weak and inexperienced leadership and administration, coupled with communal violence and a bad economic situation in the NE consequent to Partition, contributed along with the other factors to create a difficult situation. The British Forward Policy in trying to bring areas of Arunachal (NEFA) under direct control, and independent India continuing with the same policy, brought India into direct confrontation with the Chinese who also claimed these areas. The socialist movements and their success in Russia and China automatically influenced dissenters from the north-east into their fold. Chinese irritation with India over border disputes resulted in their giving wholehearted support to such dissenting groups, which included insurgents from Naga and Mizo Hills and Manipur.

The late '50s saw the start of the Naga insurgency and commitment of security forces in the Naga Hills. The Meitei insurgency started at almost the same time, with the Lushai (Mizo) Hills insurgency starting a few years later. The insurgencies were sustained for long periods due to external support and power politics, public approbation and the prevailing subversive environment all over South-East Asia coupled with poor governance. India's quarrel with

China led to the Indo-China War of '62. Western support to India against China only strengthened China's determination to help the Indian insurgent groups. India's antagonism to Pakistan gave Pakistan the resolve to support these groups through East Pakistan joining hands with China.

India's subsequent alliance with Russia, who had fallen out with China during the Cold War brought the West clandestinely into the fray against India. There was thus no dearth of external and environmental support to the above insurgencies. Though after Mao's death China has always claimed to have cut off this support, circumstances indicate that whenever we have annoyed China there has been an upsurge of insurgency, and whenever we have pleased them, insurgency has gone on a low key. Pakistan and subsequently Bangladesh, especially after the death of Sheikh Mujibur-Rehman have always supported insurgencies in the north-east. After the Naga, Mizo and Meitei insurgencies, we have seen the birth of insurgency in Tripura, Assam, Arunachal and finally in North Bengal and Meghalaya. Let us now analyse the insurgency situation in the states of the NE.

Assam

Undivided Assam, encompassing almost the entire NE, has been progressively split up into smaller states. It has access to all north-eastern areas which makes it the core of the region. Assam's population as per the 2001 census was 2,66,84,070 and has: 67.13 per cent Hindus, 28.48 per cent Muslims, 2.4 per cent Christians, 0.8 per cent Budhists, 1.8 per cent Sikhs. Assam's ethnic break-up is broadly: Assamese of Aryan origin 9 per cent, Assamese of Ahom origin 10 per cent, Assamese Muslims (pre-1901) 6 per cent, Mongoloid tribals including Bodos 12 per cent, Manipuris 2 per cent, Nepalese 2 per cent, Tea Tribes (Adivasis) 15 per cent, Bangladeshi Muslims 22 per cent, Bangladeshi Hindus 17 per cent, labour class from other parts of India 3 per cent.

Assam has a multitude of ethnic groups demanding autonomy due to socio-economic deprivation. Immigrants have swamped the state and migration, while reduced, continues. Today its indigenous ethnic groups (400-500 years old or more) constitute only about 35 to 40 per cent of its population. Whereas earlier it was predominantly Hindu, it now has 28 per cent Muslims. It still has a colonial-pattern economy - it continues to be mainly a primary-product-export region and a market for finished goods from other states. Assam has been repeatedly balkanised to create the neighbouring hill states, with each of whom it has problems—its people are not welcome in these states for fear of demographic change. While well-endowed with natural resources, the state lacks industry and markets, and has tenuous lines of communication with the rest of India. In spite of being the hub of the region, it has got embroiled in insurgency and strife due to neglect and mal-administration.

Assam insurgency has its roots in the AASU movement of 1973. The AASU felt that without agitation, the government would not listen to its demands. The movement started in Sibsagar and spread like wildfire. In 1979, hardliners of the AASU created a military wing called ULFA, with the moderates forming a political party now called AGP. The ULFA organised itself with the help of the NSCN, the ISI and DGFI, creating a Robin Hood image by carrying out social work, and simultaneously organising itself into an insurgent group. Simultaneously, the AASU started agitations on immigration and connected issues. Attempts by the Election Commissioner and the Assam government to start identification of illegal immigrants and their deportation were opposed by those with vested interests. Talks were held between the AASU and the central government. The AASU's demands included that illegal immigrants be identified on the basis of the National Register of Citizens of 1951 and electoral rolls of 1952; all others be deported and further immigration be prevented. AASU efforts failed, as the central government would agree only to a post -1971 cut-off date. The AASU started a blockade of the Siliguri corridor, continuous agitation, coupled with ethnic and communal riots. The central government finally signed the Assam Accord in 1985, agreeing to March 25, 1971 as the cut-off date coinciding with the proclamation of independence by freedom fighters of Bangladesh. Elections were then held, and the AGP came into power. The Accord did not meet the aspirations of the hardliners - there was also no progress on the implementation of the Accord or on identification or deportation of illegal migrants. From 1988 onwards, ULFA took control over Assam, and launched a terror campaign with killings galore. In 1990, the Army was called in and the situation was brought under partial control. Again in a few months, the Army had to be called in to resume operations against the ULFA. This continued till 1995, when it was felt that the Army could be withdrawn. As the authorities had failed to address the basic issue of identification and deportation of illegal migrants or improvement of the economic situation, there was a revival of insurgency and the Army was redeployed to execute CI operations. The ULFA initially head-quartered itself in Assam. However as a result of continuous pressure from the Army and the police it shifted to Bangladesh where it is located today. Media reports based on official releases by various agencies of the Indian government, my own experiences and reading on the issue indicate that the ULFA is funded through large-scale extortion carried out in Assam and through large business enterprises that it has set up in Bangladesh with the help of the ISI and DGFI. Its leadership leads a life of luxury in Bangladesh and is coerced by the ISI and Bangladeshi intelligence to do their bidding.

It needs to be noted that it has always been East Pakistan's (and subsequently Bangladesh's) philosophy of 'Lebensraum', to encourage large-scale immigration that would result in a demographic change and engineer the entire NE to secede to Bangladesh. With Bangladesh supporting the ULFA, it would therefore be apparent that the ULFA has lost sight of its original anti-immigration philosophy and the 'protector of the people's image, and is now merely a tool in the hands of the foreign powers to wage a proxy war against India in Assam. While insurgency was kept under control by the Army, the ULFA, whose bases were in Bangladesh, Myanmar and Bhutan, was under pressure from Bangladesh and Pakistan to step up their operations particularly during the Kargil war and thereafter. Diplomatic parleys were therefore held with the RBG, who agreed to throw the ULFA out of Bhutan. These operations were launched in 2004 by the RBA and led by the King of Bhutan personally; Indian Army's role was to execute border-sealing operations on their side of the border. The operation was a resounding success with ULFA and all other insurgent groups in Bhutan being thrown out. Efforts are now on to try and get Myanmar and Bangladesh to follow suit - though so far there has been little success. As a result of these operations and public pressure on ULFA for peace, they demanded a cease fire and creation of an environment for talks. This was simply a ploy to recuperate, refit and regain strength so as to restart operations as they had suffered serious losses in Bhutan. Due to resurgence in violence by ULFA the cease-fire has failed and the Army has re-launched full scale operations against the ULFA.

The ULFA and AASU movements encouraged other minority groups to agitate for socio-economic improvements, autonomy and removal of illegal immigrants. Assam has now witnessed long drawn rebellions by almost all tribes of Bodo origin, the Karbis, and Kukis. As a result of these movements the Dimasas and Karbis have been given limited autonomy and talks with the governments of Assam and the centre are in progress. Cease-fires have also been arrived at between the Government of India and a faction of the insurgents of each of these two ethnic groups.

The Bodos had started an autonomy move prior to Independence on account of their perception that the Assamese were exploiting them. They had periodically agitated for the same through the ABSU, and demanded a separate state called Udayachal. In 1980, they restated this demand. The hardliners amongst the Bodos then formed Bodo SF as an insurgent group in 1986 that started insurgency in 1990. Initial aims were for separate statehood. The Army was deployed to deal with the Bodo SF. In 1993 it was agreed that a BAC would be formed on the north bank of the Brahmaputra for the Bodos. This resulted in a split amongst the Bodos with the formation of the BLT, who favoured peaceful resolution, and the NDFB who were hardliners. The NDFB then joined hands with ULFA, took sanctuary in Bhutan and Bangladesh, and demanded secession. The BAC proposals fell through. The NDFB is also headquartered in Bangladesh and its source of funding is through extortion. After a fairly long period of insurgency it was the Bhutan operations, wherein the NDFB was severely mauled, that have largely contributed towards nudging the hardliners towards talks. The ABSU and BLT with the present government have now negotiated a Bodo Autonomous Region. Should this not for any reason sustain, insurgency would possibly resume. Unfortunately this approach by the authorities is fraught with dangers, as the Bodos form only about 30 per cent of the population of the proposed 'Bodo Autonomous Region'. The other ethnic groups, which include the Rajbangshis, Rabhas and Koches, the Tea Tribes, Assamese, Bangladeshi migrants amongst others, form the balance 70 per cent of the population, and are already agitating against this. This is coupled with the fact that some of these ethnic groups are now joining hands with people of the same ethnic origin in West Bengal to demand similar concessions and to stall the Bodo Accord. The Cease-fire arrived at between the Government of India and NDFB, also needs to be watched closely as the leadership of the NDFB is controlled by the ISI and DGFI.

The recent striking down of the IMDT Act by the Supreme Court of India has vindicated the Assamese views on the issue of migration. The IMDT Act placed the onus of proof of citizenship on the authorities which made it difficult to prove that the individual was an illegal migrant. As the Act has now been set aside, the Foreigners' Act would now apply all over the country. This places the responsibility of proof of citizenship on the individual, which would make identification simpler. While this is indeed heartening, the situation has not improved as there is no political will to implement it.

A clear policy also needs to be formulated by the authorities for handling the affairs of south Assam, which has large tracts claimed by the NSCN as part of 'Greater Nagaland'. Many of these areas are currently inhabited by Nagas, Kukis, Manipuris, Hmars, Karbis, Dimasas and Bodos. These claims and the attempts by the NSCN to enforce them by forcible occupation have led to ethnic strife between these ethnic groups that threaten to escalate out of hand. The government also has to decide on how to deal with the predominantly Bengali-speaking belt of Cachar, Hailakundi and Karimganj, which continue to indicate high Bangladeshi immigration patterns.

Nagaland

Nagaland has about 20 resident tribes (14 major), conjointly called Nagas. The population is 19,88,636 and approx tribal break-up is: Angami 9 per cent, Ao 15 per cent, Chakesang 8 per cent, Chang 2 per cent, Khiamniungan 2 per cent, Konyak 15 per cent, Lotha 7 per cent, Phom 3 per cent, Rengma 1.5 per cent, Makware 0.5 per cent, Sangtam 4 per cent, Sema 13 per cent, Tikhir 0.5 per cent, Yimchunger 2 per cent, Zeliang 2 per cent, Garos 1 per cent, Chir/Bodo-Kachari/Kuki/Mikir/others 16 per cent. Studies indicate the tribes migrated from the area of Yunnan before the birth of Christ. These tribes settled into separate areas in the Naga Hills. They have throughout been antagonistic and are ethnically, culturally and ideologically distinct from each other. They have enjoyed tribal autonomy and any threat to their individuality invited violent reaction. The Bodos, Ahoms, Mughals, Manipuris, and the Myanmarese therefore entered into agreements with them to maintain peace by allowing them autonomy; and whenever they did not do so, conducted punitive operations against them. Till the 19th century, Naga beliefs were primordial and animistic as they were relatively untouched and isolated from modern civilization. The village and clan had total autonomy in their affairs. Visits to areas outside tribal boundaries, except for limited barter trade or for raiding expeditions, was limited. Due to this their values subsisted in the simple philosophy of 'tribe - land - village - autonomy'. The sudden transition from 'tradition to modernity', that came with rapid conversion to Christianity, along with the concepts of westernisation and interaction with other communities have not yet been adapted very well. There is also the issue of looking different from the plains' people. Under British rule the Nagas were allowed local autonomy as subjugation was too expensive. The 'Inner Line Regulation' was promulgated in 1873, which restricted contacts of outsiders with the Naga tribes. This was a step taken to prevent the politics of the plains, that the British had experienced in the course of the 1857 uprising from affecting the hill tribes. This system was reiterated in the 'Home Rule Regime', promulgated vide the Government of India Act 1935 in which the Naga Hills District was declared as an 'Excluded Area'. The British tried to civilise them through conversion to Christianity and western values and culture. The effect was to partially weld them together in a fashion that no administration could ever achieve.

A.Z. Phizo, the legendary Angami Naga insurgent leader, tried to get the Naga tribes to band together to meet the threat of being swamped, culturally and economically, by plainsmen from India. This is not a truism. The Kukis were also once considered to be Nagas, and a Kuki was a signatory to the Memorandum submitted by the Naga Club in 1929 to the Simon Commission. The Naga Club was a group of 20 Nagas (composed primarily of Phizo's Angami friends with representation from only six of the Naga tribes and one Kuki) who made a representation against being bracketed with India. Today the Kukis are vehemently considered by the Naga tribes to be non-Nagas and an ethnic group to be put down by force of arms. Similarly, many of the Nagas of Nagaland do not consider the present-day Manipuri Nagas to be true Nagas, inspite of the fact that it is the Manipuri Nagas who form the preponderance of the NSCN (I and M), which in turn controls most of Nagaland. The Manipuri Nagas too do not consider many of the Myanmar Nagas to be true Nagas. There has never been generic consciousness amongst the proclaimed

Naga tribes. It is also mentioned in the memorandum submitted to the Simon commission that 'We have different languages which can not be spoken by each other .... We have no unity amongst us and it is only the British Government that is keeping us together'. This remains so even today with tribal loyalties always coming first.

There is a considerable political debate about the number of Naga tribes. The working figure is 35 Naga tribes of which 20 are in Nagaland (the 1991 census indicated 17 and earlier to that it was 14 - the numbers have increased due to ethnic politics). The remainder lives in Manipur, Arunachal Pradesh, Assam and Myanmar. According to the NSCN (I and M), Nagaland extends to the River Chindwin in Myanmar; covers almost the entire Manipur; Cachar and North Cachar Hills and the Disturbed Area belt in Assam; Tirap, Changlang and Lohit districts in Arunachal Pradesh - a huge area with a population of nearly 3 million. Two surprising aspects of claimed Naga ethnicity stand out - first is the total lack of a common language. Even today people of different Naga tribes and even clans can speak to each other only through Nagamese or English. The second issue is one of origin—despite claims of migration from South-East Asia/China which are broadly accepted, none of the tribal myths indicate migration from distant regions or from a common motherland. Anthropological evidence indicates ethnic differences between tribes and indeed some Negrito blood in a few of them. Notwithstanding these facts, attempts have been made to build up Naga ethnicity through 'Inner Line' politics which the British had adopted and by setting up of the Naga Club in 1918 and the Ao and Lotha Tribal Councils by 1928. In 1929, the Naga Club had presented their memorandum to the Simon Commission. Thereafter a Naga Hills District Tribal Council was formed. These events led to a political awakening, which coupled with exposure to the World Wars, collapse of the British Empire, partition of the sub-continent; British proposals to reconstitute the hill districts as a 'Crown Colony', successful prosecution of guerrilla war against the Japanese, further politicised them and reinforced demands for independence. Indian independence threatened loss of their culture, values and traditional administrative institutions. The new Indian leadership decided to continue with the British policy of administration-autonomy and segregation. This only alienated them, prevented their assimilation into the mainstream; reinforced their feeling of being different and superior to the plains' people and facilitated interaction with their brethren in Myanmar, who had taken up arms against their government with similar demands. Mal-administration and lack of development, attempt by the Assam Government to enforce Assamese as the state language, and witnessing the flood of Bangladeshi migration only added to their fears.

In 1946 the Naga Hills Tribal Council was converted into the NNC, but it was not representative of the Naga tribes—it became Phizo's dominant minority, which from then onwards profoundly influenced Naga aspirations. Even within the NNC, there were differing views—some favoured independence, some autonomy within India, and others a protectorate status. All Naga government servants, who in actual fact formed the majority of the Naga intelligentsia, were banned by the government from participation in the NNC. Consequently, Phizo's views prevailed. No attempts were made to allay the Naga fears on crucial issues raised by them. In 1947 immediately after the Independence, a Nine-Point Agreement was signed between the Government of Assam and the NNC, wherein considerable autonomy was granted to the Nagas but this did not satisfy them. Phizo unilaterally declared Naga independence from India in August 1947 as the self- proclaimed representative of the Nagas. There was then a power struggle in the NNC ranks between the moderates led by Aliba Imti and Phizo and their followers. Ultimately Phizo won the battle in 1950 and was proclaimed the President of the NNC. In 1951 Phizo organised a controversial plebiscite in Naga Hills District to determine whether the Nagas wanted independence or a merger with India. He claimed that 99 per cent were in favour of independence. In fact, the so-called plebiscite was held only in Kohima and Mokokchung with limited attendance, and women and other areas of Nagaland had been excluded. These realities are little known to all, including the Naga public at large. Notwithstanding these facts, it is unfortunate that the authorities ignored this plebiscite. Consequently, total alienation progressively set in.

Hostilities started between the insurgents and the government forces from 1953 with the belligerents declaring themselves the 'Peoples Sovereign Republic of Free Nagaland'. This led to insurgency and deployment of SF in the State. Violence then increased. In 1955 the NFG replaced this. By 1955 there was a rift between Phizo's extremists and the moderates, and inter-factional assassinations commenced with all those opposed to Phizo being targeted. Successful

CI operations forced Phizo to flee to Dacca with Reverend Michael Scott's help, where they received Pakistani assistance and thereafter to London. Between 1957 and 1960, there were three Naga People's Conventions held in Nagaland, which were very well-attended and sought peaceful resolution of the problem. These progressively contributed to the Govt. of India agreeing to a 16-Point Proposal by them and the state of Nagaland coming into being, and the Tuensang district of NEFA was merged with it. Notwithstanding these events, insurgency continued. The problem was aggravated by Chinese and Pakistani support to the movement. Unfortunately both the Govt. of India and Nagaland disregarded the advice that the political structure should be derived from the existing traditional Naga system of governance and internal polity. Instead, the structure existing in the other states was imposed, which has contributed to loss of Naga identity, lack of adequate representation of all the ethnic groups, corruption and poor governance. The administration gained respite in the post-1971 period, due to successful prosecution of counter insurgency operations, which forced the hostile bands to flee to Myanmar, and reduced Chinese support to the insurgents. The creation of Bangladesh, and therefore non-availability of Pakistani bases and support in that country, helped as did the Shillong Accord of 1975, wherein the NFG and NNC accepted the Indian Constitution and agreed to lay down their arms.

The respite was, however, short-lived due to the coup and military rule in Bangladesh, with consequent renewed support from Pakistan, China and Bangladesh and sanctuary in Myanmar and the birth of the NSCN out of the anti-Shillong Accord factions, as also the adoption of a common cause with Myanmar insurgents. The '80s witnessed a split in the NSCN, partially on ethnic lines and due to a blood feud leading to a power struggle between the two factions of the NSCN—the I and M and K groups to gain control over Nagaland and Naga-inhabited areas in Manipur, Assam and Arunachal. NSCN (I and M)'s Pakistani mentors managed to convince its members that success was feasible only if they operated conjointly with other insurgent groups, and that their philosophy needed to change to secession of the entire north-east! This led to NSCN (I and M) becoming the mother organisation of most of the insurgent groups in the region. Due to successful SF operations, NSCN (I and M) was forced out of Nagaland by the late '90s to bases in adjoining states and countries where they received sanctuary, which included Bangladesh, Myanmar and Thailand. It was due to these operations and public pressure that they were forced to ask for a cease-fire which has been in place since 1997. At that stage NSCN (K) controlled most of Nagaland and parts of the Naga inhabited areas in the adjoining states as well. A cease-fire was similarly brokered with the NSCN (K). The NSCN (K) was headquartered in Myanmar adjacent to Tirap and Changlang Districts of Arunachal. The cease-fire applied to both the NSCN groups but is officially applicable only to Nagaland, as other state governments refused to agree to demands for 'Greater Nagaland', wherein large chunks of Manipur, Assam and Arunachal were claimed. In reality, the SF rarely operate against the NSCN (I and M) outside Nagaland, to obviate talks breaking down, which had been initiated by the Govt. of India with NSCN (I and M) only.

With the cease-fire in place in Nagaland, talks have been in progress for some time between the Govt. of India and the NSCN (I and M). This is because NSCN (I and M) cadres are primarily Indian Nagas, and are considered to be the mother insurgent group of the north-east. It however needs to be noted that almost all the NSCN (I and M) leadership and at least 40 per cent of their cadres are from the Tangkhul Tribe of the Nagas in Manipur and not Nagaland, with another 40 per cent being from other Manipuri, Assamese and Arunachali Naga tribes - not more than 10-15 per cent or less of the cadres are from the Nagaland tribes. This is because the Naga tribes living outside Nagaland feel the majority communities in their home states are exploiting them, and that they have been socially, economically and politically deprived. As against this, the NSCN (K) has its cadres mainly from the Myanmar Naga tribes and the tribes located in areas that they control. It is because the leadership of the NSCN (K) and some of its cadres are not Indian Nagas and its power is on the wane, that the Govt. of India have not initiated talks with NSCN (K). It is for this reason that many of the Nagaland Naga tribes, NSCN (K) and other groups, view these talks with suspicion, distrust and scepticism, as they consider the Govt. of India's negotiations with the I and M to be talks with the Tangkhuls of Manipur, who are not considered to be Nagas by many of the Nagas of Nagaland, and are trying to lord over them by force of arms.The people, who are tired of violence, have used the period of the cease-fire to propagate peace. The NSCN groups have used the cease-fire to consolidate their hold over areas, strengthen themselves and eliminate their rivals. Due to the importance given to them, the NSCN (I and M) has more or less gained control over the entire state by force, with the exception of that part of the north-east which remains under NSCN (K) control. While there are popular pressures for rapprochement between both groups, this is currently unlikely due to ethnic rivalry and blood feuds. The NSCN (I and M) is the strongest insurgent group today, which has expanded to over 5000 cadres and is well equipped and armed with the latest modern weapons. It calls the shots in the region, dictates terms to most other insurgent groups, runs a parallel government and administration, collects taxes from all in both Nagaland and its claimed areas of Greater Nagaland. The NSCN (IandM) has quite obviously prepared itself for an eventuality of the cease-fire breaking down.

It should be noted that much of the ailment in Manipur, Assam and Arunachal stems from the demands of NSCN (I and M). While over a period of time there has been some rapprochement between the Naga ethnic groups, strong inter-ethnic group rivalry and clashes are likely in the foreseeable future. Those involved in policy formulation and talks with Nagas within the Govt. of India need to comprehend that coming to an agreement with only NSCN (I and M) will be seen as having done a deal with the Tangkhuls, which may be unacceptable to the vast majority of tribes, people and the state. Such an agreement is therefore unlikely to succeed. Notwithstanding the above, due to public pressure there has been relative peace in Nagaland for the last several years.

Manipur

Manipur has a population of about 23,88,634. It has Naga Tribes—Ao, Kabui, Angami, Zeliang, Khongazai, Mao, Tangkhul–13 per cent; Kuki-Chin -Anal, Chiru, Chothe, Gangte, Koira, Kom, Lamgang, Mizo, Mansang, Paite; Ralte, Sahte, Simte, Thadou, Vaiphei, Zou–14 per cent; Meitei–58 per cent; Others –15 per cent. Out of the Naga tribes listed above, only the Aos, Zeliangs and the Angamis spill across the boundary into Nagaland. Though considered part of the Naga tribes by the authorities, many of the Nagaland Naga tribes do not accept the Manipuri Nagas as part of them. The Naga residents in Manipur however universally feel neglected by the Meiteis on issues of economy, jobs, development, culture and governance, and strongly feel that the Meiteis have wrongfully seized their lands and sources of livelihood. They similarly feel that the forcible settlement of the Kuki-Chin tribals on their lands by the British was wrong. They further believe that the Govt. of India has supported the other ethnic groups against their interests, which have further alienated them. The issues of both identity and ethnicity are therefore even more pronounced than in Nagaland. They have joined together in an alliance in the form of the NFG, NSCN (K) or the NSCN (I and M) to forcibly try and resolve their problems.

The Kuki-Chin-Mizo tribes reside in a number of different pockets in Manipur. The majority is located in south Manipur in the districts of Chandel and Churachandpur adjacent to Mizoram. There are, however, two pockets in the district Senapati sandwiched between the Maos, Zeliangs, Tangkhuls and the Meiteis, and some in Imphal. While broadly of the same ethnic group, there is a great deal of sub-tribe rivalry primarily between the Kukis, Hmars, Paites, Zous, Zomis, Mizos, derived from the fact that the Mizos get preferential treatment in Mizoram, and that the demand of the non-Mizo, Kuki-Chin tribal group for inclusion in Mizoram and demands for Greater Mizoram are perceived not to have been pressed adequately. There is also the perception that the Mizos have not aided the Kuki-Chin minorities in Manipur adequately as a result of which they have suffered tremendously at the hands of both the Nagas and the Meiteis. Consequently, we have conflict between the non-Mizo, Kuki-Chin groups which are antagonistic to all other ethnic groups including the Mizos.

The Meiteis inhabit primarily in the valley floor of Manipur extending up to Moreh and along the Bishenpur axis into the Cachar district of Assam. They consider themselves superior to all the other ethnic groups in Manipur intellectually, culturally and in all other related aspects. They feel they are being oppressed to meet the demands of the tribes inhabiting the hills and are antagonistic towards them.

Manipur therefore has inter-ethnic conflict among the Naga tribes, Meitei and Naga tribes, Kuki-Chin tribals versus both the Nagas and the Meiteis, between the ethnic sub groups of the Kuki-Chin-Mizo tribals, demands for greater Nagaland and Mizoram or Valley versus Hill inhabitants. This is consequent to political, social, geographic, historical and economic instability, emanating from fragmentation and fractionalisation of polity and society, due to acute mal-administration and neglect. Today, Manipur is in a state of total anarchy where the writ of the Govt. of India simply does not run - the situation in the state is much worse than in any other part of the country. It remains out of the media headlines only on account of the fact that it is so far away from Delhi and mainstream Indian politics that no one including the media is bothered about the state.

Historically, the Meiteis are the most populous ethnic group in the state, and have ruled the state for a long period - their kingdom reportedly stretched from river Brahmaputra in the north to river Chindwin (now in Myanmar) in the south around the period of the birth of Christ. Manipur plains are the core, and the surrounding hills are the fringe regions. Hill tribes were permitted local autonomy, subject to their maintaining peace and giving tribute to kings of Manipur. After Aryan migrations into Bengal, the Meiteis became strongly influenced by Hinduism and Vedic culture. In the 16th century, they adopted Vaishnavism and became powerful in the region, along with the Bodo Cacharis who ruled from Dimapur, Mughals who ruled Bengal, Tripuris and Ahoms. From then onwards, the Kings of Myanmar who wished to expand their territory subjected them to repeated invasions. The power struggle with the Bodo-Cacharis and other powers of the region also took its toll. The Manipuri population was decimated and economy disrupted. Consequently, they were neither able to keep the hill tribes under control, nor the invading Myanmar hordes at bay. In 1824, they appealed to the British for help. The British defeated the Myanmarese, but forced Manipur to cede to Myanmar the rich Kabaw Valley. They also instigated massive migrations of Kuki-Chin-Mizo tribes, to act as a buffer between the Nagas and their plantations in the Cachar, with a view to stop the Naga tribes from raiding their newly set up colonies and plantations. Thus relations between the British and Manipuris deteriorated, leading to the 1891 Anglo-Manipur war and British annexation of the State. There was political awakening and participation in India's freedom struggle, with many Meiteis supporting the Japanese and joining the Indian National Army against the British. After partition, the Maharaja of Manipur acceded to the Indian union, which evoked insurgency amongst some Naga and Meitei groups who wanted independence. The newly created Manipur Communist party then reached an understanding with Myanmar communists, who with Chinese backing had control over the adjoining areas in Myanmar, to cede the Kabaw

Valley back to Manipur, in return for creation of an independent socialist state of Manipur that would ally it to the Chinese communists. In the '50s-'60s, due to perceived Meitei exploitation, a number of Manipur Naga tribals joined the Naga movement. Shortly thereafter, as the Mizo insurgency in Mizoram had just started, many Kuki-Chin-Mizo tribals joined their counterparts in Chin and Mizo Hills and started agitating that the Kuki-Chin-Mizo belts in Manipur be merged with Mizo Hills. They also engaged in inter-ethnic depredations for control of south Manipur around Moreh bordering Myanmar, and the lucrative trans-border drug and other smuggled goods' trade to fund their activities. By the '60s-'70s various Meitei insurgent groups had formed, who demanded revival of the Pre-Vaishnav Meitei culture and secession from India. They agitated over perennial neglect, ceding of Kabaw Valley to Burma, granting only union territory status to Manipur when Nagaland had become a state, they had been denied scheduled tribe status whereas the hill tribes had the same and finally too much attention being paid to the hill tribes who were getting preferential treatment in relation to the Meiteis simply because they had rebelled. When CI operations were launched by the SF, many groups moved out to the Chittagong Hill Tracts. Due to socio-economic deprivation, rising unemployment, and insurgency, the situation worsened. Politicians also started aligning themselves with various insurgent groups, based on their ethnic considerations, and sought their support for elections and protection. Thus political instability became the order of the day. This created an extremely complicated political situation and made governance difficult. Some respite was obtained in the '70s as the 1971 war operations had terminated Pak support, and there had been a series of successful CI operations. However, increasing frustration, corrupt and poor governance, the continuing feud between the groups and subsequent support from Pakistan and Bangladesh resulted in a revival of insurgency by the '80-'90s. To add to the complexities, Pakistan, Bangladesh and reportedly the Chinese tried to get all the insurgent groups to join hands.

Most of the Naga insurgents in Manipur are led by Muivah's Tangkhuls in the NSCN (I and M), which emerged from a split in the NSCN in '87-'88, and who have now more or less gained control of most Naga areas in Manipur and adjoining states. Besides secession and sovereignty, their demand is for merging of the Naga tribal areas of Manipur, Assam, Arunachal and Myanmar with Nagaland, which is one of the reasons for conflict with the Meiteis. Their conflict with the Kukis is for control over drug and other illegal trade traffic with Myanmar, besides the forcible interjection of the Kukis into traditional Naga areas. Some of the Naga tribals, particularly those adjoining the Chakesang belt, are part of the NFG (a derivative of the NNC), as this is an NFG stronghold opposed to the NSCN (I and M). Part of Tamenglong district in West Manipur continues to support the NSCN (K)

The Meitei-Kuki conflict is based on a number of factors such as: forcible occupation of Meitei areas by the Kukis-Chins-Mizos, demand of Kuki-Chin tribes for Greater Mizoram, encompassing all areas occupied by their ethnic groups in Manipur, south Assam and Chin Hills, control over illegal trade in south Manipur. The Kuki Chin-Mizo tribals have been alienated on the grounds that since the British settled them in these areas, it was the duty of the Govt. of India to protect them. Being from the same ethnic group as the Mizos of Mizoram and with a demand for a merging of all Kuki-Chin-Mizo areas in Manipur with Mizoram, they supported the Mizo insurgency in the '60s/'70s. In the '80s and '90s, the Meiteis and then the Nagas engaged in trying to throw out the Kuki-Chin-Mizo tribals from the areas occupied by them, and killed a large number of them. They now have organised themselves into insurgent groups, whose role is to strike back at depredations against them by the Nagas and the Meiteis and their own sub-groups, and to try to achieve amalgamation of their areas with Mizoram and Chin Hills. There is now reportedly a truce between some of the Kuki-Chin groups and NSCN (I and M), and they have joined forces against the Meiteis, with the NSCN promising them Greater Mizoram when Greater Nagaland comes through. As part of this strategy, NSCN (I and M) and allied Kuki-Chin groups are trying to strangle the Meiteis into submission, as they jointly control routes through the hills leading into Manipur. The recent blockade by the hill tribes of all routes leading into Manipur periodically for fairly long durations is part of their strategy.

After the NSCN (I and M) cease-fire came into vogue, it applied only to the state of Nagaland. NSCN's attempt was to get it extended to cover the entire NSCN (I and M) claimed areas, which included almost the whole of Manipur, major parts of south Assam and Tirap, Changlang and Lohit Districts of Arunachal, so they could gain control of the area during the cease-fire, notwithstanding the rivalry of some Naga tribes with the Tangkhuls. Delhi initially gave their approval to this proposal of NSCN (I and M). This led to extremely widespread agitation and strife by the Meiteis - Delhi was then forced to officially retract its earlier decision. There is, however, an unofficial cease-fire in the claimed areas of NSCN (I and M), between the NSCN (I and M) and their surrogate groups and the SF, apparently out of fear that talks with the authorities will otherwise break down. Consequently, the NSCN (I and M) have had a free run in the claimed areas, much to the chagrin of the Meiteis, the Kuki-Chins, the residents of these areas and the state governments. As a result of intense CI operations in Manipur against various insurgent groups, to try and bring the situation under control, many insurgent groups have shifted their sanctuaries to Myanmar, Bangladesh and adjoining states. Since the CI operations are currently only against insurgent groups who are not party to the cease-fire—primarily the Meiteis, the Meiteis are aggrieved. On account of this, coupled with the actions of the hill tribes trying to strangle the Meiteis into submission by frequent blockade of all roads leading into Manipur for long periods, the Meiteis in general find their backs to the wall. They are becoming more and more alienated and feel betrayed. This is even more so on account of the fact that the Meitei population at large has repeatedly proved their loyalty by fielding maximum people from the north-east in the national sports teams, the bureaucracy, police, Armed Forces and other central services.

The Meitei insurgent elements which are visible have in retaliation therefore launched a sustained campaign to malign the Govt. of India, the SF, the AFSPA, for violation of human rights. Their aim is to try and get the SF removed from Manipur, with a view to fight it out with the hill tribes on their own. There is also a strong nexus between the insurgents and politicians; the deep-seated political instability in the state is a fall-out of the insurgents dictating terms to willing politicians. Further, as the political majority is Meitei, due to inter-ethnic animosity, there is a lack of development in the hill districts, and a great deal of social deprivation particularly amongst the hill tribes, which only contributes further to the ethnic divide. The overall lack of law and order in the state has spawned extensive extortion by all the insurgent groups. In a nutshell, the situation in Manipur is very bad—much worse than in Jammu and Kashmir, and it is deteriorating further due to apathy and mismanagement.

Meghalaya

Meghalaya has a population of about 23,06,069 and its demographic profile is: Khasis/Jaintias/Garos–68 per cent, Dimasa/Hmar/Kuki/Karbi/Lakher/Hajong/Mon/Naga–10 per cent, Mizo–4 per cent, Others (including Bangladeshi and Nepalese migrants) about 18 per cent. The Khasis, Jaintias and the Karbis are of Austric origin, whereas the Garos, Dimasa and Hajongs are of Bodo origin. Historically, Meghalaya was insulated from the Mughal, Ahom and Burmese invasions on account of its inaccessibility. The British annexed it in 1835 and decided to set up their headquarters at Shillong, the capital of Meghalaya, for control of the north-east (undivided Assam), on account of its salubrious climate and relatively easier access. They, therefore, set up a more effective administration, while allowing limited autonomy. This area was not given a segregated 'Excluded Area' status as was done for Nagaland and Mizoram, and was amalgamated into the Assam administration. The British set about civilising the tribals through conversion to Christianity. As they were not segregated and there was greater interaction with other communities unlike the other hill states, they progressively accepted their merging with the Indian Union more gracefully, whilst maintaining their culture modified by Christian and western influence. Independence brought political awakening; demands for a separate state started from 1949. In 1952 the Khasis and Mizos led the demand for a separate tribal identity as they felt the Assam government was neglecting them. Demands for throwing out non-tribals started in 1957, particularly after observing the demographic changes in Tripura (Tripura earlier had a tribal majority, but due to excessive migration, the tribals became a minority) and Assam (the Assamese were progressively getting overwhelmed by Bangladeshi migration). Perceived social deprivation led to frustration and agitation against the Assam government. Seeing the Naga example, the youth began to agitate for insurrection to enforce their demands. Delhi decided to grant them statehood in 1972, thereby partially resolving the problem. A glance at the state's demographic profile however clearly indicates that the state also has a problem of Bangladeshi and Nepalese migration-the tribals therefore initiated out of fear a movement against non-tribals, who had migrated into Meghalaya in large numbers, which continues till date. There are also issues of economic disparity due to lack of development; the Khasis feel that areas where there has been rebellion are much better-off as the centre has poured in resources for development into those areas.

Today Meghalaya has a nascent Khasi/Jaintia insurgent movement organised into the HNLC and ANVC, with ULFA, NSCN (I and M), NDFB, Bangladeshi and Pakistani support, which propagate secession and an anti-migrant philosophy. Whereas previously the anti-migrant philosophy was primarily one of targeting the Bengalis and Nepalese, today the Khasis have also started targeting all other communities, including tribals from other NE states. There is also alienation between the Khasi and the Garo/Bodo tribals on ethnic grounds and talk of splitting the state further. In the late '90s and early 21st century the situation in Meghalaya had turned bad with extensive extortion being the order of the day. Consequently, a very large number of outsiders, who were involved in business and trade, fled the state. Fortunately the police have largely regained control and are now relatively more effective in keeping law and order under control. The anti-migrant and politically-sponsored Khasi-Garo agitations, however, continue unabated with frequent strikes and curfews consequent to which the state is unable to function effectively. There is also tremendous political instability. Meghalaya is well-endowed with natural resources, but has little industrial development. Consequently, its economic situation is poor. In a nutshell, the problem is socio-economic, and coloured by ethnic strife and nascent insurgency, which needs to be resolved by good governance.

Mizoram

Mizoram has a population of 8,91,058 and its demographic profile is: Mizos (Lushai) 60 per cent, Paite 5 per cent, Hmar 5 per cent, Riang 5 per cent, Poi 5 per cent, Lakher/Pawi 8 per cent, Chakma 7 per cent, Others including Bangladeshi and Myanmar migrants 5 per cent. Mizoram has a demographic advantage over other NE states—it is relatively homogenous with adjoining areas of Myanmar, south Manipur, south-eastern Tripura, and adjoining areas of Assam having similar Kuki-Chin-Mizo ethnic profiles. The Mizos were distinctive, fierce and warring, who started migrating from the Chin Hills in Myanmar into the Mizo Hills around the 11th century. The Bodos, and Manipuris permitted them autonomy as it was too expensive to subjugate them. It was only after the Mizos repeatedly raided British colonies and plantations in the late 19th century that the British launched a major expedition against them, subjugated them and colonised Mizo Hills. Even after doing so the British allowed them autonomy in all tribal affairs as they had done in the case of the Nagas. Administration of the Mizo Hills was comparatively simpler as the Mizo people were largely homogenous and less exposed to politics of the region. Here also the British segregated them from the plains through promulgation of the 'Inner Line' and encouraged conversion to Christianity. Like the Nagas and other isolated tribes, prior to conversion to Christianity, the religion was animism and their beliefs based on the primordial value system of 'tribe-village-land-autonomy'. Conversion to Christianity, accompanying westernisation and literacy have not changed this substantially. It is due to this that there is animosity towards other tribes and communities of the north-east, particularly against those in the plains. It is also due to these ethnic considerations that part of the demand of the Mizos has always been for a Greater Mizoram encompassing the Chin Hills in Myanmar, parts of south Assam, south Tripura and south Manipur. It is also due to these considerations that Mizoram still has some problems with its minorities.

Political groupings commenced just prior to partition–with demands being made initially for autonomy, which changed to secession and independence to form Greater Mizoram. Subsequently, after a long period of insurgency, that changed to incorporation into the Indian Union, subject to grant of greater autonomy. Unfortunately, due to faulty policy after Indian independence, the British policy of segregation through the Inner Line restrictions was continued. Governmental neglect, lack of development, mal-administration and imposition of Assamese as the state language, led to discontent and alienation. There were major famine conditions in Mizoram from 1959 to 1961, during this period the people witnessed mismanagement and lack of assistance by the government, this resulted in isolation and formation of the MNF in 1961. After building up a support base amongst the people and taking cue from Nagaland and Manipur, the MNF declared Mizoram independent unilaterally in 1966 and commenced insurrection. They received support from Pakistan, China and people from the Kuki-Chin group of tribes in neighbouring areas.

CI operations were launched immediately in 1966 to bring the situation under control. These were particularly successful after Pakistan was defeated in the 1971 war. Mizoram was then declared a 'union territory' and elections were held. With a political process having been initiated, the MNF progressively lost popular support. Talks were then initiated with the insurgents. Insurgency was stepped up again after Bangladesh came under military rule with operations dragging till 1987. The operations culminated in the Mizo Accord, with insurgents coming over-ground and surrendering their arms, accepting the Indian Constitution, forming the government, grant of statehood and bringing peace to Mizo Hills.

Since then Mizoram has progressed by leaps and bounds and is peaceful. Mizoram however does have: problems related to its minorities i.e. the Hmars, Paites, Riangs (Brus), Pois, Lakhers, Chakmas and illegal immigration of Bangladeshi and Myanmar inhabitants. It has partially resolved the problem by grant of limited autonomy to some of the minorities. Some others have been coerced into an exodus out of the state into Tripura, particularly the Riangs and Chakmas, which is adversely affecting the already delicate situation in that state. Periodic demands of 'Greater Mizoram' impel some of its people, including those in authority to assist insurgents of the Kuki-Chin-Mizo ethnic group in neighbouring Myanmar (Chin Hills) and south Manipur. It is also supportive of the NSCN (I and M)—at least conceptually, as some of those currently in power are close to them. It is opposed to migration from Bangladesh and is largely antagonistic towards it. All these aspects have resulted in strained relations with the neighbouring states/country. It is also over-urbanised (almost 60 per cent of its population are dwellers of urban areas). This happened as groupings of villages were made on the Malaysian model, as part of CI operations in the late '60s. With the grant of statehood and sudden large-scale employment avenues in the government, migration to urban areas increased substantially. In consequence, large urban areas have developed with multi-storied concrete constructions in earthquake-prone zones which are subject to frequent landslides. The urban areas have acute problems of availability of infrastructure in terms of water-supply, sanitation, roads and so on. Urbanization has also led to neglect of the agricultural sector with serious adverse effects. There is very little industrialization. Mizoram, by virtue of its geographic location and peaceful situation with little or no SF deployment, is also an infiltration route for militants of all hues transiting to and from both Bangladesh and Myanmar militant sanctuaries. There are also arms and drug-smuggling into the region again from these two countries.

Tripura

Tripura's population is 31,91,168 and its demographic profile is: Tripuri tribes (Bodo origin)–15 per cent, Riangs (Brus)–4 per cent, Jamatias-Garos (Bodo origin)–Chakmas-Mizos-Kukis-Austrics–9 per cent, Bengali Hindus–63 per cent, Bengali Muslims–8 per cent, Others–1 per cent. Presently tribal people reside primarily in the hill regions, with the plains populated by Bengalis. The predominant tribes were of Bodo origin called Tripuris, who established a kingdom in the middle ages consisting of the Arakan, Chittagong Hill Tracts, western Bangladesh, south Assam and present day Tripura. They were a power centre in the region. The population till 1921 was predominantly tribal. However, consequent to the British policy of encouraging immigration from East Bengal to under populated areas, there was extensive migrations, which continued even after the partition, independence and then again in 1971, due to which tribal percentage was reduced to about 28 per cent. The Chakmas (4 to 5 per cent) and Riangs (4 per cent) are mainly recent immigrants, who fled from Chittagong Hill tracts and Mizoram following agitation and rebellion by them against the Bangladesh and Mizoram government and the consequent clamp-down on them, when they agitated for better socio-economic conditions. The state is beset by insurgency, by tribals of Bodo origin against the non-tribals. The key factors for the insurgency are overwhelming demographic change which threaten to wipe out the tribals and their distinctive culture, dislocation of the tribals from their traditional habitats and socio-economic deprivation. The insurgency, which is essentially rural, is aided and abetted by Pakistan and Bangladesh, and aimed at trying to throw out the migrants who now rule them and has continued on and off since 1949. Unfortunately, immigration has continued, though at a lower scale. The Army had to be called out frequently to bring the situation under control. Though there have been peace talks and agreements in the past, they have fallen through due to demands not having been met and political parties using the insurgents for political ends. The state is also a major infiltration route for insurgents transiting to and from Bangladesh and gun running. A large number of SF is deployed both for border sealing and counter-insurgency operations in the state.

While the state is relatively rich in natural resources, particularly natural gas, and rubber, it has very little industry and is relatively underdeveloped. Tripura and Mizoram's geographic location and India's relations with Bangladesh create acute problems, as these states are out on a limb for surface communications with the rest of India after partition. Rationally, all transit goods should have been through Bangladesh to West Bengal or to Chittagong port and onwards. Alternatively, such an arrangement is needed with Myanmar along the Arakan coast. However, due to lack of such an agreement with Bangladesh or Myanmar, this is limited to movement by air only. Though this is cheaper for normal travel than surface communications, it is uneconomical for bulk trade. The two states therefore suffer from acute economic problems and lack of development. It is imperative that Delhi resolves with Bangladesh the issues of transit trade, Bangladeshi support to the insurgents and that Tripura resolves its problems related to the tribals.

Arunachal Pradesh

Arunachal Pradesh's population is 10,91,117. It has well over 100 ethnic groups of which 20 are considered to be major tribes. The demographic profile of its 20 main tribes is—Adis (Padam, Minyong, Pasi, Pangi etc)–27 per cent, Nissi/Dafla–22 per cent, Wangchoos–8 per cent, Monpa–8 per cent, Mishmi–7 per cent, Nocte–7 per cent, Tagins–6 per cent, Tangsas–4 per cent, Apatani–4 per cent, Miris–2 per cent, Sulungs–1 per cent, Khamptis–1 per cent, Others–3 to 4 per cent including Tibetan refugees, Chakma, Nepalese and Bangladeshi migrants. A clear ethnic division is also discernible on account of the population being split into four distinct lineages: Tibetan (Monpas/Tibetans), Indo- Burmese, Bodo origin and others. The majority of people particularly in the remote areas are all animists with primordial beliefs. The first missionaries into Arunachal were the Rama Krishna Missions, who are well liked for their efforts in the social field. Due to their missionary efforts, Arunachal today has a fair number of followers of the Hindu faith, particularly in the southern belt of north Arunachal. The tribes of Tibetan origin are all Buddhists. Christianity is also picking up particularly in the districts of Tirap, Changlang and Lohit due to the efforts of the NSCN.

Arunachal Pradesh is one part of India where one can find areas almost untouched by modern civilization, with natural pristine beauty and a population that still totally believes in its primordial value system of 'tribe-village-land autonomy', and makes concerted efforts to protect the same.

Arunachal Pradesh is a most diverse and yet relatively peaceful state, primarily due to its small population being interspersed in a huge and relatively inaccessible area, being heavily forested, under-developed with few roads, thereby ensuring relative isolation and distinctiveness for its diverse ethnic groups in most interior areas. It is also due to these reasons that the political reach of the state to these areas is limited, thereby ensuring a great deal of autonomy. It is also the most recent state to be opened up to administration. It was only in 1882 that exploration and subjugation by the British began, consequent to the British adopting a forward policy of defending its frontiers with reference to Russia and China. The British had named the area the NEF Tracts and by 1914, attempted to administer it through the NEF Tracts administration, with near total autonomy in all tribal matters. The Inner Line Regulation was also invoked and the region was given 'Excluded Area' status. After independence, India continued with the British policy. In 1954, the area was renamed NEFA and due to the border dispute with China, the Army and Assam Rifles moved in. In 1957, due to the Naga insurgency, Tuensang Frontier Division adjoining Nagaland and Myanmar Naga Hills, with a primarily Konyak Naga tribal population, was merged with the Naga Hills.

The Chinese, from the mid '50s onwards, have laid claim to the entire area of Arunachal north of the River Lohit which borders Tibet, on grounds that this entire area was directly under Tibetan suzerainty and administration prior to the forcible occupation of the area by the British. The British are also blamed for drawing up a false and illegal boundary between India and Tibet called the 'Macmohan Line' and forcing the Tibetans to accept it in 1914 though this boundary is considered unacceptable by the Chinese. After the boundary dispute became evident in the late fifties and Tibet was occupied by Chinese troops, Indian forces were moved into this area up to the perceived alignment of the Macmohan Line. This led to confrontation between the Chinese and Indian forces and ultimately resulted in the 1962 Indo-China conflict. A Border Peace and Tranquillity Accord is now in place between the two countries since the '90s, wherein it has been agreed that all disputes will be resolved through talks and a number of confidence building measures have since been instituted. Whilst talks between India and China are in progress, I have no doubt in my mind that the dispute may take quite some time to resolve. India had, however, in the course of these events seen the need to bring the area under more effective administrative control due to Chinese claims to the area. Hence the 'Panchayat system' was introduced in 1967. In 1972, Arunachal became a union territory and in 1987 it was granted full statehood.

The economy is largely agricultural, which is the mainstay of its people. It has tremendous forest wealth and in all probability also has extensive mineral deposits which have not yet been exploited. It also has great potential in the field of hydroelectric power - though yet to be exploited – and it is understood that measures are in hand to do so in the main river valleys starting with the Subansiri River Valley. Once this is done, Arunachal Pradesh will be able to supplement its income substantially through sale of power to Assam and possibly north Nagaland. A certain amount of attention is also now being paid to commercial exploitation of handicrafts, which are diverse and plentiful in the state. Its main problems are: the border dispute with China regarding the claim of the whole of Arunachal bordering Tibet; threat of change of demographic profile, due to resettlement of Chakmas and Tibetans in the state and the migration of Bangladeshis and Nepalese; lack of economic development and therefore socio economic deprivation and consequent ethnic rivalry and claims to Lohit, Tirap and Changlang districts of the State by the Nagas. As the Adis and the Nissis form the majority population in Arunachal, the minority groups complain of discrimination and neglect particularly in the districts of Tirap, Changlang and Lohit which are claimed by the Nagas. Tirap, Changlang and part of Lohit districts are affected by both the Naga and the Assam insurgency, with the NSCN (I and M) claiming all three districts right up to the Tibetan border as part of Greater Nagaland, and the area being a battle ground between the NSCN (I and M) and the NSCN (K) for control of the area. The ULFA is using the area for sanctuary and transit to their camps in Myanmar. The State is against a merging of these claimed areas with Nagaland, or for its territory to be used by any of the insurgent groups. CI operations by SF are therefore being conducted against these insurgent groups in the affected areas. The main issue in the state that needs to be attended to is the requirement for better governance, which would meet the aspirations of the minorities.

Sikkim

It has the least population amongst all the states in the country – 5,40,493. Its demographic profile is: Nepalese–80 per cent, Lepchas and Bhutias–19 per cent, Others–1 per cent. The state has no documented history earlier than the 17th century. Findings indicate that early inhabitants were Austrics, who were overwhelmed by the migratory hordes, before the birth of Christ. Legends indicate that the Lepchas migrated into Sikkim and established a kingdom. During the middle ages there were Tibetan Bhutia migrations into Sikkim. The Bhutias joined hands with the Lepchas after some time and formed a dynasty headed by the Chogyal that ruled Sikkim till 1975, when it merged with India. In the 18th century, Nepal tried to colonise Sikkim and parts of southern Tibet, which resulted in British assistance being sought and the Nepalese and Tibetans defeated. This led to Sikkim, Bhutan and Tibet being given a 'Protectorate' status and Chumbi Valley being ceded to Tibet. The British established their base in the Darjeeling district of North Bengal to control North Bengal, eastern Nepal, Sikkim and western Bhutan, and demanded that Darjeeling district be leased to them - Sikkim duly complied. The large Nepalese migration was mainly during this period. After independence, India continued with the British-era Protectorate status till Sikkim merged with India. The border dispute with China, wherein the Chinese recognised an independent Sikkim, but not its initial 'Protectorate' status and subsequent merging with India, led to large-scale induction of Indian troops into Sikkim in the late '50s and of Chinese troops into Chumbi Valley, and their being deployed opposite each other; almost eyeball to eyeball. This Army presence from both sides, though at a very reduced scale after China has recognized Sikkim's merge, continues till date.

As the state is peaceful, it has emerged as a major national and international tourist destination, this is the mainstay of the state's economy. Due to small size of the population, tourism, mining and handicraft incomes, central government assistance, extensive infrastructure development consequent to Army deployment over the past 40 odd years, and with relatively good governance the state is economically the best-off in the region. The trade opening up through Sikkim with China has also improved its prospects. There has been little cause for unrest in the state, too. Notwithstanding the above, there are reports of Western Sikkim and Darjeeling district being used as sanctuary by the 'Maoists' of both India and Nepal and some other Indian insurgent groups including the ULFA, KLO, NDFB, and even the NSCN. There are also periodic reports about Nepalese/Gurkha hardliners amongst the Maoists, with demands for a united Gurkhaland consisting of Nepal, Sikkim, Darjeeling and parts of Jalpaiguri district of North Bengal and parts of Southern Bhutan, which are causes of concern and need to be monitored and suitably addressed.

Effects of India's Internal and Foreign Policy on Insurgency/Conflict

The effects of partition of the sub-continent, besides anguish, massacres, millions of refugees, peoples split across these borders, were an unrelenting hatred and distrust between India and Pakistan. This is the backdrop to the foreign policies of both India and Pakistan since then. Creation of Bangladesh did not change the (East Pakistan) homeland concept. It made Pakistan and Bangladesh more determined, and they decided to work together towards achieving this aim. Our dispute with China resulted in their supporting the Naga and other NE rebel movements and left extremists. Pakistan took advantage of our predicament and allied with China. China from then on used Pakistan to keep India in its place and to act as its proxy to aid insurgency in India, primarily through East Pakistan/Bangladesh. China had meanwhile fallen out with USSR. With India leaning towards USSR, the Chinese stepped up support to India's NE insurgents, and the nascent Naxalite movement. The border skirmish with the Chinese in Sikkim resulted in continued aid to the insurgents through communist-controlled north Burma and East Pakistan. We also annoyed the West with our criticism of their policies and by seeking assistance of USSR, in their perception, we had joined the Eastern Bloc. Pakistan's joined the Western Bloc. Consequently, aid flowed into Pakistan which was used to fuel insurgency in the NE. Liberation of East Pakistan and Bangladesh coming into being, coupled with Pakistan's pre-occupation with the events of 1971, the Burmese reaching an understanding with China over activities in north

Burma, and the flurry of foreign policy activity to mend fences with the West and China, resulted in reduced external support to the insurgents. Consequently, the Naxalite problem and insurgency were brought under control and the situation in the NE improved.

The Pakistan Army could not accept the disgrace of defeat and consequently formulated a strategy of proxy war to defeat and balkanise India. They decided to make 'India bleed through a thousand cuts', by support to all dissident movements and through religious fundamentalism and terrorism. They therefore converted Pakistan into an Islamic State. Pakistan decided to 'go nuclear' to deter India from conventional retaliatory strikes. The Bangladesh Army took control of Bangladesh in 1975. Both the armies joined hands to try and defeat India, and achieve their original ideals. Bangladesh continued with the strategy of Lebensraum, ally with China and Pakistan, fan religious fundamentalism (they also converted into an Islamic State), build up conventional forces for defence and provide maximum support to Indian dissident groups. In 1979, Pakistan became the frontline state to defeat USSR in Afghanistan, and simultaneously instituted its new strategy. Punjab burst into flames; training of Kashmiri dissidents and other religious fundamentalists commenced; NSCN emerged in Nagaland and Manipur as did other Manipuri dissident groups; the ULFA (Assamese) and NDFB (Bodos) insurgents were born; Mizoram and Tripura insurgency and left extremist groups were reactivated. By the early '80s, the NE was in flames along with Punjab. Pakistan's nuclear bomb preparations were also on at full blast. It is impossible that the West and China did not know about all these events, perhaps they even supported them irrespective of claims to the contrary. The Indian PM's visit to China reduced Chinese support, which assisted in bringing the situation under control in Punjab, and the Mizo and Assam Accords were reached.

In 1986, the Chinese had surreptitiously occupied Wangdung/ Sumdrong Chu and Bisa Cane Bridge areas in Arunachal. Indian counter moves to try and evict them increased tensions and support to insurgents. Our pro-democracy and anti military rule policy towards Myanmar led to misunderstandings with the country, with a result that Myanmar gave sanctuary to a number of NE insurgent groups. By early '90s Kashmir was in flames; NSCN had split and been reactivated; ULFA, NDFB, Tripura insurgents revitalized and nascent insurgency in Meghalaya born. We also saw a series of bomb blasts all over the country as part of Pakistan's proxy war. As a result of foreign policy initiatives, the 'BPTA' was signed with China. By the late 90s, after successful CI operations, the Naga CF came into effect, the ULFA and NDFB were forced to shift their camps outside the country, and insurgency was brought under control. By late 1997, nearly eight years after the Soviets left Afghanistan, Pakistan had realized that as they were no longer a frontline state, the West was losing interest in them. In Jammu and Kashmir, tourism flourished again; there was development and economic progress; the majority of people turned against Pakistan; Kashmir had almost vanished from international concern. Pakistan desperately needed to bring itself back into the international focus and avenge 1971. Pakistan therefore hatched a plan to surreptitiously secure unoccupied heights across the LOC in the Kargil sector of Jammu and Kashmir and cut India's strategic lifeline to Ladakh. There would then be strong reaction from Indian forces which would have to be brought in from Kashmir, which would facilitate infiltrating Jammu and Kashmir with large numbers of terrorists. Indian Army reinforcements from the rest of India would be drawn in to remove the intrusions. Pakistan's nuclear shield and a defensive deployment were to be used to deter India from counter strikes into Pakistan. Instructions were issued to the NE insurgents, left extremists and sleeper cells amongst the minorities to keep Indian SF engaged. Indian reactions were immediate, and resulted in Pakistan eviction and defeat. The Kargil War evoked adverse international reactions against Pakistan. It however succeeded in bringing about a resurgence of terrorism in Jammu and Kashmir and insurgency in the NE, which took some time to bring under control. The events of 9/11 in the US, US decision to strike at the terrorist infrastructure and invade Afghanistan and Pakistan becoming a frontline state in the US War On Terror (WOT), made Pakistan realize they could continue the proxy war with India. They therefore staged the terrorist strike on the Indian Parliament in December 2001, and upgraded terrorist attacks in Kashmir. This resulted in mobilisation of the Indian Armed Forces and their deployment opposite Pakistan for war. The US managed to prevent escalation of violence and get Pakistan to take measures to stem terrorist activity. Meanwhile, on Pakistani request, Bangladesh stepped up support to the NE insurgents. Consequently the situation in Assam, Tripura, Meghalaya and Manipur deteriorated. Pakistan and Bangladesh prevailed on the NSCN (I & M) to increase activity levels of their surrogate insurgent groups and to increase the tempo of their activity for Nagalim. The left extremist and minority groups were also pressurised to increase their level of activities — there was an escalation in violence levels all over the country. US WOT also resulted in many of the terrorists including Al Qaida fleeing both Afghanistan and Pakistan to take sanctuary in Bangladesh. This aggravated the risk of increased Islamic fundamentalist activity to the NE. The Bhutanese operations to liquidate/destroy all NDFB/ULFA/KLO and other camps in Bhutan, with the Indian Army carrying out the border-sealing operations, were a major foreign policy and CI operation success. The KLO and NDFB were marginalized, and ULFA was forced to run back to its camps in Bangladesh and elsewhere. This facilitated giving the peace process with the Bodos a fillip in 2004, and brought temporary peace to Assam. Manipur and Tripura, however, continued to burn.

Bangladesh becoming a haven for fundamentalism and sanctuary for extremists/insurgents can only bode ill; all this would mean continued proxy war. Maoist activities in friendly Nepal pose a direct threat to us and Bhutan—it is obvious as to who is supporting them. It therefore becomes imperative for us to have a balanced foreign policy, which ensures that we retain and increase our circle of friends, while making no new enemies, and meet our challenges taking all possible consequences into account.

Let us look at how we could deal with Bangladesh particularly now that it has invisible Army rule. Its people can not help but look for greener pastures across the border. This would continue to be supported by the Bangladeshi leadership pursuing their strategy of 'Lebensraum'. It is unlikely that border fences would stop the migration, as it is impossible to police the entire borders effectively. Bangladesh still holds the ideals of Partition. Hemming them in with fences will only increase animosity. The only workable option is to undo the hatred created by the Partition, to resolve problems through discussions, economic activity, trade, people to people contact and cultural interaction. Migration can be largely resolved by adopting a work-permit system. The practice of looking the other way in the interest of increasing vote banks must stop. Bangladesh has to be prevailed upon to stop its support to various insurgent groups, and integrate economically with the region. This can only be to its advantage as it would then have a ready market for both her labour and produce. It must also provide the region with transit facilities to the coast and West Bengal, particularly the other southern states of the region. Our foreign policy options will need to cater to applying suitable pressures which may well include the threat of economic blockades, control over river waters and as a last resort the use of force. Pressures also need to be applied on them through the western world as part of the WOT.

The situation in Nepal today remains disturbing. In my view it is only a matter of time before the Maoist extremists take control of Nepal and pose us a grave national security risk. If we do not help them, we would only push them into Chinese and Pakistani laps. We need to help Nepal in taking all measures that would resolve their problems.

Our friendship with Bhutan has matured and needs to be carried forward—considering that Bhutan had put itself to a great deal of trouble and risk and has been of tremendous help to us in denying sanctuary to insurgents. We need to put in more effort towards assisting them in resolving problems they have, so that a positive message goes across to our other neighbours.

While our relations with Myanmar have had major 'ups and downs', we must ensure good relations with them irrespective of the military rule. This must be done through greater interaction, trade, economic and cultural activity, and people to people contacts. This would lessen antagonism, so that they can assist us in control of the drug menace to the north-east and insurgency. Myanmar must also be prevailed upon to dislodge Indian insurgent groups from their territory.

Internal Security Policy Issues Needing Revision for NE Problem Resolution

First, we must stop balkanising the existing states to meet demands of the numerous ethnic groups. The redrawing of state boundaries on so called ethnic lines, in the manner as has been done repeatedly, has been a major error as it gave further impetus to splintering the already fragile pluralistic civil society structure. It contributed to the creation of extremist groups like the ULFA, NDFB, NSCN, a number of Manipuri and Arunachal insurgent organisations, and an upsurge in insurgency in the north-east. Also, in the states created from the '60s onwards, it resulted in ethnic fissures and strife, with examples being the rift between Khasis and Garos; Hmars, Paites, Chakmas, Brus and Mizos; rift between the Dimasa, Karbis and Assamese, and so on. We need to switch from the existing political structure of 'majority rule' with rigid territorial boundaries and neutralisation of traditional administrative institutions, wherein the majority ethnic group exercises a high degree of hegemony over its minorities, to one of 'conciliation politics'. This calls for a very high degree of inter ethnic cooperation in managing affairs in a highly pluralistic society whilst co-opting traditional institutions. It implies a coalition of the political elites of all the different ethnic groups within the existing political boundaries. It would give all the right of veto on issues of policy; proportional representation in most fields of administration and allotment of funds; and a high degree of autonomy including traditional grass root and economic self-sufficiency for each ethnic group. If this is not done, the minorities would continue to get a raw deal from the majority, with consequent agitation and insurgency. The 'Inner Line' or 'Excluded Area' system evolved by the British today stands in the way both of integration and development which is discriminatory and hence needs to go. This is all the more so as it goes against the very tenets conciliation of political structures, and contributes to splintering the civil society, particularly when ethnic groups have been divided by artificial political boundaries. Migration and its effect on changing demographic profiles need to be attended to immediately as it is a major cause for agitation. The currently prevalent vote-bank politics of encouraging immigration for political gains must also stop. Instead, a system of work permits needs to be introduced in many cases with retrospective effect while bearing in mind that the NE is labour-deficient and would hence have to import labour for economic survival. Suitable legislation in this regard would have to be introduced and enforced. Control over all matters is currently exercised through Delhi officials, who are far removed from reality and do not even know the NE or comprehend local problems. The requirement is to delegate authority to competent Governors who can issue prompt directions within the overall policy framework issued by Delhi.

We invariably advise that development is essential for resolution of insurgency. However, development requires peace. It is unfortunate that some state governments are attempting to achieve a military solution to political problems, without bothering to remember that the root causes of the insurgency need to be addressed through good governance and dialogue, coupled with stern action only when and where required. Corruption is also rampant with the militants running a parallel government and economy through illegal taxes, smuggling and drug rackets. One frequently hears the refrain that use of force to defeat militancy does not work and is counter-productive. This is true. CI operations can only assist in temporarily bringing the situation under control to allow the state to function. There is no option but to ensure good governance coupled with dialogue. The military option must be used only when absolutely imperative for only an inescapable period, and that also with people-friendly operations and with the complete weight of the government machinery behind it. Corruption and fund-raising by militants must be ruthlessly stamped out. The state police must be made effective as it is they who must ultimately ensure law and order and not the armed forces of the Centre. Delhi must also learn to see the north-east as a composite entity, as pandering to the whims of one segment is likely to alienate the others. The answers do not lie in the politics of divide and rule, but in the conciliatory approach to politics.

Economic Aspects that Contribute to Conflict and Need Resolution

Despite huge investments, economic development has not happened, it has instead contributed to a politically-led distribution-oriented process with a result that natural resources, profits and savings are moving out to higher productivity regions, leading to unemployment and dissatisfaction. The economic failures which can be largely enumerated are: most financial receipts are from Delhi; state revenues are almost non existent; planned expenditure including that spent on security is very high; in spite of being totally agricultural, the region is deficient in food due to destructive land utilisation patterns in the form of 'slash and burn' or '*jhoom*' type of cultivation and faulty land policy, which saps the incentive to profit. Most industrial units are sick; private enterprise is limited; the region is labour scarce and consequently needs to import labour; the region is power-deficient in spite of having enormous potential; infrastructure particularly in the hill regions is woefully inadequate. The total dependence on central funds and direction has also promoted passiveness amongst the people and made armed insurgent extortion an industry and there is a parallel and huge 'black' economy run by terrorist organisations in collusion with the authorised administrative structure, in almost all the states, except Sikkim, North Bengal and to a certain extent Mizoram; there is a very high degree of corruption and siphoning off of government money; all of these seriously impede economic progress and development.

While insurgency is impeding progress, development would greatly assist in removing the causes for insurgency. The NE must switch from the present centrally-controlled economic system, to that of a regional market-driven economy, with large-scale private investments in co-operation with the state governments. However, this can not succeed if the parallel 'black economy' is not curbed. The excuse given for not clamping down on such activities is that such action would disrupt the peace. Consequently the incentive for private enterprise or investment is non-existent. Under these circumstances how can the NE develop or become economically self-sufficient? The primary focus and strategy of the national CI effort of all agencies, therefore, needs to switch primarily to denial of funds to the insurgents, as without that the insurgency will die out of its own accord. The nexus between the politician/bureaucrat/government official and the insurgents and resultant corruption need to be tackled ruthlessly and on a war footing even if this implies President's Rule being imposed. There is also a need to come down on industry and businessmen in the region as they have contributed to the insurgent exchequer through extortion and payment of protection money and failed to report the same. There are also cases where the businessmen are banking and investing insurgent group funds, and carrying out *hawala* transactions for the insurgent groups for a profit which needs to be sternly dealt with.

There is a requirement to trim the state apparatus to achieve economy in non-developmental expenditures with governments switching to the role of being facilitators. State revenues have to be increased if necessary through imposition of taxes. Presently the hill states have no income tax levies. The entire region has been living on 'doles' which find their way into insurgent coffers, which is damaging the psyche of the NE, this needs to be progressively stopped, and instead encouragement given to entrepreneurship and employment created in the private sector. The livelihood of the majority of the population in the north-east is agriculture—the focus of economic development must shift to reform in the agricultural sector and be driven by market forces. This must include horticulture, floriculture, and commercial produce of bamboo/other cash crops which will make the region self sufficient. Industrial development should target this sector and make it more productive. Slash and burn cultivation must be prohibited and land laws amended from the existing community ownership to private ownership. Similarly the 'Inner Line' must go. How can there be investment if investors cannot enter the area and land cannot even be made available on lease? Investment in power generation, water supply and road/rail/air network and other essential infrastructure is urgent and inescapable. With the region being abundant in natural resources, effort must be made to change from being a primary product-exporting region to a finished product-exporting region. The industrial climate needs to be made more efficient and effective through investment, privatisation and encouraging entrepreneurship. As the region is labour deficient, there is no option but to import labour from outside which is one of the main reasons for immigration. A rational policy will have to be framed to ensure availability of labour while ensuring simultaneously that the demographic balance is not upset. Illegal cross border trade needs to be legalised and revenue accrued. This could be done in conjunction with declaring specified areas along the borders as free trade zones. Trade with the neighbouring countries needs to be enhanced /opened including China, Bangladesh, South-East Asia, Nepal, with a view to integrating the NE with the global market. Trade transit agreements must be arrived at with Bangladesh to balance the costs of transportation along the tenuous lines of communication with the rest of India.

Military Aspects—Causes of Insurgency

Insurgency has occurred in most cases due to poor governance and neglect of minorities, and requires political solutions. The requirement is for a combination of good governance, redressal of grievances, limiting corruption, economic development, military operations, negotiations and ensuring a denial of foreign support that are imperative to end the insurgencies. Immediately after creation of Bangladesh all insurgencies in the NE went on to a very low key due to lack of foreign support, till the military take-over of Bangladesh. In all cases however the government has been using military force, without addressing the causes for grievance. In Mizoram, it is only when the government policy switched to socio-economic-political resolution of the conflict, coupled with the denial of foreign support and military operations that CI was a success. It needs to be understood that long periods of use of pure military force are always counter-productive, as it only serves to alienate the population, since there would always be some infringement of human rights and harassment of even those who are innocent. Further, if the authorities do not address the causes of grievance simultaneous to the military operations, the degree of alienation increases multi-fold. The Army is the ultimate instrument of the state and must be deployed to deal with armed rebellion only as a last resort, when everything else fails. The states should deal with such problems using the state police as they are most suited for such tasks. This means modernising and training them suitably, since there can be no doubt that no one can know the area or the people or their problems better than the local policemen. In case there is a lack of resources, the police could be backed up by CPOs/ PMF, who should preferably function under the control of the police. Our CPOs/PMF unfortunately lack the ethos, culture, training and organisation to function in such an environment, which needs to be rectified. It is only when the state police and the state administration have been totally subverted that the operational situation be handed over to the CPOs/PMF.

The primary role of the armed forces is to defend the nation's territorial integrity against external armed aggression. They also have a secondary role, to aid civil power to maintain and restore law and order in cases of strife, violence and natural calamities and catastrophes. Assistance in natural calamities is beyond the purview of this paper and is not addressed further. It is important to note that the armed forces are called upon to maintain and restore law and order only when the situation is beyond the control of the police. In the event of such an emergency, the armed forces operate in cooperation and conjunction with the civil administration. It must be appreciated that when the state is constrained to deploy the Army to bring armed rebellion under control, the Army must be given the full backing of the state in all its activities. This includes special powers, authority and legal protection to deal with the situation where the police and the administration have been rendered ineffective due to subversion, a unitary command and control structure with the Army at the helm of control, and with the state's resources where necessary placed at the Army's disposal. This implies simultaneous effort by the state to redress the causes of the conflict and re-establish its instruments of administration and control. It also implies that the state would dispense with the services of the Army as soon as the situation has been controlled adequately for the state machinery to function.

I will now cover other aspects of problem resolution and must begin by reiterating that problem resolution needs to be considered for the region in its entirety as resolution for one state would in all probability impinge on the well-being of another.

Assam

Assam is the hub of the region, Major economic progress in Assam is essential for problem resolution of the entire region. This highest priority for development in all its facets must be given to Assam for its conversion into an industrial and agricultural base for finished products and infrastructure for the entire region. The NEC should control this to ensure that the entire region's requirements are met. Assam's ULFA problem can only be resolved by a multi-pronged approach of dialogue and problem resolution with militants, dealing with migration, economic development, denial of support from Bangladesh, curbing corruption and coming down on 'Black' economy, and resolution of land and other disputes with neighbouring states. As a result of ongoing CI operations and public pressure, it appeared that talks with the ULFA would finally see the light of day. This was unfortunately not to be on account of faulty handling of the issue. Consequently the cease-fire with the ULFA broke down and progress towards talks failed. While talks with the insurgents are imperative to identify and resolve grievances, the authorities must take note of the errors that were committed in the past. ULFA's leadership has been given sanctuary in Bangladesh and has vast capital invested in businesses in that country and abroad with the concurrence of the Bangladesh government, DGFI and the ISI. ULFA cannot touch this capital without the concurrence of all these agencies; their personal security in Bangladesh is provided by these agencies; the families of these leaders and indeed the leaders themselves are puppets controlled by these agencies; they are therefore in no position to take a single decision of importance on their own accord. Any talks by the Govt. of India with the ULFA therefore will be talks controlled by the ISI/DGFI! It must be realised that there is a clear division in ULFA ranks –the leadership and their supporters controlled by the ISI/DGFI in

Bangladesh and those on the ground who still operate under at least part of the original ULFA ideals. We must deal with the latter and not the former to bring an end to the problem. In the overall and long-term context, we will at some stage in the near future have to negotiate with Pakistan and Bangladesh to find long-term solutions as the proxy war continues. The Bodo problem must be handled carefully and the aspirations of all met. The Bodo Accord must be implemented in letter and spirit as promised and a system of conciliation at politics imposed within the Bodo Council to avoid the minority groups being alienated by the Bodos. The same issues that apply to the ULFA should govern talks with the NDFB that are likely in the near future. The situation in South Assam needs to be handled with care, as this is part of the area claimed by NSCN. Conciliation politics, grass root autonomy and economic development are imperative to resolve differences between ethnic groups, otherwise ethnic strife will continue to surface. All this has to be coupled with a clamp down on NSCN and other insurgent activities and the area denied to them for sanctuary. As all insurgent groups transiting to and from Bangladesh are extensively using the area, border guarding by the BSF must be strengthened. The Assam government must also ensure development of the Bengali-speaking belt in Cachar, Hailakandi and Karimganj, failing which we could well see this area develop into a yet another fundamentalist hub. The Assamese majority must realise that though they form the ethnic majority, they form only about 40 per cent of the population with the balance being a multitude of other ethnic groups. Assam will not enjoy peace and prosperity unless it looks after these minorities as their own people. Infrastructure and industry that are to be planned for Assam must also be located and set up to cater to the needs of the entire region. This is particularly so as the hill states have comparatively small populations, whereas industry needs larger demand volumes to be cost effective. This emphasises the need for the NEC to become more effective and ensure more balanced development. The private sector and entrepreneurship must be given much greater impetus as the future lies in that realm.

Nagaland and Manipur

The major issue and stumbling block in the talks with the NSCN (I and M) is the issue of Greater Nagaland. Also, Delhi is being perceived by many as partial and wooing the Tangkhuls, who form the majority of the NSCN (I and M). Since talks have taken place only with NSCN (I and M), it is perceived as talks only with the Tangkhuls. Probably, in the long run, this will not be accepted by the other tribes, who are deeply distrustful of the Tangkhuls; and in the event of an accord with them by the centre, there may be no lasting peace. Delhi's approach therefore is fraught with danger. Delhi can not obviously agree to create Greater Nagaland, as it would have similar demands from all other ethnic groups and result in major disturbances and agitation all over the NE. It cannot also give power to the NSCN (I and M) in Nagaland, as this will amount to Nagaland being ruled by non-Nagaland tribes led by the Tangkhuls. It can again not agree to a very high degree of autonomy, as that would have repercussions on the federal structure of the entire Indian Union in general and the NE in particular. The issue now is what then is the way ahead?

One can not look at the resolution of the Naga problem in isolation, as it is intricately linked to Assam, Manipur, Arunachal, Mizoram and Myanmar in particular and the rest of the NE in general, including Bangladesh. The errors that have been made till date are in trying to find a solution for Nagaland and not for the region in its totality. Consequent to political boundaries having been created arbitrarily, with various ethnic groups being split across the same and these boundaries now becoming a highly emotive issue for all states in the region, Delhi will need to sell the idea to all those involved, that these boundaries are purely for administration and not related to the concept of territorial integrity of nation states. This will not be so easy, as the people of the region are still steeped in their primordial value system, wherein territorial integrity of the nation remains a core value; and it would be quite some time before they transit to modernity in all its facets. The answers therefore perhaps lie in the realm of transiting to modernity more rapidly; wherein integration, conciliatory politics, economic development and cultural harmony need to be given greater importance than aspects of territorial integrity and sovereignty, for all ethnic groups as a whole. Whilst doing so it should be ensured that no favouritism is shown to a single ethnic group simply because they are agitating, as this would only result in other ethnic groups rebelling against the State. This is particularly so as there has been traditionally deep-rooted distrust between the different ethnic groups, including those amongst the Nagas.

Delhi needs to first broaden the base for talks, involving various ethnic groups including, all major dissenting factions, the church, intellectuals who understand the region, and representatives of all the governments involved, and NOT simply the NSCN (I and M). President's Rule needs to be imposed in Nagaland, Manipur and areas affected by the problems in Assam and Arunachal for some time, with the approval of the Parliament, so as to be able to directly administer these regions, resolve problems and ensure rapid economic progress and development. To this end, Governors need to be carefully selected, given a free hand and if the need arises, to replace existing administrators, this should be done. All development needs to be in accordance with the will of the local people. The rule of law in all areas needs to be restored by a crackdown on all insurgent groups including the NSCN who are equally culpable for the existing state of affairs. This would mean induction of additional SF, and they need to be given a free hand with strict instructions to conduct people friendly operations with minimum possible infringements on human rights. If this means a breakdown of the cease-fire, this should be accepted. The judiciary needs to be re-activated. The police force needs to be revitalised through reorganisation, training and modernisation and progressively made effective so as to take charge of policing the state properly. Politicians continuing to play up to the insurgents should be sternly dealt with.

Extortion, drug and arms smuggling by all insurgent groups across the board should be reined in and the NSCN (I and M) and (K), and their intimidation of the local population stopped. Both the NSCN factions need to be made to abide by the terms of the cease-fire, if necessary by force; even if this means a breakdown of the cease-fire. In case this happens, the SF need to be given a free hand to deal with the situation, but at the same time ensure people friendly operations with minimum possible violation of human rights. An offensive foreign policy needs to be launched to deny external support to the insurgents. All this needs to be done by explaining the reasons for doing so publicly to the people. Extortion, intimidation and crime need to be brought under control. The SF must take all possible measures to prevent and stop inter-ethnic strife and bloodshed and wherever this occurs, ringleaders must be brought to justice. These are only the initial measures which need to be taken immediately to send a clear message to the entire population that we mean business, and that all possible measures will be taken to restore normalcy in the states, and that all ethnic groups and their problems would be handled impartially and promptly.

With ethnic emotiveness being at its peak, a concerted developmental and economic effort is required with an abundance of funds and employment generation in a balanced manner in all ethnic areas simultaneously as per the will of the local people. Private enterprise and self-employment schemes should be given impetus and private investment should be encouraged and the law and order situation brought under control. Government control over all border trade should be immediately established along with a free trade zone on the Myanmar border to facilitate trade and revenue accrual to the government. It needs to be realised that the Moreh border offers the best possible access route for trade not only with Myanmar but also the South East Asian region. This needs to be developed on the basis of top priority and capitalised upon. Manipur must get all weather road access to all neighbouring states, particularly Assam, so that the Meiteis are not intimidated by all and sundry. Manipur is rich in natural resources and trade with its neighbours must be encouraged. The rail link to Manipur, and if possible its extension up to the Myanmar border, needs to be pushed through on the highest priority. All possible interaction and measures should be instituted to counter the feeling of alienation that has crept in to all the ethnic groups alike, and to win them over through all possible measures including economic activity and development.

The widened talks suggested to attempt to resolve the Naga problem, by a 'panel' who know and understand the region, should also encompass representatives of the ethnic groups of Manipur, as a major fall out of the Naga problem is the situation in Manipur. The same Talks Panel needs also to be given the responsibility of making recommendations with regard to resolving the ethnic strife and method to be adopted for Manipur. To my mind, however with the problems being what they are, I can see no option but to create an economic and developmental federation of ethnic regions, with political boundaries being purely for the purposes of administration, coupled with conciliatory politics. Cultural and social trans-state linkages on ethnic issues can then be worked out and interwoven into the above structure to obviate the demands for greater Nagaland and Mizoram. Inter-ethnic seminars and discussions involving a maximum number of people should be undertaken to remove the causes of the ethnic strife.

Mizoram

Mizoram, though a relatively peaceful state, needs to resolve its problems with its minorities through conciliatory politics and economic development. If this is not done, agitation and strife at some stage is inevitable, as there is a perception that its minorities are being neglected. It should try to avoid involvement in the problems of the Kuki–Chin tribals of Manipur and Chin hills and issues of Greater Mizoram, as this only complicates the problem resolution of these issues. It also needs to resolve issues of disorganised development, which have resulted in neglect of the agricultural sector leading to a very large-scale migration towards urbanisation (60 per cent or more of the population is now urban), which is simply not sustainable. Today the towns are literally bursting at the seams with the infrastructure being unable to support such an influx as also the terrain and soil structure are also unable to support the high population densities that now exist in the towns. With most of Mizoram being in a high seismic zone with very high rainfall patterns, the urban areas are literally time bombs, God forbid, should a natural calamity occur! It is also very highly dependent for its survival on central assistance, with jobs being available primarily only in the government sector. It also has drug abuse problems and a high incidence of HIV. Its major problems today are in the social, economic and developmental spheres. These need to be attended to on the highest priority.

Arunachal Pradesh

Arunachal Pradesh is fortunate in having a small population spread over a huge area, thereby reducing to a degree the possibility of ethnic strife. Notwithstanding this fact, there is a fair amount of distrust and rivalry between its multitudes of ethnic groups, the majority of whom strongly feel that the 'Adi' majority is neglecting them. It is for this reason and the fact that the NSCN also claim Tirap, Changlang and parts of Lohit district, that it is embroiled in a low-grade insurgency. The only way in which such problems can be resolved is through conciliatory politics and economic development, with much more attention paid by the majority ethnic group to the minorities. The state also has a migrant problem, which needs to be addressed considering its small population size. Arunachal is again heavily dependant on Delhi for doles even though it has tremendous availability of natural resources. This needs to be progressively reduced and the state's efforts diverted towards drawing in investment, private entrepreneurship and self-employment schemes. Delhi and the NEC need to concentrate on greater efforts towards development of infrastructure, as it is woefully inadequate at persent.

Meghalaya

Meghalaya needs to attend to its migrant problem as suggested for Assam and consequently keep its low-grade insurgency under control, particularly in the Garo Hills where the ULFA, NDFB and the ANVC have sanctuary and are active. Though the police are doing a fair job, they need modernisation and training to deal with the problems adequately, particularly since the state is a major transit route for migrants and insurgents to and from Bangladesh. Here again, the problem of Bangladesh's support and sanctuary to the insurgents need urgent attention. The Khasis and Garos need to come to terms with each other and live amicably–again conciliatory politics is the need of the day. Though the State has tremendous economic potential it is financially backward. A concerted effort must be made towards economic development, employment generation in the private sector and reduced dependence on doles.

Tripura

Tripura's majority Bengali population must look after its tribal minority and give them a fair deal –all the more so since it is the migrants who today form the majority and are therefore the source of the problem. A rational social, cultural, economic and developmental package must be worked out and given to them and conciliatory politics brought to the fore. The ultimate solution would only be possible through linking hands in economic development and getting Bangladesh to desist from supporting the insurgents.

Sikkim

Sikkim is doing a commendable job in looking after its minorities –it needs to continue to do so through greater economic development and tourism. It needs to, however, take conscious note of the developments in Nepal, and ensure that West Sikkim does not provide sanctuary to Maoists and Islamic fundamentalists, or get involved in the issue of Gurkhaland. A few media reports of recent times indicate that there are attempts to do so. To this end, it needs to modernise and train its police force to handle such a situation and prevent this from happening.

Conclusion

Insurgency and conflict in the NE are a threat to development and national security. The problems of the region, though extremely complex, can be resolved through dialogue with the people of the region and by collectively applying our minds to find the best possible solution for the population at large. I would be more than satisfied if the views offered even partially contribute to the endeavours by those in authority towards problem resolution. In my view we owe the wonderful people of the NE a wholehearted and sincere effort towards resolution of their problems.

NOTES AND REFERENCES

All Central & State Government websites on the North East and its states.

Archives of Assam Tribune, North East Times, Sentinel, North East Daily, Nagaland Post, Shillong Times, Arunachal Post, Imphal Daily, Mizoram Times, The Statesman Calcutta, Daily Telegraph Calcutta, Times of India.

Anxiety and Anger in India's North East, Naga Identity, Meitei Nationalism and Electoral Politics, Peace in Naga Country, Papers presented at Centre for Conflict Development in India's North East, Gauhati.

Bareh, H.M., *Encyclopedia of North East India*, 2001.

Baruah, S.L., *Comprehensive History of Assam*.

Baruah, Sanjib, *India Against Itself: Assam and Politics of Nationality*.

Basak, R.G., *History of North East India*.

Bhattacharea, S.R., *Tribal Insurgency in Tripura*.

Bhaumik Subir, *Insurgent Cross Fire – North East India*.

Bindra, *Indo-Bangladesh Relations*.

Census of India, Government of India, 1991, 2001.

Chaherbhuj, *Tribes of North East India*.

Constantine R., *Manipur*, *Maid of the Mountains*.

Dai, Mamang, *Arunachal Pradesh: the Myth of Tranquility*.

Das, H.N., Insurgency and Development: the Assam Experience, author's paper presented at a seminar on "Addressing Conflicts in India's North East, Institute for Conflict Management, 25–27 June, 2001.

Das, Gurudas, Probable Options- Cementing the Faultlines in Assam, and

Migration, Ethnicity and Competition for State Resources: Explanation of the Social Tension in North East India, North East State Papers.

Das, N.K., *Ethnic Identity, Ethnicity and Social Stratification in North East India.*

Das, Samir Kumar, Ethnic Conflict and Internal Security – A plea for reconstructing Civil Society in Assam: and Assam Insurgency and Disintegration of Civil Society presented at a Seminar on National security Issues: Special Emphasis on North Eastern India, Omeo Kumar Das Institute of Social Change and Development, Gauhati, 22 April 2002.

Das, Samir Kumar, *ULFA – A Political Analysis: and Foreign Hand in Theory.*

Deb, Bimal J., *Development Priorities in North East India*

Dutt, V.P., *India's Foreign Policy in a Changing World*

Elwin, Verrier, *A Philosophy for NEFA*

Faultlines, Writings on Conflict and Resolution, Institute of Conflict Management, New Delhi.

Gate, E.A., *A History of Assam: and Gazeteer of Bengal and North East India.*

Gopalakrishnan, R., *The North East India: Land, Economy and People.*

Gori, Gulab Khan, *The Changing Phase of Tribal Areas of Manipur.*

Hazarika, Sajay, *Strangers in the Mist*

Horam, M., *Thirty Years of Naga Insurgency.*

Hussein, Monirul, *The Assam Movement: Class Ideology and Identity.*

Hussain, Wasbir, *Cross Border Traffic in South Asia: Demographic Inversion*

Jaffa, V.S., Ten O'Clock to Bed; and 'Insouciance in the Face of Terror', Faultlines, Writings on Conflict and Resolution.

John, Vanlalhnuna, *Church and Political Upheaval in Mizoram.*

John, W. Garver, *The China – India – US Triangle.*

Kanchan, L., *Negotiating Insurgencies: the Naga Imbroglio.*

Kumar, Anand, *A Renewed Thrust of ISI and Al Qaeda in North East; A New Destination for Radical Islamists*; and *the ULFA Business in Bangladesh.*

Lintner, B., *Land of Jade* (Banned by NSCN (I & M)).

Lt. Gen. J.R. Mukherjee, PVSM, AVSM, VSM, (Retd), *An Insiders View of Insurgency in India's North East*, Anthem Press, New Delhi, 2005.

Lt. Gen. S.K. Pillai, (Retd) *Anatomy of an Insurgency: Ethnicity and Identity in Nagaland.*

Nag, Sajal, *Withdrawal Syndrome: Secessionism in Modern North East India, Essays on North East India*, Indus, New Delhi, 1994.

Narahari, N.S., *Security Threats to North East India*; and *Socio Ethnic Conflicts in the North East.*

Nirmal, Nibedon, *The Dagger Brigade.*

Rammohan, E.N., *Manipur: A Degenerated Insurgency*

Routray, Bibhu Prasad, *ULFA; The Revolution Comes a Full Circle.*

Sachdeva, Gulshan, *Economy of the North East, Policy, Present Conditions and Future Prospects.*

Saikia, Jaideep, ISI Reaches East; Terror sans Frontiers- Islamic Militancy in North East India; and Development Challenges in India – Assam in 2015.; Articles in '*Faultlines*'.

Sanyu, Visier, What Nagaland State did to the Nagas, a Historical Perspective; A History of Nagaland and the Nagas; The Noxious Web-Insurgency in the North East.

Sengupta, Dipankar, *Insurgency in North East India: the Role of Bangladesh*

Shashinungla, *Insurgency and Factional Intransigence;* and *Nagaland the Dynamics of Extortion.*

Singh, W. Ibohal, *History of Manipur.*

Lt. Gen. S.K. Sinha, (Retd), *Illegal Immigration into Assam.*

Verghese, B.G., *India's North East Resurgent – Ethnicity, Insurgency and Governance*; and *Terror Economy in India's North East – Preliminary Explorations.*

This paper is adapted from the author's book titled '*An Insiders Experience of Insurgency in India's North East*', Anthem Press, New Delhi, 2005

Challenging the Nation-State

SECESSIONISM AND INSURGENCY

Sajal Nag

North East India poses a number of problems for the Indian state, the most serious being the problem of secessionist insurgency. It is serious as this is not merely a law and order problem but a threat to the unity and integrity of the new post colonial Indian nation-state. It not only questions the concept of one nationhood for all the communities of India but even questions the legitimacy of the Indian State to rule over marginalised communities like the Naga, Mizo, Meithei, Assamese, Khasis, Bodo, Tippera, Karbi, Dimasa and so on. They present themselves as a separate nation and demand the right to self-determination and the right to opt out of Indian Union as a separate sovereign nation state. The Government of India, therefore, had to confront serious crisis as the challenges to its authority came from rather small tribal groups. It started with the Nagas but then snowballed into many—the Mizos, the Meitheis, the Khasis, the Garos, the Bodos, the Kukis, Karbis, the Dimasas, the Tripuri tribes plunging the entire region into a killing field. Every tribe mentioned above has an underground organisation with the declared objective of seceding from India. Besides attacking the Indian armed forces and other power symbols of India, the major activity of these organisations generally involved massive extortion drives, kidnapping and ethnic cleansing of certain targeted communities. Such ethnic cleansing projects have provoked the targeted communities to organise their own underground organisation for their own protection, e.g., Bengal Tiger Force, Bengali Protection Force, Santhal Liberation Army, Kuki National Army, Bru Liberation Force, Hmar National Army, Muslim Liberation Army, and so on. In fact, there are about fifty active militant organisations in the North East.

Table 1: Active Insurgent Organisations in North East India

	Active insurgent organisation	*Ethnic Base*	*State*	*Nature*
1.	United Liberation Front of Assam	Assamese	Assam	Secessionism
2.	National Democratic Front of Bodoland	Bodo	Assam	Secessionism
3.	Bodo Liberation Tiger Force	Bodo	Assam	Secessionism
4.	Karbi National Volunteers	Karbi	Assam	Secessionism
5.	Dima Haloa Daoga	Dimasa	Assam	Secessionism
6.	Bengali Protection Force	Bengali immigrants	Assam	Protection
7.	Muslim United Liberation Tigers of Assam	Immigrant Muslims	Assam	Protection
8.	Arunachal Dragon Force renamed East India Liberation Front	Arunachalese	Arunachal Pradesh	Secessionism
9.	Peoples' Liberation Army	Meithei	Manipur	Secessionism
10.	United National Liberation Front	Meithei	Manipur	Secessionism
11.	Peoples' Revolutionary Party of Kangleipak	Meithei	Manipur	Secessionism
12.	Kangleipak Communist Party	Meithei	Manipur	Secessionism
13.	Kanglei Kanba Lup	Meithei	Manipur	Secessionism
14.	National Socialist Council of Nagaland (Isak Muivah)	Naga	Nagaland, Assam, Arunachal	Secessionism
15.	NSCN (Khaplang)	Naga	Nagaland, Arunachal Pradesh	Secessionism
16.	All Tripura Tiger Force	Tripuri	Tripura	Secessionism
17.	National Liberation Front of Twipera	Tripuri	Tripura	Secessionism
18.	Bengali Tiger Force	Bengali	Tripura	Protection
19.	Acik National Volunteer Council	Garo	Meghalaya	Secessionism
20.	Hyniew Triep National Liberation Council	Khasi	Meghalaya	Secessionism
21.	North East Red Army	Khasi	Meghalaya	Secessionism
22.	Hmar National Army	Hmar	Mizoram	Protection
23.	Bru National Liberation Front	Bru	Mizoram	Protection
24.	Kuki National Army	Kuki	Mizoram	Protection

	Active insurgent organisation	*Ethnic Base*	*State*	*Nature*
25.	Mizo National Front (since settled as a political party and wind up secessionism agenda)	Mizo	Mizoram	Secessionism
26.	Kamatapur Liberation Organisation	Koch Rajbanshi	West Bengal	Autonomy
27.	Naga National Council	Naga	Nagaland	Secessionism
28.	United Peoples' Democratic Solidarity	Karbi	Assam	Secessionism
29.	Muslim United Liberation Force of Assam	Immigrant Muslims	Assam	Secessionism
30.	Liberation Islamic Tiger Force	Immigrant Muslims	Assam	Secessionism
31.	Muslim Security Council of Assam	Immigrant Muslims	Assam	Secessionism
32.	Hynniewtrep Socialist Democratic Front	Khasi	Meghalaya	Secessionism
33.	Peoples' Liberation Front of Meghalaya	Garo	Assam, Meghalaya	Secessionism
34.	All Meghalaya Liberation Front	Garo, Khasi	Meghalaya	Secessionism
35.	Meghalaya-e-Sunna	Muslims	Meghalaya	Secessionism
36.	All Meghalaya Islamic Liberation Front	Muslims	Meghalaya	Secessionism
37.	Karbi Peoples' Front	Karbi	Assam	Secessionism
38.	Gorkha Liberation Organisation	Gorkha	North East	Protection
39.	Assam Tiger Force	Assamese	Assam	Secessionism
40.	Tripura Resurrection Army	Tripura	Tripura	Secessionism
41.	Citizens Right Preservation Committee	Non-Karbi Plains men	Assam	Protection
42.	Karbi Peoples' Front	Karbi	Assam	Secessionism
43.	Kuki National Front	Kuki	Manipur, Nagaland	Secessionism
44.	United Bengali Liberation Force	Bengali	Tripura	Protection
45.	Adivasi Cobra Force	Adivasi	Assam	Protection
46.	Muslim United Liberation Tigers of Assam	Muslims	Assam	Protection
47.	Muslim Liberation of Assam (MLA)	Muslims	Assam	Protection
48.	United Muslim Liberation Front of Assam	Muslims	Assam	Protection

	Active insurgent organisation	*Ethnic Base*	*State*	*Nature*
49.	Peoples' United Liberation Front	Meitheis	Manipur	Secessionism
50.	Hindu Liberation Army of Assam	Hindu	Assam	Protection
51.	Assam Peoples' Liberation Army (predecessor of ULFA)	Assamese	Assam	Secessionism

Very rarely these outfits came into conflict with each other even though their declared objectives clash with each other's. It is because in the underground they are collaborators and share each others booty; the north east is the field where they play.

Table 2: Terrorists related encounters with Army in North East

Terrorist related incidents in Nagaland-Manipur			
	1997-98	1995	1999
Number of encounters	64		
Extremists killed	31		
Extremists arrested	348	193	261
Arms seized	238		
Ammunition seized	278		
Security forces killed	75		

Extremists attack/violence in North East India (1997-98)		
	Incident	Civilians killed
Arunachal Pradesh	34	9
Assam	427	285
Manipur	320	233
Meghalaya	14	3
Mizoram	1	-
Nagaland	380	92
Tripura	303	205

Persons killed in Assam (1993-1998)			
	Brahmaputra Valley	*Karbi Anglong*	*Cachar*
Police	157	4	12
Army	100	23	14
Paramilitary	99	6	7
Civilians	1128	5	37

Source: Lok Sabha, unstarred question no. 1941, December 16, 1998

The Annual Report of the Ministry of Home Affairs 2000-2001 recorded that during the years 2000-2001[1], in the seven north eastern states, altogether 196 insurgency related cases were reported, 585 extremists and 153 security personnel were killed; 216 arms were looted and 574 were recovered. The number of civilians killed was 907 while 1962 extremists surrendered and 84 kidnapping cases were reported.

An NGO's report says[2] that there are about 34 underground outfits in Assam, 35 in Manipur. This report says there were a total of 800 persons killed in various conflicts in 2000 against 511 in 1999. In Manipur 237 lost their lives in 2000 compared to 231 in 1999. In Tripura a total of 405 persons lost their lives in 2000 as compared to 303 in 1999. In Nagaland despite ceasefire, a total of 13 civilians, 4 security forces and 82 terrorists lost their lives in 2000 as against 26, 4 and 124 respectively in 1999.

Arunachal Pradesh witnessed the spill over effect of insurgencies from the neighbouring states. The first insurgent organisation, Arunachal Dragon Force, made its official appearance in 2001 but its presence was known even in 2000. The districts of Tirap and Changlang were the most affected by extortions, kidnapping and attacks. In 2000, 3 security personnel, 7 civilians and 24 terrorists were killed, against 3 civilians and 3 terrorists in 1999. In Meghalaya 13 civilians, 7 army men, and 15 terrorists lost their lives in 2000 while the figures were 5 civilians and 17 security personnel in 1999. In fact on November 6, 2000, the central government declared the two active outfits HNLC and ANVC in Meghalaya as unlawful.

Table 3: Insurgency and its effects 2000-2001

States	*Militant-Army encounter*	*Militants killed*	*Civilians killed*	*Abduction*	*Army personnel killed*	*Militants arrested*
Tripura	826	38	360	558	17	NA
Assam	536	321	419	105	76	NA
Manipur	245	102	93	32	51	NA
Nagaland	195	84	13	58	4	NA
Meghalaya	74	15	11	12	7	61
Arunachal Pradesh	73		8		3	NA
Mizoram	NA	1	4	NA	7	NA

Source: Annual Home Ministry Report, 2000-2001, Government of India.

Mizoram remained largely free from the terrorist violence. But still it saw the death of four civilians, seven security force personnel and terrorists in 2000, against 2 civilians and 5 security force personnel in 1999. The two main outfits in the state are Hmar National Council and Bru National Liberation Front. The following are insurgency related figures for 1999-2000.

The turbulence created by the outfits were not confined to the above mentioned activities only. They also disturbed the civil life and political and economic activities of the region by calling 'bandhs' frequently which the frightened society was compelled to obey.

According to a report, Manipur had the highest number of bandhs, about 200 days in 2000, Meghalaya about 40 days and Mizoram 20 days. In north east 15th August and 26th January celebrations are virtually paralysed every year by a joint bandh called only by all the outfits for 36 hours (effective 12 hours preceding the day). As can be seen, the bandhs are not called by the insurgent organisations only but also by political parties as well as students' organisations and underground wings of insurgent organisations. A bandh called for 12 hours was the most common. However, longer duration bandhs for 36 or 48 hours and even 72 hours were not uncommon. According to the North East Development Finance Institution (NEDFI) study, losses in state domestic product per day have been Rs. 4,479 lakhs. The total loss due to bandhs between June 1997 and May 1998 in Assam alone was Rs. 1,255 crores.[3] There are frequent periods of partial paralysis of the civil life also like road blockade, chakka jam, non-tribal curfew and so on.

The Annual Home Ministry Report (2000-01) admitted that the ill-equipped police forces in north east India were no match for the arsenal of sophisticated weapons in possessions of militant outfits operating here. The Union Ministry had spent Rs. 184 crores to modernise and equip the police forces of the region with sophisticated weapons. The amount spent according to the report was Rs. 285 crores for a five year scheme of the Home Ministry which was put into operation since 1997-98. Besides the deployment of central paramilitary forces and Indian Reserve Battalions, the eleventh finance commission announced an award of Rs. 600 lakhs to Meghalaya for police administration besides reimbursement of security related expenditure. A sum of Rs. 321 crores had been released in 2000-01 for Meghalaya as reimbursement of security related expenditure.[4]

The Annual Report 2000-01 by the Home Ministry remarks that the militancy in north eastern region was bereft of any ideology.[5] This was the first time that the Home Ministry made such a comment on the fifty years old history of insurgency in north east India. In fact on the white paper published by the government on Naga insurgency in the early 1950s, it had declared otherwise. Though it did not approve of the Naga secessionism it did not denigrate or neglect it. It appreciated the Naga problem and hoped that in time the well meaning gestures of the Indian people will be appreciated by the Naga people. It also commented that militancy had become so rampant and easy in the region that it was like a 'cottage industry' of kidnapping, extortion and killing with the 'sole objective of making money'. The Home Ministry's report was based on the fact that almost every industry or business house, big or small, in most parts of north east make regular contribution to different underground groups.

The Home Ministry Report 2000-01 admitted that the militancy in the north eastern states had affected the very functioning of the democratic state. Accounting for the unrest, the report stated that the change from a largely tribal society to a modern society had contributed to the turbulence. The networking of various militant groups in the region relies on trans-border bases, concerted efforts to arouse aspirations for self-determination among the indigenous people and attempts to subvert the population and gain international sympathy through propaganda about alleged neglect of the region, characterised the militancy scene. The Pakistani Inter Services intelligence (ISI) had been assisting the militancy in the region. The long porous borders have facilitated movements of militant groups and inflow of illegal arms into the region, besides large-scale influx of illegal migrants into the country. The report further stated that some groups had sanctuaries in some of the neighbouring countries, and lack of employment opportunity in the private sector had fuelled the influx of neo-literate youth into militancy. Blaming the state governments for improper utilisation of funds, an alarming rise in expenditure to meet the non-plan requirements like payment of salaries, thereby reducing funds given for developmental works, the report states, "whatever funds are given for developmental needs the same are not properly utilised. Various reports of the Comptroller and Auditor General of India have pointed that works are awarded by some north eastern states without inviting tender, materials are procured at exorbitantly high rates and money is fraudulently withdrawn from government treasuries".[6]

The report also mentioned that to tackle the crisis, the Indian Central Government expressed its willingness to meet and discuss legitimate grievances, friendly relations with neighbouring countries, accelerated infrastructural development, stress on employment, good governance and de-centralisation. As to the military parts of the solution the report highlighted the deployment of central paramilitary forces and Indian Reserve Battalions. The eleventh Finance Commission announced an award of Rs. 600 lakhs to Meghalaya State for police administration besides reimbursement of security related expenditure. Rs. 3.21 crores had been released in 2000-02 to Meghalaya as reimbursement of security related expenditure.

Echoing almost an identical assessment, the Seventh Report of the National Police Commission (May, 1981) stated,[7] "The north east has been in a state of turmoil for some years now. They are posing a serious threat to the security and stability not only of this region but of the entire country...An ad hoc approach in dealing with highly complicated and explosive situation will not do. The whole country is already paying a very high price for this situation and if not effectively dealt with, may have to pay a much higher price even endangering the stability and security of the country."

Accounting for the situation this 1981 report stated,[8] "Because of the prolonged isolation of the area from the rest of the country, a feeling of separation has grown as living in isolation they have got used to living freely with minimum or no government control. They tend to resent any kind of discipline from any authority. Local grievances and aspirations have further encouraged separatist tendencies. As neglected people, the fear of being exploited by the migrants from the plains and absorbed into the neighbouring states haunts them. The fear has led to eruption of violence quite frequently. There are extremist elements among these tribals in these areas who will not be satisfied with anything short of complete separation from India. These extremist elements, it is suspected, are receiving support from some foreign countries who are interested for their own reasons in destabilising this region.... The fact that the tribals suddenly emerged from an era of isolation and extreme backwardness of the region are two major causes of this hostility. The central government has been spending huge funds to force the pace of development in this region but the benefits of economic activity have unfortunately gone only to a small section of the people. The contractors, the bureaucrats and politicians have earned most of the development benefits. The problems of the tribals in the interior areas have not been solved and they continue to suffer, even though per capita expenditure is the highest in the region. The backlog of neglect of centuries has to be wiped out and this huge task cannot be accomplished in a short time. The spread of education has not been an unmixed blessing. There is a danger that the increase of educated unemployed will outstrip the economic growth. The educated unemployed are easy prey to the propaganda of the extremist elements. The corruption and inefficiency of the administrative machinery has further created a sense of abhorrence of the outsiders in the minds of the people. The hated foreigner is known as Vai in Mizoram, Mayang in Manipur, Teppremyie in Nagaland and Dkhar in Meghalaya. There is no doubt that the solution to the problem of backwardness of the area lies in its development and not in isolation. The hatred for the foreigner has become an emotional obsession with the people and any influx, even of engineers, administrators, who are so necessary for the development work, is looked upon with suspicion. The economic backwardness of the region, poor communications and remoteness of the area are responsible for this isolation which has become emotional as well as physical. Unfortunately, pursuit of unimaginative policing, instead of integrating with the rest of the country have only succeeded in further alienating them. There is complete separation between the tribals and non-tribals living in these areas. In their anxiety to integrate these areas with the rest of the country the policy makers did not quite appreciate the historical background and the tribal social structure before deciding to introduce the central laws and systems of administration in this region. The demand for separation has taken the shape of insurgency in Nagaland and Mizoram. The situation in Manipur is also causing anxiety...."

The two reports published between a gap of twenty years (1981 and 2001) show that the understanding of the government on the subject has not changed much although within this period of 20 years the situation has worsened further. Indeed the 'Insurgency' seems like a 'cottage industry'. The ideological content of the outfits has to be judged by their involvement in extortion, kidnapping, murder and even arms dealing and drug trafficking. The sole objective is 'making money'. The demand of 'sovereignty' only appears as a cover. Even the various statistics given above would only substantiate the government's point of view. Yet it was always not so. The beginning of insurgency in Nagaland was a serious issue in the early years. The Naga movement was respected internationally and even by its adversaries. Its ideological commitment was beyond question. Since then one insurgency has turned into many. Jungle guerrilla warfare has been replaced by urban violence. The army insurgent clash has spilled over into the civilian life. Kidnapping and extortion has become rampant. How did this transformation take place? For an answer, a closer understanding of the entire history of secessionist insurgency in north eastern region is important.

The politics of secessionism was not peculiar to north east India only, and as such an understanding of the growth of secessionism and insurgency has to be against the backdrop of subcontinental political environment.[9]

The rather 'primitive' and head-hunting tribes, that bordered the eastern Indian plains, had a similar relationship of 'plunder-expedition-truce' with the neighbouring formations like the State of Ahom, Manipur, Tripura and Bengal that they had with the British.[10] The difference was that the British threatened them with encroachment upon the tribal territory and hence, the tribals did not cease to trouble them until they were actually conquered and subdued. Despite the claim of 'integrating' India, the British actually encouraged secessionist politics in British India by keeping the several areas segregated from British India under the category of 'princely areas', 'excluded areas', 'inner-line', 'partially excluded areas'. It did the same in the rest of India by the policies of divide and rule, separate electorate and so on. Hence, the politics that surfaced was also disintegrationist in nature. It is interesting to note that the imminence of British withdrawal from India led to the articulation of several 'withdrawal' schemes which if implemented would have reduced India into a conglomeration of independent states. Most important of them were the Pakistan scheme, the Azad Punjab or Sikhistan scheme, Pakhtunistan scheme, Gorkhasthan scheme, united Bengal scheme, Crown colony plan. Although Churchill spoke almost of the possibility of Princistan implying one independent state, in reality many of the 562 princely states sought to withdraw from India as sovereign entities. This was not just a historical situation but also the political climate –

often an inspiration for the small tribal and ethnic groups of north east India which had to decide their future.

The eve of British withdrawal from India was characterised by two binary opposite trends – a pan Indian sentiment seeking its culmination in the form of an integrated independent India, and the other was a secessionist tendency seeking an independent sovereign existence outside India.[11] Initially, the Indian National Congress, which was likely to assume power from the British, was not against the "Right to self-determination including secession to the constituent nationalities of India and agreed to prepare the constitution" acceptable to all sections of people and a federal one with residuary powers vested in the units. But alarmed by the impending prospect of secessionist claims it had to assert that "The Congress cannot agree to any proposal to disintegrate India by giving liberty to any component state or territorial unit to secede from the Indian Union or Federation". The post independence Indian state wanted to inherit the whole of the British Empire except the partitioned areas which would go to the post Independent state of Pakistan.

Legally speaking, except the princely states, the independent state was the legal heir of the rest of British India including North East India. The Naga-Mizo hills were excluded areas and some Khasi areas were partially excluded areas, according to the Government of India Act 1935, which excluded these from the purview of the reforms envisaged in the Act but not from British India. These areas were very much part of the British Indian territory and the successor Indian state's claim on them were legitimate. But several separatist claims and the success of Muslim League in carving out Pakistan generated a minority phobia and separatist tendencies among a section of the tribal leadership. Congress' own resolution that "it cannot think in terms of compelling the people in any territorial unit to remain in an Indian Union against their declared and established will"[12] and the eventual acceptance of the 'partition scheme' encouraged them. More so, because excluded from the participation, in the subcontinental politics, these un-Sanskritised Indo-Mongoloid tribals were confused about their true identity whether they were Indians or non-Indians. The white masters, both colonial administrators as well as Christian Missionaries and the only outsiders who they were close to, convinced them of being non-Indians, and even conceived of a crown colony to retain them under colonial rule. But the dominant leadership spurned this offer and emphasised the need of remaining with India.

In fact north east India was no exception to the subcontinental processes. Manipur, Tripura and Khasi states were princely states. The land of Nagas, Mizos and Arunachal Pradesh (known as North Eastern Frontier Agency) were excluded areas. When the British withdrawal became imminent, the tribals of the region became politically restive. They were left outside the political area by the colonial state. They now realised the urgent need of politically organising themselves. The Nagas formed the Naga National Council in February 1946. Similarly the Mizo Union emerged in April 1946, Nikhil Manipuri Mahasabha in 1934, and Tripura Rajya Gana Parishad in1939. In each of these organisations there were huge debates about the uncertainties of their future, discussions on the advantages and apprehensions of remaining within India and the fearful prospects of withdrawing from India. It is interesting to note that at this juncture of history the dominant opinions were in favour of remaining with the Indian Union. But, considering the other opinion, the Naga National Council signed an agreement with the Government of India agreeing to remain in India with provisions for safeguards of their special interests and requirements. Yet, disagreement over the interpretation of the Ninth Clause of the Agreement led to the breakdown of the Agreement. The extremist element depicted it as a betrayal by the Indian state and popularised the idea of 'independence' among the people. The hope of abolition of the oppressive institution of chieftainship under the Indian Constitution made the Mizos opt for merging with India. The Nagas finding that that the option to move out of India, incorporated in the Akbar Hydari-Naga National Council Agreement was dispensed with, also strengthened the secessionist attitude. As the Indian state tried to coerce the movement into submission, the NNC went underground, announced the formation of a Revolutionary Government of Nagaland, and tried to combat the Indian army. This was the beginning of the insurgency in Naga Hills. Caught between the crossfire of the Indian Army and the underground insurgents a section of the Naga leadership came to the negotiating table (1960). In a goodwill gesture the Indian Prime Minister, Jawaharlal Nehru, despite opposition from his own party and opposition, made the huge concession of granting statehood to a tiny Naga population, paradoxically under the Ministry of Foreign Affairs.

But this failed to have much impact on the leaders of the insurgency movement who carried on their struggle. In 1975 an Accord was signed by the underground NNC and the Indian State signifying the cessation of the Naga struggle and eventual acceptance of the Indian hegemony. But as in all insurgencies, the younger section of the underground rejected the Accord and decided to continue their struggle for freedom under a new organisation called National Socialist Council of Nagaland led by Th Muivah, Isac Chisi Swu and S S Khaplang. Subsequently, the Khaplang faction broke away to form another faction called NSCN (Khaplang) to fight the Thankhul-Sema tribes' supremacy in the NSCN. The two factions since then have continued parallel struggle for the same objective.

The Mizos were dissatisfied with the Assamese hegemony. Although chieftainship was abolished, lack of basic development, poverty, and empowerment had alienated the Mizo people, and their earlier enthusiasm to remain in India declined. The leadership dominated by the Chiefs, who wanted to opt out of India from 1946, now capitalised on this alienation and reinforced the separatist movement. The opportunity came when a periodic famine devastated the Mizo Hills (1959) without any aid or relief from Assam Government, and Assamese language was sought to be forced as official language on the tribal people, the discontent reached its peak. The voluntary organisation Mizo National Famine Front (1958) was converted into a political party. Although it had a specified secessionist objective, it contested elections for two years and as it gathered enough arms and ammunition, attempted a coup-de-etat on 1st March 1966. It provoked stern military measures from the Indian government with certain conciliatory measures like separation of Mizo Hills from Assam and creation of a Union Territory in 1978. In 1986 the MNF chief Laldenga signed an agreement with the Indian Government by which the struggle for independence was given up, and Mizoram was granted a full-fledged statehood. But this did not end the insurgency in Mizoram. The Hmar people, demanding a separate statehood, formed Hmar Peoples' convention and resorted to insurgent activities. The oppression of the dominant Mizos on the small Hindu tribe called Bru (Riang) made the latter resort to insurgency under the Bru National Army. The violent activities of the two kept the ruling MNF party on its toes till accords were signed with both the groups to halt hostilities.

Although there was a strong opinion that the princely state of Manipur and the moderate section of the Nikhil Manipuri Mahasabha had actually merged with the Indian National Congress in 1946, there were considerable debate about the final merger with India. But the rise of Communist powers in China and Burma bordering north east India and growing communist activities in Manipur and Tripura prompted the panic-stricken Indian state to use unethical means to effect the accession. The people of Manipur were appalled at the way they were ignored in enforcing the merger. Hizam Irabot Singh had already tried to establish a sovereign socialist republic of Manipur through a Telengana-like communist uprising during 1946-50. The front which opposed the merger regrouped themselves to organise a United National Liberation Front in 1964 with a declared objective of seceding from India. A breakaway faction of UNLF subsequently formed the Revolutionary Government of Manipur (RVG) with a similar objective. As Manipur reeled under poverty, famine, unemployment and political instability, more such outfits came into existence. The most powerful was the Peoples' Liberation Army (PLA) enjoying the active support of China. It was led by a few Maoist youths led by N Bishweshar Singh (1975). This was followed by the formation of the Peoples' Revolutionary Party of Kanglaipak (Prepak) and the Kanglaipak Communist Party. All of them simultaneously attacked the Indian state and launched parallel struggles to achieve the independence of Manipur. The counter-insurgency operations, the ambushes and the factional violence along with extortion drives, kidnappings and fratricidal murders made Manipur a virtual killing field.

The People's Liberation Army (PLA) is the strongest insurgent group. The PLA was organised in 1976-'77 under the leadership of N Bisheswar. The PLA had close links with NSCN and shared two camps with them in Myanmar and Bangladesh. It had an understanding with the NSCN regarding the areas of their operation; they operated without interfering with each other. It had also some Muslims in its cadre supported by Pakistan's Inter Services Intelligence (ISI). The PLA was very active in Imphal, Thaubal and Bishenpur districts. It was well armed and had a strength of about 1,000. It had a few dissenters who operated on their own and formed the People's Revolutionary Party of Kangleipak (Prepak) in October, 1977. The important leaders are Urikhimbam, Sarat and Meiraba Singh with Tajila as military commander.

The UNLF is the oldest Meithei extremist organisation formed in 1964 under Samarendra Singh. The approximate strength of this group is 700. It operates in eastern Imphal. The UNLF maintained links with NSCN until they came into conflict with each other recently in the wake of NSCN's claim of Manipuri territory in Greater Nagaland.

The KYKL was formed in January, 1994 under the chairmanship of Ibo Pishak Singh. This group has a strength of about 200. It is expanding its recruitment base.

Tripura, formerly a princely state, secured statehood under the Indian Republic in January 1972. Large scale inflow of Bengali speaking immigrants from East Pakistan, now Bangladesh, the growing pressure of land, acute food shortage, the growing unemployment among youths, backwardness of tribals generated serious socio-economic tensions and ethnic conflicts. Tripura's population composition is very different from that of any other tribal State in this region. The tribals here are vastly outnumbered by the Bengali immigrants from the neighbouring Bangladesh. It has been pointed out that the tribals in the State were never in majority. The Census report prepared by the then Princely State in 1911 put the total population of Tripura at 2,99,613 out of which the tribals numbered 1,08,526. In 1931, Tripura's population increased to 3,82,450 out of which the tribals numbered 1,86,260 and Bengalis, both Hindus and Muslims numbered 1,96,190. It was the Noakhali (East Bengal) communal riots in 1946, the partition of 1947, and communal troubles of 1963 that led to a rapid increase of Bengali speaking Hindus who came to Tripura in waves. The unabated flow of immigrants from Bangladesh weakened the basically agricultural economy of the State. The one-time self-sufficient State became a chronic deficit area, depending heavily on the Government of India for food grains every year.

The main tension was between the tribals and the non-tribals over the question of agricultural land. In the past, even in the face of a law, the tribals lost their land to Bengali cultivators who in thousands of cases got the title deed changed. But now, caught between the State's insistence on preservation of forests and opposition to 'jhum' on one side and dispossession of land on the other, the tribals demanded the restoration of their land from the non-tribals. Tripura Upajati Juba Samiti (TUJS) took up the cause of the tribals in 1967.

In 1974, the Congress Government amended the Land Revenue and Land Reforms Legislations of 1960, providing for restoration of all lands transferred by tribals to non-tribals. These legislations were, however, strongly opposed by an anti-tribal organisation known as 'Amra Bangali'; which clashed with TUJS. Widespread terror swept Tripura in the fortnight of June, 1980 like a tornado and left death and devastation all round. The CPI(M) was active among the tribal and it took up the cause of the tribals when it came to power. The Congress (I), Janata Party and Amra Bengali organisations combined to oppose the CPI(M) government's proposal to give autonomy to tribal areas. This alarmed the tribals who resorted to rioting and looting. The anti-non-tribal feelings were inculcated in Bangladesh where the TUJS militant group received their training and military hardware.

To arouse hatred against non-tribals, the TUJS gave a call for bazaar boycott for a week from June 1, 1980. In fact the trouble started from May 29 and between 29th May and 5th June, 1980 at least 12 non-tribals were killed. In 1983 there were about 50 clashes between security forces and the Tripura National Volunteer Force (TNV), and about 30 persons were killed in these clashes. In 1984 the number of clashes increased and 50 persons were killed. The TNV was receiving help from Mizo National Front (MNF) and the Bangladesh Government.

The beginning of the tribal militancy in Tripura can be traced to 1941. Between 1941 and 1983 as many as ten organisations, some of them operating underground, were set up to safeguard tribal interests. At one point of time there were as many as 24 'hit groups'. The political situation has sharply deteriorated ever since the dominant National Liberation Front of Tripura (NLFT), the All Tripura Tiger Force (ATTF) and Tripura Resurrection Army (TRA) started asserting themselves increasingly.

Among several underground units operating in Assam, United Liberation Front of Assam (ULFA) is the most active. ULFA is a militant organisation which aims to liberate Assam and the people of the state form 'Indian Rule'. It is engaged in the bloodiest and most treacherous attacks on non-Assamese Government officials, industrialists, businessmen, politicians and non-tribals, whom it considers to be foreigners and even on Central Government institutions.

The ULFA was founded on April 7, 1979. The Preamble to the Constitution of this organisation declared that independence of Assam was to be achieved through an armed revolutionary struggle. It adopted a flag of rising sun against a white background. The ULFA, which aims at secession from India, is essentially a by-product of the prolonged Assam agitation started in 1978-79 by the AGP against all non-Assamese including the business community, Hindi and Oriya speaking labour and executives working in 756 tea estates. Even people originally from other parts of the country, who had lived in Assam for generations, suddenly found themselves being looked upon as undesirable 'outsiders'. Occasionally, the members belonged to the AGP and AASU. All Assam Students' Union, which had spearheaded the 1978-79 agitation, called all non-Assamese Indians as 'Indian dogs' and served 'Quit Assam' notice on a large number of non-Assamese people.

Among those assassinated by ULFA militants were : Tankeswar Dhingia, Youth Congress (I) General Secretary and former Rural Development Minister, Ranjit Barua, the President of Jorhat Congress (I) unit and son of a former Minister of Forest Development, Rajiv Rajkhov, Chairman of the United Minorities Front; Kalipada Sen, an advocate, who was critical of ULFA activities, Sourav Bora a student leader who formed a front against the Assam Gana Parishad (AGP), the ruling party, and Surendra Pal, Chairman, Assam Frontier Tea Company (AFTC) and Daulat Singh Negi, Superintendent of Police, Dibrugarh. Kalipada Sen, an advocate and a spokesman of the Bengali speaking community in Assam was assassinated in 1986 at his residence in Guwahati within a few months after the AGP assumed office. Within the next couple of years, the toll of murders by ULFA militants was reported to be 133 and the money they collected through extortion and armed bank hold-ups was reported to be several hundred crores of rupees. Killings and kidnappings by ULFA militants were frequently reported.

But ULFA is not the only militant organisation in Assam. There are others like Bodo Liberation Tigers (BLT) and National Democratic Front of Bodos (NDFB). Both emerged from the demand of a separate state for the Bodos, the largest tribal group in Assam. The initially peaceful movement subsequently turned violent and gave rise to the underground militant organisations. The same was the case with the Dimachas of north Cachar, which resulted in Dima Halom Daoga (DHD), and Karbis of Karbi Anglong district which resulted in the United Peoples' Democratic Solidarity (UPDS) as well as Karbi National Volunteers (KNV).

Sections of Garos and Khasis, too, joined the fray of insurgency initially under the same umbrella organisation called Hyniewtrep Achik National Volunteers (HALC), which later disintegrated into two Achik National Volunteer Forces (ANVF) and Hyniewtrep National Liberation Council (HNLC) according to their tribal bases. While the Garo (Achik) based organisation demanded separate statehood, the Khasis (Hyniewtrep) demanded secession from India.

Arunachal Pradesh has been the base camp of the NSCN (K) for years. Now a new organisation called the Arunachal Dragon Force has surfaced with the avowed objective of secession from India.

The Terrorist Economy

The myriad insurgent organisations and their underground operations have economic ramifications, too. It has an adverse impact on the economy of the region, which is manifested in the stalling of development projects, flight of capital, non-entry of industries and corporate sectors in the region, growing dependence on the government for employment, growing unemployment, and escalating prices of essential goods due to parallel taxation and escape of efficient executives from the region. Despite repeated Budget declaration of tax holiday for five years and the setting up of North East India Development Finance Corporation, there has not been any encouraging response from industrialists to set up ventures in the region. In fact there is a reverse trend which is manifested in the flight of capital from the region. To meet the demands of the underground outfit, every official is taught to earn money through unfair means. This increases the cycle of corruption. In the absence of private sector enterprises, government is the only provider of employment. But due to shrinkage in its capacity the unemployment scenario is becoming increasingly bleak. The unemployed youths then become the target of underground recruitment and soon absorbed as a cog in the system of this non-state economy which is flourishing. It is a vicious cycle indeed.

What is more serious is that, it has given rise to an underbelly; a subterranean economy. It is the economy of the insurgent outfits, the features of which are parallel tax collection, arms and narcotics trade, extortion, foreign aid, profit sharing with corporate houses, diversion and siphoning off of state developmental funds. This economy grew out of the necessity of sustenance of the militant outfits which function from underground but expanded not only due to the proliferation of insurgency in the region but also due to the sheer high returns it ensured. In the process it not only undermined the authority of the Indian state but also subverted the state economy. This structure has been conceptualised as terrorist economy[13], underground economy[14], insurgent economy or warlordism,[15] illegal economy[16] and so on. Essentially it is a non-state economy functioning parallel to the state economy. In fact it is parasitic to the latter. It is amazing that from low key 'tax collection' from its isolated pockets, as was the case with Naga insurgents in its early years, and sustaining through limited foreign aid, this industry has grown to such an extent that annual budgets of some of these outfits surpass the small states where they function. They no more depend on foreign aid but have large investment stakes in the International capital market. For example, when the stock market in South East Asia recently crashed, one of the biggest losers was not any corporate house or investment bank, but the NSCN (IM) which lost over Rs. 100 million[17]. A report claimed that the ULFA, like a corporate giant, was negotiating to buy several tea gardens in Dibrugarh district and along Indo-Bangla border in the Barak Valley. Although the ULFA would fund and manage the tea gardens, the purchase would obviously be in the name of its front-men.[18] Most of the insurgent outfits of north east have shifted their base to Bangladesh where the leaders invested heavily – mostly in hotel business. The existence of such a non-state parallel economy, as it can be conceptualised, not only has serious repercussions on the state economy which is manifested in the stalling of development projects, flight of capital and escape of efficient executives from the region but also undermines the already weak political authority of the Indian state in the region.

Mobilisation of Resources

The Naga National Council or even the NSCN in its early days, or MNF of Mizoram, was careful enough not to disturb the civil life. Hence, it used to secure arms by ambushing army or police personnel and snatching arms from them. It also used to levy and collect a small amount from each government employee, professional and businessmen either local or outsiders, as 'tax' to the Government in Exile which covered its expenses for maintenance. But from the 1990's there has been radical transformation in the character of insurgency in the regions for various reasons.[19] Extortion, kidnapping, looting of treasury has become rampant in the region. Small taxes from ordinary citizens were no more enough to maintain its burgeoning expenses. Hence, extortion of corporate houses, were the prime sources of resource mobilisation. Beside the tea gardens, the public sector units like ONGC, OIL, NEEPCO, BRPL and even the Railways have to regularly shell out substantial amounts. But the biggest casualty has been the tea industry.

The Hot Brew

The 600 odd tea gardens of Assam and now even those in the Dooars in West Bengal have become a golden source for ULFA, NDFB, NSCN(IM), DHD to fill their war funds. While the NSCN concentrates on the tea gardens in upper Assam lying in the border areas of Naga hills, ULFA and NDFD concentrate on lower Assam as well. NSCN, DHD and HPC as well as some Manipur based outfits target tea gardens in Barak Valley and Jirighat area. It has been estimated that between 1990 and 1997, the ULFA has collected not less than 500 crores mostly through extortion from the tea gardens.[20] The ULFA levied 0.50 paise per kg of tea produced as the rate of extortion money to be paid by each of the tea companies.[21] As per such calculations the Tata Tea was asked to pay Rs. 90 lakhs.[22] The Nanoipur tea garden paid Rs. 20 lakhs to the Bodo Security Force (BSF).[23] The Williamson Magor Company, having the largest number of tea gardens in Assam (44) paid Rs. 1.5 crores to the Bodo Security Force.[24] The Tata Tea also had to pay Rs. 1 crore to the BSF, after its vice chairman Bolin Bordoloi was kidnapped. Subsequently both sides agreed to make such payments on a regular periodical basis, and this had to be done without the official knowledge of the government as the latter would accuse the company of collaborating with the outlawed outfits, as happened between the Tatas and the Government of Assam.[25] Hence, a system was evolved. Contractors close to the militants pay them in hard cash and raise dummy bills to the companies. This way neither the company nor the militants get caught. The rates vary. It could range from Rs. 25 lakhs for a proprietorial garden to Rs. 1 crore for a bigger company.[26] Sometimes the expenditure was shown in the annual financial statement as being spent on security. Audited accounts reveal that companies such as Williamson Magor had paid over Rs. one crore in 1994-95 and 1995-96 to NDFB. Smaller companies such as Bhergaon tea estate paid upto Rs. 25 lakh while Chandana, Mendka, Naradan Nayer, Badlapar and Ambika paid amounts ranging from Rs. one lakh to Rs. ten lakhs.[27] All these necessitated a protection force for the tea garden employees. Thus, Assam Tea Plantation Security Force of 2,500 persons was raised at the initial cost of Rs. 10 crores.[28] The companies also tried to better its image in the area by rendering social service to the people in the vicinity. The Tata Charitable Trust have spent Rs. 46 lakhs during 1995-98 in providing medical aid to Assamese children and built a hospital in upper Assam at the cost of Rs. one crore.[29] It also spent Rs. 75,000 on the treatment of Pranati Deka, the cultural secretary of ULFA.[30] But all these could not stop the murder of a number of tea officials which included Surendra Pal (brother of Lord Swaraj Pal of UK), P C Scaria, Jawaharlal Jain, Tejinder Kaur and Ms Koilee Biasnov and abduction of a number of officials.[31]

Sponsoring Satellite Outfits

The NSCN(IM) took the lead in the proliferation of insurgency in the region not only with the strategy of spreading insurgency, but also as an earning proposition. Spreading insurgency was aimed at attracting the attention of the Indian state back to it as it was losing its ground considerably over the years.[32] By creating satellite organisations it could earn a substantial amount regularly without really taking part in any action. It thus sponsored All Tripura Tiger Force in Topang, National Liberation Front of Bodoland in Assam, HNLC in Meghalaya, Karbi National Volunteers and USDP in Assam, ANVC in Meghalaya, DHD in Assam and Konglei Yawol Kanna Lip (KYKL) in Manipur. They were all supplied with arms and provided training. They would indulge in extortion, tax collection in their respective areas and share the amount on a 70:30 or 60:40 basis with the NSCN(IM).[33] Subsequently other bigger organisations also began to sponsor such satellite organisations. Thus, ULFA had a satellite in Kamatapur Liberation Organisation in North Bengal. Such satellite organisations let loose a reign of terror in their respective areas. The existence of underground outfit in every ethnic area spread insurgency in the entire region. There was a spurt of extortion, kidnapping, murder, explosions and encounters in the region. Thus, from Nagaland and Manipur, insurgency came into action in every state and every district of the region. Government officials, state or central, would pool extortion amount euphemistically called taxes, and hand it over to the representative of the outfit every month as per their demand. The higher officials and contractors had to pay a higher amount or siphon off a part of the development allocation to the outfits. Even the railways and private sector companies were not spared. Kidnapping of government officials and corporate managers are frequent. They were released after paying a substantial amount. The high ideology of nationality struggle thus progressively degenerated into a law and order problem. There are officials who never returned from abduction as their poor relatives could not pay the ransom money. Although the police often conducted raids, most of the time the police were never informed of the crimes, and deals were concluded mutually without police interference. Thus, for militant groups in north east India, the major source of financing is what the Indian state terms extortion. It might seem that many militant groups have better capacity to collect taxes than the Indian state. The slain social worker, Sanjay Ghose, found in the case of engineers of Nagaland Government's Public Works Department a concrete example: Unlike Government tax collectors who would target only the officially declared income, militants drawing on perception and rumour can impose higher taxes based on a more realistic assessment of legal as well as illegal income.[34] E M Rammohan, IPS, serving as advisor to the Governor of Assam reported:

> For the last couple of years the valley and hill militant groups have penetrated the state and central administration and carved out specific areas of influence. Every month when salaries are disbursed a percentage is deducted and paid to militant groups. In effect this was a replication of what was done by NSCN in Nagaland as also Naga districts of Manipur. Regular deductions are labelled as house tax and ration money. The militant groups reportedly interfere in the award of contracts and are also known to enter offices carrying files to secure signature of officers in question[35].

Parallel Taxation

One common case of extortion is levying taxes on commercial vehicles along the national highways. The collection of such taxes by Kuki militants is a common feature on the Imphal-Moreh, Imphal-Jiribam and Imphal-Dimapur stretches. With some 500 buses and commercial vehicles plying daily, the highways are soft targets for the militants. They have even started imposing special 'taxes' on vehicles passing through certain areas.

The NSCN has set up a tax collection gate near the Government check post at Senapati on the Imphal-Dimapur Road. Recently, three people were dragged out of a bus at Senapati and killed during an extortion drive.

But the militants are not the only one holding the roads of Manipur to ransom. Political parties and Students' Organisations resort to road block to press for their demands. The effect on the normal supply of essential times is simply disastrous. For example, the supply line was completely disrupted when the militants demanding the creation of a Sadar Hills district imposed an economic blockade on the Imphal-Dimapur stretch. This was followed by a similar blockade by those opposing the creation of the district. The security personnel are reported to be extorting money from the transport operators.

Kidnapping top officials and businessmen for ransom has become a booming business in the State. With political uncertainty prevailing in the State, militants in Manipur are increasingly resorting to kidnapping for ransom. The latest victim of kidnapping is Yambem Pishak Singh, the Managing Director of Manipur Plantation Crops Corporation. Activists of the KNF kidnapped Singh from his Office at Jiribam Tea Estate bordering Assam on 14th December 1994. The incident took place the very day Rishang Keising assumed office as Chief Minister. The kidnappers demanded Rs. 5 lakhs for safe release of Singh. According to reliable sources, a sum of Rs. 2 lakhs was paid to the kidnappers and Singh was released on the night of 19th December. The police claimed to have rescued Singh from a Kuki Village in Jiribam. In a similar incident, A. K. Srivastava, the Managing Director of the State Tribal Development Corporation, was kidnapped for a ransom. In most cases, the police try to cover up the kidnappings. Obviously, the militants are taking a cue from the experts of the banned ULFA in the business of kidnappings and extortions.

Besides, it has been reported that almost all State and Central Government employees are paying monthly contributions to the militants. The amount, ranging from Rs. 50 to Rs. 200 each, is paid at the time of salary disbursement and handed over to the militants. A lady doctor was kidnapped, her car was burnt and she was threatened with death by the militants because she refused to pay the demanded money. She reported the matter to the police but no action was taken[36].

A new 'law' allegedly promulgated by various underground Manipuri militants compels all non-Manipuris, above twelve years, to pay Rs. 100 as annual tax if they wanted to continue living in the valley. This came into force in January 1997, and specifies that the stay period may be extended after a year, only if the militants deem so. Immigrant permit cards, valid for a year, are also issued to non-Manipuris by the Revolutionary People's Front. This was disclosed by S.K. Sakshi, Secretary and spokesman for North East Indian Democratic Organisation.

Then NEIDO, a voluntary non-tribals' body, has threatened a counter-stir against Manipuri students studying outside the North East, if this harassment continued after August 31. Sakshi said, they will be asked to pay Rs. 50,000 per head to the organisation, if the atrocities do not stop. The NEIDO had sent a memorandum on this to the then Prime Minister Deve Gowda, BJP leader Atal Behari Vajpayee, Jyoti Basu and others.

Tea estate owners and managers had to pay protection money to the ULFA militants as they were stuck out in the wilds with no protection and no communication. According to the information available[37], ULFA collects more than Rs. 10 crores every year from tea companies, and the collections in foreign exchange are largely used towards purchase of sophisticated weapons and in the funding of extensive foreign trips of the top leaders of the banned outfits. Reportedly, the money is usually paid into foreign bank accounts, and it is very difficult to obtain details given the secrecy associated with it. Anybody who is found aiding or abetting the insurgents in waging war against the country must be sternly dealt with under Indian Penal Code. The tea companies are reportedly under investigation.

There are reports also that several other business houses, public sector units and State and Union government departments have been making payments to the underground outfits.[38] Documents recovered from National Democratic Front of Bodoland Ultras had shown that officers at the Srirampur check gate of the West Bengal Assam border had paid Rs. 95 lakhs to the insurgents between 1994 and 1996. Incidentally, it may be recalled that P.C. Goenka, Chairman of Assam

Carbon Ltd. and a leading industrialist of the State, says that his entire work of 32 years of building a Rs. 15 crore business from scratch had failed him on April 29, 1990 when 16 gun-totting militants walked into his house in the North Guwahati area of the State capital. They demanded Rs. 50 lakh for letting him live and continue in business. He rushed out for the police but found policemen guarding the militants' motorcycles. He left Assam for good.[39]

Trade and Industry sources say that businessmen, mostly Hindi speaking north-Indians, who control the State's economy, have coughed up between Rs. 500 and Rs. 1,000 cores as protection money since 1989. Though there had been no survey, Chief Minister Hiteshwar Saikia told *India Today* that before he became Chief Minister, about 400 traders had shifted and about Rs. 4,000 crores were transferred to new business in Siliguri, West Bengal, Bangalore, Ahmedabad and Delhi. It was reported that Prag Basmi Synthetics – a Rs. 327 crores joint venture between the Assam Government and Bombay Silk Mills – the biggest project in the State, might relocate itself from the State to Orissa after it closed down following the abduction of its Chief Executive V.G. Raghavan on December 21. Raghavan was released in March but only after the Company paid a huge ransom.[40]

Recent incidents have not done anything to counter the trend. Tata Tea executive Bolin Bordoloi was kidnapped by the Bodo Security Force and the kidnappers demanded Rs. 15 crores in dollars for his release but the Tata Tea did not succumb to pressure. Finding that Tata Tea was unlikely to pay up, the kidnappers, to gain publicity, released Bordoloi in a gesture of magnanimity, particularly, because Bordoloi happened to be the son of a previous former Assam Chief Minister. It happened only after Bordoloi's brother resumed negotiations when the Tata Tea and the State Government negotiations failed. Jayanta Chowdhury, Director of Fatemabad Tea Estate in Barpeta district and its manager, Rohini Gogoi, were kidnapped by the Bodo Security Force on June 30.

It was announced that in Guwahati Williamson Magor had paid Rs. 2 crores to militants for the release of Subir Roy, manager, of its Dimakuchi Tea Garden. Goodrick, reportedly had paid, five months earlier Rs. 20 lakhs for the release of its garden manager S. K. Bawa.

The frequent kidnapping of tea garden executives jeopardised the future of the Guwahati Tea Auction Centre, the world's largest.

On April 27, 1993, representatives of Assam Tea Trade and Industry met to express solidarity to end kidnapping for ransom.

Tea gardens are not the only places affected. A 21 member team of experts from the French Compagnie Generale du Geophysique, on an assignment for seismic studies in oil-bearing areas, had to withdraw after it received a 'tax notice' of Rs. 5 crores from ULFA in December 1992. Big projects like the Rs. 3,000 crores gas cracker project in Dengakhat in Dibrugarh district had been put on hold. Initially, the Thapar Group was keen to participate but it gave up the idea on security reasons. Bouer, a German Company, reportedly turned down a Rs. 6 crores bridge project despite Saikia's assurance of security.

Selective Killings

The army, during Operation Bajrang commenced in 1992, discovered mass graves which suggested that the ULFA had been indulging in unprecedented cruelty and mayhem. During searches, the army recovered videos of war films and guerrilla warfare and documents. Some of the documents recovered provided proof of ULFA's close links with the banned National Socialist Council of Nagaland (NSCN), Kachin Independent Army of Burma, the People's Liberation Army (PLA) of Manipur and Tripura National Volunteers (TNV).

The seized documents and interrogation of some of the arrested activists provided incontrovertible proof of the involvement of Bangladesh Government in the training of ULFA militants in Sylhet. Interrogation of some of the militants also revealed that the ULFA had finalised deals with the gun runners in Bangladesh in 1990 to smuggle firearms from across the border with the help of Pakistan's notorious Inter Services Intelligence (ISI) reported to be operating from Bangladesh.

ULFA had established their strongest bases in different parts of Dibrugarh and Tinsukia districts because of the support the militants received from the rural area. After the Congress (I) came to power under the Chief Ministership of Hiteswar Saikia, the army operations were discontinued from July, 1991. The ULFA activists resorted to hit and run tactics. They kidnapped several persons, and refused to come to the negotiation table when requested by Chief Minister Saikia. Operation 'Rhino' had first been launched by the army in September, 1991 and was suspended in April 1993. The immediate provocation for the revival of this operation was the assassination of the Minister for Rural Development, Nagen Neogi, and nine of his security men by ULFA militants. The manner in which the ambush was carried out by the ULFA seemed to indicate that the ULFA militants had been helped by the National Socialist Council of Nagaland (NSCN).

The killing of Nagen Neogi was no isolated incident. On 25 April, 1993 the Congress candidate Binu Chetia and five other travelling with him lost their lives in a similar ambush in the Tinsukia district of upper Assam. Then, on 28 April, a senior army official Lt. Col. Devendra Tyagi, was gunned down by ULFA activists in the premises of the Kamakhya Temple. In a press statement on 10th May, ULFA's central publicity secretary M. Daimary justified Neogi's killing saying "All those politicians involved in anti-national activities for their narrow personal gains will meet a similar fate".

The ongoing army offensive against the ULFA in the Jorhat district of Upper Assam was reported to have been successful in gaining substantial inside information. The documents seized from hardcore ULFA militant, Srimanta Bora, yielded vital information. Srimanta was injured in a shoot-out with the army in January 1997 at Lahdoigarh near Jorhat.

In order to intensify their struggle for a Bodoland, the Bodo militants had been on a war path since 27th May 1990 when a bomb blast in Tinsukia killed 50 people. On 19th June, 1990 a police vehicle was blown up in Bongaigaon, killing 12 policemen. In September 1990 a bomb blast in Assam Transport bus in Barpeta killed 20 people. On 13th October, 1992 a blast ripped through two compartments of an Arunachal special passenger train near Barpeta, killing 21 persons. On 10th May, 1994 a bridge over Gormari river in Lower Assam was blown up by a powerful remote control device. Four policemen, including the driver of a police vehicle, were killed. On 19th November 1995 a bus was blown off near Sonitpur district with the help of a hand grenade, killing 8 persons. On 23rd November 1995 a bus was blown apart by a remote control device near Udalguri police station in Darrang district, killing 6 persons including 5 Assam police personnel.

The Congress Government in 1991 was greeted with the kidnapping of 14 senior government officials the day after it assumed office. The newly installed AGP Government was welcomed by militants with a spate of brutal killings. The AGP which swept to power with four of its allies and assumed office on 15th May, 1996 perhaps did not expect the militants to strike so soon. But the banned ULFA, bolstered by fresh recruits and emboldened by in-flow of sophisticated weapons, struck, the day after the AGP came to power.

The militants ambushed the Tinsukia Superintendent of Police (SP) Ravi Kant Singh and killed him and four others with ruthless efficiency. The manner in which Singh's three vehicle convoy was attacked left no doubt in the minds of the security agencies that the ULFA had matured into an efficient striking machine. Singh became the second SP to be killed by ULFA militants. Earlier, Daulat Singh Negi had fallen victim to the ULFA in 1989. Negi was killed in the neighbouring Dibrugarh district. The two districts of Tinsukia and Dibrugarh were ULFA strongholds in the late Eighties, but the militants suffered severe reverses following an army crackdown. But Singh's killing and the attack on Binu Chetia, a Congress (I) candidate for the Margherita Assembly constituency, two days before the elections on 27th April pointed to the fact that the ULFA had managed to regroup again.

Close on the heels of Singh's assassination, came another attack by unidentified gunmen who shot dead Parag Das, Executive Editor of the State's highest circulated daily, *Assamiya Pratidin*. Das was attacked in the heart of Guwahati city and killed in broad day light. Death of Das provoked strong protests from journalists and ULFA. The journalists took out a procession through the city demanding adequate protection. The police failed to identify the killers. The needle of suspicion pointed to SULFA (Surrendered ULFA) members as Das had been scathingly critical of their actions ever since they quit ULFA in March, 1992.

The killings of Bimal Bhuyan, Principal Information Officer, Government of Assam, in Guwahati on 13th March 1996 by unknown persons, S. Solanki, R.G. Patel, Parban Singh, Judhi Prajapati, all employees of a private power company in Thelamara, Sonitpur district on 17th March 1996 by Bodo militants, Binu Chetia, Congress (I) candidate and four others in Ulup village, Tinsukia district on 25th April 1996 by ULFA militants, Lt. Col. Devendra Tyagi in Kamakhya temple, Guwahati on 28th April 1996 by ULFA militants, Ravi Kant Singh, SP, Tinsukia, in Tinsukia on 18th May 1996 by ULFA militants and Parag Das, Journalist in Guwahati city on 17th May 1996 by unknown assailants terrorised the people. A report from Guwahati disclosed that security in and around the oil installations in Assam had been beefed up following a threat from the outlawed ULFA to blow them up. The ULFA activists had demanded immediate ceasefire by the army. The army warned that they would be "forced to retaliate if the Assamese people continued to be harassed" by the destruction of vital installations.

In November 1996, the ULFA blew up an oil pipe at Ulubari in Nalbari district. The impact of the blast was so intense that it partially blocked a parallel pipeline carrying finished petroleum product by causing a 'bend'. In the last week of March, 1997 they had killed a Lt. Col. of the army and the wife of a tea garden manager[41].

On 13th April 1997 a driver of the army vehicle was shot dead by the suspected ULFA militants, while skirmishes between army jawans and insurgents in the foothills of Bhutan continued on 14th April in Nalbari district. With insurgents holed up inside the Bhutan territory as border patrolling was stepped up, both the ULFA and Bodo militants were routinely attacking army personnel. An army patrol party was fired upon near Jamuguri on 14th April morning when they were returning from Nagrijuli to the brigade headquarters at Tamulpu in Nalbari district. The encounter lasted for about 25 minutes, with both sides using heavy fire but there were no casualties. In another incident, the driver of an army vehicle was shot dead by suspected ULFA militants on 14th April at Goalpara. Official sources said that 'cat and mouse' ambushes, are used by the ULFA leaders holed up in these camps to try to sneak into India. The ULFA seemed to have decided to follow NSCN which collects an annual 'tax' from a cross section of the State's people.[42]

The new Chief Minister, Prafulla Kumar Mahanta of the AGP, was already shaken by the fast deteriorating law and order, and he was in for further shock when simmering tension between the Bodos and the Santal tribals in western Assam's Kokrajhar district erupted into open ethnic strife that left over one lakh homeless and hundreds dead in five days of rioting in May 1996. Mercifully, a Nellie-type of massacre of over 5,000 persons, which occurred in February 1983 near Guwahati, was averted through the timely intervention by the army which had some units stationed in the vicinity as part of its revived Operation Rhino, though just two days before the AGP Government took over, a party delegation had submitted a memorandum to the State Governor, seeking withdrawal of the army from the State. It was felt that had the army actually returned to the barracks, there would have been a major disaster, as the State Government was then left with barely 37 companies of paramilitary forces as against 80 companies it had during the elections. Realising that the situation was grave, the army deployed two brigades to contain the situation. About 8,000 soldiers fanned out to remote areas in Gossaingaon sub-division of the district to prevent further violence.

The most shocking was the reported death of Sanjoy Ghose in the custody of ULFA militants. At the time of his abduction by the ULFA militants on 4th July 1997, the Association of Voluntary Agencies for Rural Development in the North East (AVARD-NE), led by Sanjoy was engaged in anti-erosion schemes and social upliftment programmes in Majuli, the largest riverine island in the world. Both Sanjoy and his wife Sumita made village Mekheli in Majuli their home for over one year, and motivated the people of Majuli to engage in voluntary work to save the island from being washed away.

The press note issued in Guwahati by Mithing Daimary, the Central Publicity Secretary of ULFA, claimed that Sanjay Ghose was in the process of being released when Ghose had met with an accident somewhere in the hilly terrains of Arunachal Pradesh. In the note dated 5th August 1997 the ULFA outfit blamed the army for launching an offensive, forcing a situation which caused the 'unfortunate incident'.

In a fierce counter-attack, the army accused ULFA of killing Sanjay Ghose in 'cold blood'. In a strongly worded press release from its 4 Corps headquarters in Tezpur, the army categorically stated that no operations, whatsoever, were conducted anywhere in the vicinity of Arunachal Pradesh during the period from 1 July to 5 August 1997.

As the ULFA and the army slugged it out, the curtains came down on Ghose. Sanjoy Ghose had been abducted by ULFA militants on 4th July. For days, nothing was known of Ghose's whereabouts till the night of 22nd July, when faxes arrived at some newspaper offices in Guwahati announcing the 'death' of Sanjoy Ghose in ULFA custody. But the very next afternoon, an 'official' communiqué from the ULFA outfit claimed that Ghose was 'alive and well'. And by the beginning of August there were positive signs from ULFA that it was willing to set Ghose free. This gave hope to all those who were waiting for Ghose's safe return.

While referring to a statement issued by the 4 Corps Commander, Lt. General R.K. Sawhney, that Ghose died at about 4 pm on 4th August

1997, Chief Minister Prafulla Mahanta reportedly said "we have our doubts". Apparently intelligence officials at the 4 Corps headquarters in Tezpur had intercepted two radio messages at 7 pm and 7.30 pm on 4th August stating that Ghose had died in a fall from a cliff somewhere in Arunachal Pradesh, and the media be informed that he had been killed in an encounter with the army.

Sanjoy Ghose attracted the attention of ULFA which suspected him of being a 'government agent' and it accounts for his abduction and subsequent killing. There was strong reaction from every political quarter throughout the country and more specifically in Assam. The ULFA militants were called upon by different political parties to lay down arms.

The ULFA had simultaneously launched a propaganda war in a bid to demoralise the army and paramilitary forces. The modus operandi of the ULFA militants is to mobilise the rural populace especially women. With war between the two groups the army also began to treat the Assamese as hostile people. The cases of secret killings, encounters, rape and molestation of women, abduction, torture of innocent villagers, began to increase. While the ULFA used such incidents as oppression by the Indian State, Civil Society groups were formed to protect the civilian people from army atrocities. The transformation of the Indian army from protector to perpetrators of violence only succeeded in alienating the common people of Assam further.

Changing Nature of Insurgency

The advent of the last decade of the twentieth century marked a transition in the history of insurgency in North East India. Transition here meant a fluid state where the future course of insurgency was uncertain. Following this phase was a transformation in the character of insurgency in the region. To be precise, this transformation became evident from 1995. As such 1995 was a watershed in the history of insurgency, because it ushered a metamorphosis in the nature of insurgency and the insurgency-related activities. Insurgent activities, so far, involved guerrilla warfare with the Indian armed forces, formation of a Government in exile, training and camping in the jungles and occasional killing of officials representing the Indian State. In other words, the confrontation between the Indian State and the insurgents, which were confined mainly to the jungles and remote areas, hardly ever disturbed the civil life. In fact, it was the army which disturbed the life of the civilians during their counter insurgency operations. Thus, insurgency was viewed by the commoners as a struggle for lofty ideals, in course of which supreme sacrifices were made for a sacred goal, and insurgents were seen as *haloed* people to be helped, supported and emulated. But from 1995 the activities of the insurgents changed to extortion, kidnapping, abduction, looting of banks and exchequers, collection of exorbitant and arbitrary amounts of money in the name of taxes, bomb blasts and killing of civilians. These acts were resorted to mainly by NSCN (IM) and the insurgent outfits it sponsored. Thus, insurgency had come down from jungles to the urban areas and from lofty sacrificial acts to an ordinary law and order problem. It obviously has meant a massive change in the character of insurgency in North East India. In this section of the paper, we study the change and try to account for it. We shall also discuss the latest developments that constituted the history of insurgency in North East India till date.

The collapse of the Soviet system, its impact on the Eastern European Communist conglomerations, disintegration of the old nation states making way for the new ones, were significant new developments in the world. In the late '80s it was the break up of Russian, Yugoslav and Czechoslovak states into a number of new nations. It also saw the unification of the divided Germans, Vietnamese and the Yemens. It witnessed the independence of South Africa and the secession of Eritrea. It saw the return of peace in Ireland and autonomy for Scotland. These new developments had its due impact on India, too. India did not have any *perestroika* or *glasnost*. But, plagued by secessionism, subnationalism, communalism and provincialism, it had its insecurities as a nation.[43] This insecurity was evident when, in the wake of the disintegration of Eastern Europe, there were deliberations whether India, too, was going to break up. Several newspapers carried articles on the possible areas, which might secede, states that could form independent nations, and even the possibility of formation of commonwealth of Indian nations. Several academicians participated in the decade to provide a serious dimension to the debate.[44] On the other hand, it also raised hopes among communities which were struggling to secede from India that perhaps they would be able to secede from the Indian Union. Among them were the Nagas who felt that, pressurised by the international political climate, the Indian State would now allow them to form an independent nation state. The admission of the NSCN (IM) to the Under-represented Nations and Peoples Organisation raised the hopes further. But no such thing happened. As the situation in Eastern Europe settled down, the international pressure on India eased out and the hopes of the Nagas petered out. The time was, therefore, for retrospection, regrouping, rejuvenation and working out new strategies. This explains the lull during the period 1993-94.

The events and developments in the subsequent period, that is 1995 onwards, indicate a new phase in the history of insurgency. It was marked by activities, which were hitherto not associated with the insurgents. These were essentially criminal acts, which amounted to the breach of law and order. This change in the nature of insurgency related activities were not really unplanned, nor did it mean any dilution of the ideologies of the insurgents, or any change in their declared goal of Naga sovereignty. A careful study and analysis of the nature of transformation suggest that such change was the result of a carefully worked out strategy. Such a strategy was necessitated by the Indian State's policy of perpetually ignoring the struggle of the Nagas or Mizoram as long as it did not affect the developments in the rest of India. As far as the north east region was concerned, the Indian state was content in imposing a semi-permanent presence of army and paramilitary force in the affected areas. It was accompanied by a liberal dose of cash inflow to the state government which instead of facilitating development, bred corruption and uneven distribution of wealth.[45] Such non-attention to the Naga or Meithei problem only protracted their struggle with no hopeful picture of the future. The East European developments also did not have the desired impact on the Indian State as far as the Naga or Meithei aspirations were concerned. Moreover, the successful achievement of an Accord, and the consequently rapid pace and prosperity in Mizoram also unleashed a debate about the necessity of peace and tranquillity in Nagaland and Manipur, too. In such a situation the NSCN (IM) could no longer remain quiet and wait for the Indian State to initiate a move to resolve the Naga problem. It evolved a strategy of disturbing peace in not just Nagaland, but the entire north eastern region, so as to attract the attention of the Indian state and compel it to negotiate the Naga problem more seriously than it ever did. To spread insurgency throughout the region, create law and order problem for the government, sponsor terrorism and internationalisation of the Naga problem, were some of this carefully evolved strategy.

Spreading Insurgency

The 1990s saw a sudden spurt in the rise of new insurgent outfits in the north-eastern region, and a consequent increase in the terrorist violence. These outfits were in addition to the already existing ones, and they emerged in the so far most peaceful of areas, representing ethnic/tribal communities which never showed any sign of discontent with the Indian state. Some outfits also emerged where some assertive democratic movements were going on. For example, the failure of the six-year long foreign national movement in Assam led to the crystallisation of the United Liberation Front of Assam (ULFA). It was organised in 1979, but its presence was beginning to be felt only from the 1990's. The Indian army sources reported that it was the NSCN (IM) which strengthened the ULFA by supplying arms and training to it. Similarly the Bodos and the Karbis were in the thick of a peaceful democratic movement demanding separate states for themselves. The rejection of their demands had brewed discontent among the two tribes. But the movement became violent as there appeared underground wings, which resorted to terrorist methods to attract the attention of the government. With the emergence of Karbi National Volunteers (KNV), the demand for autonomy graduated to secession. There emerged two insurgent organisations among the Bodos, thereby unleashing terror in the region. Similarly, Tripura had experienced massive violence during 1980-1985 for which the outfit called Tripura National Volunteers (TNV) was responsible. After the Accord, between the TNV and Government of India, peace was expected to follow. But in Tripura too, two new insurgent outfits appeared shortly – the All Twipra Tiger Force (ATTF) and National Liberation Front of Twipra (NLFT). At least one of these – the NLFT was engineered by the NSCN(IM). Another such area was the Karbi Anglong district of Assam, which we have already mentioned, the other being the North Cachar Hills of Assam. North Cachar hills are inhabited by one of the most peaceful tribes of North East India – the Dimassas, who had not articulated discontent so far. The NSCN (IM) first used this area as a transit route for their guerrillas, and subsequently set up their base in the dense forests of the hills.[46] This was followed by the organisation of an underground organisation named Dimassa National Security Force (DNSF). Under the chairmanship of Bharat Langthasa, this outfit advanced secessionist demands but its main activity was extortion and extortion related murders. But soon NSCN (IM) withdrew its favour from the outfit, and formed a counter outfit call Dima Halom Daoga under the chairmanship of Jewel Burman. This outfit, too, mainly indulged in extortion from businessmen and government employees. It was reported that DHD was a front organisation of the NSCN (IM), and seventy per cent of the money collected through extortion was to be deposited with the NSCN (IM). The seeds of insurgency were also sown in the peaceful hills of Meghalaya, where the NSCN (IM) sponsored two organisations – the Achik National Volunteers Council (ANVC) to operate in the Garo hills, and Hyniewtrap Achik Liberation Council (HALC) to function in and around the city of Shillong. Although both were secessionist in their claim, the main activity they indulged in was extortion and murder of businessmen and officials. In Manipur, although a number of such outfits were already in existence, the NSCN (IM) sponsored another outfit called Kanglei Yawol Kanna Lup (KYKL).

The NSCN (IM) did not declare its policy behind the sponsorship or expansion of insurgency in the region. But it seems that it had a two fold motive: one, to have as many front organisations as possible through which it could collect its finances; two, to create acute turbulence in the region, through these organisations. Both would attract the attention of the Indian State to the region and compel it to negotiate with the NSCN (IM) as solution to the Naga problem would neutralise other outfits too. The immediate attention of the Indian State was sought also because the Naga issue and the Naga underground movement had been too protracted with no sign of any prospective solution. In the mean time the prolonged struggle had eroded its mass base and resulted in dwindling cadre structure.[47] As against this a large chunk of the Nagas has been frustrated, and had settled down to the fact of being the sixteenth state of the Indian Union.

Turbulence in Civil Life

Throughout its history, the NSCN (IM) had so far never disrupted the civil life or inflicted violence on the common people, or resorted to extortion from the Naga or non-Naga citizens of the Naga hills. The only 'extortion' it indulged in was the collection of an annual amount from the government servants working in Nagaland as 'taxes', which was a source of revenue to run the underground movement. The amount was small and collected with due receipt without any threat or violence. But significantly, from the 1990's it not only indulged in widespread extortion, threat, violence and abduction, it also resorted to bomb blasts which killed innocent civilians. It thus marked another change in the pattern of insurgency: degeneration to criminal activity and shift of insurgency from the jungles to urban areas.[48] It was no more the army only which had to deal with insurgency; from now on the State police force was also involved in combating insurgency as it concerned the law and order situation. For example, on the 25th of February 1995, there was a massive bomb blast in a train near Nailung near Lumding.[49] The army reported it to be a handiwork of the NSCN (IM), which the NSCN (IM) did not deny.[50] In Karbi Anglong and North Cachar hill, the NSCN (IM) and its front organisation had launched a massive extortion drive from the businessmen and government and bank employees. The situation was so bad that the banks operating in the area were seeking to withdraw from the region, and the employees working in the area sought immediate transfer. The business houses were either shifting to safe areas or closing down. On 5th February 1995, a massive bomb exploded near the Manipur Raj Bhavan at Imphal.[51] Following the deterioration in the situation, General Shankar Roy Choudhury, Chief of the Indian Army, toured the north east and hinted at large scale army deployment. But he emphasised that a military solution would provide only a temporary relief; for a permanent solution to the insurgency problem, dialogue with the insurgents was essential.[52] On December 27th, 1994 their was a massive shoot out between the NSCN (K) and the Indian army in the Mokokchung town of Nagaland, resulting in the death of seven people including civilians.[53] On 5th March 1995, an army convoy coming from Imphal to Kohima was fired upon by the NSCN (IM) (subsequently, it was reported that there was no firing but the sound of a tyre burst from the nearby area). The panic stricken Rashtriya Rifle personnel resorted to open fire in the middle of the Kohima town, resulting in the death of eight civilians.[54] This act of the army earned widespread condemnation. But by March 1995 more than 150 persons, including 13 policemen, 18 army men and 112 civilians were killed by the underground forces in the renewed escalation of terrorism and violence.[55] This compelled the Government of Nagaland to promulgate the Disturbed Area Act, 1958 in the state with immediate effect (3rd March 1995). As the situation became volatile, the army launched Operation Golden Bird by which it flushed out 200 ultras from the Mizoram-Myanmar border, and compelled them to abandon their traditional transit routes along the Mizoram-Myanmar border. The simultaneous escalation of violence in Manipur led the army to launch Operation Sunny Vale there from August 4th, 1995. This operation was to counter the Meithei insurgent groups like PLA, UNLF, PREPAK, KYKL, which were operating in Manipur. But the situation showed no signs of improvement.

Another shift in the activity of the NSCN (IM) was observed when it was seen to be active in the tea gardens of Assam along the Assam-Nagaland border. It served extortion notices to a number of tea gardens to deposit exorbitant amounts or face dire consequences. On 17th October 1995 a tea garden executive was kidnapped from Nowgong.[56] On 19th October another tea executive was kidnapped.[57] A powerful bomb exploded in Diphu town on 29th of October reportedly by KNV.[58] The United Liberation Front of Assam had also begun to extort a large number of tea planters. As a consequence panic gripped the tea industry of the region.[59] The NSCN (IM) also involved itself in the border dispute with Assam. It supported the concept of greater Nagaland, which amounted to disturbing the territorial integrity of Assam and Manipur. The NSCN (IM) claimed a large chunk of Assam territory as part of Nagaland, which was objected to by its erstwhile comrades in the ULFA.[60] Apprehending disturbance of the territorial integrity of Manipur, all the Meithei insurgents also protested against the NSCN (IM).[61] As a follow up of its claim in the Assam territory, the NSCN (IM) attacked a border post at Lakhimijan near Sibsagar, killing some state police personnel.[62] It was also involved in the ambush of an army convoy in Halflong, killing several civilians in the process which included a lady and a nine-month old baby.[63]

Such disruption of the civil life was resorted to not only by the NSCN (IM) but other outfits like the ULFA, NDFB, BLTF, ANVC, NLFT, KNV and the DHD too creating a volatile situation in the entire region. A sense of terrible panic gripped the minds of the people as life became insecure. Bomb blasts and explosions were rampant, dead bodies were found frequently. Besides the army launching counter-insurgency operations throughout the region, paramilitary forces were patrolling the affected areas round the clock. Railway authorities rescheduled the departure and arrival timings of the trains to avoid night operation.

The newer forms of terrorism and violence led the Human Right activists to denounce the acts of the insurgents. It was significant because all along these bodies were a severe critic of the army and their modes of operation, and who sympathised with the undergrounds. The National Human Rights Commission Chairman Justice Ranganath Mishra stated that the insurgents, too, were guilty of human right violations, because all violence was an anti-thesis to human rights.[64]

Establish NSCN (IM) Hegemony

As is evident from the narration above, the insurgency scene in the North East was entirely dominated by the NSCN (IM) from 1995. While Mizoram had settled down to peace and development after the Accord, the Meithei outfits were confined to Manipur valley only. As against this the NSCN (IM) which was hitherto confined to the Naga Hills now extended their operations throughout North East India. In some areas it functioned directly while in others through its front organisations like KNV, DHD, NDFB, ANVC, HNLC and NLFT. In doing so it not only spread insurgency but also had established itself as the premier insurgent outfit having its hegemony over the others. In fact the NSCN (IM) had been struggling to establish its supremacy over others all along its history. After the Shillong Accord (1975) it broke away from the NNC and formed NSCN (IM), but it still had to contain the NNC as its rival organisation. Shortly NNC was relegated into insignificance but the NSCN (IM) itself broke into two factions – the Isac Swu Muivah group and Khaplang group. Since then the two factions had been fighting an extremely bitter battle to establish their respective supremacy. Now, by having so many front organisations who looked up to NSCN (IM) as their parent body, it finally established its hegemony in the region. To further strengthen its position it tried to set up an umbrella organisation under which all the insurgent outfits of the region would function and where the NSCN (IM) would be supreme. One such umbrella body, the Indo-Burmese Revolutionary front, was already there. In this body the NSCN (K) had the supremacy. Therefore, the NSCN (IM) now formed the United Liberation Front of Seven Sisters (ULFOSS) in which the other members were the United Liberation Front of Assam, Hmar Peoples

Convention, United National Liberation Front (Manipur), Peoples Liberation Front of Manipur.[65] These outfits could now buy arms and ammunition form the Bangkok and Singapore markets through this body. The Indian army sources reported that the Inter Services Intelligence of Pakistan was also involved in this regrouping. The ULFOSS was formed in December 1993. Subsequently, on November 30, 1994 it redrew its strategy by forming another umbrella organisation called the Self Defence United Front of South East Himalayan Region to coordinate the activities of the constituents.[66] According to the Sokemn declaration signed by twenty-three individuals, representing various outfits, its objective was to "fight Indian expansionism and the Indian State terrorism". The signatories were the NSCN (IM), HALC, NLFT, KNV, HPC, KYKL.[67] It can be seen the constituents of this body were the outfits which were sponsored by the NSCN (IM) itself. Needless to say, therefore, NSCN (IM) was the commanding voice in this organisation.

The other method of establishing hegemony which was adopted by the NSCN (IM) was to form counter organisations against the existing ones. Thus, it created NLFT against the ATTF in Tripura, NDFB against the BLTF in the Bodo area and KYL against the other Meithei outfits in Manipur. It first created the DNSF in North Cachar Hills but when it fell out with it, it countered by creating the DHD. In fact, some outfits were able to see through the games of NSCN (IM). In a press statement, the United Liberation Front of Manipur accused the NSCN (IM) that it was trying to create divisions not only among the Meitheis by creating front organisations like the KYKL, but also trying to destroy the traditional bond between the Nagas and Meitheis in Manipur.[68]

Internationalisation

Since the beginning of the movement, the Nagas were trying to internationalise the Naga issue. It was imperative to create international diplomatic pressure on the Indian State to release the Nagas. This internationalisation process was started by Phizo himself. The NSCN (IM) continued the effort. It was a major achievement for the NSCN (IM) when it got admission to the Unrepresented Nations and Peoples Organisation. As a result of their persistent endeavour, the NSCN (IM) was able to raise the Naga issue at the United Nations Commission for Human Rights Conference[69] held at Geneva in

December 1996 and the Working Group on Indigenous People around the same time and the International Convention of Ethnic People in Geneva in July 1994.[70]

Crackdown in the Neighbouring Countries

Simultaneously with the military operations against the underground in India, there were crackdowns on them in the neighbouring countries too from the 1990's. Such crackdown created immense difficulties to the insurgent outfits because most of them had their main base office and training camps in the neighbouring countries like Bangladesh and Bhutan. As the pro-democracy movement was resuscitated in Myanmar from 1994, the Military Junta in Myanmar began its suppression drive again. The various Myanmarese groups like the Karens and the Kachins, who were leading underground movements to secure independence from Myanmar also became victims of this suppression drive. The NSCN (IM), both Khaplang and Swu-Muivah factions also had to leave the area as a result of their persecution. The situation worsened with the change in the Government of Bangladesh. The previous Khaleda Zia government was favouring the Indian underground outfits to establish their bases in the Bangla territory. But the then government headed by Sheikh Hasina sought to improve its relationship with India. As a goodwill gesture the Hasina government decided to disallow the insurgents to use the Bangla territory against India.[71] As a first step, the bank accounts of the insurgents were frozen[72] and the ultras were asked to leave the Bangla territory by April 15, 1997.[73] The two governments then agreed to jointly fight the ultras. In February 1997, the Bangladesh government officially launched a crackdown on the ultras and their base camps were busted.[74] The ultras were reported to be shifting their bases back to the jungles of Myanmar[75], while the Brahmaputra Valley based ultras like the ULFA and NDFB were moving to Bhutan.[76] To add to the woes of the ultras, the Government of India negotiated with the Government of Bhutan not to allow sanctuary to the Indian insurgents. As a follow up the two governments agreed to launch a joint operation against the ultras from November 1997.[77] The operation in Bhutan by the Bhutanese government took place in 2003. It was a very successful operation in which the entire ULFA hide out was blasted and its cadres either killed or flushed out. Before ULFA could recover from this setback, the Myanmarese government, on the request of the

Government of India, started flushing out operation against the Indian militants in 2006-07. These developments were serious setbacks to the undergrounds, because without these base camps outside India it was immensely difficult for them to operate.

Peace Process: End of Insurgency?

While the ultras were on the run outside and facing combined military operations inside India, the commoners in North East India were facing more hardship. Caught between the insurgents and the army, repeated curfew and counter-insurgency operations their normal life was paralysed. Such a volatile situation created a strong urge for peace and normalcy in the minds of the people. The Nagas, especially, sought an urgent solution to the fifty year old Naga imbroglio. The change in the government in New Delhi facilitated the peace initiative when the then Prime Minister H.D. Devegowda, during his visit of North East, invited the underground to come for negotiations.[78] It was later confirmed that the Prime Minister had actually met some insurgent leaders to initiate the peace process.[79] The prominent Naga citizens and organisations decided to seize the opportunity and strengthen the initiative. In a significant move, the Naga commoners decided not to leave the initiative either to the government or the underground alone, and create pressure on both the parties to settle the Naga issue once for all. Since the Government of India had expressed its willingness to talk to the underground the onus was now on the NSCN (IM). The only problem was the factionalism of the Naga underground.[80] The Naga people decided to take initiative to get the NSCN (IM) agree to unify and then sit for talks. Thus, the Naga Hoho (the summit conference of the Nagas) along with prominent NGOs like the Naga People's Movement for Human Rights, Naga Mother's Association, Naga Student Federation and Church leaders held discussions to start the peace process. A United Naga Conference was held on February 6, 1997 to deliberate on the subject.[81] On 4th March 1997, the Prime Minister announced in the Lok Sabha that he had met some insurgent leaders to discuss the Naga issue. The Home Minister Indrajit Gupta subsequently told the Rajya Sabha that the Prime Minister's talks with the underground on secession from India was unacceptable to the government.[82] As a result of this failure, the Indian army expressed its doubt over NSCN (IM)'s sincerity in holding talks with the Centre. "Our past experience shows that this sort of move (acceptance of talk offer) was used by militants as a reprieve and also to redefine and consolidate their present position".[83] The NSCN (IM), too, expressed its dissatisfaction over the Centre's attitude. It set certain preconditions for further discussions. (i) that the talks be held in a third country, (ii) the negotiations be settled by a third country.[84] In the mean time, the Kukis (a tribe in constant conflict with the Nagas) urged that they be included in the negotiations because any settlement had to take care of the future of the Kukis.[85] The Khaplang faction of the NSCN (IM) dissociated from the talks.[86] But despite these bottlenecks, the first round of talks between the NSCN (IM) and the Indian officials were held in Bangkok in July 1997, which proved to be an adequate ice breaker.[87] As per the desire of the Naga Hoho and as a goodwill gesture to create a congenial atmosphere for negotiations, the Government of India offered a cease-fire agreement to the NSCN (IM) which the latter accepted. As a result cease-fire came into effect in Nagaland from August 1, 1997. After almost fifty years guns were silent in the hills of Nagaland.

Meanwhile, the Naga Hoho and NGOs kept up their pressure on the NSCN (IM) so that the peace initiated did not fizzle out. The Baptist Fellowship of America organised a convention of Nagas at Atlanta (USA) in August 1997 to mark the 125th year of the advent of Christianity in Naga Hills. The convention wanted to use this opportunity to thrash out a lasting solution to the Naga problem. The Naga Hoho made the NSCN (IM) agree to participate in the convention. In fact, it even got to Khaplang faction to agree to come to the convention. The eight day long convention was attended by about 10,000 Nagas and had a successful deliberation on the Naga issue. Its major success was to get the Khaplang and Swu-Muivah faction of NSCN (IM) to join the peace process and not to impede solution to the Naga issue.[88] Addressing a UNPO Conference at Geneva (15th session), Isaac Swu of the NSCN (IM) stated that the Government of India had agreed to the NSCN (IM) condition that (i) talks between them be held without either side stipulating any preconditions, (ii) that the talks be held at the highest level (Prime Ministerial) and (iii) at a venue anywhere outside India or Nagaland.[89] In pursuance of the agreement, the second round of talks was held in Geneva. The date and deliberations of the meetings were not known as they were kept secret. But the Government of India and the Naga Hoho were hopeful about the progress of the negotiations. To continue the peaceful atmosphere the Government of India extended the cease-fire further which continued up to the middle of 1999. There were hopes all around that the half a century old Naga problem was going to be solved, and the insurgency and violence was giving way to peace and prosperity.

Meanwhile, the United Front Government was dislodged from power and a new government led by Atal Behari Vajpayee assumed power. But this change did not affect the peace process. The new government extended the cease-fire and appointed Swaraj Kaushal, a prominent lawyer and former Governor of Mizoram, as Prime Minister's emissary to the negotiations. Talks were subsequently held in Manila, Zurich and Amsterdam. The Amsterdam talks were held in March 1999. A joint Ceasefire Monitoring Cell was constituted by the NSCN (IM) and the Government of India to monitor the progress of ceasefire, and breaches, if any. The next round of talks were scheduled at the end of June 1999. This time the Government of India wanted to hold the talks in any Indian city, but the NSCN (IM) insisted still on a foreign country.[90]

The period under discussion acquired more significance for further reasons. Due to the pressure of Naga Hoho, the Khaplang faction of NSCN (IM) agreed to participate in the ceasefire. It now appeared that the Naga Hoho emerged to be in a position to control the Naga situation. It agreed with the NSCN (IM) to observe May 16 as the 'Plebiscite Day', and accordingly it was solemnly observed throughout Naga areas. In May itself (May 8, 1999), the Naga underground leaders Th. Muivah and Isaac Swu returned to Nagaland after 33 years, and since then were camping there to monitor the ceasefire, peace process and to assess the ground realities in Nagaland. In an interview Isaac Swu said, ''since we are entering into serious discussions with India (after initial rounds) we have come here for consultations''.[91] Muivah stated "the people here are very anxious about the developments taking place outside. Our movement as such is people based and unless people understand what is going on there will be gap".[92] While in India, the NSCN (IM) renamed itself as National Socialist Council of Nagalim (Lim stood for land). Expectedly the visit of the underground leaders raised the hope of the Naga people about the imminence of a lasting solution of the Naga imbroglio and advent of long awaited peace and tranquillity, so that they could lead a normal life, which had so far eluded them. But the conflicting statements issued by the two parties raise doubts about the end of the insurgency. The Naga leader declared that they could not accept any solution that is not 'honourable' after fifty years of struggle, and sovereignty was inalienable.[93] The representative of the Indian State, Swaraj Kaushal, ruled out sovereignty for the Nagas.[94] He stated that any solution was to be within the framework of the Indian Constitution.[95] With both the parties refusing to negotiate 'Naga Sovereignty', it was feared that the talks were heading for a deadlock. This would mean despair and agony for the Naga people. But the question remains, can the Naga undergrounds and the Indian State continue to ignore the Naga peoples' urge for peace and right to normal life.

However, in the July-August (1999) peace talks, the ceasefire was again extended, this time for a year signalling another positive development. There were a number of meetings between the NSCN (IM), and the Government of India negotiator Swaraj Kaushal in Bangkok, Zurich and Paris and twice in Amsterdam. But then suddenly Kaushal resigned from the post of negotiator. Internal politics within the Bharatiya Janata Party of which Sushma Swaraj, wife of Kaushal, was a prominent leader was said to be the reason. K. Padmanabhaiah, retired Home Secretary, was then appointed as representative of the government in the peace talks. He continued the peace discussions with the NSCN leaders. In a meeting held on 29-30 July 2000 in Bangkok the two parties agreed to extend the ceasefire by another year. But following this an unfortunate event took place. The NSCN leader, Th. Muivah, was arrested by Thailand Police on charge of travelling on a fake document and put him in jail. With the leader in jail the continuation of the peace talk was in peril. There was another lurking danger to the peace process: the question of extension of ceasefire in all the areas of north-east where there is a preponderance of Naga population.

Ceasefire and Greater Nagaland

On 26 August 2000, Mr Isaac Swu of NSCN (IM) wrote to the Prime Minister of India, accusing his government of betraying its commitment on the ceasefire issue. Padmanabhaiah had reportedly agreed to the extension of ceasefire provision to all the Naga inhabited areas of North East, not just Nagaland. The NSCN argument was that observing ceasefire only in Nagaland, but continuing the fight between NSCN and the Indian Army in other areas, did not prove meaningful.

It vitiated the atmosphere for the continuation of peace discussion. Swu warned that the NSCN (IM) would no longer be under any obligation if the Indian Government does not officially implement the ceasefire in all Naga areas by 5th September 2000. In reply on 11th September 2000, K. Padmanabhaiah, replied to Swu stating that none of the government representatives had agreed to extend the ceasefire in all Naga areas. He also pointed out that the Government of India would consider extension of ceasefire with NSCN (IM) to other areas in north-east subject to the condition that NSCN (IM) accepts and agrees to issue a statement that extension of ceasefire to other areas will not be interpreted by them as a step towards recognition of their claim to Greater Nagaland.

Padmanabhaiah's statement had a context. The Naga underground organisations have long been demanding that all the contiguous areas of Nagaland, which have a preponderant Naga population, such as those in Assam, Arunachal Pradesh and Manipur, should be amalgamated into a single Naga unit. From this emerged the concept of greater Nagalim. In fact, for these organisations it was not just the sovereignty of Nagaland but carving out a greater Nagaland was also part of the goal. But problems resulted from the opposition from those states—Assam, Manipur and Arunachal Pradesh which protested and opposed the idea of greater Nagaland, and refused to part with even a fraction of their respective territory. As soon as the Swu-Padmanabhaiah dialogue became public, there was vociferous objection from these states, which compelled the Prime Minister to convene a meeting with the Chief Ministers of these states. In this meeting of 28th September 2000, the Chief Ministers of Assam, Manipur and Arunachal Pradesh opposed the extension of ceasefire in their respective states on the ground that this would legitimise the claim of the Nagas on the territory of these states in future. In fact it would become the basis of their future claim of Greater Nagaland. Secondly, the ceasefire extension over these areas would provide free access to the NSCN to construct their camps, carry on their tax collection and extortion drives, recruit local youths in its cadre, and give birth to dummy insurgent outfits. All these were sure to disrupt these otherwise peaceful areas. In fact, even the Nagaland Chief Minister S.C. Jamir, in his meeting with the Home Minister L.K. Advani, said that the extension of ceasefire beyond Nagaland was fraught with dangerous consequences.

But the NSCN (IM) was not ready to continue peace discussion without such extension. Since it decided to call off the negotiation, if ceasefire to all Naga areas were not implemented, the Government of India in a significant move on 14th June 2001 decided to agree to ceasefire 'without territorial limits'.

The Fall Out

The fall out of this extension of ceasefire over areas of other states was cataclysmic. The state of Manipur was up in arms. Led by the students' union, the state experienced unprecedented violence in the form of protests. The State Assembly building was burnt, legislators threatened and Government establishments attacked. The uprising continued unabated for almost a month. With more and more people joining the protest, women and youth coming into the forefront and defying State's repression and prohibitory orders, the movement continued to gain strength. Gradually the protest movement spread in other areas of the region too viz. in Assam and Arunachal Pradesh. While student organisations and political parties protested against the government's decision, it threatened to become violent when insurgent organisations like Dima Halom Daoga and United Liberation Front of Assam also joined the protest. The situation became volatile and threatened to erupt in large scale violence. In Manipur the enmity between the Meithei and Nagas was also on the verge of breach. Terrified of violent attacks on them, the Nagas of Imphal Valley evacuated to safer places. The Kuki and Vaiphei, etc., the non-Meithei tribes of Manipur also supported the protest of the Meitheis.

Taken aback by the unprecedented protest, the Government of India convened a series of meetings with the protesting groups as well as the Naga organisations. On 27th July 2001, a high level meeting was held at 7 Race Course, New Delhi at the Official Residence of the Prime Minister. Subsequent to this, the Home Minister announced that while ceasefire continued, the words in the agreement 'without territorial limit' were being withdrawn. In other words, the status quo was maintained and ceasefire would be continued only within Nagaland. It was also added that the Government of India representatives had discussed the matter with the NSCN (IM), which was agreeable to the decision.

While the announcement quelled the disquiet in Manipur, Assam and Arunachal Pradesh, it had the expected repercussion on Nagaland.

The people of Nagaland as well as the Nagas of Manipur rose in protest against the about turn which they termed as 'betrayal'. To make matters worse, the NSCN (IM) stated that, contrary to the statement of the Government of India, it had not agreed nor is agreeable, to this 'reversion'. The breach of agreement was done unilaterally by the Government of India. Although the latter insisted that, despite the setbacks, the negotiation with the NSCN (IM) would continue, the future seemed to be uncertain yet again. The only hope was the Naga Hoho, Naga Mother Association and Naga People's Movement for Human Rights, which were making untiring efforts to bring the peace process back to its track.

For the next round of meetings, the Indian Government was keen that instead of holding the negotiations in a third country, the NSCN (IM) leaders should come to India. It facilitated their visit by withdrawing the ban on the organisation. Responding positively to the invitation, the NSCN (IM) leaders, T. Muivah and Isaac Swu, reached New Delhi on January 8, 2003. This visit marked a historic day as it was the first occasion since a Naga team talked to the then Prime Minister Indira Gandhi in 1967. The two parties held a series of negotiations. While it is not known what transpired, the signals were positive. The Naga leaders assured that there would be no more fighting between the Indian Army and the NSCN cadres. It also expressed its satisfaction at the progress of the discussions.[96]

The negotiations between the two parties were observed euphorically by the people of the North East, believing that the dawn of peace would arise soon in the region. Following NSCN, the Bodo Liberation Tigers of the Bodos, the Dima Halom Daoga in North Cachar and United Peoples' Democratic Solidarity in Karbi Anglong of Assam also declared unilateral ceasefire and expressed their desire to come to the negotiating table. This confirmed that there is a fatigue in the rank and file of all the underground outfits in the region. Moreover, the problem associated with the jungle life, like shortage of food stuff and medical care for the lower cadres, desire for a family life and no immediate sight of achievement of their goals had brought despair in them. This was caused by the constant hunt of the counter insurgency forces as well as growing public opinion against the insurgency in the region. In fact, the BLT participated in the negotiation with the Government of India, and achieved autonomy for their area by signing an Accord with the Government of India in

February 2003. Although most of the region is still restive, any breakthrough with the NSCN (IM) could usher in the long-cherished and elusive peace, tranquillity and development of the region. Every concerned party, therefore, was keeping their fingers crossed.

Conclusion

From a simple resistance movement launched by a tiny tribal community in remote Naga hills to massive violent uprisings encompassing the entire North Eastern region, insurgency has come a long way over the last sixty years of Indian independence. It not only challenged the might of the Indian state, but undermined its authority, subverted the economy, and embarrassed it internationally by publicising it as an oppressor nation. One insurgency has multiplied into many; jungle warfare has spilled over to the civil life. It has forced the State to reconsider its counter-insurgency strategy from using military solution to prolonged negotiations and signing of bilateral accords. But peace has eluded the region so far. The Indian state has therefore realised that mainstreaming of marginal communities could neither come through military solution or cultural standardisation. Equitable economic development and democratization of power-structure perhaps could to some extent integrate the region with the rest of the country. Hence there is a splash of activities in the region initiated by the Central Government. Massive funds are being sanctioned for infrastructural development and efforts are being made to link it to the flourishing South East Asian economies through a 'Look East' policy. A long neglected and ignored region has suddenly become a centre of attention.

NOTES AND REFERENCES

1. Annual Report of the Ministry of Home Affairs, 2000-2001, Government of India, New Delhi, 2001.
2. Institute of Conflict Management, New Delhi, South Asian Terrorism Portal.
3. Ibid.
4. Ibid.
5. Ibid.
6. Report of the National Police Commission, (Seventh), May 1981, New Delhi.

7. Ibid.
8. Ibid.
9. Nag, Sajal, *Nationalism, Separatism, Secessionism*, Rawat, Jaipur & New Delhi, 2000, pp. 169-293.
10. See Dev, Laxmi, *Ahom-Tribal Relations*, Gauhati University, Gauhati, 1968 for details
11. For a detailed discussion see Sajal Nag, *Contesting Marginality : Ethnicity, Insurgency and Subnationalism in North East India*, Manohar, New Delhi, 2000.
12. Ibid.
13. Sahni, Ajay, 'The Terrorist Economy in India's North East : Preliminary Explorations', in *Faultline : Writings on Conflict and Resolution* , vol. 8, New Delhi, April 1, 2001, p. 127-148.
14. Ibid
15. Saikia, Jaideep, 'Revolutionaries or Warlords: ULFA's Organisational Profile' in *Faultline*, vol. 9, July 2001, pp. 105-129.
16. Sahni, Ajay, *op. cit.*
17. North East Vigil, issue no. 1.20, 16, March, 2000 in http/ www.north eastvigil.com/newssearch/16.03.2000.
18. *The Sentinel*, Guwahati, June 9, 2000.
19. Discussed later in details
20. Dasgupta, Anindita, 'Small Arm Proliferation in North East India : A Case Study of Assam' in *Economic and Political Weekly*, January 6, 2000, pp. 59-64.
21. Gokhale, Nitin, *The Hot Brew: The Assam Tea Industry's Most Turbulent Decade 1987-97*, Spectrum, Guwahati, 1998, p. 32.
22. Ibid.
23. Ibid., p. 54,
24. Ibid., p. 55.
25. Ibid., pp. 55-56.
26. Ibid., p. 79.
27. Ibid., p. 81.
28. Ibid., pp. 7-8.
29. Ibid., pp. 122-124.
30. Ibid., p. 123.
31. Ibid., pp. 146-147.
32. See later in the section 'Changing Nature of Insurgency'
33. *The Sentinel*, 26, April 1995.
34. Ghose, Sanjay, *Sanjoy's Assam: Diaries and Writings of Sanjoy Ghose*, edited by Sumita Ghose, Penguin, New Delhi, 1999.
35. Rammohan, E.M., 'Manipur : a Degenerated Insurgency' in *Faultlines*, vol. II, April, 2002.

36. *Sunday*, 8-14 January, 1995.
37. *The Asian Age*, 10 September, 1997
38. *The Asian Age*, 15 September, 1997.
39. *India Today*, 31 July 1993.
40. *India Today*, *ibid.*
41. *The Telegraph*, 23 March, 1997.
42. *The Asian Age*, 15 April, 1997.
43. Nag, Sajal, *Nationalism, Separatism, Secessionism*, New Delhi, Rawat, 1999.
44. Nayar, Kuldip, 'Defiance by the Nagas' in *The Sentinel*, 8 March, 1995.
45. *The Sentinel*, 27 February 1995.
46. *The Sentinel*, 26 May, 1997. It was reported that to attract young men, the NSCN(IM) was offering Rs. 5 lakhs to each recruit.
47. *The Sentinel*, 23 March 1995.
48. *The Sentinel*, 26 February, 1995
49. Ibid.
50. *The Sentinel*, 27 February, 1995.
51. *The Sentinel*, 10 February, 1995.
52. *The Sentinel*, 9 February, 1995.
53. *The Sentinel*, 28 December, 1994.
54. *The Sentinel*, 6 March, 1995.
55. *The Sentinel*, 23 March, 1995.
56. *The Sentinel*, 18 October, 1995.
57. *The Sentinel*, 20 October, 1995.
58. *The Sentinel*, 30 October, 1995.
59. *The Sentinel*, 18 October, 1995.
60. *The Sentinel*, 24 August, 1997.
61. Ibid.
62. *The Sentinel*, 3 February, 1996.
63. *The Sentinel*, 8 February, 1996.
64. *The Sentinel*, 4 November, 1996.
65. *The Shillong Times*, 27 December, 1993.
66. Kamrupi, 'NSCN (IM) Redress Its Strategy' in *The Sentinel*, 21 February, 1995.
67. Ibid.
68. *The Sentinel*, 23 February 1995.
69. *The Sentinel*, 6 January, 1997.
70. *The Sentinel*, 26 April, 1995.
71. *The Sentinel*, 26 July 1996.
72. *The Sentinel*, 14 September 1996.
73. *The Sentinel*, 18 April, 1997.
74. *The Sentinel*, 19 April, 1997

75. *The Sentinel*, 1 March, 1997.
76. *The Sentinel*, 4 March, 1997.
77. *The Sentinel*, 20 June, 1997 and 26 June, 1997.
78. *The Sentinel*, 25 October, 1996.
79. *The Sentinel*, 5 March, 1997.
80. *The Sentinel*, 26 May, 1997. The main fight was between the Khaplang and Muivah-Swu faction. Khaplang was a Myanmarese Naga while Isaac Swu was a Sema and Muivah was a Tangkhul. The bulk of the cadre were Konyaks. In 1988 the Konyaks murdered 88 Tangkhuls, leading to the separation of the Khaplang and Muivah factions.
81. *The Sentinel*, 18 February 1997.
82. *The Sentinel*, 15 May, 1997.
83. Quotes in *The Sentinel*, 19 December, 1995.
84. *The Sentinel*, 30 December, 1996.
85. *The Sentinel*, 21 May.
86. 30 July, 1996.
87. *The Sentinel*, 3 July, 1997.
88. *The Sentinel*, 31 July, 1997.
89. 2 August, 1997.
90. *The Telegraph*, 12 June, 1999.
91. Interview with Isaac Swu and Th. Muivah in Nuland, Dimapur, Nagaland May 27, 1999 in *North East Sun*, June 15-30, 1999.
92. Ibid.
93. *The North East Daily*, 4 June, 1999.
94. *The Telegraph*, 12 June, 1999.
95. Ibid.
96. *North East Sun*, vol. 8, no. 12, January 15-31, 2003.

Section V

Role of Institutions and Media in North East India's Development

Religion and Colonial Politics

ASSAM, MYANMAR AND BUDDHISM

Swapna Bhattacharya (Chakarborti)

India is a country of varied religions, social traditions and institutions, which have prospered and experienced various ramifications through ages. Historically, Hinduism and Buddhism are considered as indigenous religions, whereas Islam and Christianity are seen as more of an exogenous nature. Nevertheless, Christianity and Islam entered India at quite an early period. People responded to the call of the preachers and got themselves converted. Sometimes, people were hardly aware that they were being "converted". They continued to adhere to their old faith, showing, however, due regard to their new religion as well. Multiple identity of a single individual is something very common in Indian tradition. One of the major factors which is directly responsible for such a development in the domain of Hinduism and Buddhism, to some extent in Islam also, is the extreme popularity of Mahayana Buddhism in large areas of eastern Bengal, Bihar, lower Myanmar and Arakan. In contrast to orthodox Theravada (also called Hinayana) Buddhism, Mahayana Buddhism allows a Buddhist to worship Hindu Gods and goddesses without any problem. In the forefront of this divine world stood Lord Shiva and Lord Vishnu, both of whom found their followers among the Buddhist population of modern Myanmar, Thailand and Cambodia. A large number of archaeological evidences stand witness to this influence. Equally important are the inscriptions found in these countries written partly in Sanskrit, but in major part, however, in their indigenous languages. This eastward movement of Indian people, mainly from coastal provinces of eastern and southern India, and, overland, from eastern India experienced a westward turn, whenever people from China and

Tibet moved downward creating pressure on land and resources. Myanmar over centuries had to absorb this movement, the process of which was not always peaceful.

Compared to other parts of India, the North Eastern states, Bengal and Assam were the regions most open to this influence coming from countries, such as Myanmar (Burma), Thailand (erstwhile old Siam) and Cambodia. In all these three countries, from quite an early stage, Buddhism[1] experienced such openness. Colonial expansion in India and Myanmar had to face the challenge of this cultural asset of Asia. Lalrimawia rightly described the situation: "The cross followed the British flag"[2]. Meghalaya, Nagaland and Mizoram remarkably experienced a sudden but rapid spread of Christianity.

In this paper, an attempt is being made to demonstrate that the missionary activities of the western preachers happened to take place exactly when there appeared to be a resurgence of Buddhism in India and Myanmar. Though in a different context, in the context of the tribal society of middle India, one of the most outstanding anthropologists of modern India, Professor Nirmal Bose, has shown such cases in his book The Structure of Hindu Society. Let me quote this great anthropologist and Gandhian: "The nineteenth century witnessed a number of social movements among Mundas, Oraons and related tribes. The *Pax Britannica* brought in Christian missionaries, Hindu money lenders and land grabbers from the plains. One important consequence of these threats to the old established ways of life was the emergence of revivalist movements of various kinds. Such movements reveal very clearly the dilemmas faced by these relatively isolated communities on being suddenly exposed to the full onslaught of a highly sophisticated cultural system"[3].

The present paper sets the tune in tracing some remnant elements of important Buddhist cults and existence of pockets of Buddhist population in Assam, and some other parts of the North Eastern states. A few examples given in the pages below will reveal how the Annexation of Assam, development of Tea Industry in Assam, demand for Burma Teak, Pacification of the Lushai Hills, Three Anglo-Burmese Wars in 1824-26, 1852, and 1885-1886, administrative centralization of the Chittagong Hill Tracts[4], intensive missionizing activities, occurred in rapid succession and in intensive interdependence, in the entire region. The paper pleads for taking up inter-disciplinary projects by social scientists from all concerned nations, particularly, India and her eastern neighbours to explore this lost link.

India has developed a rich school of Buddhist scholarship, but, in most cases, the research is focused on texts and theories. Works dedicated in tracing how Buddhism accommodated rising Islam, or Vaishnava thought, or how Buddhism remained existent in local cults at grass root level, or how high Buddhism got "tribalised", remained unexplored. In the case of Buddhist Bengal, the only exception is perhaps the 'religion' of the Bauls of Bengal, which attracted the attention of scholars for its highly syncretic nature.

This paper also questions the validity of the concept of a tribal society, which often implies as if the tribal society does not possess elements of any established religion, let alone Buddhism. Buddhism was a vast system and accommodated within its fold various beliefs and thoughts[5]; Myanmar Buddhism is a remarkable example. The tag "tribal" is a British 'gift' to post independent India. The extreme case of such a fallacy is visible when communities from North Eastern Indian states, with a strong Buddhist identity and a long civilizational background are designated as 'tribes'. Such a qualification approved by the Indian Constitution may benefit them in various ways and means, yet, no one can deny that such methods of identification may appear as enigma for a country where Buddhism was born, prospered and from where the religion traveled to various parts of the world, in the countries of immediate neighbourhood, in particular.

Part I

Myanmar History Reinterpreted in the Context of the History of Assam and the North East

There is a marked similarity between the history of Myanmar and the history of India as regards the colonial expansion. Neither country was annexed and occupied overnight. Instead, it took several hundreds of years, until a relatively firm hold over land and people could be established by the colonial rulers. We are acquainted with the nationalist movements[6] which actually were centered on the heartland, while, in remote areas, partly inaccessible, lying deep in the hills and jungles, a different kind of struggle was going on. A full-length history of such struggle is yet to be written. This is true in the case of India, as in the case of Myanmar. One of the most remarkable features of colonial expansion and occupation is the sudden and fast spread of

Christianity in certain regions of modern Myanmar (Karen and Kachin States, Chin Hills, etc) and North Eastern India. This change in religious conviction brought in major changes in the social life of the concerned people. A large number of converted Kachins, Karens and Chins served in the British Army. In most cases, the converted people felt socially secure and came close to the rulers. The states of Meghalaya, Nagaland, and Mizoram experienced such social changes, which show remarkable resemblance with the Myanmar scenario. The races like the Burmans, Shans, Arakanese and the Mons remained with their religion, i.e., Buddhism. Buddhism became a major inspiration for anti-colonial struggle in Myanmar.

Indeed, social changes, migration, discarding of one's old home, occurred even before the advent of the British. Constant invasion and intrusion of Sanskritic people, with what they perceived as their 'legitimate authority', cornered the actual sons of the soil, whom we call today the *adivasis.* A large number of this people belongs to the Austric group, the languages (Grierson) and cultures of which are less explored compared to high cultures of the heartland. These groups were deprived of their land and resources, but continued to remain within the greater Hindu domain, as Hinduism possesses a great power of absorption. It was only through conversion to Christianity that they could enjoy the privileges that during the colonial period the urban middle classes used to enjoy. In this paper, we are concerned not with the examples of state formation in the classical tribal belt of eastern and middle India[7], rather we are to concentrate mainly on one of the neglected areas of North Eastern India , i.e., Mizoram. The area was known as the Lushai Hills[8] (Sir R. Reid, 1978). To understand the religion and politics in the Lushai Hills areas[9], we have to take into consideration the adjoining areas of other states from modern Bangladesh and Myanmar.

North East Indian states[10], especially Manipur, Tripura, Arunachal Pradesh and Mizoram are situated directly along the trade and religious routes connecting the people of Myanmar and eastern India, including Bengal. In the 18th and 19th centuries, British administrators and military officials took long journeys along several such trade routes, which went up to China, to find out for themselves the best possible opportunities for trade and commerce in this entire region. Mizoram is unique in the sense that Mizoram, the Lushai Hills, as the region was known in the past, became a confluence of people from the Chittagong Hills of Bengal[11] on the one hand, and the Chin Hills and beyond in Myanmar, on the other. Rail link had always been in the British plan, though it never materialized. Instead, Bengal was linked up with British Burma through water ways, where steamship navigation companies made huge profits. This slowly created a mental isolation between the Buddhist communities in Burma and eastern India. However the Bengal connection of Mizoram, we should not loose sight of, as the Lushai Hills meet Chittagong hill Tracts, a strong centre of Buddhism. Strong military presence of the British forces in Chittagong helped them to pacify the South Lushai Hills, while the North Lushail Hills were controlled by the forces in Assam. Learning of tribal languages by the preachers and administrators alike is known throughout colonial history. Such academic adventures inspired the sons of the soil. For example, the first Mizo grammar was written by a Bengali Christian in the year 1884. His name is Brojanath Yalva[12].

The countries like Myanmar, Thailand and Cambodia on the mainland Southeast Asia, and Indonesia on the Island Southeast Asia, stood in multiple contacts with Buddhist eastern India. The immediate neighbour, Myanmar, appeared to be a meeting ground of the various branches of the Sino-Tibetan people, whom various names were given in the Indian tradition. The name *Kirata*[13] is the most widely known one. Mongoloid in feature, this band of people came down from Tibet and China in continuous flow from time immemorial. Their white (yellow) complexion, the strength of their number, and their business acumen impressed the people of the countries in which they entered. Nevertheless, their aggressive advance from Tibet and China down to the plains and river valleys of Myanmar and North Eastern and eastern India, as far as North Bengal in this side, and Chittagong on the other side, brought in massive social and cultural changes. Mixed marriages between the indigenous population and the Mongoloid people took place. This was obvious as the area was largely unpopulated with vast tracts of partly very fertile lands.

The Mon-Khmer people, one of the most important groups, bearing a very old and uninterrupted tradition of Buddhist faith, got continuously marginalized by the continuous pressure from above. If the history of Myanmar[14] is a history of constant assimilation of various ethnic groups, it is also a history of a marked conflict between these two major groups: the Sino-Tibetans and the Mon-Khmer people of Austric origin. Early trade between coastal Myanmar and central Thailand (old *Dvaravati* kingdom) as also coastal southern and eastern India[15] brought the Indian people to this shore, called *Ramannyadesa.* The Burmans owe their Buddhism to these Mons. Those who have been in Pegu (Bago), the capital of the Mon kingdom, must have witnessed in the edifices and archaeological remains, how deeply embedded Buddhism was in this part (Pegu-Thaton-Martaban area) of Myanmar. This Buddhist kingdom in the lower region of Myanmar was known as the *Suvarnabhumi* (Golden Island), the eastern limit[16] of which may be stretched as far as eastern Bengal (*Bengala*). One of the major ports of this region Thaton (*Sudhammavati* in Sanskrit) was established by a merchant, who was a follower of Lord Buddha. The Mons[17] are believed to have sidelined the Pyu people, who were also Buddhists in their faith.

The classical period of Mon history came to a halt, if not an end, in 1757, when the great warrior king Alaungpaya defeated the last Mon ruler of Pegu. It is believed that thousands of Mon people were driven out and took refuge in Ayuthaiya, the old capital of the Thai kingdom. It is quite probable that these displaced groups of the Mons also entered the Indian subcontinent, covering large distance, either through plains and Hills of Chittagong or by the Upper Burma route. Nevertheless, the foundation of the modern Myanmar state owes a lot to this warrior king, who is known as the 'Shivaji of Burma'. Among Alaungpaya's successors, king Bodawpaya (1782-1819) appears to be the most impressive. Buddhism experienced a resurgence during his reign. This resurgence automatically meant a solid political relation with India with a strategic plan to stop the expansionist design of the British power based in India.

Both Vaishnavism and Shaktism have deep roots in Assam and other parts of North Eastern India. Vaishnavism in Manipur, for example, is a living force and played an important part in bringing Myanmar and India together. Navadvipa in the modern Nadia district of West Bengal, was a centre of Sanskrit learning. After the fall of this centre and entire Bengal for that matter, to the Turkish invading army, Brahmins migrated to Upper Myanmar, in the capital cities like Ava. These learned Brahmins and Pundits known by the name *Ponna*,[18] came not only from Bengal and Arakan, but also from Manipur and other parts of India. Vaishanvas of Bengal in large numbers found home in Manipur and from Manipur to Ava and Upper

Burma. Ava was the capital of the Burmese Empire before it was shifted to Mandalay.

Manipur's close contact with Ava is echoed in the words of Thant Myint U: "In 1743 the famed Manipuri teacher Maha Tharaphu arrived in person at Ava, intending to instruct the Burmese king in the ways of Hindu faith"[19]. Manipuri astrologers, for example, were highly patronized in the royal courts of Myanmar. Intensive process of state formation with a centralized power structure of the Meities[20] isolated them from the Kukis and Nagas, a large part of whom embraced Christianity. The link with Upper Burma remained as before. Indeed, social and religious intercourse between Manipur and Upper Burma became so intensive that Manipur became in later days a bone of contention between the British and the Burmese kings. The kings of the Alaungpaya dynasty placed their claim over Manipur, and the British came up to declare what they considered their legitimate claim. In 1764, Manipur was invaded by the army of Alaungpaya, which was, however, only a temporary victory, for, according to the Treaty of Yandabo, all the regions, including Assam and Manipur, had to be surrendered to the British.

One has to place all the three Anglo-Burmese Wars in the context of the commercial, social and strategic encroachment of the British in Assam and the North East[21]. The economic considerations were high in agenda, for example, the establishment of Tea Industry in Assam. Within a few years from the time of the first Anglo-Burmese War (1824-26), in 1839, Assam Tea Company was established. The first phase of Christian missionary activities started in the Naga Hills and Lushai Hills exactly during the time when plans for annexing Burma part by part got a concrete shape. One must not forget that the Nagas[22], one of the most powerful races of India, have a long history of independent existence. The Ahoms of Assam, who entered the valley of the Brahmaputra in the 13th century ruled a large area of Assam and parts of North East for a very long time. Yet, they could not subjugate the Nagas.

Like in the Lushai Hills, so also, in the case of the Naga Hills, missionary activity started in the 19th century; the American Baptist Naga Mission initiated its work in 1836, which brought a feeling of solidarity among the Nagas. An Assamese Christian, Godhula Brown[23] took up missionary activities in 1842. Though politics of post-colonial Nagaland and the Naga insurgency do not constitute the topic of the present paper, yet, it may be relevant to mention here that a considerable part of the deeply religious people of Nagaland have failed to identify themselves as Indian nationals. As a result, the struggle of the Nagas for their separate home land continues. For me, it appears to be a paradox as the Nagas were one of the most indigenous people of India.

Part II

In Search of a Lost Asset: Remnants of Buddhism in the Societies of Bengal, Assam and Other Parts of North East

The entire region between the plains of Assam up to the upper Burma (Mandalay -Pagan region), plains of Dhaka and Chittagong up to Arakan Hills, and from Tripura to Arakan (modern Rakhine state), are actually full of hills and plains. It is very difficult indeed to divide the area into broad categories like Hills and Plains. Here people live from a wide range of ethnic affiliations, linguistic groupings, and religious schools. The archaeological remains in the Mainamati Lalmai range in the Comilla district of Bangladesh[24], in the western Myanmar state of Arakan[25], in Tripura, in Arunachal Pradesh, in certain places of Manipur and of course in Assam and Bengal demonstrate that the kind of Buddhism which enjoyed popular support was not actually orthodox Theravada Buddhism. It could not be so, as eastern Indian kings and people shifted from the line of orthodoxy. Vinaya rules observing monks were certainly highly regarded in the society, but the kings could not afford to adhere to orthodoxy; the popular support for monks with unnatural power touched the grass root. Thus, the kind of Buddhism, which rose in this entire region was of highly mixed character, allowing rituals from Saivite and Tantric fold, where human body was considered as a means to achieve the 'salvation'. This complicated, yet simple and 'lax' ideology, made the ground fertile for rapid spread of Islam in the littoral state, particularly in Chittagong[26]. The role that Chittagong played in the spread of Islam in Bengal had its impact on the northern part of Arakan as well[27]. To understand this mixed and somewhat unorthodox nature of Islam and Hinduism in eastern Bengal, one has to refer to two major works: Enamul Haque's[28] *History of Sufism in Bengal* and Shashi Bhusan Dasgupta's[29] *Obscure Religious Cults*. Many beliefs and social practices of Mahayana traditions were absorbed into Islam in lower Bengal. Islam in Bengal was quite accommodative, which went to the extent of identifying oneself as

Muslim and Vaishnava at the same time. The history of the Chittagong-Arakan region carries a tradition of parallel existence of Buddhism, Islam and Hindu religious schools. The worship of Kali, Durga and Vishnu was more a rule than exception. While the people of the Lushai Hills got isolated from their co-brethren, the Buddhist Shans of Upper Burma[30], a large number of Buddhist people of the Chittagong Hills, could continue their relation with their Buddhist brethren across the border in Arakan. All three emient scholars Lalrimawa, Lalthangliana and Malsawma are of the opinion that the Lushais (Mizos) lived for quite a long time in the Shan State.

To give an example of mixed religious affiliation with the Chakmas from CHT, Chakma Raja Dharam Bux Khan became a king in 1812. As it shows, he took a Muslim name, being himself a Buddhist. Dharam Bux Khan was initiated into Hinduism by his Bhattacharya priest. One of the queens of Dharam Bux Khan was Rani Kalindi, whose name is still cherished by the Chakmas as one of the most popular rulers of the Chittagong Hill Tracts. Kalindi popularized the Mahamuni legend and inspired the Chakma people to be true Buddhists[31]. Her welfare works like building of temples, digging of ponds and arranging of Mahamuni Mela were parts of her aspiration to revive the Hindu-Buddhist traditions in the face of the rising political power of the British in India, especially in the eastern India and Myanmar. One can see in the Rani's endeavor a clear political dimension.

Though the Mahamuni legend is known among Buddhist scholars, yet, an elucidation is needed exactly here as we will see how the Mahamuni cult wandered around, and landed even in Assam. Lord Buddha, inspired by his disciples, once felt an urge to visit Arakan as the king Candrasuriya desired to pay Him a homage. He was confronted by the problems that the long journey from Sravasti to Arakan is hazardous, with regions ruled by the *nagas*, serpent demons. Relating this to his disciple Ananda, he flew with his 500 disciples and landed at Selagiri Hill, opposite Kyauktaw. A sacred image of Buddha was constructed by Indra and Visvakarman. Lord Buddha himself brought life into the image, which was His own. His unique act immensely impressed the common people and the King. This Mahamuni image thus became a symbol of Buddhist Arakan, indeed a symbol of legitimacy to rule as a Buddhist king. When Bodawpaya, the king of the last Myanmar dynasty, annexed Arakan in 1784, he took the Mahamuni image with him to Mandalay, his new capital. This incident indicates as if the possession of Mahamuni gives one the true authority to rule anywhere in this vast tract of land. With the Mahamuni, the Hindu worshippers were also taken to Mandalay. Even today, Mandalay is standing proud and prominent with this Mahamuni image. Rani Kalindi's leaning towards Mahamuni tradition and her efforts to rejuvenate Buddhism with the help of this legendary tradition, indicates Chakma people's close contact with the Rakhine (Arakanese) Buddhism.

To quote another example of continuity of Mahamuni tradition; in this case, nearer home is from Assam. The temple of Madhav at Hajo in Kamrupa district of Assam[32] is the case. It is said that originally the temple was a Buddhist shrine, only to become a place of worship for the Hindus. Interestingly, the temple deity is known as Mahamnuni. Now, it is a place of pilgrimage for Hindus and Buddhists alike.

There are established Buddhist communities in India, like the Khamptis of upper Assam and Arunachal Pradesh. The Khamptis of Arunachal Pradesh are direct descendants of the Buddhist Shans of Upper Burma, who came down in not so distant past, only a few hundred years ago. They joined their predecessors, the Ahoms of Assam, who swept over the entire Brahmaputra valley in the 13th century. The Ahoms are of Tai-Shan origin. They soon embraced Hinduism and became a part of the great Hindu tradition. The Khamptis possess language and script of their own. A detailed description of the Khampti society and Khampti culture, kinship and language in the context of their link with Myanmar has already been dealt with by me earlier[33]. Like the Chakmas and Marmas of Chittagong Hill Tracts, like the Maghs and other Buddhists from Tripura, Arunachal Pradesh and Mizoram, the Khamptis attracted the attention of many scholars[34] partly due to their aristocratic heritage and long continuity in Buddhist faith.

There happened to be two major types of migration of the Buddhist population into the plains and Hills of Assam and North East from Myanmar: one that came in large numbers whenever there was any attack or disaster. The other movement was of individual people in splinter groups, who came in search of better life. There could even be a third possibility where the original group remained in the Indian soil. One such group (either of the last two types) is the Man Buddhist community[35] found in the state of Meghalaya. Here is a state with a

Mon-Khmer population, the major part of whom were converted to Christianity even before the Lushais were converted.

Indeed, the people of Meghalaya ethnically belong to the Mon-Khmer group. The Mon language, is unlike the Myanmar language, a non-tonal one. Their script was derived from the old Pallava script of South India, which the Burmans later borrowed from the Mons. This small group of the Buddhists, numbering only 1,000 (one thousand) with the name 'Man' may be identified as one of the splinter groups of the Mons who were, as has been shown above, constantly being cornered by the Burmans from the Upper regions. Lalthangliana makes a broad category of four groups of the Tibeto-Chinese: Man, Karen, Tibeto-Burman and Tai-Chinese[36]. Suhas Chatterjee[37] expresses the opinion that during the political unrest triggered off by the Maomaria Rebellion, the "Ahom General Badan Chandra invited the Burmese (Mans) to Assam"[38]. The Mans of Meghalaya[39] (K.S Singh, Meghalaya, 133) profess Buddhism of Theravada school. In the houses of the Mans, the images of Lakshmi and Saraswati are also worshipped[40] (K.S Singh, Meghalaya,137). They observe the Buddhist norm of following Panch-Sheel (abstinence from five vices) and also Astha Sheel (eight principles). The image of lord Buddha, which the Mans worship in their Vihar (monastery), has a yogic posture. This substantiates our view of the existence of a mixed, sometime esoteric, and in any case, liberal tradition of Mahayana Buddhism prevailing in large parts of what was known as the *Kokiland.*

Part III

British Explorers encountering the Buddhist Past of the Kokibhumi

Earlier, mention has been made of the commercial and strategic motivation behind engagements of the British in North Eastern India. The political compulsion was to create a barrier between the mighty Myanmar Empire of the Alaungpaya dynasty (based in Upper Burma) and equally formidable frontier tribes. Such a design finds expression in the following words written by R.G. Woodthorpe: "The Govt. does not wish to exterminate these frontier tribes, but by converting them into our allies to raise a barrier between our frontier districts and other more distant races"[41]. Quite often, the administrators undertook long journeys, describing their experiences with the people of such frontier regions. They left behind their personal experiences with the local people, their habits and customs, kinship system, and their religions. During the years of the first Anglo-Burmese War, Captain Wilcox took a journey through Upper Assam to Khampti Long, or Bor Khampti (also known as Putao) the place where the Buddhist Khamptis belonging to the great Shan race came from. He appears to be much impressed by the Buddhist priests roaming around in the region. He described them in the following way: "The only sign of population that we saw on our journey were parties of Priests (Khamptis) moving from one village in the jungle to another"[42].

Francis Buchanan's Account on his journey in March 1798 is equally interesting. Buchanan's interest was to explore the southeastern Bengal (Chittagong, Noakhali, Comilla) and adjoining areas of North Eastern India and western Myanmar. Crossing Noakhali and later passing Chittagong, Buchanan reached the shore of the river Naaf. The river Naaf, as we know separates Chittagong from Arakan. The Hills of Chittagong impressed him immensely. Therefore, he went to Hill Chittagong, crossing Karnafuli and landed in Barkal, which is so very close to the Lushai Hills. Again he went back to Chittagong. For over two and a half months he toured around in southeastern Bengal, leaving behind a very vivid picture[43] of all the people of this vast region. There were Arakanese (Buddhist Rakhines) who entered southeastern Bengal (Chittagong, Comilla etc) since their kingdom was annexed by the Burmese king Bodawpaya who took away, as we have seen before, the pride of the Arakanese people, the Mahamuni image. Buchanan was perhaps eager to feel the pulse of the people of this region (Arakan-Chittagong region) in the aftermath of this great political and cultural shock. In Comilla, Buchanan saw the ruins of Mainamati Buddhist Vihars, though he could not assume the date of this Buddhist civilization, which is actually of 8th-12th century origin. It is important to mention here that Buchanan was very much interested in visiting Tripura. Yet, he did not dare to take up the journey. But, he got himself informed about this important kingdom with a strong Hindu-Buddhist tradition. He had a long discussion with the priest of the king of Manipur who was the father-in law of Tripura's king. Buchanan got information about the road connection to Tripura-Manipur and from there along the Chindwin river to north-west Burma. He also got information about the latest occupation of Manipur by the Burmese king, and about political developments, in general, in North Eastern India[44].

Almost one hundred years after Buchanan, appeared captain T.S. Lewin whose administrative skill ultimately pacified the Lushai Hills and brought the administration of the Lushai Hills and the adjoining areas of Chittagong Hills to a sound footing. The expedition[45] of the Lushai Hills itself is a very significant one, for it took place in the 1870s, which falls in the period between the second (1852) and the Third Anglo-Burmese wars (1885-86). Like the Myanmar people (Burmese), the Lushais also did not accept the imposition of the British rule over their territory. There were wars of resistance. At last, the Lushais could be pacified with intensive military operations. In 1890, British supremacy was established. Pacification of the Lushai Hills appeared to be of immense significance in the context of the military intervention in Upper Burma, which brought the entire kingdom of Burma under the British occupation. Viewing from this perspective, the attachment of the annexed Burmese Empire to the already established British Empire in India appears to be only too natural, indeed the only alternative. In 1898, North and South Lushai Hills were amalgamated and made one single District. Parallel developments in the neighbouring Chittagong Hill Tracts is equally impressive; to centralize the system of administration, a Regulation was passed in the year 1900, which is unique in the sense that it effectively centralized the colonial administration.

After the pacification of the Lushai Hills came the massive missionary activities, of which mention has been made right in the beginning. The Lushai people were so much attached to their original religion, what is called animism, that they simply refused to embrace Christianity which appeared to them as an unknown and alien religion. Rev. Williams, one of the early Presbyterian missionaries, who earlier worked in the Khasi and Jaintia Hills, arrived at Aizawl in 1891 and distributed pictures of Christ among the Lushai people[46]. Later, in 1890s, other preachers came in and visited remote villages across Lushai Hills. Two important personalities were Rev. D.E. Jones and Rev. Edwin Rowlands. The personal contact with the people of the remote areas must have been very effective; the number of converts, as Lalrimawia shows, increased rapidly in the early years of the 20th century (1900-1905). It may be relevant to mention here that it was exactly in those years that the colonial Burma was experiencing a Buddhist resurgence movement with YMBA (Young Men Buddhist Association) being founded in 1906. The London Baptist Missionary

Society and the Welsh Presbyterian Mission, both, were engaged in missionary activities in the Lushai Hills. While the northern part of the Lushai Hills was looked after by the Presbyterian Mission, with its headquarter at Aizawl, the Baptists confined themselves mostly in the southern part, in and around Lunglei.

With the Churches established, the people were encouraged to read the *Bible*, slowly motivated to make peace with the alien rulers. The British were relieved of the raids perpetrated upon them by the hostile Lushais, who were also called *ukis*. According to the British documents, the first reference to disturbances perpetrated by the Kukis is mentioned in 1777[47]. The pacification of the Lushai Hills placed the administrators in a remarkably advantageous position to administer Upper Burma and the Chin Hills[48], the plains and Hills of Arakan and last, but not least, the Chittagong Hill Tracts. The tribal people of the Chittagong Hill Tracts, the majority of which belonged to the groups like Chakmas and Marmas, could not be converted, as Buddhism was deeply embedded in the area[49]. Even in the plains of Chittagong, like the Cox's Bazaar area Buddhists continued to live. More over, Buddhists of Chittagong Plains and Chittagong Hill Tracts carefully maintained their contacts with Buddhists of Arakan.

It is most interesting to note that exactly the time during which the British power was engaged in Lushai Hills, with military, and later missionary activities, a very strong Buddhist resurgence movement was visible in the kingdom of the last Myanmar royal dynasty, in modern Sri Lanka and in Eastern India. The Mahabodhi Movement of late 19th century is what is meant here[50]. King Mindon Min (1853-1878) was responsible for various reforms in the Buddhist order and thus set the right atmosphere for the movement that started later on. In the forefront of this Buddhist resurgence movement stood the Sri Lankan monk Anagarika Dharmapal. This great monk, who had many well-wishers in India, had also his patrons in America and Europe. He made possible a well established nexus operating between the Buddhist centers in Calcutta, Bodhgaya, Colombo, Akyab (capital of Arakan) and Chittagong. When the first mission, consisting of four monks from the Mahabodhi Society of Colombo, which was founded in 1891, reached Bodhgaya, they took shelter in a Burmese Rest House which was previously built by Mindon Min[51]. This Buddhist axis proved to be a very precious asset for the nationalist movement in Myanmar and India.

The most distinct feature of the British policy during the 19th and 20th centuries in India and Myanmar is reflected in the classification of people into various groups, giving them various nomenclature. Interestingly, these names did not mean much, as various names were used for the same tribe by various people. For example, the Lushais, who had in themselves various groups, were also called by the ethnic name, 'Kuki'. To laymen, the name *Kuki* is just like any other name(s) for tribes of India. Now, if one refers to the work by the famous Buddhist monks Lama Taranath and Sumpa Makhan Po, we encounter very interesting information regarding wide popularity of Buddhism in the Kokiland. The work by the first monk-author is History of Buddhism in India and the second one wrote the work History of the Rise, Progress and Downfall of Buddhism in India[52]. Taranath included Pukham (Pagan), Rakhan (Arakan) and Hamsavati (Pegu) in the geographical jurisdiction of Kokiland. Even, mention has been made of countries as *Cakma* and *Kamboja*.

Though Taranath lived in the 16th century, yet, his knowledge of the history of Buddhism seems quite impressive. According to Taranath, in Kokiland, Buddhism flourished as early as during the time of the king Ashoka. Though originally Theravadin, Buddhism was increasingly becoming Mahayanist, in this part of eastern world, just as it happened in Tibet. The Kokiland has been identified by historians and linguists as the land where a hill tribe with the name Kuki was living. The area of these Kukis are the frontier areas of Assam, Arakan and Upper Burma[53].

We know from various sources that already by the 8th-9th centuries, the monasteries of Bengal and Bihar like Vikramasila, Odantapuri and Nalanda[54] became centers of Mahayana-Tantric practices. The land route between upper Burma and Bengal went straightway cutting across the hills and plains of Assam and almost all the North East Indian states. The parallel existence of Theravada (Hinayana) and Mahyana Buddhism was more a rule than exception. This is why the North Eastern states and Assam could become strong centers of Shaivism, Shaktism (for example in Assam) and Vaishnavism (Manipur). A large number of the Chakmas, Marmas and Riangs from Mizoram and elsewhere in North East worship Hindu Gods and Goddesses.

Conclusion

The innovation of the word 'tribe' goes to the credit of the British. The word has been used more in the case of India, than in the case of British Burma. Nevertheless, a large part of British Burma, where indirect rule was operational, was called Frontier Area, in contrast to Ministerial Burma, where the rule was direct. Quite often such expression as 'wild' has been used to mark the people, whom apparently the rulers wanted to protect from the exploitation of the moneylenders, contractors, petty officers from the plains. Prior to that, however, military expedition in the Hills and Plains inhabited by the tribes was justified by the argument that the tribes (for example the Kukis) were raiding the British territory. This principle of 'protection' urged them to take out what they called tribal areas from the mainland. After successful completion of this the second step was to designate such territories as 'Totally Excluded Areas', 'Excluded Areas' and 'Partially Excluded Areas'. Different rules and regulations were passed and implemented in these areas, which indeed caused physical and mental separation between the mainland and the periphery. The concept of periphery is indeed relative, for what today is periphery, was yesterday a bustling business and trade centre. One can quote numerous examples from Lower Burma, Arakan, Manipur and Tripura.

The policy behind such administrative separation aimed at weakening the high tide of nationalism in the mainland, where Buddhism became a great inspiration. One only has to think about the Pongyi movement in colonial Burma, and the movement's close link with India.

Through Government of India Act 1935 Lushai Hills area was declared as 'Totally Excluded Area', whereas in the case of the Chittagong Hill Tracts, problems arose, whether CHT should be considered a 'Totally Excluded Area' or 'Partially Excluded Area'. The theory of 'tribe', creating of separate administrative units, such as 'Hill Tracts', excluding the areas from the Mainland, or creating the concept of 'Mainland' and 'Frontier'—all went on along with consolidation of economic and strategic bases in the same region, the *Kokiland*, the lost Buddhist land.

As discussed by me elsewhere, the tribes were further separated by the creation of further categories like 'Valley Dwellers' (Kyoungtha) and 'Hill Dwellers' (Taungtha). Out of this rather imaginary division between the 'Valley Dwellers' and the 'Hill Dwellers', appeared further the notion that those tribes who are designated as 'Hill Dwellers' (for example, the Kukis who were also known with the name Lushais) were less civilized than, for example, the Chakmas or Marmas of Chittagong Hill Tracts. By virtue of being Kyoungth affiliates, the Chakmas and Marmas were considered more as belonging to the category of 'Valley Dwellers'. This certainly created division between the up-hill people like the Mrus of CHT and the Chakmas. Long continuity in Buddhism in the Chittagong Hill Tracts, and the close geographical and spiritual contact of the people of CHT with Buddhist Arakan, and also existence of a large number of Buddhist communities (for example Baruahs) in the plains of Bengal[55] closed the door of conversion in that area.

Contrastingly, in the case of Mizoram, as the missionary activity was successful and a feeling of unity was slowly visible, a new name tag 'Mizo' was awarded to them. The people of the Lushai Hills were benefited by this act, for their identity experienced a honourable transformation; the word 'Mizo' actually means the 'Highlanders' (more sophisticated Kyoungtha!). Their past as 'Kuki Raiders' was taken under the carpet, and soon forgotten.. Renowned anthropologist L.G. Loeffler, whose works on the Chittagong Hill Tracts and the adjoining areas are widely known, wrote how Pacification of the Lushai Hills caused upward mobility of the Lushais, which further led the ultimate award of the name 'Mizo'[56].

Mizoram today is one of the most peaceful states of North Eastern India, almost free of insurgency. It is often said that Mizoram can show the path to other North Eastern states. Social progress and advancement in other fields, like education, women's education in particular, health sector etc., are remarkable. The churches play an important role in mobilizing the people towards peace, integration and prosperity. India is a country, which offers a fertile ground for religions of varied directions and schools to progress and prosper. The inner dynamics of our civilization gives an individual, no matter to which social category he/she belongs, an endurance to maintain multiple identities. After all, as I have attempted to demonstrate in this paper, Mizoram and the adjoining areas of Myanmar and Bangladesh have a long tradition of survival of various religions and thoughts amidst all social and economic challenges. Before the Lushais got converted to Christianity, they, like many other racial groups

(I want to avoid the term 'Tribe') including the Lushais were worshippers of various nature Gods, which remind us of the Nat worship prevalent in various forms at local levels in Buddhist Myanmar society. Mizos, as good Christians can perhaps try to go back to their past and could hear the whispers of history, for, after all, all of us have to live with nature.

NOTES AND REFERENCES

1. Dutt, Sukumar, 1962, *Buddhist Monks and Monasteries of India* Delhi: Motilal Banarasidas
2. Lalrimawia, Mizoram, 1995, *Mizoram - History and Cultural Identity.* Guwahati: Spectrum Publications
3. Bose, Nirmal Kumar, 1996, *The Structure of Hindu Society*. N. Delhi: Orient Longman (translated from Bengali with an introduction and Notes by Andre Beteille).
4. Mey, Wolfgang, 1996, *Parvatya Chattagramer kaumasamaj. Ekti Arthasamajik Itihas* Calcutta: Firma KLM for International Centre for Bengal Studies, (translated from original German into Bengali by Swpana Bhattacharya Chakraborti).
5. Spiro, Melford. E. 1982. *Buddhism and Society. A Great Tradition and its Burmese Vicissitudes*. Berkley: University of California Press.
6. Bhattacharya (Chakraborti), Swapna, 2007, 'Some observations on Political Systems, Religion and Culture of Western Myanmar, North Eastern India and Southeastern Bangladesh in the Context of Present Trends in India-Myanmar Relations *Asia Annual* New Delhi: Standard Publishers: pp. 193-222 (Annual Journal of Maulana Abul Kalam Azad Institute of Asian Studies, Kolkata)
7. Sinha, Surajit (ed), 1987, Tribal Politics and State Systems in Pre-colonial Eastern and North eastern India. Calcutta; K.P Bagchi & Co.
8. Reid, Sir Robert, 1978 (first pub. 1942), *The Lushai Hills*. Calcutta: Firma KLM on behalf of Tribal Research Institute, Aizawl
9. Lewin, Capt. T.H., 1978, (first pub. 1870) *Wild Races of Southeastern India*. Calcutta: Firma KLM on behalf of Tribal Research Institute, Aizawl, Mizoram
10. Singh, K.S. (General Editor), 1994, *People of India: Nagaland.* Calcutta: Seagull Book. Anthropological Survey of India
11. Bhattacharya (Chakraborti), Swapna, 2007, *India-Myanmar Relations 1886-1948*. Kolkata: K.P. Bagchi & Co.
12. Singh, K.S., (General Editor), *People of India: Mizoram*, 1995, Calcutta: Anthropological Survey of India.

13. Chatterji, Suniti Kumar, 1974, Kirata Jana Krti The Indo-Mongoloid: Their Contribution to the History and Culture of India. Calcutta: The Asiatic Society.
14. Thant Myint U., 2007, *The River of lost Footsteps*: *Histories of Burma* London: Faber & Faber
15. Majumdar, R.C., 1991, *Hindu Colonies in the far East*. Calcutta: Firma KLM
16. Bhattacharya (Chakraborti) Swapna, 2005, 'Buddhism in Myanmar: Interpretation from Indian perspective' *Journal of the Asiatic Society* (Kolkata), Vol. XLVII, No. 4., pp. 65-81
17. South, Ashley, 2005 (first pub. 2003), *Mon Nationalism and Civil War in Burma*. London: Routledge
18. Leider, Jacques, 2005-06, 'Specialists for Ritual, Magic and Devotion: The Court Brahmins of the Konbaung Kings (1752-1885)', *Journal of Burma Studies,* vol. 10, pp. 159-202
19. Thant Myint U., 2007, *The River of Lost Footsteps*: *Histories of Burma* London: Faber & Faber.
20. Hodson, T.C., 1989, (first pub. 1908), The *Meiteis*. N.Delhi: Low Price Publication
21. Banerjee, Anil Chandra, 1964 (first pub. 1943), *The Eastern Frontier of British India 1784-1826*. Calcutta: A. Mukherjee & Co.
22. Horam, M., 1992, (first pub. 1977), *Social and Cultural Life of Nagas*. Delhi: Low Price Publication
23. Singh, K.S. (General Editor), 1994, *People of India: Meghalaya.* Calcutta: Seagull Book. Anthropological Survey of India.
24. Morrison, Barry. M., 1974, Lalmai A Cultural Centre of Early Bengal. Archaeological Report & Historical Analysis. Seattle: University of Washington Press
25. Gutman, Pamela, 2001, *Burma's Lost Kingdoms: Splendours of Arakan.* Bangkok: Orchid Press
26. Eaton, Richard, 1997, (first pub. 1993), *The Rise of Islam and the Bengal Frontier. 1204-1760*. N. Delhi: OUP
27. Bhattacharya (Chakraborti), Swapna, 2002, 'Myth and History of Bengali identity in Arakan' in J. Gommans & J. Leider eds. *The Maritime Frontier of Burma,* Leiden: Koniklijke Nederlandse von Wetenscherpen, Amsterdam, pp. 199-212.
28. Haque, Enamul, 1975, *A History of Sufism in Bengal.* Dhaka: Asiatic Society
29. Dasgupta, Sashi Bhusan, 1947, *Obscure Religious Cult*. Calcutta
30. Lalthangliana, B., 1975, *History of Mizo in Burma.* Mandalay University M.A. Thesis., Pub by Zawlbuk Agencies, Aizawl
31. Sattar, Abdus, 1983, *In the Sylvan Shadows*, Dhaka: Bangla Academy

32. Singh, K.S. (General Editor). *People of India : Assam*. Calcutta: Seagull Book. Anthropological Survey of India. (vol 1, pt. I)
33. Bhattacharya (Chakraborti) Swapna, 2005, 'From Mahabodhi Movement of the 19th century (1891) to neo-Buddhist Revival (1956) in Post colonial India', *Myanmar Historical Commission Conference Proceedings*, Pt. 2, Ministry of Education, Union of Myanmar, Yangon, pp. 339-364
34. Bhikkhu Kondinya, 1986, Monastic Buddhism among Khamptis of Arunachal. N. Delhi
35. Singh, K.S. (General Editor), *People of India : Assam*. Calcutta: Seagull Book. Anthropological Survey of India. (vol 1, pt. I)
36. Lalthangliana, B., 1975, *History of Mizo in Burma.* Mandalay University M.A. Thesis. Pub by Zawlbuk Agencies, Aizawl
37. Chatterjee, Suhas (Dr. Suhas Chatterjee), 1990, *Mizoram Encyclopedia.* Vol. 1, Bombay: Jaico Publishing House
38. Chatterji, Suniti Kumar, 1974, Kirata Jana Krti The Indo-Mongoloid: Their Contribution to the History and Culture of India. Calcutta: The Asiatic Society.
39. Singh, K.S. (General Editor), *People of India : Assam*. Calcutta: Seagull Book. Anthropological Survey of India. (vol 1, pt. I)
40. Singh, K.S. (General Editor), *People of India : Assam*. Calcutta: Seagull Book. Anthropological Survey of India. (vol 1, pt. I)
41. Woodthorpe, R.G. Liuet, Royal Engineers, 1978 (first pub. 1873). *The Lushai Expedition 1871-1872.* Calcutta: Firma KLM on behalf of Tribal Research Institute, Aizawl
42. Wilcox, R. 1980. Memoir of a Survey of Assam and the Neighbouring Countries. Executed in 1825-6-7-8. New Delhi: Cosmos Publication
43. Van Schendel, William (ed.), 1994, *Dakshinpurva Banglay Francis Bukhanan (1798).* Publication in the Series: International Centre for Bengal studies, Dhaka University (translated from English by Salahuddin Ayub)
44. Ibid
45. Woodthrope
46. Lalrimawia. Mizoram. 1995. *Mizoram - History and Cultural Identity.* Guwahati: Spectrum Publication
47. Tripurar Lushai Kukider Itikatha, 1980, Gaveshana Adhikar: Upajati o Tapashili Jati Kalyan Bibhag, Tripura, Agartala, Tripura Sarkar
48. Lehman, F.K., 1963, *The Structure of Chin Society,* Calcutta: Firma KLM Published on behalf of Tribal Research Society-Aizawl
49. Charney, Michael, 2002, ' Beyond State-centered Histories in western Burma: Missionizing Monks and Intra-regional Migrants in Arakan Littoral c. 1784-1860' in: The Maritime Frontier of Burma' Leiden:

Koniklijke Nederlandse von Wetenscherpen, Amsterdam, pp. 213-224

50. Bhattacharya (Chakraborti) Swapna, 2005, 'Migration, Acculturation and Integration of Myanmar Tribes in India: Khamptis and Singhphos of Arunachal Pradesh' in Mahavir Singh ed.
51. Bapat.P.V., 1997, (first. Pub 1956), *2500 Years of Buddhism* (Delhi: Ministry of Information and Broadcasting, Govt. of India.
52. Chattopadhyaya, Debiprasad (ed), 1970, *Taranatha's History of Buddhism in India*. Simla: Institute of Advanced Studies (translated from the Tibetan by Chimpa Lama and Alaka Chattopadhyaya).
53. Ray, Niharranjan, 2002, (first pub. 1936) *Sanskrit Buddhism in Burma*. Bangkok: Orchid Press
54. Niyogi, Puspa, 1980, *Buddhism in ancient Bengal.* Calcutta: Jijnasa
55. Khan, Abdul Mabud, 1999, The Maghs: A Buddhist Community in Bangladesh. Dhaka: UPL
56. Lorenz G. Loeffler & Claus Dieter Brauns, 1990, *Hill People on the Border of Bangladesh.* Basel: Birkhauser.

Mizoram and the Role of the Presbyterian Denomination

Margaret L. Pachuau

This paper seeks to denote the profound changes that have occurred within the parameters of the Mizo society after the advent of the Christian Gospel.Where religion has often been suspect and controversial the world over, this paper reflects on what would perhaps be tantamount to complete transformation within the Mizo society. The focus here is on the Presbyterian Church of Mizoram, the largest Christian denomination within Mizoram.

At the very outset one must mention that Mizos, as a tribe, were predominantly animists, the faith of the pre-literate people. Mizos worshipped spirits or 'ramhuai',who were cruel, malicious and not at all beneficient.They were said to be present in large trees, high mountains and rocks. They were also deemed to be easily offended if men were to trespass upon their domain. In fact, if such an instance occurred the priest or 'bawlpu' would be summoned and sacrifices would be offered to appease the spirits. It was within the backdrop of such a scenario that the Presbyterian Church of Wales first set foot in Mizoram, in order to extend their mission. The Arthington mission sent missionaries, J. Herbert Lorrain and F.W. Savidge, members of the Highgate Baptist Church in London, and they arrived on 11th January 1894, at Sairang, Mizoram. Development was enhanced almost right from the very outset. The two missionaries were highly meticulous in terms of their habits and routine. Initially they both devoted their time to learning the Mizo language, and they wrote books in Mizo and they also translated parts of the New Testament. Prior to their coming, Mizo was not a written language and they both devised an alphabet using Roman lettering.[1] It was modified slightly later, but in principle it remained the same. In 1895, the Assam government produced and printed the first book in the Mizo language. It was a Child's Primer, and later Lorrain, who had special flair for languages, composed the Lushai-English Dictionary of several thousand words; the text was later published along with a grammar of language. 1940 saw the publication of the complete dictionary comprising 33,000 words.[2] As Savidge himself had been a school master in London, he set up a school in Aizawl in 1895, despite much parental resistance. With this, the Mizo passion for education grew by leaps and bounds. The missionaries inculcated in the Mizos not merely a desire to learn, but also a desire to teach and share with others various aspects of learning.

J.M. Lloyd, a missionary to the Mizo hills, also documents that Sunday schools gave additional impetus to the process of elementary learning. Access to books as well as contact with the minds of people in other lands had a magical as well as transforming influence on the land. In order to enhance the development of education, a missionary by the name of Edwin Rowlands, decided to establish a school of a more permanent nature, and he chose the Khandaih village, four days journey from Aizawl, with over four hundred houses. Later on the government granted it recognition in 1904. So great was the impact of progress in the school, that the government school that had been established earlier was shut down, and the monthly grant of fifty rupees was subsequently transferred to the mission school. This occurred under the tenure of the Chief Commissioner of Assam, Sir Bamfield Fuller. By 1952, under the missionaries, every Mizo village comprising a hundred houses was provided with its own school.[3] The Church provided the required basic infrastructure, and this included a brass gong that was suspended at the entrance of every school. The teachers were also provided salaries with the assistance of the Church. Religion thereby has not only been a reliable leader of the community but has provided influence in a time of rapid change for the Mizo community. Literacy was greatly enhanced, and the missionaries also recognized that in order to set up and maintain literacy, new and interesting books had to be maintained. Accordingly, a press was set up in Aizawl in 1911 by Dr Fraser. It was a small hand press and the first one within the hills. The impact of development was not confined to literacy alone. Major attempts were also made by the missionaries to create model villages, and training was imparted to the people in terms of sanitation, health and hygiene, rearing of domestic animals, prevention of fire and construction of houses.[4] Subsequently, Christian medical work also had a great impetus and especially towards 1930-31, preparations were rendered by the mission towards a new hospital building.

The Presbyterian Mission thereby brought about a radical change in terms of socio-economic parameters even as far back as the pre-independence era. The development thus generated has been consistently reflected in the sensibility of the Mizos. Mizoram remains one of the few states within India that can claim to be predominantly Christian. The Church draws the people together and contributes towards a fabric of cohesion in their lives. In Mizoram especially, the citizens have been largely attracted towards the precepts of Christianity from the very outset. These could be related to certain relevant issues, such as the manner in which the faith was propagated, and also nuances related to pre-Christian beliefs[5]. I shall not go into an in depth exploration of these factors but will choose to concentrate upon the arenas of development that the missionaries have contributed to. Especially after the establishment of a permanent mission station by the Welsh Presbyterian missionaries in 1898, it was realized that the response to the faith was overwhelming, and by the mid twentieth century all those who considered themselves as Mizos were Christians. Christianity as a religion has succeeded in creating a new world order for the Mizos, especially in terms of socio-political-economic cohesion[6]. It has helped to uphold the moral and ethical values as well as traditional norms of society. With the advent of Christianity, the old beliefs in the evil spirits of the world were gone, and the mission taught the Mizos that development in religion was related not merely to a personal commitment. It denoted a necessary reflection in terms of social action groups, action-reflection processes especially, in order to usher in a new dawn in terms of development and radical transformation in Mizo society.

At the advent of the new millennium, Mizoram rates a statistical high of 86.97 per cent in terms of a Christian populace. The spread of Christianity, especially by the Presbyterian denomination, has indeed made significant inroads towards the struggle for justice, peace and development. The same denomination has also made consistent attempts to reach out to groups and peoples both in terms of organization and mobilization[7]. It has established many cells and committees through which it attempts to monitor both human as well as societal development. For instance there are bodies within the Presbyterian Synod that focus consistently upon arenas of overall development. I will focus upon certain fundamental bodies related to the same. For instance, The Synod Literature and Publication Board was established in 1930 in order to enhance the growth of publishing in Mizoram[8]. By the year 1978, a translation cell had been formulated under the same board. The board functions with several full time workers. It has subsequently published relevant books to enhance literacy, and it conducts training and seminars towards the same. It has published, apart from Bible dictionaries in Mizo, several books on Mizo grammar as well as Mizo historical texts. Another predominant factor in terms of monitoring a coherent social ethic remains the Synod Social Front, which was set up in 1979. Its main purpose is to garner a sense of development in terms of prosperity and solidarity on various arenas. It also attempts to generate guidance and education for the citizens against the physical and mental effects of substance abuse. This is done in terms of rendering education to the members of the Church in order that they promote aspects of good citizenship. It also imparts participatory measures towards relief and rehabilitation, in order to help and provide support to victims of sexual abuse. Action is also rendered to help facilitate the mentally, spiritually and the physically handicapped in order to initiate and activate community participation in terms of social defence programmes. Developmental awareness is rendered through seminars, workshops, consultations and publications. Interrelated to the same is the continuing aspect of educational development. Interestingly enough, the Presbyterian Church took measures related to the same, especially in order to generate awareness about the decline in terms of education in the state.[9] The Mizo Presbyterian Synod has also collaborated with the State government since the year 1992. This project undertakes tasks such as visits to schools as well as meetings with officials. Pamphlets are distributed in order to render greater awareness. It appeals to Churches to organize their own educational development programmers at grassroots levels. Awards are given to successful students, and weaker ones are given stipends. The recommendations and findings of the committee are submitted to the Mizoram government, and research information that is collected subsequently has greatly contributed towards enhancing literacy percentage in the state. Currently two schools are run by the Synod: The P.C. Girls

School and The Synod Higher Secondary School.[10] These schools are in fact regarded to set enhanced parameters in terms of academic credibility. Economic development, which is intrinsically relevant in terms of a developing state and society, has also been focused upon by the Presbyterian denomination. In 1992, the Mizoram Presbyterian Church announced a 'decade for self sufficiency'. Seminars, workshops and consultations were conducted in order to fulfill the same. The Government of Mizoram and the committee collaborated towards several agricultural research projects, and recommendations were made towards the enhancing of terrace farming, rice plantations, and use of organic fertilizers. Various agencies and companies outside the state have in the process approached the committee in terms of their willingness to help and participate in such measures.[11]

The menace of alcholism, drugs and AIDS has also been confronted by the Presbyterian mission at an early stage. Research has been conducted systematically on this front. It has also associated with Mizoram State Aids Control Society (MSACS) in conducting awareness campaigns that cover the entire geographical domain of the state. It visits private as well as governmental rehabilitation centres, and organizes training for counselors. Due to pressure from the Synod Social Front Committee, the Mizoram Liquor Total Prohibition Act (MLTP), was implemented by the Mizoram government in 1996. It has succeeded in curbing the menace of liquor and alcoholism to a certain extent within the state.[12] In order to facilitate rehabilitation of drug abusers, the Presbyterian mission has established the Synod Rescue Home, in September 1987, at Durtlang.The home has three separate units for patients in terms of detoxification, rehabilitation and after care. Therapy is implemented in terms of personal as well as group counselling, work therapy, physical exercises, and Bible studies. In almost the same lines it must be mentioned that Medicare has also received a coherent focus. At the outset the Presbyterian mission established the Presbyterian Hospital in 1908. It was first established as a small dispensary by Dr. Peter Fraser, a Welsh missionary and some years later, in 1928 it became a full fledged hospital by the name of the Welsh Mission Hospital. Much later it was renamed as The Presbyterian hospital. In 1994, the Presbyterian mission established a Nursing School which offers a course in General Nursing and Midwifery (GNM). Charitable clinics are conducted by the hospital on a weekly basis.[13] These are accounted for from the charity fund, set aside by the hospital. Doctors with various fields of specialization render health care to all, regardless of caste or creed or social status, in the spirit of Jesus. The hospital also has a de-addiction ward and a rehabilitation centre known as Khawngaihna Ward (K Ward). This functions as a hospice centre for HIV patients (in collaboration with the Mizoram State Aids Control Society).The mission has also established a drop in centre in Aizawl for the treatment of addiction related problems and a hospice centre for HIV patients has been established in collaboration with Mizoram State Aids Control Society.[14]

Aspects such as environment are also not neglected. An environment cell has been set up in order to monitor the preservation of the environment. Booklets and pamphlets are prepared and awareness seminars are organized in collaboration with the Forest and Environment Department of Mizoram. Systematic research has been done and it has made a positive impact on both the governmental as well as non governmental sectors. In the process, land ceiling and land reform cells have also been implemented. Seminars and consultations are held on relevant topics in order to garner awareness.

The Synod has also implemented an Endowment Fund programme. It had been initiated as the Centenary Endowment Fund in the year 1994. Various Churches as well as individual Church members can contribute towards the same, and it has been implemented especially in order to help the economically backward classes and uplift their standards of living. It also grants scholarships to economically backward students in order to promote higher education. Apart from this, the main thrust of the fund remains focused upon the enhancement of the standards of living of the poor and the needy in society.

Mizo women have also been empowered, especially by the developmental measures undertaken by the Presbyterian denomination. Catherine Jones, wife of the missionary Rev. D.E. Jones, began working with the women since the year 1904. Ladies were taught practical arts and craft and the alphabet. As the need for developmental concerns were tremendous, some of the women were trained on a full time basis for evangelism and for the enlistment of the people. They were sent to different districts to serve alongside the pastors, and they were known as Bible Women. The Women's Fellowship has made a tremendous headway ever since then. Efforts are made to build good

Christian homes, and effective campaigns and seminars and other special programmes are held to establish the same.[15] The Women's Ministry has also contributed towards an enhanced literary reading public, especially as they have published a monthly magazine that has wide readership. An orphanage has also been established by the Women's Ministry in 1986. It also takes up several projects and it contributes financially towards various centers such as: the Synod Mission Board, the Presbyterian Hospital, the Synod Rescue Home, as well as several extension programmes. Christianity has thus brought about significant changes in the lives of Mizo women.

The political arena has not been neglected by the Presbyterian mission, and the political education has also been imparted by the Church at many levels. The Church as a religious body has continued to monitor various aspects that are related towards state level politics in many ways. Intensive campaigns have been undertaken, and the masses have been educated in terms of the ethical as well as fundamental precepts of politics. At the same time, it has also helped to decipher demerits and layers of party politics. Mizoram has been tremendously influenced due to these measures, especially in the creation of peaceful polling at the time of elections. A politics cell has also been formed under the Presbyterian Synod, in order to generate a certain level of political awareness and accountability amongst the Mizos. The Mizoram Peoples' Forum was also established for that very purpose, and it continues to stand as the official organ of the Mizoram Presbyterian Church Synod in terms of political reform. Religion has also remained a significant instrument in the insurgency movement and the subsequent peace accord of Mizoram. I shall only make a brief mention here of the same issue. From the very outset, the Mizo National Front (MNF) had tried to capitalize upon the concept of a single Mizo Christian identity in order to safeguard the land, the nationality as well as the religion. Right from the very outset the intention of the rebel groups was concentrated upon, amongst other aspects, a focus to protect Christianity. The rebel groups often accused the Indian government of attempts to wipe out Christianity, the sole religion of the Mizos. One can thereby clearly comprehend the fact that identity as well as religion played a very dominant role within the Mizoram political scenario. So strong was the movement that many pastors rendered moral support by taking up arms after relinquishing their posts as ordained pastors. Equally worth noting is the fact that in the face of such a scenario, the Mizoram Presbyterian Church became the first religious body to raise critical objections towards the violence of the insurrection. Within a couple of weeks of the shoot-out in the major towns of Mizoram, it issued a proclamation, condemning the acts of violence as it felt that it was contradictory to the precepts of Christianity. Due to these measures, other denominations, too, followed suit in terms of condemnation. Later, a much more detailed message to the MNF, known as "The Mizoram Presbyterian Church Declaration" was issued by the Mizoram Presbyterian Church on 1st August 1967.[16] It generally denounced the bloodshed and violence, and declared that violence was against the theology of Christ. The Mizo National Front then responded by prohibiting all further writings against the party. However, the Church remained undaunted and continued to maintain a stronger stand. It must also be realized that while the condemnation of violence grew, the Churches also initiated a positive move towards finding a peaceful solution for the political disturbance. Eventually, it did succeed in garnering positive outputs towards the peace process, and it must also be noted that the role of the Presbyterian denomination has proved vital in time of the insurgency, especially as it was the first to condemn the violence and the first leading instrument with a focus towards ushering peace.

Development has made inroads within Mizoram, especially with the assistance of the Presbyterian denomination. At the same time, the Presbyterian denomination still has many miles to go and several challenges remain to be met in terms of development. Goals especially addressed towards the empowerment of youth, through education and employment could perhaps be focused upon at length by this denomination, even as its influence remains at intrinsically higher parameters upon Mizo sensibility than the state government. These issues continue to remain vital to the needs of the hour as far as developmental goals are concerned. These aspects of development remain integral, not merely in terms of furthering Mizo society but in the realization of a predominantly more pan Indian, global development that would emphasize an enhancement of the Mizo outlook. My essay has attempted to focus upon the state of Mizoram and its uniqueness, and in the process has denoted that a broader, developmental dynamic remains in terms of religion and society, even while the focus remains inherently upon the human resource nexus within the state.

NOTES AND REFERENCES

1. As elucidated by J.M.Lloyd, *History of the Church in Mizoram.*
2. Ibid.
3. Ibid.
4. Ibid.
5. Rev. Zairema had denoted aspects related to the same in his text God's *Miracle in Mizoram*
6. Rev. Khuanga had stressed upon these parameters in his essay *Towards a Tribal Theology*
7. The same aspects could be traced in the essays compiled in the text *Towards a Tribal Theology*
8. The Presbyterian Synod has made consistent attempts to focus upon enhanced notions of development.
9. Education both in terms of quality as well as quantity for the Mizos has been of utmost importance for the Presbyterian Synod.
10. These schools have produced students with consistently good academic record. Emphasis has been laid upon a wholistic approach towards learning as well.
11. Several companies and firms within and outside the state have also expressed a keen interest in terms of enhancing market as well as enterprise.
12. The Church was one of the first to set up notions concerning the fact that drug abusers as well as reformed characters should not remain ostracized by society at large.
13. The practice continues till today, with professionals of different specializations imparting medicare, on a weekly basis even as the hospital is situated at a far flung locale from the city.
14. Nurturing, has been rendered to all patients who seek aid. At the same time, programmes such as these promote a sense of awareness in the society.
15. Regular visits are made by the same groups,in terms of promoting and honing the sensibilities of the public at large.This group monitors accountability levels of the families as well.
16. Sangkima in his essay had elucidated upon these aspects. Also interviews with Rev.Lalngurauva, one of the key persons in the peace mission have continued to focus upon the role of the Church in an intrinsically positive manner.

Primary Sources

1. Kipgen, Mangkhosat, *Christianity and Mizo Culture,* Jorhat, 1996.
2. Lalrinawma, V.S., Mizo *Ethos Changes and Challenges,* Aizawl: 2005.

3. Lloyd, J.M., *History of the Church in Mizoram,* Aizawl, 1991.
4. Ninan, George, A., *Church and Society,* New Delhi, 2001.
5. Păchuau, Sangkima, *Ethnic Identity and Christianity* Frankfurt, 2002.
6. Siama,V.L., *Mizo History Aizawl*, 1991.
7. Sangkhuma, Z.T., *Missionary te Hnuhma* Aizawl, 1995.
8. Thanzauva,K. (ed) *Mizo Miziaa Pathian,* Thu Aizawl, 1988.
9. Zairema, *God's Miracle In Mizoram,* Aizawl, 1978.

Articles

Towards a Tribal Theology: The Mizo Perspective Jorhat:1989.
Seminar on Calvinism: Aizawl Theological College,Durtlang:2007.

Electronic Sources

www.mizoramsynod.com.

Challenges Before the Media

Subir Bhaumik

The media in North East India has reported on the conflicts in the region and those beyond its immediate borders, but rarely has it been under the kind of pressure that it now faces. At a time when it is seen as a force multiplier in conflict, the media in North East is a target. Both the governments and the rebels fight them, the vested interests and the parties in conflict want the media to be on their side. They try to suborn the media and when such attempts fail, the media persons are threatened, kidnapped and even killed. And an attack on media persons in the region rarely stirs the professional community elsewhere in the country.

The growing threat media persons face in North East India has best illustrated by the abduction of six newspaper editors in Manipur on 15th April 2006. They were freed on 17 April after their newspapers published a statement by the separatist Kangleipak Communist Party (KCP) that they had earlier refused to publish. The KCP also announced that it was banning publication of the *Imphal Free Press*, an English-language daily, for three months for supposedly misrepresenting the content of its statement. The newspaper has continued to publish in defiance of the ban, but the editor Pradip Phanjoubam and his staff live and work in fear.

On 18th April, all the newspapers left their editorial columns blank in a show of protest, while journalists staged demonstrations. The next day, none of the papers appeared. "If no newspapers have been published today, it is because we want to tell the world that press freedom cannot be restricted," said Rajesh Hijam, the editor of the English-language *Sangai Express*. In February, the KCP claimed responsibility for an attack in which Ratan Luwangcha of the daily *Poknapham* was badly injured. At least four journalists have been murdered in Manipur state since 2003.

The attack on the journalist in Imphal followed the mysterious death of a young reporter of a newspaper in Assam in the same month. Prahlad Goala, 32, a reporter of *Assamiya Khabar*, a local language daily published from Assam's main city of Guwahati, met with an unnatural death. *Khabar*'s editor Atanu Bhuyan said Goala was brutally killed for writing a series of stories exposing corruption and a nexus between a forest warden and timber smugglers. Police later arrested the forest warden K.Z. Zaman Jinnah on suspicion of getting Goala murdered. The two incidents within a month exemplified the pressures under which media persons are now working in the North East India.

The separatist United Liberation Front of Assam (ULFA) has often targeted some editors and journalists as 'agents of Delhi', threatening them with dire consequences. In February 2007, the ULFA took the extreme step of asking the NE TV, a multi-lingual television channel based in Guwahati, to leave Assam unless they could prove a story they had done about the ULFA. The NE TV story had claimed the ULFA had quietly agreed to lift the ban on the Indian national games after receiving a huge payment of fifteen crore rupees from the Congress led ruling government of Assam. It is true that the NE TV story carried no real evidence of the supposed payment and that the group's owner have direct political interests, that the ULFA is opposed to. But the ULFA's threat of direct action put scores of journalists and camerapersons who work for NE TV at grave risk.

Scores of journalists in Assam have earlier suffered arrests by police on charges that they were close to the ULFA. This includes some leading editors of the state. While some of these journalists and editors adopt an editorial line that is seen as close to the separatist stand, arrest on mere suspicion is unwarranted. The media in North East therefore is under pressure from both sides of the divide.

PSYOPS and Force Multipliers

In the past one decade, as the separatist struggles in India's North East has multiplied leading to intensified counter-insurgency action, the media in the region has found itself in the midst of a tug-of-war between the government and the insurgents. Both sides have tried to cultivate the media and suborn it and when that did not work, the media came under threat. The key question here is how personal a journalist can afford to get with his or her source. Some of them do become friends but beyond a personal level, whenever they offer a story, that needs to be closely tested out against other sources. The more personal a reporter's relationship with a source, the more closely a story offered by him or her should be scrutinised. The 'motive analysis' of a source (of a source-turned-friend or a friend-turned-source) needs to be done at all levels of a story offered by him. If the source is a kin, it is preferable the story is handed over to another reporter in the bureau. This is to avoid allegations of bias in future. Reporters have often been trapped by interested parties and have run a plant without realising it was one. Journalists, unlike intelligence services, do not get to work with huge source funds so 'buying off' sources is rarely possible. It is therefore desirable that the journalist impresses on his or her source (a) the sincerity of purpose (in our case, reporting as truly as possible) (b) the unacceptability of favours of a material kind – just to get this across to a rebel leader that you value his interview or access to his base for pictures than the gifts he may offer. But there are elements who try to influence the coverage by leveraging the access he is offering. The Indian army has managed to get favourable coverage from TV channels by just leveraging the access to crews in remote areas. Some rebel groups have done the same.

If the army flies TV crews to remote Siachen or anywhere in the conflict zones of the North East, as it often does, it ensures the channels give them 'positive publicity'. It is often left to a probing newspaper or magazine reporter, under no obligation to the army for flying in crews and providing "great pictures" by firing artillery pieces for the mere show of it, to write on the massive damage to the environment in and around Siachen and the possible shrinking of the Siachen glacier as a result of the huge military deployment. A probing eye, a still camera, few notepads and lot of research often yield a better investigative story than a dozen camera rolling to military orders. But, as I have sometimes found, some interested parties have better media management instincts. They will take advantage by offering a real story that a journalist cannot reject for fear of being scooped out by the competition.

The ULFA military wing chief Paresh Barua gave me critical information about the fall of his bases in southern Bhutan during the Bhutanese military offensive in December 2003. There was no way I could get these information any faster from Bhutanese or Indian military sources. And all the information turned out to be correct. But no military commander, rebel or regular army likes the admission of defeat. So why would Barua give me such information? A careful analysis revealed that Barua's disclosures would obviously make headline news and would find its place in many BBC broadcasts including the Bengali evening time news at 7 PM Indian time. That is one news broadcast all ULFA commanders listen to. Since the ULFA's wireless network suffers from limitations and it is important for the rebels to know which base has fallen and which has not, one of the quickest way for Barua to inform his people on ground is to pass on the information to the BBC correspondent. As a reporter desperate to stay ahead of competition, I am not in a position to overlook such information. So though my broadcasts would prove useful to the ULFA, there was no way I could overlook it or not use it so long as the information was correct.

But though I have known Barua for the last two decades and have trusted his information, I have often not used many of his inputs in stories – either because the information could not be confirmed by a second source, preferably an official source or because his claims were not obviously true. But many other reporters who interviewed Paresh Barua were reckless. An NDTV correspondent, introduced to Barua by me, asked him about his location in an interview. Barua promptly replied he was somewhere in Arunachal Pradesh, in the mountains, 16,000 to 17,000 feet above sea level. That was a lie. But Barua obviously could not own up his location in a neighbouring country. I felt his location in that interview was redundant – what he said about the ULFA plans was more important. But I was astounded to see that portion of the interview going intact into the telecast. When asked, the NDTV correspondent startled me by her answer: " Modern television is all about effect. Rebel chiefs speaking from high mountains over a satellite phone would create a great image, so we ran all that." As a BBC correspondent for more than a decade, I have done my bit of television along with Radio and now Online. I thought good television was about true images, not false ones.

A recent AP story from Guwahati on "24 North East Indian militants killed in Dhaka" was a classic case of Psyops (the abbreviated version of Psychological Operations). A senior police official targetting ULFA military wing chief Paresh Barua for years offered the story to the AP stringer who carried it without cross checking with any source or even his own bureau in Dhaka. The AP later killed the story and removed it from their tickers. This was a clear case of Psyops to put pressure on Bangladesh to act against North East Indian rebels by exposing their presence in the neighbouring country.

The Psyops aims at converting the media into a force multiplier for their cause. In India's troubled North East, characterised by a huge deployment of army, para-military and police forces fighting a host of separatist rebel armies, 'Psyops' has come to loom large on journalism in the region, like in some other conflict-ridden zones of India. The army and para-military forces, the intelligence agencies and even the state police have their own budgets for Psyops and their own dedicated personnel.

While most organisations use their intelligence units or public relations officials to perform the task, the Indian army has a full-fledged Psyops cell in the Directorate of Military Intelligence. Officers working for this cell print visiting cards that proudly declare their identity, I have one of Major Manoj Kumar Singh, General Staff Officer-2 (Psyops), Army Liasion Cell, Directorate of Military Intelligence, South Block. Bigger intelligence agencies like the Research and Analysis Wing (RAW) employ 'media directors', mostly drawn from the Indian Information Service. Some state governments in North East India have 'Psyops' specialists on their role.

And what do they do? Plant and push stories that run down the enemy and their image, promote their own cause and image, cover their tracks on a secret killing or blame it falsely on others (routine for them to pass off a secret killing done by their assets as 'infighting amongst rebels'), create a feel-good atmosphere about their own operations. It could be a one-off story or a campaign, often designed and crafted to run for a while. 'Psyops' planners carefully take into account the capabilities of their 'media assets' and the reach of the media they work and whether the intended 'plant' would hit the target. It is war through the media; whoever said pen is mightier than sword is vindicated, but at the cost of professional journalism. Even good journalists shy away from exposing Psyops because they would have to expose colleagues and as they say, crows don't nibble at crows.

The US during the two Gulf Wars lend respectability to 'force multipliers' by formalising a structure of 'embedded journalism'. During its long involvement in counter-insurgency, where 'winning hearts and minds' are seen as a priority, the Indian army and its paramilitary forces as well as intelligence agencies have quietly developed a culture of Psyops by developing "media assets" who are used as 'force multipliers'. After carefully studying the use of the media by the Pentagon as 'force multiplier' in the 1991 Gulf War, the Indian army initiated a phased army-media interaction seminar – at the levels of divisions, or, regional command and in Delhi. Reporters and editors were invited to interact with officers. I attended two such seminars – one in Tezpur (Assam), the other in Calcutta. The army used the classic teacher-bully combination to find 'force-multipliers' and willing sources who could then be converted into media warriors. Most military officers would tout the CNN's role in the Gulf War, and how its coverage boosted the Allied war effort against Iraq.

Identity Barrier

But apart from the pulls and pressures of the government and the rebels, there is a serious problem afflicting the media in North East India. It is internal to the professional community there but it does affect accuracy and objectivity, two important goals of any serious media operation. For those of us who hail from North East India and have reported the region , the first professional challenge was to rise above this problem – the problem of the 'identity barrier'.

I was a college teacher, not a journalist as yet, when my home state Tripura was gripped by violent ethnic riots in June 1980. Tripura's demography has undergone the most profound change since the Partition of India. In the last fifty years, the indigenous tribes people have been reduced to a minority and Bengali settlers from East Pakistan, now Bangladesh, have come to account for more than seventy per cent of the state's population. The tribes people have lost out on lands, jobs and other opportunities and have been marginalized in politics and the economy of the state. Since the late 1970s, younger generation of tribesmen have formed underground rebel groups and unleashed much violence against the settlers. Over the past decade, kidnappings and killings have increased sharply.

During the 1980 riots, the Bengalis suffered heavy losses. Hundreds were killed – nearly four hundred in one village Mandai and thousands were rendered homeless. The newspaper industry in Tripura is totally dominated by the Bengalis. All the Bengali vernacular and English dailies and weeklies are owned by Bengalis, the reporting corps is almost wholly Bengali and there is no newspaper or local cable channel in Kokborok, the language of the tribes people. During the 1980 riots, the reportage in the Tripura newspapers (there was no local cable TV channel in those days) was an endless string of stories about the massacre of the Bengalis, their woes in refugee camps and so on. Into the second week of the riots – and I was witness to this – the tribals were also suffering heavily. The Bengali-dominated police was wreaking vengeance wherever it could and Bengali goons backed by them were on an orgy of loot and violence in the tribal villages.

This was one side of the story that went almost wholly unreported, except in one small left wing weekly *Agami*. Anyone could see that the sufferings of the tribals were no story for the Bengali-dominated newspaper industry in Tripura. An editorial in the largest circulated *Dainik Sambad* even went to the extent of lambasting the Tripura chief minister Nripen Chakrabarty for his alleged 'softness for tribals'. The language he used was plainly abusive – the chief minister, the editorial said, "would not be spared because he was sucking up to the tribespeople". In such a surcharged atmosphere, any journalist reporting on the atrocities perpetrated on the tribals was a likely target for Bengali vigilantes in the towns, from where the newspapers are published. No wonder, the 'Agami' folded up soon after the riots.

The newspapers from Calcutta, catering to a largely Bengali audience in West Bengal, also played up the 'Bengali angle' almost shamelessly. They picked up scores of unsubstantiated stories from the Tripura papers, of gory massacres that had not happened, of "scores of bodies flowing down the rivers", of "villages being burnt down one after another". Calcutta's largest circulated *Ananda Bazar Patrika* even talked of 'helicopter and tanks' chasing the rebels, when no such thing was happening. The army had been called out by the Tripura government in aid of the civil authority but only infantry columns were out on a confidence building role. Tripura's only rebel group at that time – the Tribal National Volunteers – were armed with locally made muzzle-loaders and tanks and helicopters were surely not needed to combat them. The rest of the Indian media was slightly more balanced and there were stories looking at the causes of the conflict. But between themselves, the local, the regional and the national media perpetuated the stereotype of the tribesman as the violent rebel, the merciless killer, the 'anti-national insurgent'. The image has stuck, but nothing could be farther from truth.

Like the Bengalis, the tribals suffered heavily during the riots. They lost their homes, many of them were killed and they suffered at the hands of the police. Now, they suffer as much at the hands of the security forces as at the hands of some insurgent groups like the National Liberation Front of Tripura, who have punished tribal families with death and rape for not heeding their appeal to convert to Christianity. In the very first month of my job with the *Dainik Sambad*, which I joined the year after the riots, I raised the issue of balance with the editor, who, like most others in the state, was also the owner of the paper. "I have to take care of my circulation, my sales," he was quick to add. The hint was obvious: since most readers of *Dainik Sambad* were Bengalis, it was necessary for the paper to play up the 'Bengali angle'. Since that was the message from the top, the newsroom would usually go a step further, double-guessing the emperor.

Later when I joined the Press Trust of India in Agartala, my senior colleague Manik Chakrabarty told me the amazing story of the state Congress chief Asok Bhattacharya walking into his office at the peak of the riots and claiming that "eighteen thousand Bengalis have been slaughtered." Mr Chakrabarty questioned the story and demanded what were such claims based on and who would be a possible source for such claims. "Quote me if you want and ascribe the story to me," thundered the state Congress chief, "but for heaven's sake, write that eighteen thousand Bengalis have died. Otherwise, Delhi will not sit up and take notice." At that time, the state government was confirming the deaths of around eight hundred people, more than two-thirds of them Bengalis. Unofficial estimates varied between fifteen hundred to two thousand, but here was the Opposition leader in the state assembly claiming a death toll nine times as much! Mr Chakrabarty refused to carry the story for good reasons.

This incident raises three key issues – (a) how far can a journalist in a delicate conflict situation trust his source, however well-placed he or she may be (b) how he or she is to handle an obviously 'biased' source but one who is important like the Opposition leader of Tripura assembly, (c) how will the journalist maintain balance and fairness in such a surcharged atmosphere. For a young journalist with no real-life experience or training to handle conflict situations, this was baptism by fire. I derived some clear lessons and set myself four professional tasks : (a) to rise above the 'identity barrier' and recognise that all involved in the conflict have a point of view that deserved media attention, (b) to develop a wide range of acquaintances and sources in all communities in the shortest possible time, (c) draw on a wide range of sources and report with appropiate attribution , so that the reader could get a balanced version of events, (d) wherever and whenever possible, avoid second-hand sourcing and report from the spot , since presence and access is key to insight on such events. One could then avoid reporting claims – even preposterous ones like the one made by the Tripura Congress chief.

Actually, there are reporters who would carry such a story. One of my junior colleagues suggested that the PTI should have carried the story and sourced it to the Congress leader to avoid direct responsibility. But I would go with Mr Chakrabarty in not reporting the claims which were obviously false and unsubstantiated – no area-wise break-ups were given by the leader to back his claims. Journalists are paid a salary to assess a story and report it with context rather than play the postman distributing mails around. This is not a question of value judgement that might kill a possible story, it is a question of what is possible and should be reported and what is not. Fairness, mobility, wide source-network and a sense of responsibility emerged as key values in those early days in Tripura and Assam that have remained part of my professional make-up. Over the years, I have realised that these are no wasteful luxuries, no high-sounding pompous display of liberalism, but a sound investment for professional success.

In reporting conflicts, fairness and balance is the key to greater access and acceptability. And greater access and sourcing is key to good comprehensive coverage. In conflicts, more than in other situations, a journalist may run the risk of getting one-sided with sources.So it is important to (a) create consciously the widest possible network of sources, (b) to assess the sources on a continuous basis, discard dubious ones (those who try to plant stories) and reinforce ties with credible ones, (c) to keep reaching out to diverse communities within the region and across the borders (in my case, the normal progression was to first reach out to communities other than my own in Assam and Tripura , then do the same in Nagaland, Mizoram and Manipur, and finally to the Chakmas in Bangladesh and Kachins, Chins and Arakanese in Myanmar, and round off the exercise by building adequate "mainstream contacts" in Myanmar and Bangladesh) (d) to make source-building a continuous exercise – so if one is weak in an area or does not have enough sources within a community or an important organisation, there must be a conscious attempt to reach out (e) it is important to be fair and come across as fair, because that is the key to wider networking and source-building (f) handle the sources through continuous interactions, periodic assessment and a balanced personal relationship that does not affect the journalist's objectivity, but ties the source and the journalist in a bond that transcends the attraction of material benefit.

The Content Problem

The other problem the media faces in the North East is that of content– which, in a way, is linked to resources. The print and electronic media in North East operates in a small market. The circulation of the largest Assamese or Bengali newspapers in the region do not exceed fifty thousand, with one or two exceptions. The circulation of the largest circulated Bengali paper in neighbouring West Bengal is twelve to fifteen times as much. The largest English daily *Assam Tribune* has crossed the seventy thousand mark, but it is beginning to face stiff competition from metropolitan dailies now bringing out editions for North East India. Again, the circulation of *The Telegraph* in Calcutta is four to five times that of *Assam Tribune.* The smaller languages like Mizo, Meitei, Khasi or Garo can only sustain newspapers with the circulation of a few thousand.

With paper sales and advertising revenue very limited by the size of the market, the media in the North East has very little funds to invest in newsgathering. Papers run with ill-paid journalists cannot be expected to produce great content with consistency and accuracy. The more promising of these journalists only bide time for an opportunity in the burgeoining national press and the desertion rate from the regional media is very high. The *Sentinel* started in Guwahati in 1983 as a challenger to the *Assam Tribune* with a team of bright young regional journalists. More than two decades later, there is only one or two of the original recruits still working for the paper. Most of the rest have graduated to good positions in the national press or branched away into more lucrative professions.

Since most newspapers in the region run on shoestring news budgets, they produce very little local content worth it. A study of content in six newspapers of North East India between June and August 2006 done by me (with assistance from two students of Calcutta

University) revealed that sixty-two per cent of the content was 'national news' – news from states of India outside the North East or news from the national capital. Much of it was picked from agencies like the PTI, the UNI or Indo-Asian News Service. Twenty-one per cent of the news was from the state where the newspaper is based and only three per cent was from neighbouring North Eastern states. The rest was foreign news. The nation clearly weighs heavily on the region in terms of media output. The scene will not change unless the low-cost model of regional newspapers and magazines change. The scene is no different in the fledgling electronic media of the region. And matters would be worse when the national media penetrates the region, which it has started doing.

Educational Indicators of Human Development

AN ANALYSIS

Lalhmasai Chuaungo

Human development is the main concern for the world. It may not be an exaggeration to say that all our efforts are directed towards the realisation of human development. Generally, education, health and income are considered as important indicators of human development. The United Nations Development Programme (UNDP) has emphasized education and health instead of conventional indicators like the Gross National Product (GNP) as indicators of human development and progress.

The importance of education for human development cannot be over-emphasized. It is indeed the key to all the processes of human development. From the mere literacy of the masses to the highly professional skills, all forms of education contribute towards overall development of a nation. A country educationally developed is also developed in all other respects. Numerous studies conducted by social scientists have shown that a nation remains underdeveloped so long as its people remain deprived of education. Frederich Harbison conducted a study on 75 countries and found the coefficient of correlation between the rate of literacy and the GNP of these countries to be as high as 88. Many cross-country studies have also demonstrated the significant impact of education, especially primary education, on economic growth rates (Barro 1997; Krueger and Lindahl 2000; Gylfason and Gylfi, 2001). Aggregate production function studies had shown that an additional year of education for the labour force was associated with increases in income and output. Similarly, farm productivity rises with the educational level of farmers. Even more, the prospects of raising the growth rate of the economy to the level achieved by the 'tigers' of East Asia hinge crucially upon all children completing at least elementary schooling.

Generally, North-Eastern India is accepted as a backward area with multifarious problems and frequent social and political unrest. Increasing violence, insurgency, terrorism and separatist movement work as a deterrent to peace and progress. The primary factor responsible for this state of affairs is diagnosed as the under-development of the region. Therefore, all efforts should be made to hasten the process of development. In this process, human resource is going to play the most crucial role. At a time when efforts are being made to expand educational facilities of the region by establishing more universities, technical institutions, IITs etc., one should not forget that it is elementary education which lays the base on which the superstructure of education rests.

Keeping in view the indispensability of basic education including adult literacy for human development, it is felt necessary to present and analyse selected educational indicators at elementary level in North-East India that have direct or indirect bearing on human development.

Data Presentation and Sources

Data on key educational indicators for human development in North-Eastern India are presented in Tables under the following main heads:

Table – 1 : Literacy rates by sex and overall, over various censuses

Table – 2 : Access and Gross Enrolment Ratio (GER).

Table – 3 : School-related indicators. (schools in rural and urban, type of school building, student-classroom ratio, single teacher school)

Table – 4 : Facilities in Schools.

Table – 5 : Enrolment-based indicators.

a) Enrolment and Gender Parity Index (GPI)
b) Apparent survival rate
c) Examination result

Table – 6 : Teacher-related indicators.

a) Distribution of teachers, pupil-teacher ratio and academic qualification
b) Professional qualification and training

Data on literacy rates by sex and overall over various censuses that have been compiled from Statistical Abstract (various issues), Government of India, are taken from a book "Elementary and Mass Education in North-East India". Data on Access and GER presented in Table 2 are compiled from the Seventh All India School Education Survey – Provisional Statistics – 2005. All other data presented in Tables 3, 4, 5a, b, c, and 6a, b are collected and compiled from the District Information System on Education (DISE) 2004 data (for 25 States and UTs of India) presented in a book form in Elementary Education in India : where do we stand? However, data for Arunachal Pradesh and Manipur are not included in the DISE 2004 data probably due to non-receipt of report from these states; therefore, the names of these two North-Eastern States do not appear in the Tables except Table 1 and 2.

Analysis of Data

1. *Literacy Rates by Overall and Sex*

Table 1 reveals that literacy levels still need some improvements in North-Eastern region. The level of literacy according to the 1991 census was more or less consistent with the national average with the exception of Mizoram which recorded the second highest level in the country. While Mizoram retains the status of being the second highest literate state in the country in 2001 census, still there are three states (Arunachal Pradesh, Assam and Meghalaya) that have registered the lower rates than national literacy rate of 65.38 per cent. Literacy rates among female population are still lower when compared to that of male population.

2. Access and Gross Enrolment Ratio (GER)

Table 2 indicates that many habitations in North-East India are still without schooling facility. The states with percentage of habitations having primary school facility within 1 km, lower than the national figure of 86.96 per cent, are Arunachal Pradesh, Assam, Manipur, Meghalaya and Tripura. The GER (percentage of enrolment to target child population) for boys and girls and girls only are lower than the national figures of '93 and '91 respectively in Assam and Nagaland. The percentage of rural habitations, served by upper primary schools within a walkable distance of 3 km, lower than the national percentage of 78.11 are Arunachal Pradesh, Manipur, Meghalaya, Mizoram and Nagaland. The GER for total, and girls only are lower than the national average of 58 per cent and 54 per cent respectively in Assam, Meghalaya and Nagaland.

3. School Related Indicators

In India, 87 per cent of the total of 9,31,471 schools that impart elementary education in the country are in the rural areas. Table 3 shows that all the North Eastern States except Mizoram have higher percentages of schools in the rural areas.The distribution of schools by type of building shows that the range of percentage of schools having pucca buildings is only 11.61 (Mizoram) and 32.18 (Assam), whereas the national percentage is 69.29. This clearly shows the poor condition of the region in this regard. All states from the North-Eastern Region have comfortable student-classroom ratio. The ratio is as low as 17.67 students per classroom in the case of Mizoram. Whereas 12.93 per cent schools in the country have only one teacher, all the North-Eastern States record lower percentages than the national ones that show its good point.

4. Facilities in Schools

With regard to facilities in schools, the position of North-Eastern States as shown in Table-4 is far from satisfactory as the region records lower percentages than the national percentages. The situation is all the worse in the aspects of facility such as drinking water, girls toilet, book bank and medical check-up as the states' percentages of schools having these facilities are all much lower than the national ones. Other facilities like common toilet, blackboard, computer, playground, development grant and teaching-learning material grant are also inadequate in the schools of the region.

5. Enrolment – Based Indicators

(a) Enrolment and Gender Parity Index (GPI)

The percentage of enrolment in rural areas shown in Table 5(a) reveals that the same is significantly low when considered with respect to the share of the total number of schools in these areas. The range of percentages of enrolment in rural areas is from 65.4 (Nagaland) to 90.47 (Assam), whereas the percentages of elementary schools located in rural areas range from 78 (Mizoram) to 95 (Tripura). Table 5(a) further shows that GPI ranges between 0.92 and 1.04 in North-Eastern States while it is 0.88 at the national level. Meghalaya (1.04) has more girls in elementary classes than boys. Although boys outnumber girls in the rest of the North-Eastern States, the difference in the enrolment rate is not much. The situation of the region in this regard is better than that of the national.

(b) Apparent Survival Rate

One of the crude indicators to know the retaining capacity of the system is apparent survival rate. In other words, the survival rate also reflects on the status of efficiency of the education system. Table 5(b) reveals that a large number of children drop out from the system before reaching class V. While more girls survive upto class IV in all the North-Eastern States, more boys survive upto class V in Assam and Mizoram. All the North-Eastern states except Tripura have lower survival rate upto class V than the national rate of 64.72 per cent for boys and 61.56 per cent for girls. The lowest record is made by Meghalaya where it is only 30.36 per cent and 33.01 per cent for boys and girls respectively. The low survival rate implies high rate of drop-outs at the primary level that further implies a low level of human development in the region.

(c) Examination Result

In India, the learners' achievement is considered as one of the significant indicators of quality of education. However, there is no mechanism to collect information on learners' achievement on a regular basis. In the absence of learners' achievement data, alternatively, the results of examination conducted by schools are considered as one of the proxy indicators of quality of education which are being collected under DISE every year.

A cursory look at Table 5 (c) tells us that the performance of students in examinations at primary and upper primary levels is poor. The percentages of boys and girls passed and the percentages of boys and girls passed with 60 per cent marks and above, in all the North-Eastern States except Mizoram (in the case of boys and girls passed in upper primary Examination) are all lower than the national percentages. Taken as a whole, girls perform better than boys.

6. Teacher-Related Indicators

Tables 6 (a) and 6(b) reveal the satisfactory position of North-Eastern States in relation to number of teachers per school and pupil-teacher ratio as well as the unsatisfactory position of the region with regard to teachers' academic and professional qualifications and training.

(a) Distribution of Teachers, Pupil-Teacher Ratio (PTR) and Academic Qualification

Table 6 (a) shows that the average number of teachers per school in each state of the region except Meghalaya is higher than the national average of 3.94. Distribution of female teachers is lower than the national figure (38.18) except in Meghalaya and Mizoram. In terms of PTR that influences classroom transaction, the position of the region is quite satisfactory as the ratios in different states are all much lower than the national ratio of 39. The lowest PTR (14) is observed in Mizoram. The low ratio may be attributed to the thin population of the state as compared to other states of the country.

Elementary teachers in North-Eastern States are less qualified when compared with the national scene. The percentage of teachers with below secondary level of education in each state of the region is much higher than the national percentage of 3.28 for male and 3.67 for female. At the same time, the percentage of teachers having high qualification in each state is lower than the national figure of 14.49 and 13.67 for male and female respectively.

(b) Professional Qualification and Training of Teachers

Professional qualification of teachers shown in Table 6 (b) indicates that North-Eastern region has low percentage of teachers having professional qualifications. When teachers are classified under below B.Ed level, B.Ed or equivalent and M.Ed or equivalent, the percentages of teachers having these qualifications are less than the national figures in almost all the cases. We cannot expect quality education without teachers equipped with professional qualifications. The percentage of male teachers who have undergone in-service training in each state except Assam is lower than the national percentage of 33.09. Female teachers are better in that a larger number of them has undergone the training and the figure in each state except Tripura exceeds the national figure of 44.7 per cent.

Summary of Findings

When selected educational indicators for human development in North-Eastern states are analysed against the national scene, the region is in satisfactory or almost satisfactory condition in the following areas:

- Gross Enrolment Ratio.
- Distribution of schools in rural areas.
- Student-Classroom Ratio.
- Percentage of single teacher school.
- Gender-Parity Index and girls enrolment
- Average number of teachers per school.
- Pupil-Teacher Ratio, and
- In-service training of female teachers.

The position of North-Eastern States is unsatisfactory in the following areas :

- Spread of literacy
- Access/habitations having primary school within 1 KM and upper primary school within a walkable distance of 3 KM.
- Type of school building.
- Facilities in schools such as drinking water facility, girls' toilet, book-bank, medical check-up; and also common toilet facility, blackboard, computer, playground, teaching-learning material.
- Percentage of enrolment in rural areas.
- Survival rate
- Students' performance in examination.
- Academic qualification of teachers
- Professional qualification of teachers and
- Training of teachers.

Suggestions

In view of the findings stated above, a few suggestions have been made as given below :

1. Efforts have to be made for raising the general level of literacy of people. Literacy certainly raises awareness especially among parents, and hence it is the main support base for childrens' education leading to human development. Special emphasis should be given to female literacy and education

as this correlates closely with women's choices in life, the number of children they have, the survival rate of their infants, how their children perform at school and how productive their livelihoods subsequently become. This has a direct bearing on human development. In imparting literacy, caution must be taken that it does not end up with mere ability to read and write, but functionally integrated with the life of the learner.

2. There are still many habitations without primary school within 1km and upper primary school within 3 km in different states of North-East India. SSA has special provision to conduct surveys to identify the unserved areas for providing schooling facilities. The findings of such surveys are to be considered in establishing new schools.
3. There should be proper norms for opening schools with regard to availability of funds, buildings and basic facilities; and these should be strictly regulated and implemented.
4. The low percentage of enrolment in rural areas in relation to the percentage of rural schools together with the low survival rate in the region may indicate that the rate of dropout at elementary stage is still high. This calls for serious attention to improve the living conditions in the area. The tough life style in rural areas of the region is a great impediment for children, especially girl children, to attend schools or to survive in schools. It is necessary to initiate actions at various levels. Good child care centres to relieve older children from taking care of their young siblings, part-time education and open schooling for rural children, are some of the avenues which need to be made more effective. Augmentation of the overall infrastructural development like road, power, housing, health, etc. enables children to take benefit of educational facilities. Media and communication have a great role to play in disseminating the message regarding the value of education to people. But more important is direct interaction with the people. The resources of social institutions and community as a whole should be effectively exploited.
5. Since results of examinations conducted at the end of primary and upper primary levels in different states do not give us a sound base for comparison of the learners' achievement in

different states, Baseline Learners' Assessment Studies should be conducted. Each state may utilize the service of SSA mission as there is a provision for conducting this kind of studies in SSA. The expertise of individual researchers and SCERTs in the region may be utilized to see whether elementary school children have achieved Minimum Levels of Learning (MLL) prescribed by NCERT or not. To improve learners' achievement, curricular innovation, practical and activity oriented teaching-learning method and continuous and comprehensive evaluation system need to be introduced in our education system.

6. The region as a whole presents a rather dismal picture in respect of teachers' academic as well as professional qualifications and training. In teachers' recruitment, professional qualification in addition to good academic qualification should be given due emphasis. Apart from clearing the huge backlog of untrained teachers, there should be continuous cycle of teacher training to improve the quality of instruction. The NERIE, NCERT, Shillong, has to take necessary steps in this regard by continuously giving training and resource support to SCERTs and DIETs in North-Eastern states.

Conclusion

As the present paper reveals a considerably miserable situation of North-East India in achieving the targets of quality education for all, a high level of human development cannot be expected. Hence, continued efforts have to be made for improvements, particularly in the areas where the position of the region is still unsatisfactory.

NOTES AND REFERENCES

Bhattacharya, R.K. et.al. (Eds), 2003, *Human Development*. Delhi : Kalpaz Publication.

Lyndem, B. & Bhattacharjee, D.S., 2005, *Elementary and Mass Education in North East India. (A study of Meghalay & Sikkim)*. Gauhati, DVS Publishers.

Mehrotra, S et.al., 2005, *Universalizing Elementary Education in India : Uncaging the 'Tiger' Economy*. New Delhi, Oxford University Press.

Mehta, Arun, C., 2005, *Elementary Education in India: where do we stand?* New Delhi: NIEPA.

NCERT, 2005, *Seventh All India School Education Survey: Provisional Statistics*. Department of Educational Surveys and Data Processing, New Delhi.

Singh, V.P., 2006, Rural Elementary School Education in North East States of India : A Report Card in *Journal of Indian Education*. Vol. XXXI, No. 4.

Female Work Participation Rate in Mizoram

AN ANALYSIS FROM DEVELOPMENT PERSPECTIVES

Lalhriatpuii

A country can achieve a high rate of economic development through the best and the fullest use of its resources. In a developing country like India, burdened with a huge population, an ideal strategy would be to utilize its human resources to the maximum for rapid economic growth of the nation. This would necessitate optimum participation of women in the various sectors of economic activity[1]. The development of an economy cannot only be measured in terms of GDP, per capita income and wage, it needs to be seen also in terms of effective participation and utilization of the capabilities of both men and women as an effective human resource potential[2]. In this context, the economic role of women cannot be isolated from the total framework of development. Equal participation of women is a pre-condition for the development of not only the women but also the country as a whole.

Female Work Participation Rate (FWPR) in Mizoram

Women constitute almost 49 per cent of the total population in Mizoram, with almost 43.7 per cent of the total female population working according to the 2001 census. A majority of the population are engaged in the informal sector and therefore are subjected to the discrepancies, which exist in the labour market. Traditional handicrafts, like weaving and bamboo works occupy a prominent place next to agriculture. In Mizoram the impact of developmental activities on women during the post-independence period is significant. The role and status of women have undergone notable changes with the improvement in literacy and awareness that comes along with development and change in the social and economic life. Yet inequality of status persists in different aspects of economic, social and family life. Inadequate employment opportunities compel women to concentrate in the unorganized sector and women lag behind men in employment in salaried jobs and in sectors, which involve decision-making and exercise of power.

Table 1: Work Participation Rate

Year	*Detail*	*India*			*Mizoram*		
		Number	*%WPR*	*AG%*	*Number*	*%WPR*	*AG%*
1971	TW	186405113	32.91	-	149576	45.61	-
	FW	36711290	19.69	-	65843	44.02	-
	MW	149693823	52.50	-	83733	55.98	-
1981	TW	251455499	36.8	3.49	224364	45.44	5.0
	FW	49788188	19.8	3.56	97823	43.6	4.86
	MW	201667311	51.09	3.47	126541	56.4	5.11
1991	TW	314121370	37.6	2.49	337360	48.91	5.04
	FW	89767563	22.05	8.03	151205	44.82	5.46
	MW	224363807	51.08	1.13	186155	55.18	4.71
2001	TW	401289511	39.1	2.77	467159	52.6	3.85
	FW	126802251	31.59	4.13	204151	43.70	3.50
	MW	274487260	68.40	2.23	263008	56.29	4.13

WPR : Work Participation Rate
AG % : Annual Growth with reference to last available record
TW : Total Worker, FW : Female Worker, MW : Male Worker — : Not Available
Note : Saiha District 1981 & 1991are undivided i.e Chhimtuipui district record. 2001 is Saiha District record.

Source : Census Reports 1971, 1981, 1991and 2001(India & Mizoram), Statistical Hand Book 1981 (Chhimtuipui District)

Female population constitutes a strong force in Mizoram, and the proportion of female workers in work participation shows an improving trend like the rest of India. The latest census reveals that work participation in Mizoram is much higher than in India, as a whole. The total work participation is 52.6 per cent as against 39.1 per cent in India as a whole. The FWPR, according to the 2001 census, is 43.7 per cent as against 31.59 per cent in the whole of India for the same period. MWPR in Mizoram during the 2001 census was 56.29 per cent as against 68.4 per cent in India, as a whole.

There has been an increase in the proportion of workers in India and Mizoram, although this could be due to an absolute increase in the number of male and female workers in all areas. Increase in female workers during this period may be counted for a growth in the literacy rate between the period from 1971 to 2001, and also due to a greater social awareness among the people to seek monetary value for the services rendered.

In the overall analysis the following facts emerged:

- The FWPR is much lower than MWPR in India and the same trend obtains in the state of Mizoram.
- Female work participation is poor in India.
- The growth of female work participation rate in Mizoram has shown an improving trend during 1971–2001, the growth rate is higher than the All India growth rate during the same period.
- Another feature reveals that although annual growth rate, both for male and female work participation, has shown varying trends during the period of our analysis in India and Mizoram, there has been a discernible trend towards a decline in the WPR of both males and females as revealed by the 1991 and 2001 census. The decline in MWPR happens to be more or less uniform and gradual in 1991, but the growth rate of FWPR has been showing an upward move during 1991. This could again be mainly attributed to changes in the definitional concept of FWPR in the census; women's frequent entry and exit as well as re-entry may also distort the real picture of female participation rates.

Depending on the needs and requirements of the household, a woman needs to oscillate between wide varieties of tasks, whether productive or unproductive. As chastity and frequent motherhood prevent women from entering the labour market and in situations where they do, it is because of compulsions of economic condition like poverty and deprivation. While the economic necessity and the need for supplementing family income could be the major factors for women to enter the labour market, economic transformation could also be cited to constitute an equally important reason[3]. It is important to

Table 2: Occupational Distribution of Female Workers (Main)

Year	Total Female Workers			Cultivators			Agricultural Labourers			Household Industry Workers			Other Worker		
	Number	% of total	AG%	Number	% of total	AG%	Number	% of total	AG%	Number	% of total	AG%	Number	% of total	AG%
MIZORAM															
1971	65843	100	-	63486	96.42	-	177	0.27	-	-	-	-	2180	3.31	-
1981	97823	100	4.85	84431	86.31	3.30	2113	2.16	109.38	1027	1.05	-5.29	10252	10.48	-
1991	151205	100	5.46	112043	74.10	3.27	4506	2.98	11.33	1905	1.26	8.55	32751	21.66	21.95
2001	137022	100	-0.94	89861	65.6	-1.98	4130	3.0	-0.83	1625	1.2	-1.47	41406	30.2	2.64
INDIA															
1981	44806000	100	-	14826000	33.09	-	20764000	46.34	-	2046000	4.57	-	7170000	16.00	-
1991	62922000	100	4.04	21533000	34.22	4.52	2827000	44.93	3.61	2220000	3.53	0.85	10899000	17.32	5.2
2001	72857170	100	1.58	25367090	32.9	1.78	22378045	38.9	-2.08	4697071	6.5	11.2	20414964	21.7	8.7

% of total : Total Share as a percentage of the Total Female Workers for the year.
AG % : Annual Growth Rate with reference to the last available year.
Source : Census Reports of Mizoram and India 1971, 1981, 1991 and 2001.

analyse female work participation rate (FWPR) in the context of improving the status of women which does not necessarily increase with an increase in the participation rate but along with an increase in the ability to claim wages and to take an active part in the decision making process.

Occupational Distribution of Female Workers

The occupational distribution of workers in the table above reveals that the largest concentration of female workers has been as cultivators in Mizoram throughout the reference period. But the annual growth rate of cultivators has been declining from 3.30 per cent in 1971 to – 1.98 per cent in 2001. On the other hand, the participation of women as agricultural labourers has been increasing throughout the reference period.

Increasing women participation as agricultural labourers is due to lack of economic opportunities and choices, which force women in this area to engage themselves as agricultural labourers[4]. In India the rate of female participation as cultivators has been increasing from 33.09 per cent in 1981 to 34.22 per cent in 1991, but declined to 32.9 per cent in 2001. Female participation as agricultural laborers has been declining from 46.34 per cent in 1981 to 44.93 per cent in 1991, and further declined to 38.9 per cent in 2001 (Table 2). This decline may be due to the increase in agricultural productivity or a decline in the cultivated area.

The rest of the workers are unevenly spread between household industry workers and other workers. Further, it may be added that various promotional government schemes have led to the diversification of economic activities at the all-India level in the rural areas, causing a decline in the primary sector[5]. But such schemes have failed to take shape in Mizoram. This may be responsible for a continuous increase of female participation as agricultural labourers. In Mizoram, the dominance of FWPR as agricultural labourers may be due to lack of opportunities in the organized sectors, and the absence of employment opportunities in other alternative sectors.

Rural-Urban Distribution of FWPR: A Comparison

Table 3 below attempts to highlight the rural – urban difference in the WPR among males and females as estimated by the decennial census conducted during 1971-2001. For entire India, the urban female WPR, which is merely 9.2 per cent in the 1991 census, has been considerably lower than the rural FWPR of 26.70 per cent for the same period. In the 2001 census also the urban female WPR is 3.24 per cent, which is lower than the rural female WPR of 22.39 per cent for the same period. This may be due to the difficulty in combining work with household and other duties in urban areas[6]. In contrast in rural areas, work in the family or in the family enterprises constitute the main activity, leading to a rise in WPR. Moreover, in rural areas unmarried girls, young wives, busy mothers as well as older women are being forced by difficult economic situations to seek some kind of employment. In such a condition of survival, work opportunities are uppermost in their minds, and this enables them to detach themselves from the social stigma attached to work in the field. As a result FWPR in the rural areas is much higher than the participation rate in the urban areas in the whole of India and Mizoram.

In recent years, men have increasingly moved to the urban sectors in search of job opportunities, mainly due to low remuneration from manual work of cultivation in rural areas. These jobs are left to be done by their womenfolk, leading to a rise in rural FWPR. This is one of the crucial factors responsible for feminization of agriculture. This in no way means that the position of rural women workers has improved, since it is only due to a fall in the relative returns to agricultural labour. This has resulted in a fall of marginal productivity of agricultural labourers and a similar decline in wage rate. As a result male workers, who had at one time flocked this sector, have started moving from this sector leaving it to their female counterparts.

Studies also revealed that there was a rapid expansion in public activities particularly in the health and rural welfare services, during the eighties, in the rural sector. Women have been the chief beneficiaries of those activities, which might also be another factor responsible for the rising level of FWPR in rural areas. Post reform period has also witnessed diversion of land from food crops to cultivation on a much larger scale of non-food crops like floriculture and horticulture, all of which employ a growing number of female workers. This trend may therefore be another reason leading to a rise in FWPR in the rural sector. Other notable features are that (i) MWPR has been maintaining the near zero or even slightly negative growth rate in both urban and rural areas in the 1991 and 2001 census; and (ii) a rise of FWPR in the urban sector from 8.3 per cent to 9.2 per cent, and from 23.2 per cent to 26.7 per cent in rural areas between 1981 and 1991, and to 17.5 per cent in the urban sector, and to 31.6 per cent in rural areas in 2001. This could also mean a better coverage of women workers in the census reports.

Table 3 : Work Participation Rate of Females in Urban and Rural Areas in Mizoram (in percentage)

Area	M /F	URBAN					RURAL				
		1981	1991		2001		1981	1991		2001	
		%	%	AG%	%	AG%	%	%	AG%	%	AG%
India	F	08.3	9.20	1.08	17.5	9.02	23.2	26.70	1.51	31.6	1.84
	M	47.1	48.90	0.38	82.5	6.87	53.8	52.50	-0.24	68.4	3.03
Mizoram	F	5.25	12.91	14.59	20.25	5.69	27.38	21.05	-2.42	27.29	2.96
	M	10.73	21.80	10.32	27.04	2.4	37.4	27.78	-2.57	30.24	0.89
Aizawl	F	6.38	15.75	14.69	28.57	8.14	26.66	17.34	-3.5	14.55	-1.6
Lunglei	F	2.92	9.5	22.53	15.27	6.07	26.05	23.99	-0.8	31.65	3.19
Saiha	F	2.35	2.95	2.55	6.71	12.75	32.86	35.68	0.86	33.74	-0.5

AG% : Annual Growth rate with reference to last available record.
Source : Census of India and Mizoram, 1981,1991 and 2001.
Statistical Handbook of Mizoram, Directorate of Economics and Statistics, 1981, 1991, 2001.

The growth rate of FWPR in Mizoram, like the rest of India, is found to be increasing at a better pace in the rural areas in the urban areas when compared between 1981 and 2001. This implies that women are engaged in agriculture and allied activities, which are subject to discriminatory wages. The factors operating at the all-India level leading to this trend of FWPR in the labour market may also be operative in this region. It has also to be noted further that the handloom and handicraft, which were predominantly household activities, are now becoming highly commercialized. This has necessitated employing a larger number of labourers in these household activities at a wage rate, expressing preferences for female labourers. For women, this dependency poses an additional problem, because this sector of the economy is largely characterized by irregularities of jobs, seasonal nature of work, and with lack of fixed hours of work. In this case, the burden of women is immense as work in this sector is often combined with full time household work. In the urban sector, male participation has recorded a slight increase during the period from 1981 to 1991, and a further increase in the 2001 census, implying that there has been a gradual shifting of male workers from the rural to urban sectors, leaving the female workers to survive under conditions of discriminatory wages. The economy of Mizoram being primarily agrarian, a majority of the woman workforce is still concentrated in agriculture and allied activities. Paddy being the principal crop requires and employs more women for sowing, transplanting and harvesting.

Determinants of Female Work Participation Rate in Mizoram

To examine the factors that determine the pattern of female work participation rate we selected various socio-economic variables. The socio economic variables selected for the purpose of our study have been Female Literacy, Sex Ratio, Freedom of Decision making of Females, Attitude of Males towards working Females, and Male Literacy. In order to analyse the determinants of female work participation rate, and to assess the impact of such variables on the participation rate, we use the following models.

Since the level and structure of employment are often affected by the degree of literacy we assume female participation rate to be an increasing function of the level of education. Therefore, the first model that we specify is as follows:

Model: $W_F = a + b_1 Lit_F + e_1$ ...(1)

Where W_F : Female Work Participation

Lit_F : Female Literacy

e_1 : Error

Sex ratio or the number of females per thousand males is also an important factor to determine the growth of female population over the years. Growth of female population contributes to the supply of female labour. Therefore, there is a need to assess whether this change in the supply of female labour as a consequence of higher sex ratio results in an increase in female work participation. We therefore specify the second model as follows:

Model: $W_F = a + b_2 S_R + e_2$ ...(2)

S_R : Sex Ratio

e_2 : Error

Freedom to take decisions in family matters automatically entrusts some degree of authority to the person who is capable of taking a decision. The greater the autonomy in a woman's ability to take decision, the greater is her freedom to make a choice about her decision to work. The decision making ability of women will be judged through primary data. We therefore specify the next model:

Model: $W_F = a + b_3D_F + e_3$ ...(3)

D_F : Freedom of Decision Making of Females.

e_3 : Error

Irrespective of the nature of society, male attitude towards working women play a significant role in deciding womens' entry in or exit from, the labour market. We therefore formulate the next model as follows:

Model: $W_F = a + b_4M_A + e_4$ ...(4)

M_A : Male Attitude towards Female Work Participation.

e_4 : Error

Along with female literacy, male literacy is also assumed to create a positive impact on the participation of women in work. Higher male literacy is assumed to remove the cultural and social taboos associated with womens' work created by the patriarchal ideology. Accordingly the next model formulated is as follows:

Model: $W_F = a + b_5Lit_M + e_5$ ...(5)

Lit_M : Male Literacy.

e_5 : Error

To determine the relative strength of all the independent variables for the purpose of ascertaining the structure of female participation, we have incorporated each of these variables using multiple regression analysis in the following models:

$$W_F = a + b_1Lit_F + b_2S_R + e_1$$

$$W_F = a + b_1Lit_F + b_2S_R + b_3D_F + e_2$$

$$W_F = a + b_1Lit_{F\,+}\, b_2S_R + b_3D_F + b_4\,M_A + e_3$$

$$W_F = a + b_1Lit_F + b_2S_R + b_3D_F + b_4\,M_A + b_5Lit_M + e_4$$

Results of regression models tested with the help of regression analysis, reveal that the best indicators of female work participation rate in Mizoram are (i) female literacy, (ii) freedom to work and (iii) positive attitudes of males towards female work in the labour market.

Conclusion

An analysis of female work participation has shown that though womens' participation has been increasing over the years, their position is lower than their male counterparts. The women folk are engaged in various works along with men in both agriculture and household farming, but the nature of most of these works reveal that these works are small time works confined within the household, and are yet to find sufficient exposure in the market.

Overall, it could be said that female workers in Mizoram like the rest of India are restricted to marginal status in the workforce and gender participation in home-based and traditional production needs to be comprehensively estimated and accounted, which could ensure a better picture of womens' participation rate in the area. The pattern of low female work participation as compared to male as examined in Mizoram, is consistent with the character of gender relations in different parts of the country. The north western states are distinguished for their highly unregulated gender relations and distribution of work patterns between males and females. High literacy rate, which is a characteristic feature of the state of Kerala, which also has a distinguishing history as a liberated society. This has in return enhanced the social standing of women in the state, and has brought about significant changes in terms of social achievements, less unequal gender relations, less patriarchal kinship systems, less male dominated property rights and greater prominence of women in influential social, political and economic activities. Similarly, the rapid transformation of the women of South Korea and China, brought about by enhancing the educational status of women, and equipping them with necessary training skill, has created a transformation in the participation of women in the economic sphere. The success of these states and countries could be taken as an example to illuminate the social standing and position of the women of Mizoram, which also dominates in aspects of literacy among females and high sex ratio. These regional contrasts provide a useful means of investigation in different aspects of womens' participation in the area, and these experiences are but important lessons to emulate and adopt them in practice.

NOTES AND REFERENCES

1. Bagchi, J., 1995, *Indian Women Myth and Reality*, Sangam Books, Hyderabad.
2. John E. Mary, 1996, Gender and Development in India, 1970s–1990s some reflections on the constitutive role of contents, *EPW*.
3. Boserup, Ester, 1970, *Women's Role in Economic Development*, George Allen and Unwin, London
4. Fong M.S., 1975, *Measuring Women's Work in Agriculture*, Seminar Paper, Institute of Social Studies, New Delhi.
5. Raana Haider, 'A Perspective in Development: Gender Focus', *Indian Journal of Gender Studies*, January–April 2006.
6. Beneria Lourdes, 1978, Production, Reproduction and the Sexual Division of Labour, ILO.

Contributors

Abhijit Choudhury, Head, Department of History, St. Edmunds's College, Shillong.

Ishani Naskar, Lecturer, Department of Political Science, Rabindra Bharti University, Kolkata.

Toki Blah, Development Specialist, Shillong.

Shyamananda Bhattacharjee, North Eastern Council, Government of India, Shillong.

James L.T.Thanga, Research Scholar, Department of Economics, Mizoram University, Aizawl.

T.C. Nunga, Professor, Department of Economics, Mizoram University, Aizawl.

Rakhee Bhattacharya, Fellow, Maulana Abul Kalam Azad Institute of Asian Studies, Kolkata.

Vanlalchhawna, Reader, Department of Economics, Mizoram University, Aizawl.

Kausik Bandyapadhaya, Fellow, Maulana Abul Kalam Azad Institute of Asian Studies, Kolkata & Senior Lecturer Department of History, North Bengal University, Darjeeling.

L. H. Rawsea, Lecturer, Aizawl Theological College, Aizawl.

Sajal Nag, Professor, Department of History, Assam University, Silchar.

Lt. Gen. J.R. Mukherjee (Retired), Kolkata.

Swapna Bhattacharya (Chakarborti). Fellow, MAKAIAS and Reader Department of South & Southeast Asian Studies, Calcutta University, Kolkata.

Margaret L. Pachuau, Lecturer, Department of English, Mizoram University, Aizawl.

Subir Bhaumik, BBC's Bureau Chief for Eeastern and North Eastern India.

Lalhmasai Chuaungo, Lecturer, Department of Political Science, Mizoram University, Aizawl.

Lalhriatpuii, Research Scholar, JNU, New Delhi.

Index